A CONTINENT DECIDES

KARACHI.   25TH JULY 1953.   FAILURE OR COMPROMISE?

INDIA AND PAKISTAN

A Continent Decides

By

LORD BIRDWOOD

by Frederick A. Praeger, Inc.

FREDERICK A. PRAEGER
NEW YORK

BOOKS THAT MATTER

Published in the United States of America
in 1954 by Frederick A. Praeger, Inc.,
Publishers, 105 West 40th Street,
New York 18, N. Y.

Library of Congress Catalog Card Number: 54-9289

Printed in Great Britain

DEDICATION

To men and women in these lands who serve
in silence rather than in speech

It was with deep regret that, since this book was submitted to the Publishers, the death of Dr. S. P. Mukerjee was recorded in Srinagar on 22nd June 1953.

Dr. Mukerjee had been an element of embarrassment for the Government of India for a long time, particularly in his activities within the State of Kashmir. But his fearlessness and integrity of purpose had undoubtedly won the respect of his opponents, and tributes came in from all shades of political opinion including the Prime Minister of Kashmir. It was fitting that his body was cremated on the banks of the River Hooghly on 24th June, the last rites being attended by many thousands of his devotees.

Breathes there the man with soul so dead
Who never to himself hath said
   " This is my own, my native land ! "
Whose heart hath ne'er within him burned,
As home his footsteps he hath turned
   From wandering on a foreign strand?

SIR WALTER SCOTT

CONTENTS

PART III
Kashmir

APPENDICES

MAPS

[1] These appear in italics in the text.

INTRODUCTION

WHEN on an evening in November 1944 I had watched the Bombay silhouette become one with the horizon from the stern of a troopship, I made up my mind that a chapter in life which had covered twenty-five years was closed. Ahead lay all the doubts and insecurities which are the common experience of officers of the Army when they discover suddenly that a lifetime of healthy soldiering is no necessary qualification for success in the hazards of search for employment.

The India I left was one big question mark. It was quite certain that the kind of life which the British had secured for themselves had gone for ever. The daily round of the civilian or soldier, with its set plan for work and play, had already been lost in the war years, and the spacious secure days of a parochial routine would obviously never return. But that was the only certainty. The thousands of Englishmen who came and went through the Forces in India during the war knew nothing either of the country and her problems or of the settled happy times we ourselves had enjoyed between the wars. They therefore treated India as a staging camp and, as such, contributed to the general uncertainty and sense of insecurity. The Working Committee of the Indian National Congress were in political confinement, but it was quite obvious that their release after the war would revive a situation similar to that of 1919, charged only with a greater urgency and danger.

These were the circumstances in which I and many others watched at a distance with academic interest the gathering pressure of events which heralded the 15th August 1947. For myself, I felt a mild frustration. I had in no way whatsoever contributed to the shaping of policies; and yet I felt that my experience in the eastern Punjab and my knowledge of many of the local leaders could be put to use.

Somehow it was difficult in England to take in the fact of a momentous transformation. Political India obviously did not believe that we were leaving, and in spite of our own assurances we seemed almost to be deceiving ourselves. But late in 1947 and throughout 1948 the stream of Englishmen returning prematurely from the Indian continent served to confirm the reality of the greatest experiment in nation-building ever made. In sadness and bewilderment we heard of the murder of an old servant, the wreck of the Punjab Mail or the desertion of good troops from good regiments.

In my father's room at Hampton Court I can remember turning the pages of faded photograph albums on an afternoon in the autumn of 1949. There were pictures of elegant young men and ladies in square-cut tweed coats and tight-fitting riding-habits relaxing in picnic groups on the fir-clad Simla hills. There was my mother on a favourite pony, her face lost in the shadow of an immense topee. There was the magnificence of the Curzon Durbar and a group of that small band of brothers, the personal staff at Snowdon in 1907, with Kitchener towering in the middle. Not quite so yellow with age were the familiar groups of my father's staff, British and Indian, of the nineteen-twenties, with a set of photographs of my family and a proud household in the garden of the Commander-in-Chief's house just completed in New Delhi. A few hours later, in an illustrated weekly, I chanced on a photograph of Pandit Nehru digging up the same garden in encouragement of a food-growing campaign; and a mood of wistful re-creation of the past was sharply dissipated! Nevertheless, when you have lived all your life among the relics and reminders of a tradition covering five generations of service it is not possible lightly to adjust the mind to sudden swift changes. One explanation of this book is therefore that it is a manifestation of a sincere claim to have made that adjustment. We cannot put the clock back, nor should we wish to do so. But we can at least go forward carrying the lessons of this experience and applying them to future not dissimilar situations.

This was my own reaction to much bitter contemporary comment. For my father's generation it was different. There was far too much evidence to support those who could say " I told you so ", to expect a former generation to accept the great change. Even those who had come away from India within the last few years were obviously dubious. It was therefore not unnatural that their fathers should be frankly horrified. In the Service Clubs they spoke of the abandonment of power and the break-up of Commonwealth and Empire, the beginning of the end. More particularly officers of the Indian Army foresaw the rapid deterioration of Army institutions, of Mess life, and the gradual decay of a mighty brotherhood of arms, with its history rich in traditions of honour and adventure. The Mess trophies would find their way into the homes of Indian officers, and the Mess would become a kind of hostel for stray friends and relations of the Commanding Officer!

These were opinions freely expressed whenever two or three gathered together in the clubs. No less concerned were the civilians who foresaw the slowing down of the administration and the spread of corruption, graft and nepotism. *Does* the Deputy Commissioner now only exist to satisfy his near relations? *Is* the Mess silver clean? *Is* the great Indian National Congress but a travesty of its former united strength and integrity? Change, yes: but for better or worse? To discover the answer was one of the reasons for my return to India. I had written out a previous assessment in circumstances of an unknown future,[1] and 1951 seemed to beckon with a finality which demanded the sequel.

[1] *A Continent Experiments.* Skeffington and Sons, Ltd., 1946.

But there were many other matters on which I wanted information, and only personal investigation could satisfy my curiosity. In retirement after an unsuccessful and not very enthusiastic effort to enter business, I took to the study of international affairs. Nine months in Germany with the British Red Cross on civilian relief work had whetted my appetite. To anyone working in Germany in 1947 divorced from the official attachment of either the Army or the Control Commission, the imminent division of the world became not merely apparent but inescapable. It was too late to study the clash of two ideologies from an academic approach and to start reading *Das Kapital*. But there was at least time to see something of the practical effect. I visited Yugoslavia in 1950 and Czechoslovakia in 1951, and learnt something of the methods of the police State. If we are to live with this separation of the human race for many years—and the evidence is to this effect—then it seemed to me that in studying India and Pakistan afresh I could perhaps contribute something in a field of inquiry not receiving overmuch attention; namely, the part which the great sub-Continent may play in the international drama. Will Indian influence in the East be exerted to control not only temporary situations, but the course of history? Will Pakistan increasingly and naturally assume the role of leadership in the Middle East? Once again I wished to discover the answer.

There was another and more appealing problem which I think has been neglected. We are all uncertain of the position which two nations, ancient in culture but on the threshold of their political existence, will occupy within the framework of our Empire and Commonwealth. True to tradition, we leave clear definition alone, and it is a matter of bad taste to raise awkward questions concerning the relationships of members of the family. India elected to become a sovereign independent Republic, and by virtue of a special formula it was found possible for her to remain a member of the Commonwealth. Pakistan was content for her membership to conform to the normal pattern of Dominion status. We left it at that. If India and Pakistan had been launched as friends, all might then have been well. But from their date of birth the twins struggled, fought and kicked each other in mutual distrust, and in such conditions the nature of their relationship within the family has become obscured. If the self-governing countries of the Commonwealth had known anything of the Indian continent before the emergence of two new members, many subsequent doubts and difficulties might have been obviated. Instead, overnight, countries such as Canada and Australia found themselves on a basis of equality with the new States of India and Pakistan. Their leaders had to learn something of a number of colleagues of whom they had previously never heard. The element of colour in equal co-operation was new and unknown. Will the new nations settle down to a relationship of family loyalty? Or as the years go by will they tend to regard themselves only as protectors of Asia from the encroachment of Western capitalism? Will we just drift on in some kind of compromise of opportunism by which Pakistan and India receive the privileges but avoid the obligations of family membership? These and many allied problems are now emerging to confuse our hazy, modern conception of Empire and Commonwealth, and I wished to discover at first hand what Indian and Pakistan leaders thought of such matters. As a lecturer for the Central Office of Information I knew that the British public themselves were ill-informed, and seemed, alas, only too ready to forget that within the self-governing countries of the Commonwealth about five persons in every six are Asians. I desired passionately to awaken and quicken interest in these problems. Certain it is that the process of making our Commonwealth a vital factor in world affairs is mutual. If Britain, the heart and nerve-centre, fails to supply the energy to pump the blood to the distant portions, the body will wither and die in so far as those particular limbs are concerned.

With these vague thoughts in mind the chapters on Commonwealth and International Relations emerged, and I would ask indulgence for some overlap of argument in the effort to separate external relations by chapters into two components, International and Commonwealth. Inevitably the position of India and Pakistan within the Commonwealth affects their relations with their neighbours. I would justify the separation with the plea that our Commonwealth in its present form is so unique in the history of mankind's social development as to deserve an attempt at special treatment.

But this great experiment on the sub-Continent is surely a gauge by which we may measure future success or failure elsewhere; and I should like to feel that this book is some contribution to the solution of the problems ahead in a great Colonial Empire. There is a world of muddled thinking on the nature of trusteeship, due to the misapplication of a familiar term, " exploitation ". The word has come to be regarded as an accusation when in fact it describes more often a normal process of natural progress. My book has given me the opportunity I have long sought to set out some thoughts on Britain's obligations to her less-developed territories. If sometimes it could be the means by which teachers in schools may pause before they present the familiar apology for their country—which, alas, too often prefaces the lesson on current affairs—then indeed I should be happy.

Apart from the theoretical approach, an unbiased account of the last six momentous years has yet to be written. There have been valuable contributions, but they have been recorded too close to the events of 1947 to be able to place both India and Pakistan in perspective against the judgment of time. And yet I in no way claim this contribution to be recorded history; for there is little chronological record to balance the personal flavour. Rather is it to be regarded as a series of essays, sometimes fact, sometimes theory, sometimes just the random impressions from a diary.

I have claimed that there is need for an unbiased account. That need is aptly reflected in the simple fact that in England instinctively many still speak of the great sub-Continent as "India". It is a habit which not unnaturally irritates Pakistanis. And yet the impersonal term "sub-Continent" conveys nothing of history, past or present, nor of geography. Ian Stephens, the recent editor of *The Statesman*, has seriously suggested that we should invent a new name—"Delkaria"—containing sufficient suggestion of Delhi and Karachi as to convey the area we knew as India.[1] The difficulty could not have arisen had India adopted "Hindustan" as her identification. One day, when India and Pakistan have settled their differences, we shall perhaps refer to the two countries separately. At present their difficult mutual relations result in a sound rolling off the tongue which usually emerges as "Indianpakistan"!

As time went by I felt increasingly that the pressure of ever-changing phases and events in Pakistan and India would mean that the day would come when it would be too late to study changes intelligently. My associations with the continent are still green enough to enable me to relate the present and the future to the past. But in a few years the personal machine of deduction will slow down. I had to write of these events while I was still able to relive the past, and thus assess the new continent accurately in relation to the conditions I had known.

Above all, I wanted once again to return to a hundred small scenes of past memories: a bungalow compound; a polo ground where I had spent hours trying to do justice to ponies deserving of a better player; the rocks of the frontier where I had shot chikor, or a glimpse of the Kashmir my mother had loved to sketch. I wanted, too, to wander again into the villages round Jullundur and Lahore, and decide for myself whether in fact the common *zemindar* had in any way changed with his change of allegiance to Bharat or Pakistan. How did he now view the Pax Britannica? Would that change be a reality in his daily life or just a dim, distant matter of opportunism in politics? I knew that countless situations would be sad and haunted, and I was both afraid and fascinated by the prospect.

There was therefore a long list of questions waiting to be answered, and this book is the result. In *A Continent Experiments* I wrote, "The quality of truth needs to be realised. It is seldom either black or white, but is found in varying tones of grey, sometimes dark or sometimes pale." My object has been to search for truth and record it. That principle must surely guide all historians. But in the present case the circumstances of the past six years demand a careful interpretation of this simple formula. Apart from the fact that if truth is recorded brutally, without discrimination, one often hurts good friends, there is a very grave responsibility on anyone who delves into the maze of accusation and counter-accusation which confronts the historian of the sub-Continent of India between the years 1945 and 1951. We all of us wish now to see these two countries go forward in mutual harmony as willing members of the

[1] Article in the *Spectator*, 22nd August, 1952.

British association of nations. Indeed, I regard the strengthening of an
Inter-Commonwealth relationship between Britain, Pakistan and India
as a solemn obligation, and not the least of reasons for writing.

The need for tact in the interpretation of truth does impose a certain
technique in recording personal comment and criticism. May I cite
an example? If I record that nothing less than three Divisions of British
troops could have controlled the Punjab situation in August 1947, then
I am reflecting not only my own opinion, which is incidental, but also
that of a senior officer who played a leading part in the control of events
at the time. The reader may therefore assume that frequently controversial expressions of opinion are based on the many talks I had with
Englishmen, Indians and Pakistanis who were the officials responsible in
the actual situations.

It is perhaps a matter not so much of running away from truth, for
eventually to face truth cannot be wrong. But whereas the historian of
the future may hope for a happier background which could resist the
repercussions of a strict and critical record of the past six years, to write
at this moment demands some control of opinion better left over for a
few more years.

The questions I have suggested for answer fall logically into distinct
fields of separate enquiry, and with the exception of the Kashmir chapters
it should therefore be possible for readers to select any chapter and read
through it without relation to other chapters. Nevertheless it is as one
complete contribution to history that I hope the work may be regarded.

To tell of the emergence of two countries in one coherent narrative
presents a number of difficulties, and it would have been simpler to have
written two books. Yet if we believe that the destinies of India and
Pakistan are irrevocably interlocked, it is logical to continue to regard
their history also as inseparable. There is the advantage, too, that the
need for repeated contrast ensures equal consideration being given to
both countries. We are so frequently criticised for alleged partisanship
and it is important that this vital corner in the story of our Commonwealth should be recorded without favour for either Dominion.[1]

I make no apology for the full use of footnotes. The footnote is often
regarded as a device of the lazy writer to cover up an afterthought in his

[1] Ever since the Commonwealth Relations Office took charge of the self-governing
portion of the Empire and Commonwealth, the word "Dominion" has been regarded
with suspicion. I have yet to meet the Australian or Canadian who is worried by
the term, and I use it freely in discussing our common problems. The words
"Dominion status" were used in the announcement known as the "3rd June Plan",
and at the time Lord Mountbatten's comment gives the truth. "Somehow people
seemed to have some doubts about this word 'Dominion status'. It is absolute
independence in every possible way with the sole exception that the member states
of the Commonwealth are linked together voluntarily. In fact they look for support,
mutual trust and, in due course, affection."
(Since this comment was written, the new style and title of Her Majesty the Queen
proclaimed at the end of May 1953 omits the word "Dominion". The Queen is
accepted by both India and Pakistan as "Head of the Commonwealth".)

composition which he is unwilling to insert in a reconstructed paragraph. In fact, it is a quite logical method of adding information which is redundant to the main narrative, but which may be of particular interest for one who reads in a spirit of serious research. Frequently it is the means by which statistical detail can be separated from the main argument.

Both in India and Pakistan the old titles of British India have disappeared and in their place indigenous terms have been adopted. Thus Pandit Nehru is today known as " Shri Jawaharlal Nehru ", and Pakistan's Foreign Minister is recognised as " Chaudhri Zafrullah Khan ". I apologise for using the terms familiar to Englishmen. I have done so mainly because I was frequently in doubt as to where and when new names are now in use.

My first intention had been to devote a single chapter to Kashmir. But once on the ground, it became increasingly clear that here was the key to agreement over the whole range of controversy between the two Dominions. There would be no need for an ineffective trade pact or the nonsense of a modern journey from Lahore to Amritsar if this one problem was solved. In Karachi or Delhi sooner or later all political discussion is subordinated to the Kashmir theme. It can make or mar dinner-parties, and a modern history of the sub-Continent could logically be written around this gloomy but vital issue. It is to place it in perspective for a British public unconscious of its scope and meaning that the story has expanded to cover eight chapters.

It remains only to thank a countless number of officers of the Indian Civil Service and the Army, retired and serving, who gave me their time and advice in long hours, or supplied me with valuable memoranda. In India such busy men as General Cariappa and Sir Gilbert Laithwaite found time not only to deal with my questions but also to arrange for me to see others. Nor should I forget the great assistance I received from the Information Officers at India House and Pakistan House.

Where there is criticism in these pages, I ask those against whom it is directed to believe that I expect from them that same tolerance which in England enables political opponents in the midst of their thrusts and counter-thrusts to hold each other in respect, even affection. This I believe is the spirit of maturity in which India and Pakistan can and must go forward from strength to strength.

PART 1

INTERNAL PROBLEMS

CHAPTER ONE

YEARS OF UNCERTAINTY

IT is an unkind provision of fate which directs that man, in his endeavour to free himself from the shackles of his folly, usually chooses the aftermath of a war as the time for launching schemes of Utopia. War is regarded as a kind of cauldron in which all manner of previous ideals, political, social or economic, are pooled; and from which subsequently a new and vital opportunity beckons us to put our homes in order. My belief is that after a war we should all just sit back and do nothing. By that I do not mean that we should make no effort to repair the shattering physical effects of modern war. But the great machine of human thought needs time to recover. Whole nations have lived through a period of "nervous breakdown", and quiet convalescence is needed. That is the psychological aspect. It was evident in our efforts to establish the United Nations Organisation at the one time in history that was the least promising for its inauguration: when passions ran high and the world thought only in terms of victor and vanquished. No less convincing are the economic considerations. To attempt the luxury of the Welfare State when the till is obviously empty breathes good intention but hardly wise finance.

In India every factor demanding a pause for clear thought and economic recovery was present. If the leaders of the Congress and the Moslem League could have come to a standstill agreement for a year or so, the sub-Continent might today be a happier land for its 400 million inhabitants. The British Government were just as impatient to hand over power as Indians were to accept it. Yet to decide to whom to hand it defied the patience and diplomacy of Lord Wavell and his advisers. This is an attempt to tell the political story of those difficult days. It is neither an exciting nor uplifting kind of narrative: yet, since it closed a chapter in the history of our British Commonwealth, it needs to be told with accuracy and understanding.

On 14th June 1945 the long-awaited announcement was made by Mr. Amery in the House of Commons and by Lord Wavell in India. Simultaneously the Working Committee of the All-India National Congress were released. The Viceroy's former Executive Council was to disappear and in its place a new Council representative of the Congress, the League and the other main parties would be chosen by the Viceroy from names which the parties were to submit to him. The offer which Sir Stafford Cripps had brought to India in March 1942 remained open "in its entirety without change or qualification". From the old order only the Governor-General himself and the Commander-in-Chief would remain. There followed the Simla Conference to settle the matter.[1] The Conference failed, mainly on the issue of the nomination of the Moslem representative. Mr. Jinnah claimed the exclusive right to nominate all Moslems to the Council, a right which would immediately have excluded Maulana Abul Kalam Azad, the Moslem President of the Congress, from accepting a seat in the Council. The Congress maintained their attitude that as a body representing all communities they had the right to include two Moslems among their nominees. Yet on all sides the wisdom and breadth of the Government's proposals were recognised. The Council, with the exception of the Commander-in-Chief, would have been composed of Indians nominated by Indians. The controversial portfolio of Foreign Affairs would have been in the hands of an Indian. In recognition of a new situation of embarrassment in which the Viceroy might be representing both British national interests and the interests of India, the appointment of a United Kingdom High Commissioner in Delhi was announced.[2]

Had it been possible to persuade the Moslems to join the new Council, we might well have seen another pattern to the subsequent course of events. The war was still being fought against the Japanese. In the final days of its prosecution a group of Ministers selected from the two great parties might have worked in harmony for a common good.[3] I sometimes wonder if at this stage it was not fear of Congress friendship which may have subconsciously played its part in influencing Mr. Jinnah.

In the meanwhile in England a Labour Government had taken office. It was natural that Congressmen should associate a sense of urgency over their future independence with Mr. Attlee and his colleagues. In fact it was a Coalition Government under Sir Winston (then Mr.) Churchill which had sent Sir Stafford Cripps to India in 1942, and it was hardly appreciated that the "Cripps proposals", with their promise of independence after the war, had formed the basis for all subsequent discussion.[4] In any case, the British electorate was apathetic and ignorant of Indian affairs, and in so far as India's future was an election issue, the view was loosely held that we should no longer continue to shackle anyone who wanted freedom.

In September 1945 Lord Pethick-Lawrence, the new Secretary of

[1] For an account of the Simla Conference see *A Continent Experiments*, Chapter XIII.

[2] Mr. T. A. Shone, C.M.G., was appointed in September 1946.

[3] The representation proposed for Congress, League and other parties was on a percentage basis of 40 : 40 : 20, thus giving the much smaller Moslem population parity with the Hindus.

[4] In 1942 at the time of the Cripps Mission, S. Vallabhbhai Patel had said : " We would rather be ruled by Dacoits than by the British ". An interesting contrast is his statement three years later (30th June 1945, Bombay) : " We have no enmity against the British people. If there is a change of heart in our British rulers we shall not pursue our quarrel."

State, announced that elections to the Central and Provincial Assemblies would be held as soon as possible. It will be recalled that since the beginning of the war, when the Congress Provincial Ministers had withdrawn from office, five of the eleven Provinces had been administered under Section 93 of the Government of India Act. As a matter of administrative convenience it would have saved a lot of trouble if that situation could have continued, so that with the transition, independence could have been grafted directly on to efficient, if unrepresentative, bureaucracies. But the leaders accepting office would have had no mandate from the people, and so an election was unavoidable. It had the effect of reviving slumbering passions, both communal and anti-British, on a scale without precedent. The Congress leaders released from prison had shown remarkable restraint in adjusting themselves to the strange role of taking British proposals seriously, and here was an election to set the people of India about the game of slinging mud at the British and each other, when, left to themselves, they might have kept their senses. On 16th November 1945 the *Statesman* aptly put the case in these words :—

> " With avidity born of long-sustained rancour, racial and political leaders and newspapers of the Congress party have of late seized on every happening in India or abroad capable of anti-British use and exploited it to the full. British progressives reading day after day the twisting against their own country of every possible news item, Indian or foreign, may turn away, heart-hardened from sympathy for India's problems. We sense a graver estrangement between Britain's and India's biggest political organisation than has yet existed. British folk in India, military and civil, are very naturally tired and irritable. But World War II has been fought by them not merely for survival, but for principles. It was the noblest, grimmest, least self-interested struggle in their history. Let them not in the inevitable phase of post-war weariness now upon them, lose grip upon those ideals."

This, from the leading English newspaper in the country, was no understatement. No matter what the pretext—Indonesia, Palestine, the Indian National Army trials, or an innocuous announcement of a Parliamentary delegation to pay India a friendly visit—wild and vindictive abuse was hurled at the Administration, whether in Delhi or Whitehall.[1] Yet the elections of 1945 probably had their long-term significance; for it may have been in the light of harsh experience that the particular measures to conduct the far greater operation of 1952 were so carefully elaborated.

Closely following the announcement of elections on 19th September, Lord Wavell, who had returned from consultations in London, broadcast further proposals from Delhi. After the elections it was the Viceroy's

---

[1] See " Indecision in India ", by the author, *Nineteenth Century*, March 1946.

intention to consult representatives of those elected. For the first time the Indian States were to be drawn into the discussion. Together in conference they would work out the form a Constitution-making body should take. A treaty could then be concluded between the British Government and the Constitution-making body. Notwithstanding the failure of the Simla Conference, an Executive Council was to be formed with the support of the main parties. The Congress greeted the Wavell Plan with suspicion. The absence of the word " independence " and the use of the less specific term " self-government " raised doubts, so that when they came to throw themselves into the heat of the election battle, it was the old " Quit India " resolution of 1942 which formed the rallying point for their campaign. In effect this would have left a continent in turmoil without a Government. For the League, Mr. Jinnah stood uncompromisingly on the demand for Pakistan. In the circumstances the appointment of an Indian, Sir Chandulal Trivedi, as Governor of Orissa passed unnoticed.[1] Sir Maharaj Singh, the leader of the Indian Christians, commented with gloomy accuracy, " Elections will worsen rather than improve relations between the two major communities ".

The results of the elections were a foregone conclusion. The Congress and the League carried all before them at the expense of such feeble manifestations of opposition as Mr. M. N. Roy's Radical Democratic Party, the Communists and the Hindu Mahasabha.[2] The dilemma was complete with the Moslem demand for their own State firmly established and the Congress refusal of its recognition. In Delhi the ten British members of Parliament who had arrived on a mission of goodwill were told by an Indian journalist that they were regarded as " a huge joke "!

The elections to the Provincial Legislatures were not concluded until February 1946. The results revealed few surprises. The Moslem League, however, were unable to confirm their claim to Assam, while in Sind, Nationalist Moslems supporting the Congress were returned, creating a dangerous balance of twenty-seven Moslem seats to twenty-six of the Congress. In the Punjab an uneasy Coalition of the old Unionists, the Congress, the Moslem League and the Akali Sikhs took office. The supremacy and sanity of the Unionists had been undermined. To vote " Unionist " was to oppose Pakistan, and at that stage it was beyond the

[1] Announced in October 1945. Assumed office on 31st March 1946. Sir Chandulal Madhavlal Trivedi, K.C.S.I., C.I.E., O.B.E., was Secretary, War Department, 1942-46. His signature to Army Instructions will be familiar to many British officers of the Indian Army. He entered the Indian Civil Service in 1917.

[2] The elected element in the new Legislative Assembly became

Congress.	.	.	.	56
Moslem League	.	.	.	28
Akali Sikh	.	.	.	2
Independents	.	.	.	5
European	.	.	.	8

power of the Punjab Moslem Unionists to swim against the current of a demand which had so swiftly spread throughout the rest of India.

In an atmosphere of complete frustration the British Government, announced its intention to send out a Cabinet Mission. Accordingly Lord Pethick-Lawrence, Sir Stafford Cripps and Mr. Alexander sailed for India in March. Sir Stafford's reputation alone was such that high hopes were inevitably entertained of their ability to produce a settlement. For the Congress this meant the abdication of power by Britain within weeks. For the League, any negotiation which did not recognise the claim for Pakistan was meaningless. Yet it was as conciliators with an open mind that the Mission arrived. The magnitude of their problems became evident when they realised that it was months since the rival leaders had met in the same room. For Sir Stafford Cripps this was not a new experience. In 1942 he had journeyed 7,000 miles to find that the leaders would not walk across the road to meet each other in his presence. Lord Wavell had been no more successful. The Mission at least were able to induce the leaders to come together in the cool atmosphere of Simla. Alas, to meet was not to agree; and it was in no spirit of optimism that the Mission published their ingenious but complicated plan on 16th June. They had narrowed the gap, they had preserved unity, but they were no nearer to finality than their predecessors.

First and foremost the plan reaffirmed the need for an interim Government to be established with the support of the major political parties. There were many urgent matters of daily administration which could not wait on the ponderous process of formulating a new Constitution. Not the least was the grave danger of famine. A Union with a central Executive and Legislature was to be formed embracing both British India and the States. It would retain the subjects of Foreign Affairs, Defence and Communications. Any question raising a communal issue was to require not only a total majority vote, but a majority of the representatives present, and voting of each of the two major communities.

Pakistan was not conceded. But in order to satisfy the desire for Moslems to get together and avoid direct domination by a Hindu Government, the Provinces were to be free to form groups each with their own Executive and Legislature. It would then be for each group to determine the allocation of subjects as between the group and the Province within it. After ten years a Province could reconsider its position within the Constitution. It was an elastic arrangement, and with goodwill certainly represented a workable compromise between unity and vivisection. Its weakness lay in the inevitable decentralisation of economic power and consequent loss of control over services which demanded firm central direction in the interests of the Indian peasant. But it was only a suggestion, leaving the details of a Constitution to be thrashed out by separate machinery. For this purpose a Constitution-making Assembly was to be voted into power on a basis of one delegate to every million of the population, the main communities being thus represented in proportion to their numbers. The Assembly thus formed was to comprise 292 delegates from British India and ninety-three from the States. To them would fall the task of framing the Constitution in detail first for the Provinces and then for the Union. The plan for the formation of a Constituent Assembly was outlined in a previous statement of 16th May. In view of subsequent misunderstandings it is important that this should be borne in mind. As regards the Princes, the British Government could no longer exercise the powers of paramountcy, and they would be free to join an Indian Union or attempt a precarious independence.

In presenting these proposals the Mission made a pessimistic forecast of the results if they were refused. The alternative, they said, would be " a grave danger of violence, chaos and even civil war. . . . It is certain that it would be a terrible disaster for many millions of men, women and children." They were right.

This time the reaction of Indian leaders was by no means the familiar and immediate refusal. The objections, sure enough, appeared. But the scope of the problem was now well established in the minds of all, and an off-hand refusal was recognised as not enough. The Moslems on reflection required two Constitution-making bodies, one for Hindu Provinces, the other for the remaining Provinces and the Centre. There was disagreement over the powers of the Centre to raise revenues. The Mission had purposely left a number of issues untouched, since it was in the general interest that as many matters as possible should be settled by mutual agreement. Yet it was clear that if the principles of this three-tier Constitution were accepted such issues as a centrally controlled food policy to avert famine would immediately call for consideration.

By far the most determined reaction came from the Scheduled Castes, whose leader, Dr. B. R. Ambedkar, immediately sent a telegram of bitter protest to Sir Winston Churchill.[1] It will be recalled that when the 1935 Government of India Act was under consideration Mr. Gandhi's threat to fast to death had sufficed to keep this reluctant community within the Hindu fold. Nevertheless, Dr. Ambedkar has never abandoned the idea of their separate representation, and his efforts recently culminated in his resignation from Pandit Nehru's Ministry.

By June the Moslem League had surrendered sufficiently to be able to endorse the Mission's plan for grouped Provinces, and the Rulers of the States had declared their willingness to co-operate in an All-India Government. The time was ripe for setting up the Constitution-making machinery, and once again Lord Wavell began the task of forming an

---

[1] " Cabinet Mission's proposals are shameful betrayal of the cause of 60,000,000 untouchables. No representation in Constituent Assembly. No representation on Advisory Committee. No protection by treaty. Untouchables all over India are grateful to you for your speech in Parliament. Future of untouchables very dark. Depend upon you for safeguarding their interests."

interim Government previous to elections for the Constituent Assembly. Immediately he experienced the old difficulties of agreement on the composition of his Council. He therefore attempted the expedient of issuing personal invitations in the proportion of five seats to the Congress, five to the League and one each to a member of the Scheduled Castes, a Sikh, a Parsee and an Indian Christian. Having failed to collect a team, he accepted the only alternative, which was to appoint a stop-gap Executive of officials. Meanwhile arrangements to elect the Constituent Assembly went ahead. Once again between 11th and 28th July 1946 elections were held, the method being that of indirect election by the Provincial Assemblies on a system of proportional representation. Reluctantly the Congress decided to enter the contest, making it clear that their interpretation of the functions of a Constituent Assembly was that of a sovereign independent forum bound only by its own decisions for the attainment of complete independence for a united India. In effect this would have negatived the powers of the Viceroy and the existing Council. They also were emphatic that the conception of the grouping of Provinces was not accepted. The Sikhs, who saw in the proposal their own political eclipse, refused all form of co-operation. In the circumstances, and with a view to an attempt to reconcile the Congress attitude with the Mission's plan, the Viceroy postponed the summoning of his elusive interim Government. Not unnaturally the Moslem League summoned a meeting to reconsider their attitude. The League newspaper *Dawn* accused the Mission of a " double-cross ", and Lord Wavell received the unkind attention of the cartoonists. Nevertheless the elections for the Constituent Assembly went ahead, the two main Parties being overwhelmingly returned, the one in bellicose mood with a complex in regard to the prospect of an imposed treaty with Britain,[1] the other regarding the Congress approach as a repudiation of the Mission's plan to offer the Moslem minority a form of self-determination. The whole trend of Moslem sentiment at the time received encouragement from the resulting composition of the new Assembly. The Congress held 211 seats in a House of 296, and with his memory of bitter years of Congress domination, Mr. Jinnah was not likely to view the future in a spirit of co-operation. In the meanwhile the original function of the Constituent Assembly, which was to create a Constitution, had been lost in the various demands and reservations. Lord Wavell, persevering in an unequal contest, decided to snatch at such prospects of implementing the Mission's plan as were practical and called on Pandit Nehru, as the representative of the majority party, to form an interim Government. A Government was accordingly announced and was effective from 2nd

---

[1] " If the British Government presume to tell us that they are going to hold anything in India because they do not agree either in regard to the minorities or in regard to the treaty, we shall not accept that position. It would become a *casus belli*. We shall have no treaty if they seek to impose anything on us, and we shall tear up any treaty they try to impose."—Pandit Nehru.

September.[1] But no member of the Moslem League accepted office. In a broadcast announcement the Viceroy made it clear that he would welcome the co-operation of the League if they should change their mind. "They can propose to me five names for places in a Government of fourteen, of which six will be nominees of Congress and three will be representatives of minorities." At the best, it was a precarious Government, for Pandit Nehru still claimed sovereignty for the Constituent Assembly, while the Viceroy if challenged would have obviously exercised his power under the existing Constitution.

The Moslem League's protest now took an ominous and tangible form, and a day of "Direct Action" was called for 16th August. For four days Calcutta accordingly witnessed scenes of hooliganism and barbarity which should have sobered Mr. Jinnah. In a fit of utter irresponsibility the Bengal Moslem League Ministry took the opportunity to declare a public holiday, and their reward was a casualty list of 4,000 killed and another 4,000 in the hospitals. In Delhi Sir Shafa'at Ahmed Khan, a Moslem member of the new Ministry, was stabbed, but recovered. A curious twist in the approach of such a confirmed enemy of Britain as Mr. Sarat Chandra Bose was his reflection on the lack of responsibility of the day. He who had previously insisted on the withdrawal of the British Army from India now demanded the resignation of the Governor, Sir Frederick Burrows, for failure to take adequate measures, to be followed by the dismissal of the League Ministry and the handing over of authority to the Army!

Much as we deplore the senseless sacrifice of life which followed on "Direct Action", it is difficult to avoid sympathy with the Moslem League in the treatment which circumstances dictated for their embitterment. As the party and power with a numerical majority, the Congress were receiving common justice. But it was a justice which could only cut across the Moslem sense that their acceptance of a British plan offering them a modified form of their demands had been discarded in appease-

---

[1] Pandit Jawaharlal Nehru.   Congress President.
 S. Vallabhbhai Patel.   Congress Working Committee.
 Dr. Rajendra Prasad.   ,,   ,,   ,,
 Mr. C. Rajagopalachari.   ,,   ,,   ,,   (formerly Premier of Madras).
 Mr. Sarat Chandra Bose.   Congress Working Committee (Congress Leader in Legislative Assembly).
 Dr. John Matthai.   Indian Christian. Managing Director, Tata Chemical Works.
 S. Baldev Singh.   Sikh Member of Punjab Ministry.
 Mr. Asaf Ali.   Congress Moslem. Deputy Leader, Congress, in Legislative Assembly.
 Sir Shafa'at Ahmed Khan.   Former High Commissioner, South Africa. Non-League Moslem.
 Mr. G. H. Bhaba.   Parsee.
 Sayed Ali Zaheer.   Leader, Shia Moslem Congress.
 Mr. Jagjivan Ram.   President, Depressed Classes League.

ment of the greater numbers. It was the birth of an intuition which has persisted into the years after partition. With the arrival of the Cabinet Mission, for a time there had been an artificial sense of hope. The plan for a Constituent Assembly had been accepted by both the Congress and the League. But on a detailed analysis it became apparent that the two parties were really agreeing to quite different things. The whole object of an interim Government was surely to teach the representatives of the two parties to work together. A Cabinet which contained only members of Congress and their fellow travellers was meaningless if it failed to attract League membership. Conversely, the argument that the Viceroy should have turned to the minority community, as having accepted the plan in principle, and asked it to form a Government was equally divorced from reality. It will be recalled that the Mission's statement on 16th May outlined the method of forming a Constituent Assembly. The subsequent declaration of 16th June misguidedly provided that in the event of the Viceroy failing to assemble a willing and representative interim Government, he should proceed to select a Government " as representative as possible of those willing to accept the statement of 16th May ". Since this statement referred to the formation of the Constituent Assembly, to which both parties had already agreed, the scope for misunderstanding and legal cross-purpose argument became illimitable.

For six weeks a Congress Ministry was in office before the Moslem League decided to enter the Government. When finally on 26th October their five nominees [1] accepted vacancies on the Executive Council, the resulting team was in no sense a Coalition working for the good of India. Rather was it two blocs engaged in a sparring contest, each determined not to retreat from their own interpretation of the Cabinet Mission Plan. In an effort to bridge the gulf Mr. Gandhi produced a formula covering the right of the League to represent Moslems throughout India. But it was not happily worded and led to a further confusion of claims and accusations. Nor with this curious qualified co-operation could the Moslems bring themselves to take their seats in the Constituent Assembly when it met in session on 9th December. It was therefore in an Assembly dominated by the Congress, without representatives of either Moslems or the Princes, that Pandit Nehru secured an overwhelming majority for the resolution defining an " Independent Sovereign Republic " as the goal for the new India. The resolution presented on 13th December was finally carried on 22nd January 1947, after a delay to allow the Moslem League to enter the Assembly if it so wished.

The entry of the Moslems into an interim Government involved the

[1] Liaquat Ali Khan   U.P.
I. I. Chundrigar.   Bombay.
Abdur Rab Nishtar.   N.W.F.P.
Ghazanfar Ali Khan.   Punjab.
Jogendra Nath Mandal.   Bengal, Scheduled Castes.

resignation of three members.[1] The new arrivals who took their place represented a surprise, in that Mr. Jinnah, following the precedent of Mr. Gandhi, remained outside the Cabinet. The inclusion of Mr. Jogendra Nath Mandal, who had been a member of the Bengal Moslem League Ministry, was a clever move to indicate the League's solicitude for minorities.

In this general period of uncertainty, Pandit Nehru took the opportunity to fly to Waziristan, where, in spite of Congress assurances of the end of the days of punitive expeditions, he was given a chilly reception. After firing on his plane, the *jirgah* at Miranshah told him they would " avenge the ill-treatment of Moslems in India ". The episode is of interest in the light of India's relations with Afghanistan today and the latter's encouragement of tribal autonomy. Meanwhile in Bengal the aftermath of " Direct Action " was taking its toll. In East Bengal, where Moslems predominated, hundreds of villages were set on fire and the first streams of refugees took to their wagons. In Calcutta troops and the police were out every day firing on riotous mobs, while British troops were hurried to Patna in Bihar. Pandit Nehru, who had previously condemned bombing by air as a weapon against frontier tribes, did not hesitate to threaten its use against the Bihar rioters.

On 20th February 1947 in the House of Commons Mr. Attlee made his historic statement to the effect that, come what may, power would be transferred to responsible Indian hands not later than June 1948. Furthermore, if the Moslem League did not join the Constituent Assembly as envisaged by the Cabinet Mission Plan, the British Government would have " to consider to whom the powers of the Central Government in British India should be handed over, on due date, whether as a whole to some form of Central Government for British India or *in some areas* to the existing Provincial Government or in such a way as may seem most reasonable and in the best interests of the Indian people ". Simultaneously it was announced that Lord Wavell would be immediately succeeded by Lord Mountbatten.

Here was the first official reluctant recognition of the inevitability of two nations. Here, too, was at last the naming of a date on which to base plans and a guarantee—if it was still needed—that, for better or worse, Indians would in sixteen months' time take complete control of their own destiny. June 1948 was to be the focus for a new sense of urgency. Alas, it did not have that effect. Instead it drove leaders farther apart. Those " areas " which sensed the coming severance from a Government in Delhi were suddenly restive. Hindus in Bengal saw themselves as the victims of primitive Moslem savagery and clamoured for the partition of their Province. In Assam and the N.W.F.P. the Congress Ministries stood their ground. But in the Punjab the League finally dislodged the

---

[1] Sarat Chandra Bose.
Sir Shafa'at Ahmed Khan.
Sayed Ali Zaheer.

short-lived Coalition Ministry, and the Governor took over the Province under Section 93 of the Government of India Act of 1935.

In England debates in both Houses of Parliament revealed consternation at the prospect of what seemed a British abandonment of responsibility before a real settlement could be achieved. In the Upper House Lord Templewood, who had piloted the Act of 1935 through Parliament, spoke of "unconditional surrender at the expense of many to whom we had given specific undertakings". He was supported among others by the great authority of Lord Simon. It fell to Lord Halifax to urge that there should be no division. While it was easy to say what was wrong, it was not so easy to say what was right. The fact was that no one had a better solution; and their Lordships reluctantly accepted the wise counsel of a great servant of India.

In the House of Commons the Opposition were not so acquiescent. Sir John Anderson,[1] a former Governor of Bengal, moved a resolution which, while reaffirming agreement on the principle of the transfer of power, criticised the fixing of an arbitrary date. Sir Winston Churchill naturally supported the resolution with all the eloquence of one whose whole life had been an assertion of the mission of Britain to lead nations forward by processes of gradual development and consolidation.

Sir Stafford Cripps for the Government put the case clearly as a choice between remaining to govern for another fifteen years with a reinforcement of British troops, and a further effort to bring Indian leadership together with the warning of a time limit. The Opposition resolution was lost by 337 votes to 185.

Lord Wavell's return was presented as the result of his own decision to resign, and all demands by the Opposition for explanations were resisted. Nor is it possible at this stage to offer a full vindication of one whose great contribution to this vital moment in history has not yet been acknowledged. In a reference to Lord Wavell's hurried consultations in London in November 1946 it has been suggested that he had nothing to offer as a solution.[2] This is no justice to Lord Wavell. It would be nearer the truth to deduce that he had a plan which nevertheless involved a gradual transition and attempted to save at least the unity of defence from the debris of British India. The truth must await the passing of years to lessen the impact of controversy.

On 24th March 1947 the last British Viceroy was administered the oath by Sir Patrick Spens, the British Lord Chief Justice, the Durbar Hall finally reflecting all the splendour of generations of viceregal ceremonial with the central figure and his consort worthy of the dignity of so dramatic an occasion. In characteristic fashion Lord Mountbatten threw

[1] Now Viscount Waverley.
[2] "Wavell, he [Mr. Attlee] said, had come back with nothing more constructive than a military evacuation plan." *Mission with Mountbatten*, Chapter I, p. 17 (Alan Campbell-Johnson).

himself into the problem before him, lavishing on it the dynamic energy and efficiency which had come to be recognised as his equipment in problems of either diplomacy or naval precision. But there seems to have been one limitation on the manner of his initiative. Its nature can perhaps be illustrated by quoting a small incident. Alan Campbell-Johnson records that on 25th March, in his first interview with Pandit Nehru, he asked the latter for his estimate of Mr. Jinnah.[1] At the time Nehru was the head of a Government with an Assembly in which Moslems refused to sit and a Cabinet of doubtful Moslem loyalties; and in normal times it would have been natural for the Head of the State to turn to his Chief Minister for an opinion on any personality in the political situation of the day. But the times were not normal; for they demanded nothing less than the very difficult condition that the Viceroy should be on terms of complete equality with both Mr. Jinnah and Mr. Nehru. The mere fact that the Viceroy found himself discussing one leader in consultation with the other three days after his arrival suggests that the association never got away to an initiation by which the two leaders were regarded as unknown quantities to be judged from personal impressions which could start from scratch.

Lord Mountbatten immediately inaugurated a series of discussions and interviews with Indian leaders of all shades of opinion. The urgency of the times will be appreciated if it be remembered that his Cabinet were far more concerned with internal dissension than with the government of the country. It might, for example, be considered somewhat fantastic if the Chancellor of the Exchequer was openly to attack the Prime Minister of the day.[2] Yet this was exactly the manner of conduct of government. Meanwhile British officers of the services anxiously awaited a development on which they could base their future. Many normal matters of administration awaited decision. Yet no one could be bothered to decide. Frequently it was difficult to know from whom to take orders. In the circumstances it was only natural that the administrative machine should slacken to a sluggish crawl which was a travesty of its former efficiency. Uncertainty brought cynicism. Yet there could be no indifference, for the plight of the country was making the highest demands on the patience and physical endurance of the harassed administration. Everywhere the spectre of communal madness was looming over the land. Arson, loot and murder in a hundred cities taxed a police force which itself was fighting to keep clear of contamination. In the third week in April deaths from rioting were reported from

[1] *Mission with Mountbatten*, Chapter III, p. 44.
[2] On 21st April 1947 the Finance Minister, Liaquat Ali Khan (who was also General Secretary of the Moslem League), described certain statements of Pandit Nehru as " most thoughtless ". He added : " If the spirit of arrogance exhibited by Mr. Nehru is to be the guiding principle of Congress policy in the future, then God help those who may choose to cast their lot with Congress ". (The occasion was a warning by Pandit Nehru to the Princes.)

Calcutta, Delhi, Lahore, Cawnpore, Amritsar, Bannu and Dera Ismail Khan. It was as if a mighty river was about to burst its banks. Feverishly men of goodwill strove to stop the gaps. But the pressure was soon to sweep aside their labours, and waters of despair were to drench the entire country.

By the middle of May Lord Mountbatten had seen and heard all that usefully could be contributed by Indian leadership and had formulated his proposals. He accordingly flew to London for their final confirmation with the British Government. In his absence, Mr. Jinnah addressed the Press in Delhi and called for " friendly and reciprocal " relations between India and Pakistan. In the same breath he said that the Moslem League would " fight every inch " to resist the partition of Bengal and the Punjab, the inference being that the two Provinces should be included in their entirety in Pakistan. He added the demand for a corridor across India to connect the separated limbs of the new State. But it is difficult to believe that he was really serious.

On 30th May the Viceroy returned to Delhi. Even at this late hour it seems that Mr. Gandhi had not reconciled himself to the inevitable, for at his prayer meeting on 31st May he condemned those who were working for the division of India and urged that Britain should be held to the Cabinet Mission Plan. On 2nd June Lord Mountbatten summoned the leaders and handed them the Plan which was to set the seal on the creation of two States and the partition of India. On 3rd June the Plan was broadcast to the Indian people by the Viceroy.

The ingenuity of the " 3rd June Plan " lay in the manner in which, having provided for partition, it in no way prejudged further Pakistani or Indian decisions. Even at that late hour, could the leaders agree, there was nothing to preclude negotiations for a united India. The future relations of India and Pakistan with the Commonwealth and with each other were for the new States to decide, even though Dominion status would naturally be first assumed. The Indian people were themselves also to decide that most controversial of problems concerned with the geography of partition; namely, the fate of Bengal and the Punjab. For this purpose the Legislative Assemblies of the two Provinces were to meet in two separate portions representing respectively districts with Moslem majorities and those without. If either portion were to opt for the partition of the Province, then partition would take place. The Districts were classified according to the 1941 census. Subsequently a Boundary Commission would settle the details. In the N.W.F.P. a referendum was to be held to decide whether or not the Province was to join Pakistan. With the lapse of paramountcy the States would be free either to enter the Constituent Assembly or to plough their own lonely furrow. The British Government could recognise no Indian State as a separate Dominion.

The outline of the Plan was clear and inevitable. That it was at this stage the only way out is indicated by its reluctant acceptance by all the

C

leaders. "It is with no joy in my heart that I commend these proposals, though I have no doubt in my mind that this is the right course," was Pandit Nehru's verdict. Even Sardar Baldev Singh, whose community, the Sikhs, had the most to lose by the partition of the Punjab, had to admit that there was no alternative. If therefore I find myself unable to accept one vital reservation which was made, it is in no way to deny full recognition of the Plan itself.

The anticipated date of the transfer of power in June 1948 had hitherto governed all discussion and thought. Yet on 3rd June 1947 the Plan stated that provision would now be made for the transfer, on a Dominion status basis, within the current year. A few days later we were to learn that 15th August had been fixed as the day on which power would pass. There was thus left just under two and a half months in which to complete the greatest political and administrative operation in history. The dividing of resources, of the Civil Service and, alas, of a great Army, had to be driven forward at a speed which, though it commanded admiration as conveying to all concerned a sense of vitality, inevitably resulted in the emergence of the new State of Pakistan in the utmost confusion.

On 4th July the Indian Independence Bill was introduced in the House of Commons. The Bill was hustled through its various stages, and passed its third reading on 15th July, receiving the Royal Assent three days later. In the meanwhile the members in the Punjab and Bengal Assemblies had confirmed the partition of their Provinces.

In the N.W.F.P. the referendum was finally taken in July, after heated argument. The circumstances in which the desires of an essentially Moslem area required confirmation are not usually understood. The mere fact that Moslem authority was not challenged had led to the emergence of a body of political thought outside the Moslem League. The case for the protection of Moslem interests did not arise, and it was therefore natural that politically minded Moslems should harness their loyalties to the Indian Congress. The result was the Red-Shirt movement under the redoubtable leadership of Dr. Khan Sahib and his brother, Khan Abdul Ghaffar Khan. But it was obvious that, situated within the geographical limits of a new State—Pakistan—the position of a Moslem Province attempting to exist in political isolation would be quite untenable; hence the referendum. The final decision does not appear to have been taken until 23rd June, when the reluctant agreement of the Congress to the referendum was at last forthcoming. At the time Dr. Khan Sahib, who led the Red-Shirt Ministry in the Province, threatened to resist. But on Gandhi's advice he accepted a peaceful abstention. The Governor, Sir Olaf Caroe, applied for leave, and the Governorship and conduct of the referendum were placed in the hands of a soldier, General Sir Rob Lockhart. There had been some unkind criticism of Sir Olaf Caroe, and his application for leave was a graceful gesture in the public interest to dispel bazaar rumours concerning his impartiality. Thus a Province which had been intimately linked with the fortunes of the Army was to turn to the Army for vital assistance in deciding its future.[1] The result of the referendum was a foregone conclusion. On 20th July it was announced that 289,244 persons had voted to join Pakistan against 2,074 who had voted for India. The Red-Shirts abstained. For a while Dr. Khan Sahib clung to his responsibilities. But on the establishment of Pakistan and his refusal to take the new oath Mr. Jinnah removed him. He and his brother then had to accept the same confinement which he had previously bestowed on the Moslem League leaders. Released from gaol, Khan Abdul Qayyum Khan, who at one time had been a Moslem member of the Central Assembly on the Congress ticket, formed a Ministry. The fortunes of the Frontier Province have rested ever since under his somewhat unpredictable but firm control.

In the meanwhile the Boundary Commission under Sir Cyril Radcliffe had begun its work. Four High Court Judges from the Punjab assisted in the case of the western problem and the same number from Bengal tackled the eastern boundary.[2] Since the Punjab delimitation raised the more acute controversy and concerns an area with which I was once closely concerned, I will not touch on the Commission's work in Bengal. But we may assume that the same kind of difficulties were experienced in the east as in the west.

In the Punjab, Radcliffe's assistants were two Mohammedans, a Sikh and a Hindu; and it was a sad reflection on the state of the country that four High Court judges divided their judgment exactly according to communal sentiment.

The terms of reference of the Commission were as follows:—

> "To demarcate the boundaries of the two parts of the Punjab on the basis of ascertaining the contiguous majority areas of Moslems and non-Moslems. In doing so, it will take into account other factors."

Sir Cyril certainly gave those other factors their full consideration. They were not unimportant. The orientation of railways, canals and a hydro-electric system were the main arguments cutting across the satisfaction of communal sentiment. In a chapter on the fighting in Kashmir I have more conveniently referred to the apparent departure from the principle supported in the "3rd June Plan", by the award of most of the Gurdaspur District to India.[3] In this particular case a glance at the map will reveal that to have awarded the Pathankot *tehsil* to Pakistan would

---

[1] The actual conduct of the referendum was entrusted to Brigadier J. R. Booth (commander of the Wana Brigade).

[2] Sir C. Radcliffe, G.B.E. Now Lord Radcliffe of Werneth (cr. 1949), Director-General, Ministry of Information, 1941–45; Vice-Chairman, General Council of the Bar, 1946–49.

[3] Chapter XVI, p. 235, and the map of Kashmir should be noted.

have placed the headworks of the Upper Bari Doab Canal at Madhopur under Pakistan control.[1]   The canal irrigated the Lahore, Amritsar and Gurdaspur Districts, and of these Amritsar held a Hindu majority, besides representing the religious stronghold of the Sikhs. It was a case of the needs of an area artificially created by a canal against the sentiments of a majority of the inhabitants.

According to Mr. Din Mohammed, who was one of the two Moslem members of the Commission, Radcliffe's main reason for awarding the Batala and Gurdaspur *tehsils* of the Gurdaspur District to India was that their award to Pakistan would have isolated the important Amritsar District from surrounding Indian soil. To the east the District was bounded by Kapurthala State, which, though ruled by a Sikh Maharaja, at that time contained a narrow majority of Moslems. If we contemplate the check-like pattern of *tehsils* on the map, we will appreciate Radcliffe's difficulty. That his decision covering the Gurdaspur District was sincere we should not doubt. But it is also fair to Pakistan to recall again that had the Gurdaspur District not been awarded to India, India could certainly never have fought a war in Kashmir.

The further suspicion, even conviction, of Pakistanis that Radcliffe, with Lord Mountbatten, was guilty of a plot to deprive Pakistan of Kashmir, is most unfortunate. Mr. Din Mohammed, for one, will doubt our good faith for many months to come. Yet it would be wrong for Englishmen who stand outside the controversy not to believe in Sir Cyril Radcliffe's sincerity of intention or fail to appreciate his dilemma when he wrote: ". . . differences of opinion as to the significance of the term ' other factors ', which we were directed by our terms of reference to take into account and as to the weight and value to be attached to those factors made it impossible to arrive at any agreed line." We are told that Lord Mountbatten issued strict instructions that his staff were to have no contact with Sir Cyril Radcliffe during his difficult task, while he himself equally avoided a meeting.[2] Accusations of collaboration are therefore certainly not to be accepted.

But there is one aspect of the Radcliffe Award which calls for comment; and that is the timing of its publication. Independence Day was deliberately avoided, and the verdicts for both Bengal and the Punjab were made known a day later, on 16th August.

The fact that the final demarcation of these very controversial frontiers was not announced until the day after they should have been recognised indicates the complete absence of any conception of an operation involving population exchanges. With communal tension increasing all

---

[1] The " 3rd June Plan " did not specify that Districts with Moslem majorities were to go to Pakistan. It merely used the distinction of Moslem majorities and non-Moslem majorities as the basis for deciding the issue of whether or not to partition the Punjab. But in doing so it naturally implied that the principle of the composition of a District would govern its allotment to either country.

[2] *Mission with Mountbatten*, Chapter XII, p. 152.

YEARS OF UNCERTAINTY

over the country, ever since the Moslem League's instructions for
" Direct Action " in August 1946, it might have been anticipated that
the act of partition would hasten the tempo. Could it not have been
foreseen that the motives of primitive fear and revenge gripping millions
in Pakistan and India would drive the minority communities to seek
shelter in the land across the border which they identified with the safety
of their own religious persuasion? For a moment let us indulge in the
luxury of wisdom after the event. Name a date for partition, not two
and a half months but at least six months ahead of the first decision.
Arrange for the Army to remain undivided under neutral orders for six
months after the setting up of the two new States. Place a Boundary
Force on the frontiers, not of one Division, but of a Corps made available
from the Army, with British troops sharing the responsibility in large
numbers. Set up a Boundary Commission to publish its award at least
two months previous to partition. Make all arrangements to register
and remove those millions who desire to be removed. Carry through
the exchange of populations to a time-table elaborated with all the
precision of a " D " Day operation. Finally, divide the Army, with the
retention of British troops until the last moment. Only some plan on
such a scale could have rescued the north of India from the misery in
which it was to be engulfed. Nor need it in any way have jeopardised
the passing of constitutional power on the named date. Many reasons
have been advanced for the unreality of a Master Plan. But one, at least,
requires to be questioned. It is said that it would have been impossible
to retain British troops in the country. In England the public were
pressing for their return, while in India the constitutional position would
have involved placing troops of the British Army under Indian and
Pakistani orders. The first reason is a lamentable reflection on the
judgment of the British public, assuming that they could and should
have been informed of the issues at stake. As to constitutional questions
of command, had the conduct of a plan been made the responsibility of
an Army answerable to neither Dominion, but to His Majesty's Government, for the period involved, there could have been no doubts. In fact,
Field-Marshal Sir Claude Auchinleck was appointed Supreme Commander from 15th August, answerable to a joint Defence Council
consisting of himself, the two Governors-General and the two Defence
Ministers. But he was given no responsibility for law and order, with
only operational control over troops in transit. In an extension of his
powers of command together with the allocating of his final responsibility to an authority outside India lay the only hope of smooth transition.
We are told that both sides insisted on military independence as a condition of settlement.[1] Such independence would eventually have come,
and it would have been worth risking some harsh words to have answered
insistence with equal determination. A Boundary Force arrived. In
effect it was the 4th Indian Division hurried up from the south of India.

[1] *Mission with Mountbatten*, Chapter X, p. 125.

But it found itself involved in a task for which it was quite inadequate, and it was hardly fair to expect Indian soldiers to remain immune from communal sentiment when so closely associated with it on the spot.[1]

The whole pattern of development can really be traced back to the decision to squeeze the administrative headache of partition into about seventy-five days. Circumstances had to fit into a plan rather than a plan be adjusted to the circumstances. The question we ask therefore hardly concerns such considerations as to whether portions of the British Army could or could not have been placed under the orders of either the Governors of East and West Punjab or the two Governors-General; since we maintain that no constitutional or administrative difficulty, however uncompromising, should have been allowed to stand in the way of a plan so vital to a peaceful partition. The real issue, then, narrows down to whether or not chaos in the Punjab could and should have been predicted. The orgy of slaughter did not break upon us as a sudden elimination of human control. It had been smouldering and gathering force for many months all over the land. Was it not clear that it would approach its climax so soon as the Radcliffe Award was known? For the refugee movement had already begun. We ask ourselves whether British officers on the spot could foresee the scope of the problem. We hear stories of civil and military officers with long experience of India being taken completely by surprise. I myself had known and worked in that most controversial of areas, the Jullundur District, where Hindu and Mohammedan villages are interspersed in close proximity; and yet I would hesitate to give any firm assurance that I would have prophesied the events of August. In that doubt must rest some exoneration of British authority and their decisions.

It will be recalled that the Cabinet Mission in the previous year had made it clear that paramountcy must lapse.

> " This means that the rights of the States which flow from their relationship to the Crown will no longer exist and that all the rights surrendered by the States to the paramount power will return to the States. Political arrangements between the States on the one side and the British Crown and British India on the other will thus be brought to an end."

Thus ran the decree of the Cabinet Mission presented to the Chancellor of the Chamber of Princes on 12th May 1946. The " 3rd June Plan " confirmed that statement. There followed those high-pressure negotiations with the Princes which have been described elsewhere, and which were to result in their eventual absorption into the new India.

Within one chapter it is not possible to trace the administrative story of partition in detail. A Partition Committee gave way to a Partition Council with power to take policy decisions. But the main work fell

[1] I have dealt more fully with the military situation in Chapter V. Here, in the interests of clarity it is necessary to repeat the main features of the problem.

on a Steering Committee of two; and fortunately they proved the right men for the task. H. M. Patel, the Cabinet Secretary, and Mohammed Ali,[1] Adviser in the Military Finance Department, were Civil Servants of outstanding ability, ready to work together for the satisfaction of seeing a great responsibility through to its conclusion. Even so, they and the various committees which were set up could never have tackled their heavy responsibility with the confidence of success had they not been able to draw inspiration from the dynamic personality in control. Armed with wide powers under the India Independence Act for effecting partition, the Viceroy was able to impart that extra sense of urgency to the machine which alone could make partition a practical achievement within the time.

The Independence Act allowed for those transitional powers to extend to 31st March 1948, it being further provided that a Governor-General be appointed by the King for each of the two new Dominions. It remains only to note the controversy which arose in the implementation of the Indian desire to retain Lord Mountbatten as Governor-General of India and Mr. Jinnah's wish to assume the Governor-Generalship of Pakistan.

Early in July Mountbatten was turning over in his mind the difficult issue of the future of the two appointments. It had been thought that Jinnah would wish to assume the more powerful appointment of Prime Minister; and it came as a surprise to discover that this was not the case. Meanwhile the Congress had paid Mountbatten the unique tribute of requesting him to remain on as Governor-General after partition. Apart from the fact that here was a gesture of tremendous significance for the British Commonwealth in view of the past years of bitterness, it seemed that India and Pakistan would more probably be launched in some harmony if Mountbatten, rather than a member of the Indian National Congress, was available to accept the responsibility for direct relations with Jinnah. Mountbatten was at first reluctant. He feared that a diminution in status might bring in its wake a loss of goodwill from both Hindu and Moslem. General Ismay flew home to place the issue before the Cabinet. The views of the Opposition were sounded, and Sir Winston Churchill lent the great weight of his verdict in favour of Mountbatten remaining on for the transitional period. But the effect of a logical decision taken in good faith was hardly up to expectations. Pakistanis felt that one whose personal understanding with Indian leaders had appeared in marked contrast to his relations with Jinnah was, in his new position, able to influence the British Government in exclusive favour of the India of his choice. Mr. Jinnah had come forward with the unconventional proposal that Mountbatten should be appointed as supreme Governor-General with powers of control over both Dominions in regard to such matters as the division of assets. The British Government would not consent. Perhaps the constitutional difficulties were too formidable. A neutral Governor-General would certainly

[1] Later Finance Minister, Pakistan.

have needed to live within his own self-made enclave of neutral territory. But to dismiss Jinnah's proposal as insincere is ungenerous. Had it been a practical possibility it might have saved us all some bitter recriminations. The legacy of the arrangement was later to emerge as an acceptance of the Mountbattens with an emotional adulation in India, in contrast to undisguised hostility at the mention of their name in Pakistan. These contrasts of sentiment have continued on with surprising persistence into the subsequent years.

If personal friendships played some part in confusing loyalties, the circumstances by which one community desired partition while the other resisted it would inevitably and naturally influence Englishmen who strove to rescue the semblance of unity until the last. Partition was against every instinct of the Power which had covered the land, with a common administration, a common railway system, with roads and canals which took no thought of Hindu or Moslem, and with one Army for defence. Until the end Mountbatten struggled to retain some form of Indian unity, and the Cabinet Mission Plan was kept before the leaders in face of such startling demands as that of Mr. Jinnah for a corridor. It was not until 2nd June, in the momentous meeting with the leaders, that the seal was finally placed on the decision to partition British India and the Plan was reluctantly unfolded.

Once that decision had been taken there followed the danger that the interim Government might not hold together until the ratification of partition by Parliament at home. For a few days Mr. Jinnah maintained the attitude that the Plan would need the approval of the Moslem League. The Sikhs were restive in anticipation of the division of their community. The fate of the States after the lapse of paramountcy was uncertain, and as late as 15th June the issue of Dominion status was unsettled. The difficulties confronting the Viceroy might well have shaken the will of a less confident man at the helm. Yet I think Lord Mountbatten would be the first to admit that his task bore that seal of finality and purpose which made the way clearer than it ever would have appeared to his predecessor. Nor could he have seen the great transition through without those previous tireless negotiations of Lord Wavell which had brought the true nature of the conflict into the light of day. Mountbatten was navigating across unknown seas. But he was fortunate always to know his destination. Where men of greater capacity for research and profounder experience might have hesitated, he was able to ride forward in buoyant optimism, watching his fences before he took them, yet never allowing the eye to linger long enough for those doubts to take control which might have harassed a statesman of greater caution and orthodoxy. India in 1947 was a country susceptible to the power of personality. It looked for a man who carried his heart on his sleeve. It was impatient with one who appeared to hide his mind in defensive circles of reserve. Indeed, when in September Mountbatten attempted to withdraw from active participation and assume the more leisurely role of a constitutional Governor-General he was recalled from Simla to Delhi by Nehru and Vallabhbhai Patel, who saw in him alone the salvation of a crumbling situation. Such was the spell which the last of a long line of British Pro-Consuls was able to cast over Indian leadership at a time when many years of drift would seem to have confirmed the loss of all hope of a happy ending. Not the least of achievements was the capture of the friendship of Mahatma Gandhi. Once the mind of the great Indian leader was with him—and particularly must this apply in the Mahatma's final acceptance of partition—then the conquest of India was confirmed. We are still near events. But I am so bold as to suggest that in no small measure was the subsequent decision of an Indian Republic to seek membership within the Commonwealth due to the influence of the Mountbatten stewardship.

And yet it will be many years before we can regard the ending as entirely happy. It may be that the first seeds of partition were sown way back in 1909, when a Moslem delegation met the Viceroy of the day to request separate Moslem electorates.[1] It may be that ever since that event the gathering political antagonisms of the Congress and the League had been moving to this climax. If so, the subsequent bitterness and recrimination were certainly beyond the power of one Englishman to harness and control. Time alone will, then, prove the healer; time and the leavening of human experience. Men are foolish, and often learn only by their own follies. But they *do learn*. In that belief we look to the immediate and bitter legacies of the events of 1947 one day becoming lost in the limbo of time.

[1] Delegation to Lord Minto headed by H.H. the Aga Khan.

CHAPTER TWO

YEARS OF CONFIRMATION

THE new Indian Government were certainly not slow in setting about the business of governing. A Drafting Committee under the chairmanship of Dr. Ambedkar was formed on 29th August 1947, and immediately entered on the task of drafting a new Constitution. In just under six months they managed to draft the longest Constitution in the world, complete in 395 articles and eight schedules. The achievement constituted a monumental contribution to India's future on the part of the distinguished Chairman. Thereafter, clause by clause, the draft was submitted to the scrutiny of the Constituent Assembly. By 16th November 1949 they had disposed of the final amendments, and on 18th November Dr. Ambedkar was able to move that " the Constitution, as settled by the Constituent Assembly, be passed ". On 26th January 1950 India formally adopted her new Constitution, and a milestone in the political evolution of mankind was thus erected for all who press forward on the quest for political progress.

The Constitution of India is that of a " Union ", a term which was used previously by the Cabinet Mission, and which allowed for some elasticity in the relations between the Centre and its twenty-eight Component States.[1] That elasticity was necessary was indicated by the very different degrees of political and administrative competence in various States. Thus the group which included the small hill Principalities now grouped together as " Himachal Pradesh " could hardly expect the same form of responsible government as Bombay; and in general the whole problem of the integration of the India of the Maharajas connoted a structure in which the federal components were necessarily uneven.

The pattern for the future was indicated to the Princes in the Memorandum addressed by the Cabinet Mission to the Chancellor of the Chamber of Princes on 12th May 1946. In this it was made clear that the British Government could no longer exercise the ambiguous function known as paramountcy after British authority had withdrawn. It was tactfully suggested that the States, so far from seeking to hinder developments in British India, would wish to contribute to the making of the new Constitutional structure. " To do this doubtless the States

[1] The structure comprising Parts A, B and C States is more conveniently described in Chapter VI. Part D consists of the Andaman and Nicobar Islands and the State of Sikkim. In a work of this scope a detailed analysis of the Indian Constitution is not attempted. In particular the whole aspect of financial arrangements between Centre and States is not touched. This is covered in Part XII of the Constitution. See also Appendix I.

will take certain steps to set up their own administrations according to the highest standard." Since the British Government would not hand over paramountcy to a successor Government or Governments, it would be necessary to make certain "interim arrangements" with those in control in India at the time for the continuation of the *status quo*. These were the "standstill agreements" which in the case of the Kashmir agreement were to be the focus for much controversy. The Princes were advised to set up a "negotiating committee" to meet representatives of the Constituent Assembly when formed, and this they agreed to do.

There followed the mingled process of coercion and persuasion by which the States signed their various Instruments with the Indian Union under the impression that the commitment was for Union control only of Defence, Communications and Foreign Relations. As late as 5th July 1947 Sardar Vallabhbhai Patel, as States Minister, had confirmed that Congress would scrupulously observe the autonomous existence of the States and would not interfere in their domestic affairs. It proved otherwise, and we are left wondering whether there was ever any real intention to honour the limited contract. In the White Paper published by the Indian Government in March 1950 the process is accepted as the mere pressure of circumstances.

> "With the formation of the Union of States the necessity of enlarging the content of the accession of States was more acutely felt. . . . All the Rajpramukhs . . . subsequently signed fresh Instruments of Accession by which they acceded to the Dominion of India in respect of all matters specified in the Federal and Concurrent Lists, excepting those relating to taxation, and eventually taxation was included also."

The above passage tells us nothing of how the Rulers were persuaded to surrender powers which for generations had come to be regarded among their order as almost of divine origin. Nor does Sardar Patel's own testimony enlighten us as to the individual negotiations. Speaking to the Constituent Assembly of the assurance that was given to the Rulers that accession would involve only the three accepted subjects, Patel skilfully indicated that the Princes had in magnanimity and wisdom conceded their powers, and thus saved the Government the embarrassment of acting in contradiction to their obligations :—

> "These commitments had to be borne in mind when the States Ministry approached the Rulers for the integration of their States. There was nothing to compel or induce the Rulers to merge the identity of their States. Any use of force would have not only been against our professed principles but would have also caused serious repercussions. If the Rulers had elected to stay out they would have continued to draw the heavy civil lists which they were drawing before and in a large number of cases they could have

continued to enjoy unrestricted use of the State revenues. The minimum which we could offer to them as *quid pro quo* for parting with their ruling powers was to guarantee to them privy purses and certain privileges on a reasonable and defined basis. The privy purse settlements were therefore in the nature of consideration for the surrender by the Rulers of all their ruling powers and also for the dissolution of the States as separate units. . . . The capacity for mischief and trouble on the part of the Rulers if the settlement with them would not have been reached on a negotiated basis was far greater than could be imagined at this stage. Let us do justice to them : let us place ourselves in their position and then assess the value of their sacrifice. The Rulers have now discharged their part of the obligations by transferring all ruling powers and by agreeing to the integration of their States. The main part of our obligations under these agreements, is to ensure that the guarantees given by us in respect of privy purses are fully implemented. Our failure to do so would be a breach of faith and seriously prejudice the stabilisation of the new order." [1]

If there was no other evidence available, this one statement would surely confirm that the whole nature of negotiation was that of a hard-driven bargain. Technically there was nothing to prevent a State from remaining in aloof isolation as an island of sovereign autocracy in the midst of a republican sea. Nor was there any statutory limitation on a State in the middle of India to prevent it from acceding to Pakistan. But it was clear that India could, without force, have reduced the administration of such a State to a farce. In return, if the States had chosen to stand together and insist collectively on their independent status, they could seriously have restricted the economic life and development of India. On the same occasion as already quoted Patel said :—

" The situation was indeed fraught with immeasurable potentialities of disruption, for some of the Rulers did wish to exercise their technical right to declare independence, and others to join the neighbouring Dominion. If the Rulers had examined their right in such an unpatriotic manner, they would have found considerable support from influential elements hostile to the interest of their country."

An operation so delicate, yet so immense, could have been seen through only by such a combination of force and experience as was represented by Sardar Patel and his Secretary of the States Ministry, Mr. V. P. Menon. Patel was shrewd enough to see that at all costs the Communists must not be admitted. He realised that many of the Princes held the respect and affection of their subjects, and that open methods of drastic

[1] *Constitutional Assembly Debates*, Vol. X, No. 5.

dictatorship might create just that vacuum which would admit Communism among the most gullible and ignorant of India's communities.

If we look at the old map of the sub-Continent we usually see British India outlined in pink and the territories of the Princes in yellow. It will be seen that, with certain prominent exceptions, the yellow masses form either contiguous areas or areas which with adjustment could be made contiguous. Hyderabad, Mysore, Travancore and the Orissa States formed islands. Nevertheless there would have been some justification for regarding a third Dominion of the territories of the Princes as a practical proposition. Had this been put forward in the Cabinet Mission statement of May 1946, or indeed in any subsequent plan, it is probable that the Princes would have rallied to the suggestion, would have sunk their differences, surrendered certain of their powers in the common interests of the new Dominion and the British Commonwealth would most certainly have gained a very loyal partner.[1] This is not necessarily to support the proposal. It is merely to point out that the alternative, if discussed, was quickly negatived; and in the absence of its official recognition the Princes were in no position to press it on their own behalf. In the event they took the only course which was open to them. They rescued their titles and their privy purses.[2] Today it is a precarious retention. So long as the same political party is in power which included the late dynamic Vallabhbhai Patel, their remaining rights will be scrupulously respected. But if control in Delhi were to pass to the Left, we could expect to see the last lingering symbols of autocracy swept aside.

With the democratisation of the States the Indian National Congress have realised the fulfilment of their hopes which found expression many years ago. Nor is the passing of the Princes viewed by many in England with that dismay which retired officers of the Indian Political Department felt at the time. Nevertheless the immediate result has by no means been to introduce everywhere the blessings of an impatient democracy. The process of accession in many cases involved either the assumption of power by local Congressmen who had lived as citizens in the States or the arrival of men from outside to take over the administration. In both cases they frequently proved very poor material as compared with those whom they displaced. As an example of the kind of process which governed the methods of change, one State in Rajputana was given five days' notification of the arrival of its new administrator. He proved to be a former deputy Customs official, now faced with the task of taking over the responsibility of directing the affairs of a small but complete kingdom. The retiring Chief Minister was given no time to effect a

[1] In 1942 representatives of the Princes approached Sir Stafford Cripps on his Mission to India with an enquiry as to whether they would be free to form their own Union.
[2] The Privy Purse was worked out on a basis of 6 per cent of the audited revenue of the previous three years up to a maximum of 10 lakhs.

proper hand-over. No detailed time-table was received from Delhi, nor was there time for its local preparation. Subsequently administrators came and went at frequent intervals. Not unnaturally the Ruler's active interest in his former subjects ceased. Indeed, it could not have been maintained. He was forced to retire to the confines of his palace and the few surrounding acres of countryside which he had retained. The administration of the State was put back many years and the people suffered. As for the young Ruler, his womenfolk, who were quite incapable of comprehending the nature of constitutional change, regarded the State's misfortune as the result of his incompetence. Time may iron out the anomalies of theoretical progress. But four years after 1947 my impression was that those States which had developed in unquestioning loyalty to a wise but all-powerful autocracy were still in some confusion, administrative and psychological; while others which had been so primitive as to have nothing to lose had benefited from the change.

Apart from the merits of the issue, the Princes probably received more than they had anticipated, and their assessments of private property and buildings were generally accepted. The blow was as much to their pride as to their material resources. Perhaps the saddest aspect of change was the severing of their treasured association with the Crown. Many of them had regarded the Royal Family with a reverence which was touching in its simplicity and which in the nature of the circumstances had to go without a thought as to the psychological effect of destroying such firm devotion. The symbols of loyalty are not easily surrendered. I recall a small stronghold of former kingship where the Union Jack is still hoisted surreptitiously on the palace and the State buildings on the occasion of the official Royal birthday.

Weighing the position of the Princes against the inexorable march of events, it seems impossible to conceive of any other solution than that sought by Sardar Patel. There is so much to regret in their eclipse; and a Ruler such as the Nawab of Bhopal, who so jealously guarded the welfare of his subjects, is deserving of our sympathy. He and many others may now find too little scope for active minds. Others who earned the reputation of absentee landlords have only received their deserts. Good Rulers have suffered in the common interest, and we can only hope that their sacrifice will eventually reap some reward hardly yet apparent.

With the process of accession completed, the consolidation of the States into contiguous administrative areas and their democratisation could be undertaken. Four distinct methods were employed. Some States were merged with adjacent Provinces, such as Bhopal. A few, for varying reasons, were merged with the centre.[1] Others which already shared contiguous borders came together to form Unions, such as Rajasthan. Finally, four large States—Hyderabad, Mysore, Travancore—

---

[1] Manipur, Tripura and Kutch were placed under the Centre for frontier security reasons until more peaceful conditions prevail.

Cochin and Kashmir—continued as separate administrative units.[1] In each of the large units so formed the executive power of the new State is vested in a *Rajpramukh*, who under the Constitution has powers similar to those of a Governor. In each case the *Rajpramukh* is a former Ruler of influence and prestige; and since he now enjoys a Governor's salary in addition to his Privy Purse, it cannot be said that his position is inadequate as compared with his former independence.

We pass on to consider the greater structure with which Princely India has now merged its identity. I have referred to the unequal nature of the family of twenty-eight States which form the Indian Union. The Government have already been under pressure to remove the distinction between the different categories, particularly in regard to the upgrading of Part C States.[2] Rightly they resisted, and, with certain concessions, each group remains with the type of Legislature suited to its needs. A student of Commonwealth relations might be forgiven if he drew attention to the fact that it is just this inequality in political education and social structure which is the problem before British Colonial administrations sprinkled over the world, and in meeting which we are sometimes criticised in the Indian Press.

In drafting the Indian Constitution the authors drew on many resources. Not the least was the Government of India Act of 1935; but the Constitutions of the United States, Eire and Australia all received attention. The tone is set effectively in the Preamble. " We, the people of India . . . enact and give to ourselves this Constitution." Thus is introduced the most comprehensive statement of government yet attempted, with the emphasis on true democracy as its background. It was democracy rather than independence which was to be the keynote; for the latter, once achieved, could be taken as inherent in the former. " It is conceivable that a Republic may not be democratic. . . . The House will notice that in this resolution," said Pandit Nehru: and that is the simple explanation of the substitution of the word " democratic " for the original adjective " independent " which by some was thought to have a special significance.[3]

But while this devotion to democracy commands our admiration, it has not been without its penalties. It resulted in the inclusion of much conscientious material concerning the protection of fundamental rights which has frequently led the Legislatures into difficulties in the last few years. Part III of the Constitution sets out in elaborate detail rights of all descriptions which can be enforced by law. They are supplemented by Part IV, which contains the " Directive Principles of State Policy ". These lay down certain principles of political and social policy which,

---

[1] Five hundred and fifty-two States were affected by integration schemes.
[2] The argument was pressed home in the debate on the Government of Part C States Bill, during the Budget session of 1951.
[3] " Independent Sovereign Republic " was the goal defined in Pandit Nehru's Declaration of Objectives moved on 9th December 1946.

though regarded as fundamental, are not covered by legal enforcement. These two aspects together protect the rights of the individual citizen in almost effusive solicitude.   Yet in August 1952 the Prime Minister was confronted with the task of piloting the Preventive Detention (Second Amendment) Bill through the House of the People in face of some stiff opposition.   The original Preventive Detention Act was due to expire on 1st October 1952, and the new measure sought to extend its life to the end of 1954.   It was necessitated by the fact that the Communists in Southern India had refused to surrender arms which they were known to possess and which placed them in a position to blackmail the Government.[1]   " I cherish the freedom of the individual and I do not want, even in the name of the State, the freedom of the individual to be crushed. But undoubtedly the freedom of certain individuals has to be curbed for the safety of the State, if occasion arises," said Mr. Nehru.   There is little doubt that he was right.   Nevertheless the measure was hardly in keeping with Article 22 of the Constitution, which covers the conditions under which the individual is to be arrested, informed, defended and produced before a magistrate within twenty-four hours.

A more noticeable example of constitutional intransigence is found in the right to Freedom of Religion (Article 25).   Liberty of belief, faith and worship is indeed written into the Preamble.   Articles 14–18 protect the right to equality, prohibit religious discrimination and sweep away untouchability through the abolition of the old discriminative practices.   This is understandable when we recall that Dr. Ambedkar, the traditional champion of the scheduled castes, was in charge of the drafting of the Constitution.   And yet these very praiseworthy and precise provisions have even now not taken effect in the countryside.   On 31st October 1951 Mr. Jagjivan Ram, Minister of Communications and a member of the scheduled castes, addressed a meeting of the All-India Scheduled Castes Convention at Nagpur.   Although the Constitution had declared untouchability to be unlawful, and although local laws sought to remove the social and civic disabilities under which the scheduled castes had always suffered, " these have mostly remained a dead letter and have not been put into actual practice ".   The Minister went on to point out that while a time-lag between legislation and its implementation was inevitable, in the meanwhile the scheduled castes were becoming more and more conscious of the humiliations under which they had suffered for centuries.

Yet another example of aspirations which have proved unpractical relates to the Press.   Article 19 (1) (a) gave all citizens the right to free-

[1] The measure was passed by 296 votes to 61 in the House of the People and by 100 to 23 in the Council of States.   In the latter, the Communist leader, Mr. P. Sandarayya, sought to justify his resistance by claiming that Communists in southern India would surrender arms if they were promised exemption from subsequent detention or arrest.   The Home Minister, Dr. K. N. Katju, was quick to note that Mr. Sandarayya's speech was the most effective justification for the Bill.

dom of speech and expression. In the summer of 1951 the Government
sought to qualify Article 19 by an amending Article 19 (2), giving the
State the right to impose certain restrictions. These included the right
of the Government to demand the pre-censorship of a newspaper and
the submission of financial security before publication, the deposit to be
subject to confiscation. The measure was attacked energetically by the
All-India Newspaper Editors' Conference. Mr. C. Rajagopalachari,
the Home Minister, met their protests in a spirit of compromise. The
result was the submission of the Press (Incitement to Crime) Bill. Pre-
censorship was withdrawn and the demand for security was transferred
from the executive to become a judicial responsibility. These concessions were not regarded as sufficient to satisfy a hard core of resistance
in the House of the People based on a contention that fundamental rights
were in danger. The Bill, they maintained, sought to create one law
for the people and another for the Press. The term " objectionable
matter " as a yard-stick to measure an offence was open to many interpretations. In meeting the attack of Pandit Kunzru and others the Home
Minister showed patience and resource. It was not against the Press
collectively that these powers were sought but against a small section
operating without regard to their public responsibility. Where the
written word was concerned the Government had to differentiate between the intention of the writer, which might be correct in law, and the
effect of his words on the reader.

The sections of Part IV which comprise the " Directive Principles of
State Policy " might be regarded as somewhat platitudinous. The
health and strength of workers are not to be abused. Childhood and
youth are to be " protected against exploitation ". The State must
" make provision for securing just and humane conditions of work ".
These are all admirable but rather obvious sentiments. They were
borrowed largely from the Constitution of Eire, and one cannot avoid
being reminded of a jurist's conclusion that " the necessity for the insertion of declarations of rights in constitutional charters is a striking
testimony to the weakness of popular government ". For India,
launching her first indigenous Constitution, it was probably not unwise
to start with declarations of high intention. Moreover, some of the
obligations in this short section draw attention to matters of practical
importance.[1] Article 40 enjoins on the State the duty of organising
village *panchayats* as units of self-government; and if a written but
unenforceable instruction did in fact serve to remind both the Government and the people of their intentions, then certainly the Article was
worth insertion. Other enjoinders cover a varied assortment of matters,
from the prohibition of alcohol to equal pay for equal work for both
men and women. The inclusion of the latter (Article 39 (*d*)) might seem
a little unreal in a country where the status of women is, as yet, so far
removed from professional competition with men as understood in the

[1] Part IV consists of fifteen Articles (36–51) which cover only three pages.

D

West. Yet it is kinder to regard it as a brave recognition of the truth and a determination one day to overcome conditions which have for centuries circumscribed social life and structure. In contrast, the obligation to prohibit alcohol has taken full effect in Madras and Bombay. " The State shall endeavour to bring about prohibition of the consumption, except for medicinal purposes, of intoxicating drinks. . . ." The wording leaves us with the feeling that the Government were not going to commit themselves to a definite pledge, and it is probable that the experiment in two States is being carefully watched with a view to its adoption or refusal in many other areas.

Part V of the Constitution describes the whole substance of the central structure and its operation. In five chapters it deals with the President and his Powers, the Council of Ministers, Parliament, its composition, the conduct of its business and the Union Judiciary. This is followed by a similar statement in Parts VI and VIII for the States. It is here that the pattern of the Government of India Act, 1935, is continually reflected.

The student who turns these pages of careful and complete definition will seek immediately for the relationship between the Centre and its components. Unlike the American States of the eighteenth century, the units of India were not sovereign States seeking a federation, nor was the Indian Constitution born of a conflict between the rights of the Centre and those of the States. There was thus the opportunity to build the new edifice on a strong centre to prevent internal disintegration and meet external aggression. Wisely the occasion was seized, and the result is a compromise between a Federation and a unitary State. This is reflected in many ways. A State cannot frame or alter its own Constitution. In contrast, the Centre can alter the boundaries of a State or change its name by a simple majority decision. A common citizenship is given to all. A National Planning Commission takes no heed of State boundaries. The President possesses wide powers. He " appoints " Governors and " recognises " *Rajpramukhs*, the distinction being only one of theory. Under the Emergency Provisions (Part XVIII) he can assume to himself the functions of the Government of a State. India is therefore building on a foundation which in normal law-abiding circumstances offers no encouragement to those who would seek State autonomy. It is only the abnormal and the unpredictable which could ride rough-shod across the written instruction; and that this is recognised is inherent in the elaborate Emergency Provisions. Section 93 of the Act of 1935 came in for some trenchant criticism in days gone by. Nevertheless the new Constitution fully recognises the need to cover particular, if infrequent conditions.

Chapter IV of Part V deals with the Judiciary. One of the doubts of sceptics in the past related to the alleged difficulty of establishing in free India a Judiciary which would be completely independent of the Executive. Much of the nature of partisanship in previous days, whether in legislation or in any other aspect of government, derived from the communal bias. On partition this disappeared, and in so far as the administration of justice was previously affected, the communal element can now be forgotten. We have only to note that the Chief Justice of Bombay is a Moslem.

While it is gratifying to record the truly secular nature of the Judiciary, it should not necessarily be regarded as due to any inherent virtue. Once a minority has accepted the inevitability of its status as such, the problem is solved. Its identity is merged with that of the majority in a quick and natural assimilation.

A Supreme Court is established with powers hitherto enjoyed by the Privy Council. It consists of a Chief Justice and not more than seven Judges. Beneath it the High Courts in the States support the Constitution and, in so far as a layman can judge, I would maintain that they are independent of the State Governments. Indeed, the independence of the Judiciary does appear to have been successfully achieved. Upon the Supreme Court devolves the function of jurisdiction between the centre and any of the States, and between one State and another. This was to have been the role of the Federal Court which was set up under the Act of 1935. But since one of the partners—the Princes—remained outside the intended federation, whole sections of the Act never came into operation, and the old Federal Court was hardly extended in meeting its day-to-day commitments.

The independence of the Judiciary is secured, first, in that the President appoints all Judges in consultation with the Chief Justice of the Supreme Court; secondly, in that the status of Judges is protected by securing them their tenure of appointment with substantial privileges and rights.[1] On the shoulders of the Supreme Court rests the responsibility of enforcing the coveted "fundamental rights". It was in the discharge of this duty that in the early days of the Constitution the Court was overwhelmed with applications for relief. In fact those difficulties arising through an over-emphasis on fundamental rights to which I have already referred are concerned exclusively with the Courts and their interpretation of those rights in relation to enactments of the Legislature. The conflict was sufficient to enforce an Amendment Act to the Constitution in 1951.[2] That amendment was necessary will be appreciated when

---

[1] A former Chief Justice of India, Sir Patrick Spens, K.C., M.P., has pointed out that in his time there was nothing to prevent the Viceroy from transmitting his recommendations to England for approval of appointments of Federal and High Court Judges without reference to the Chief Justice of India. Sir Patrick secured the right of consultation from two successive Viceroys, which may have been instrumental in having the right written into the new Constitution.

The Chief Justice receives a salary of Rs. 5000 per mensem and the Judges receive Rs. 4000 per mensem. A residence free of rent is provided for each of them and they hold office until the age of sixty-five years.

[2] Constitution Amendment Act 18th June 1951. A second Amendment Bill was referred to Select Committee on 11th November 1952. This sought to relax the

we recall that one of the High Courts had declared invalid the law which punishes sedition and the promotion of enmity between the sections of the people, on the ground that it conflicted with the fundamental right of freedom of speech, and " The right to freedom of speech has been held by some courts to be so comprehensive as not to render a person culpable even if he advocates murder and other crimes of violence." [1]

For those of us who are not prepared to pursue the matter into the realm of complex relations as between a government and the judiciary it creates, it is enough to note that India's Supreme Court represents a strongly entrenched guardian of the Constitution, yet avoids the danger of becoming its master. In presenting the Amendment Bill the opportunity was taken by the Government to include a number of other corrections. For example, in the States the validity of their various *zemindari* abolition laws had been challenged, with the result that implementation had been held up.

In passing his Bill to a select Committee, the Prime Minister was not allowed to escape without some forceful criticism from Dr. S. P. Mukerjee, who had resigned some months previously from the Union Cabinet. To come forward with proposals for drastic changes after only eighteen months of operation was " cutting at the very root of the Constitution ".

I have returned to this aspect of the Indian Constitution since it is of much interest and concern for us in days when new nations are constantly emerging to claim their sovereign independence. Particularly is it of significance in contrast to Pakistan, where the Government have to meet the charge that they have been dilatory in presenting the nation with its new charter. It will be recalled that the first Pakistan Assembly was formed from the more active Moslem members of the Delhi Assembly who came over to Karachi. As a token of impartiality, and presumably for Indian consumption, a Hindu untouchable was elected as temporary chairman. When India produced her Constitution there was undoubtedly a feeling among Pakistanis that the Government of the first Prime Minister, the late Liaquat Ali Khan, had been dilatory in producing similar results. Yet time will surely prove that it was wise to hasten slowly.

In 1951 Pakistan procured the advisory services of an eminent Commonwealth jurist, Sir Robert Drayton. Before his arrival in 1949 Parliament had already accepted an " Objectives Resolution ", which had been prepared by the Cabinet and introduced by Liaquat Ali Khan. It might have been thought that a statement of objectives for a new State very conscious of its exclusive Islamic nature would prove of some

---

upper and lower limits of a parliamentary constituency in view of the increase in population. It came in for some harsh treatment.
[1] I quote from Chapter IV of Mr. B. N. Bannerjee's admirable commentary, *New Constitution of India. A Political Hand-book* (A. Mukherjee & Co., Ltd., Calcutta).

embarrassment to an English jurist approaching his task. In fact Sir Robert discovered a short impressive resolution in which Islam is mentioned only twice and which will appropriately form the preamble to the Constitution when it comes into operation.[1]

> "In the name of Allah, the Beneficent, the Merciful; whereas sovereignty over the entire universe belongs to God Almighty alone, and the authority which he has delegated to the State of Pakistan through its people for being exercised within the limits prescribed by him is a sacred trust. . . ."

The hard-headed Westerner is inclined to regard the introduction as too dramatic to be of honest and practical application. It is difficult for those who have never travelled beyond Port Said to appreciate that in the world of Islam, the law as established in the Holy Quran is life itself. Inheritance, marriage, divorce, theft, gambling and prohibition are some of the matters which fall within its purview. It has regulated life in Moslem countries successfully or unsuccessfully, according to the manner in which the ruler was able to combine the roles of spiritual and temporal leadership. In at least three Moslem States it is still the basic law of the land; and so there is certainly nothing unexpected in the brave words which herald in the future Constitution of Pakistan.

Sir Robert Drayton's opinion was that, in view of the difficulties into which India had been led, the delay in finalising the Pakistan Constitution was wise. In particular, he held the view that the emphasis on fundamental rights would lead India into further trouble.

The speech of Mr. Liaquat Ali Khan on 7th March 1949 which introduced the Objectives Resolution was mainly concerned with an explanation of its particular nature. He insisted that, in accordance with the spirit of Islam, authority was to be delegated to the people, "and to none else". For this reason it was wrong to look on the new State as a theocracy. The theocratic State had come to mean government by ordained priests, yet Islam denied the authority of a priesthood. The Prime Minister went on to draw attention to the traditional tolerance of Moslem communities, reminding his listeners that it was under Moslem patronage that the first translations of the Hindu scriptures were made from Sanskrit into Bengali. "Wherein the principles of democracy, freedom, equality, *tolerance* and social justice as enunciated by Islam shall be fully observed. . . ." Thus is the third obligation of the resolution recorded. Nevertheless the Basic Principles Committee which was subsequently set up made concessions to religious leadership, and a direct acknowledgment of the influence of religious leaders was implied in an instruction which says that "no legislature should enact any law which is repugnant to the Quran and the Sunna". Furthermore, the head of the State, who must be a Moslem, is to constitute a board of not

---

[1] See Appendix II.

more than five experts in Islamic law to advise him in the interpretation of this instruction. These provisions, as we shall note, are by no means welcome to progressive public opinion.

At this point it is sufficient to note only that the subsequent support proffered by Sir Zafrullah Khan on 12th March followed much the same course, though Sir Zafrullah elaborated his argument with erudite quotations from the Holy Quran. Reading these two speeches and those of the limited opposition, one is aware of a note of defence.[1] A new Islamic State is on trial, and it is up to those who are to frame the Constitution to prove that doubts as to its secular nature are un-justified.

Following on the acceptance of the Objectives Resolution a number of Committees were set up. One of these, the Basic Principles Committee, had produced an important interim report by September 1950, and its final report was presented to the Constituent Assembly on 22nd December 1952. The Committee appointed three sub-Committees to frame re-commendations on Federal and Provincial Constitutions and the distri-bution of powers, on franchise and on the judiciary. By 7th September 1952 only the report of the first sub-Committee had been received. It seems clear that with the Constitution of India available for study, the Basic Principles Committee were not averse from drawing freely on the Indian example. Names are altered. The Council of States becomes the Council of Units. The Units prefer to continue as " Provinces ". But the pattern of the Executive is much the same. Thus the executive power of the Federation is vested in the head of the State, who is to be elected by both Houses of the Central Legislature. As in India, the head of the State is empowered to declare an emergency, and similarly he appoints the heads of the Provinces. But in two respects there appears to be an intention to depart from the Indian practice. The Budget and all money Bills are to be considered jointly by both Houses of Parliament. The nature of the two Houses follows the Indian pattern, in that election to the Upper House is to be by the indirect vote, while that to the Lower House is to be direct. The units are to have single chambers. The two Houses of the Central Legislature are to represent complete parity as between East and West Pakistan, and already there are signs that the equal status of the Eastern State is by no means acceptable to the West. The other matter of complete divergence from the Indian practice is the intention to have separate representation for the minority communities. In the House of the People seats are to be reserved for scheduled castes, for Hindus other than scheduled castes, for Christians, even for two Buddhists from East Bengal. The preservation of separate electorates invited much criticism from India, while within Pakistan it was challenged by the small Hindu representation in the Assembly. The leader of the Opposition, Mr. S. C. Chattopadhyaya, presumably saw the same kind

[1] Opposition came from two Hindus, Mr. S. C. Chattopadhyaya and Mr. B. C. Mandal, both formerly representing General constituencies in East Bengal.

of objections to the distinction drawn between scheduled castes and Hindus as had been upheld in India.[1]

The interim report included some miscellaneous items of interest. The State is not to grant titles, nor are titles to be accepted from the head of a foreign State. Awards for valour in the Defence Services and Police will remain. Urdu is to be the national language. The decision concerning titles will have been unwelcome to a large influential section of Moslem society. I know of at least one Nawab who was quite overcome with emotion at the thought of never again wearing his treasured decorations. It was probably one of those gestures to idealism which are made in moments of brave resolution and subsequently so often regretted.

The franchise is open to every citizen at the age of twenty-one. Pakistan thus sets the example in the Moslem world in allowing women to vote, which, with the exception of Syria, has hitherto been frowned on in Moslem countries.

Three annexes to the report set out the lists of subjects which, as in the case of India, are classified as federal, provincial and concurrent. On 6th October 1950 the report of another Committee—that on fundamental rights—was also adopted by the Pakistan Constituent Assembly. It is a brief document of sixteen articles, the sixteenth being an unusual denunciation of untouchability which should receive sympathetic recognition in Delhi. Five sections are devoted to various aspects of the freedom of religion.

This, then, represented the extent of progress up to February 1952. Sir Robert Drayton's task was not to frame a Constitution. That is left to the Constituent Assembly. It is for the Cabinet to press home the time-table they require as practical and call in the experts when their task is completed.

[1] *Proposed Composition of Pakistan's Parliament.*

	House of Units.	House of the People.
East Bengal	60	200
Punjab	27	90
Sind	8	30
N.W.F.P.	6	25
Tribal Areas	5	17
Bahawalpur	4	13
Baluchistan	2	5
Baluchistan States . . .	2	5
Khairpur State . . .	2	4
Capital of the Federation . .	4	11
Total	120	400

Note.—Schedule II to the Report of the Basic Principles Committee gives details of the separate representation of minority communities in the Lower House. Thus the 200 members from East Bengal include twenty-four of the Scheduled Castes, twenty Hindus, one Christian and two Buddhists.

But there is one factor in the business of framing Constitutions which remains undetermined. It is true that Pakistan as constituted is a full and very welcome member of the Commonwealth; but the last word has not yet been said. Until the Constitution is written and accepted the country is free to remain a Dominion or leave the Commonwealth, or equally free to accept a monarchical or republican status. It would perhaps be more accurate to say that until these great decisions are taken the Constitution cannot be completed.[1] The greatest factor in influencing the future is the problem of Kashmir; so that in one way or another it may be later rather than sooner that the Pakistan Constitution will see the light of day.

Meanwhile an Assembly which was primarily intended to frame a Constitution is given legislative powers to carry on the government of the country by a special interim measure. The Opposition, which includes some Hindus, sometimes accuses it of being " unrepresentative ". Hitherto provincial elections have been held in the Frontier Province and the Punjab. It remains for general elections over the whole State to confirm or expel the present Moslem League Ministry; and it may be that these great issues will be left for the people to decide.

Pakistan has chosen a federation as the definition of her future status, " an association of provinces, the Chief Commissioner's Province and such States as have acceded or may accede to the federation ". We should here note that the Pakistan view in regard to the Princes was previously in contrast to the attitude of India. Only twelve States were involved in the case of Pakistan, and the initial understanding was that they remained as independent islands of sovereignty within Pakistan's territory. " We are bound by the terms of the Instruments of Accession executed by the rulers of the acceded States and we are morally and legally bound to honour them." These were the words of Mr. M. A. Gurmani, the Minister for States and Frontier Regions, and they represent the strictly constitutional and correct attitude which Pakistan has hitherto adopted. In April 1952 four of these States came together to form a Union, complete with its own Legislative Assembly of twenty-eight elected members. These were Kelat, Mekran, Las Bela and Kharan. Together they now form the largest single unit of Pakistan. The new Province will be entitled to receive financial assistance from the Central Government. It will certainly need it. Baluchistan has been described

---

[1] In January 1953 the Karachi daily *Dawn* published a report to the effect that a declaration of a Republic by the Prime Minister was imminent. The present position appears to be that no declaration can be made until the report of the Basic Principles Committee is accepted. Since the report has raised so many controversial issues, its final acceptance has been indefinitely postponed. (See also Chapter IX.)

Part X of the Interim Report of the Basic Principles Committee stated that it should be made extremely difficult to alter the Constitution. There followed recommendations to ensure that it is implemented. It is regarded as imperative to be quite certain that basic principles are first accepted as irrevocable before the Assembly finally assents to its new charter.

as a land on which the clouds rain stones, and it is difficult to think of it as other than a permanent financial liability. The Khan of Kelat becomes its first President with the title of 'Khan-I-Azam'. The other rulers receive a Privy Purse as a specified annual payment from the Union revenue on much the same lines as pertains in India. There has recently been talk of a similar union of the group of small kingdoms known as the "Frontier States".[1] But the Pakistan Government have made it clear that they do not intend to exert any pressure, and it is for the rulers themselves to decide.

For a limited period the particular status of Bahawalpur State was in doubt. Attention was drawn to the ambiguous situation when, early in 1952, a civil action was brought against the Ruler, Amir Sadiq Mohammed Abbassi, for damages for breach of contract. In spite of an appeal to the High Court in the King's Bench division, a ruling was given that the Amir was immune from the jurisdiction of the Courts. This seemed to confirm his status as an independent ruler. Yet at the same time the State was in no way recognised by the Commonwealth Relations Office as a separate Dominion, and in fact it had acceded to Pakistan after partition. With the advent of constitutional reforms and an elected Legislature in the State, ambiguity has been removed. Bahawalpur is now a unit of Pakistan, although the Amir undoubtedly enjoys a position of distinction as compared with that of the Princes in India. An official from Karachi now resides in Bahawalpur and acts as Liaison Officer with the Central Government. In the case of the smaller State of Khairpur there is a movement for its absorption into either Sind or Baluchistan.

In January 1953 the report of the Basic Principles Committee was due to be discussed by the Constituent Assembly. But in the month which had been available to review matters since the publication of the report certain sharp differences of opinion had emerged. In particular the West Punjab felt that its prestige would suffer and its identity be lost in the general process of federal equalisation. For years Lahore has tended to regard Karachi as an artificial growth which developed through the handling of entrepôt trade. The history and culture of the Moslem North are centred, they claim, in the capital of West Punjab. Others heartily disliked the influence which religious leaders may exercise. But more vital was the clamour from certain quarters for a republic. Many Englishmen will hope and pray that leaders who themselves would unwillingly yield to the demand may have the strength and courage to stand firm. In another chapter I refer to the circumstances by which India was enabled to reconcile her republican status with membership of the British Commonwealth. The immediate effect on Pakistan was to create a sense of a penalty imposed for their closer adherence and loyalty to the normal Commonwealth relationship. Among a limited but vocal section of informed opinion this feeling has persisted. We cannot avoid

[1] Chitral, Hunza, Dir, Swat, Amb.

the reflection that Britain has done little to remove this sense of injustice. It is a delicate matter, and it is easy enough to slip into a lazy process of thought which would dismiss the issue as merely one of labels. Certainly the material advantages of Pakistan's full membership are not evident. What, then, is in a name? We can only argue in terms of sentiment. The desire to create a republic is a symptom of drift; and once drift begins one wonders where it will end. It is a process which must affect others in the British Commonwealth who are pressing forward to nationhood. With such reflections in mind how can an Englishman view the republican tendency with apathy? [1]

Quite recently I happened to see a letter from an Englishman in Karachi written with a view to attracting the attention of Ministers in the British Government. It complained of the indifference of the small English community in Pakistan to their responsibilities. I know what he meant. It was just that many Englishmen seem unaware that they live among a highly sensitive community and that every contact made throughout the day is in the nature of an influence to strengthen or weaken the association of Pakistan with their own country. Particularly

---

[1] This chapter was completed when news of a constitutional crisis was received. On 17th April 1953 it was announced that Mr. Ghulam Mohammed, the Governor-General, had relieved Khwaja Nazimuddin's Cabinet of its responsibilities and asked Mr. Mohammed Ali (Pakistan's Ambassador in America) to form a new Government. For some time it had been realised that the Government had lost the confidence of the country.

On the only occasion on which I met the outgoing Premier he was frank and approachable. He was known and appreciated as a keen patron of cricket. Maybe that an infectious geniality which he imparted was hardly the quality to rescue his country in an economic crisis. Particularly was a very grave food shortage the means by which public suspicion of faulty administration and lack of Cabinet leadership was roused. Apart from the facts and figures of a situation which involves the importation of nearly 1,500,000 tons of grain in 1953, together with shrinking reserves and a desperate exchange position, there are matters of a deep divergence of thought in framing policy. It would seem that the new order represents success for a forward-looking policy of international co-operation at the expense of the narrow doctrine of those who follow the mullahs. The new Cabinet includes Khan Abdul Qayyum Khan, Chief Minister of the Frontier Province, who successfully imparted a sense of urgency and enthusiasm for modern development schemes in his own Province. He now takes charge of the portfolio for Industries.

Mr. Nazimuddin went in protest, complaining that his removal was not constitutional. He accepted it, however, with a sense of the inevitable, and was awarded a pension of Rs. 2000 a month on condition that he renounced all activity in public life. This presumably affects his position as President of the Moslem League.

The crisis resulted in a general reshuffle, Mr. Amin-ud-Din going from the Sind Government to be Governor of the Punjab and Mr. Chundrigar moving on to Delhi as High Commissioner, where his previous Bombay associations will be an asset in Indo-Pakistan relations.

A tribute is due to the courage of Pakistan's Governor-General in undertaking a move involving risks and hostility from certain quarters. He could, however, depend on the support of the two services who appreciate the value of efficiency—the Civil Service and the Army. These remain the background to Pakistan's future strength and our confidence in her ability to win through.

will this apply to officers of the three armed Services who may be destined to spend a year or so on contract in Pakistan. Let the War Office and Whitehall therefore see to it that men, not only of professional ability, but who are aware also of certain social and political responsibilities, go out to assist Pakistan in these critical formative years ahead.

CHAPTER THREE

BOMBAY DIARY

THE adventure of return was governed by the obvious situation of a comparison. The instinct was to look for something different in the profusion of life in the Bombay streets. Yet the message of what is seen by the eye was much the same as it had been eleven years ago. Perhaps the evidence of the gap between wealth and poverty was a little sharper. There were as many motor-cars hooting round the streets, and their shapes and sizes seemed more extravagant than ever before. In overwhelming contrast there was as much poverty and squalor and disease. Indeed, since Bombay appears to be regarded as a kind of talisman attracting refugees from as far afield as Orissa and Bengal, it has not escaped the refugee invasion. But by and large there was little physical evidence to mark the British exit and the Indian entry. It was only when I came to talk to people that the nature of a profound psychological change was certainly vivid and real. Within twenty-four hours I had exchanged views first with an old friend, an elderly Parsee lady of wit and precision, and later with the sincere and charming Prime Minister of the Bombay State.[1] The former, in the freedom of an elaborate cocktail party, spent half an hour assuring me that India's only salvation lay in a British reconquest! The latter, a true and complete disciple of Mahatma Gandhi, with equal assurance and sincerity held that Britain's departure had been her greatest and only victory. Between these two approaches it was sad to feel, as I did, that the great mass of opinion, in so far as it was articulate, floundered in doubt and difficulty with loyalties of confusion and profusion. The elections were only a week or so away, and at the street corners the candidates competed for wall-space with their bewildering wealth of appeals. At a lunch party I asked a British housewife how her domestic staff were taking all this political medicine. She said she had asked them herself, and the reply had been a candid confession. *"Memsahib, yeh kya ghar-bhar hai ?"* ("Madame, what is all this fuss about?"), adding as an afterthought that they would vote as Madame directed in the matter.

The 1951 monsoon had failed, and the place was as dry as a bone. The green lawns of the Mahalaxmi race-course were parched and dry. Yet the colour and the crowds were as vivid as ever. The reformers of the Bombay Congress will certainly go out of office if they attempt to abolish the Bombay races. Of the standard of racing, having seen the

[1] Dr. G. D. Kher. Appointed to succeed Mr. Krishna Menon as High Commissioner in London in July 1952.

splendour of the pre-war years, it is only possible to lament the decline. The Arab races with their hazards have disappeared, and with them have gone those elegant ruffians from Baghdad who added colour to the race-course. Nor is the fine stock of the Punjab studs now available: the efforts to breed Indian horses and train Indian jockeys therefore reflect much of what is happening in other spheres. But it would have been quite wrong to take the changes very seriously, for a Newmarket standard is, after all, not so important as the spirit of good sport; and there was plenty enough of that.

When one is busy dashing round the town seeking interviews with people who offer many conflicting opinions, it is easy to miss the normal experiences which can speak for themselves. A cup of tea at the Taj Mahal Hotel or the reservation of a berth on the train can mean much if there is time to pause and remember their significance. The service of tea at the Taj would hardly have been passed by Mr. Banerjee, the exacting manager of my time; while it would equally have startled me ten years ago to find the railway reservation office of the B.B. & C.I. entirely in the hands of sophisticated young Gujerati women.

That busy cosmopolitan life round the Gateway of India which the war brought has gone. Prohibition has killed the night life in and around the Taj. But, in contrast, the crowds by the Stadium for the Test Match were greater than ever before. There was in fact usually something to balance out the losses.

I suppose the first and greatest irritation for the Europeans is Prohibition. Any social gathering—a meal of four or a cocktail party of forty—is a chance to poke fun or let off steam. I sought out Dr. Gilder, the retiring Minister of Health. He had been responsible for Prohibition in the first Bombay Congress Ministry in 1937. His politics appeared to be a loose Socialism with the additional obstinacy of the idealist. Arguments that the Bombay State surrendered sixteen crores of revenue through Prohibition left him unmoved. "But look what the people save," he retorted, and he proceeded to illustrate the point with a story of an experience of many years ago in London while practising as a gynæcologist. It appeared that he had attended at the birth of the fourth child of the wife of a crossing-sweeper. He had been impressed by the cleanliness and modest prosperity of these humble people. The wife had said that her husband had not touched alcohol after the birth of the first child. To this was attributed the condition of the family. Doubtless he was right. But his one happy memory was hardly a contribution to a question of great magnitude, as represented in the wisdom of the State direction of a people's morality. A few miles up the coast from Bombay the boats come in with the drink. The police arrive, and the smugglers move on a dozen or so miles. An arrest is in any case meaningless. What does it matter to a fisherman if he spends a few weeks in gaol? He has a roof over his head and a ration to eat. Indeed, there is a story of a village which has divided itself into gangs of a dozen or so, who

solemnly ply the drink trade and court arrest in turn.   The remainder of
the village watch the interests of the missing batch, and the village as a
whole share out the profits.

A curious immunity is enjoyed by the Defence Forces; and the Army,
Navy and Air Force can drink to their hearts' content.   I do not blame
them for pressing their case.   Good luck to them in success.   But I
fail to follow the logic of permission to one section of the community
exclusively to drink and the refusal to all the others.   Permits are available to enable those with medical certificate to procure drink, and for
non-residents in the Bombay State who pass through.   This has created
a stampede to discover any obscure excuse for the doctor's certificate.
If the young ladies running the advance booking-office of the B.B. &
C.I. astonished me with their helpful efficiency, I was certainly reminded
of the other side of the picture in the Customs office which handles drink
permits.   In Britain we dislike the local Food Office and everything to
do with it.   But I can assure readers that our irritations are nothing
compared with the impositions on the good citizens of Bombay in the
matter of procuring alcohol.   The defence is, of course, that, since
alcohol is prohibited, the local Government are not going to worry
overmuch about applicants whom they presume to be hypochondriacs or
medical parasites on the State.   In practice we witness an overcrowded,
understaffed room of files and forms in chaotic profusion.   When
Prohibition first returned it took fifteen days to obtain a permit from this
gloomy asylum of bureaucracy.   An illiterate *chaprassi* had to be bribed
to hasten the process.   The puritans overcame the difficulty by posting
up on the wall a short Gujerati sermon on the evils of bribery.   Fortunately time was on their side, and as the months went by, and the
thousands of applicants either received the doctor's strange prescription
or gave up the unequal contest, the queue became manageable.   Even
so, the place was a madhouse.   I spent an hour each morning for three
days negotiating the units to which I was entitled.   In triumph, I finally
presented the fruits of my labour to my kind Parsee host.   Yet I enjoyed
in Bombay quite the most lavish distribution of champagne within
my memory of the past dozen years.   The members of the Diplomatic
Corps enjoy complete immunity; and if you happen to know a friendly
Ambassador and you want to throw a party he will help you out.   Drink
in a great city such as Bombay was never a monopoly of one class at the
expense of another.   The toddy-shops have suffered together with the
whisky agents, and the sad reflection is that it all becomes something of an
undignified obsession once the State steps in to reform its citizens.   Good
European families who would normally not have worried overmuch
about a forgotten glass of whisky in the evening appear as childish addicts
when they know that it is forbidden.

The population of greater Bombay is now reported to number three
and a half million, and to the north innumerable mushroom industries
are ever adding to this great human tide.   Biscuits, sweets, printing,

resin and the cinema trade are some of the outlets to the people's will for industry. As I drove out through an uncontrolled expanse of new factories and the bazaars which follow in their wake, it seemed that here was India's problem of the future all around me. How to harness this ever-expanding avalanche of humanity?

If you talk to the Bombay business-men you will find that they at least have a refreshingly practical approach to the city's dilemma. Mechanical power, and even more of it, they say, is the answer. My friend Wilfred Russell [1] went so far as to insist that the country should forget all political issues. Elections were a waste of time. The course was set for a great industrial reorientation of all life, and industry needed power. Power, then, was the key to the absorption of a vast, parasitic, unproductive community seeking employment, for power alone could satisfy the needs of industry, which in turn could drink in the millions of idle citizens who defy the ingenuity of generations of planners. While in no way accepting this thesis as the whole truth, I was grateful, in that it led me to inquire into the absorbing issue of the Bombay power cut.

In November 1951 the Bombay Government announced a 33⅓ per cent cut in power. They sought cover in blaming the monsoon for a failure to supply water in the catchment areas. In December 1951 Dr. J. N. Mehta, the Minister for Public Works, was able to announce a partial restoration for large industries, but not before the cotton textile industry had been threatened with a loss estimated at Rs. 25 crores and the total loss to industry was calculated to be double that figure.

The development of hydro-electric power in Bombay has for years been in the secure hands of the Tata Hydro-Electric Power Supply Co., Ltd., and the establishment of a grid around the city was the work of that great pioneer of Indian industry, Mr. J. N. Tata. It is to the Tata Grid that the city turns for the expansion of the light industries on its northern suburbs. As early as December 1948 Tata's drew the Government's attention to the need to increase capacity. At that time they were not only supplying power to industry but, due to the increased demands of the Bombay electrified railways, they were also under contract to supply the Central and Western Railways [2] with power. Five years ago Tata's gave the railways formal notice of the termination of power supply, the power being required for new consumers, and immediate steps should then have been taken by the Railway Administration to increase the capacity of their own thermal station at Chola, outside Bombay. Instead they slept on the situation for twenty months. Finally, when the Bombay Government and the Railway Board combined to order machinery for Chola, they turned to Germany and Japan, and it is hardly surprising that those countries have only recently been able to start delivery.

[1] A well-known member of the firm, Killick Industries, Ltd., author of *Indian Summer*.
[2] Formerly the G.I.P. and B.B. & C.I. Railways respectively.

The effect of the power cut on the private consumer was that each household was on a ration. In Bombay, where fans and domestic cold storage are something more than a luxury, the family in its home certainly could be excused a few rough words for the State Government. Yet such is the lack of publicity in these matters that I doubt if the power shortage ever figured as an issue in the election campaign.

Behind this situation is a long story involving a vital principle of conflict between Government and private enterprise. The Bombay Government which came to power in 1937 was a Congress Government with worthy obsessions of certain forms of social advancement, but little experience of industry and commerce. The Government which again assumed control after the war was of the same complexion. The new India, intent on building its house on firm foundations of Socialism, sought governmental control of the main services, and Bombay was second to none in the crusade. With one eye on the mighty structure of Tata's, with doubts concerning the renewal of the Tata licences, they engendered a loss of confidence within industry in general, and within Tata's in particular, without creating any of the necessary public enthusiasm required to raise the money for Government power schemes to replace the existing sources created by private enterprise. The Government have a vast irrigation-cum-power scheme—the Koyna Valley Project in the Deccan Highlands—which, in providing 580,000 kilowatts at 75 per cent of maximum load, will double Bombay's supply. But a Government which lightly surrenders Rs. 16 crores through Prohibition is unlikely to interest the public in loans for such a scheme as the Koyna Project, particularly if it relies on its own resources for technical advice and direction.[1]

It was the hope and expectation of the Bombay industrialists that once the elections were over the new Government would show its hand. It was believed that it would profit and learn from past mistakes and that generally it would turn to the established and experienced agencies of industry, and work through them rather than seek to displace them.

The Tata group of companies were at the time waiting in suspense to know if their licences were to receive extension up to 1970. In the circumstances it was generous of the Tata Hydro Group to come forward with suggestions which, if accepted, would bridge the gap until power under the Koyna project is available in seven years from the day work is started. They accordingly advocated the Kundalika Project of their own, a scheme costing eight crores and capable of completion within four years. As a joint enterprise by the three big Tata companies,[2] the finances would be forthcoming from the investing public.

---

[1] Power for Ahmadabad, the great textile centre 300 miles to the north of Bombay, has been stepped up through the trust reposed in Killick Industries, Ltd.; and in the last five years nearly three crores were raised for power expansion with a dividend offered of 6 per cent tax free. When the Bombay Government tried to raise two crores for a scheme in the Tapti Valley, the public subscribed only 60 lakhs.

[2] Tata Sons, Ltd.; Tata Hydro-Electric Agencies, Ltd.; Tata Iron and Steel, Ltd.

The project would tide over the period of short supply until power was available from the Koyna project, perhaps in 1960. In their approach to the whole problem, and in particular in their attitude to Tata's, the Bombay Government could perhaps recall that the Government of India recently concluded an agreement with the Standard Vacuum Oil Company for an oil refinery in Bombay, with immunity from nationalisation for a period of twenty-five years.

Behind all the permutations and combinations of this argument is a situation which has been inherent in Bombay for generations. Geography dictated the circumstances by which Bombay would inevitably develop into a gigantic concentration of trade and industry. Yet the Province was also the home of those Gujerati leaders of a puritanical nationalism through which they were associated with the championship of the Gandhian ideal. I do not attempt here to moralise on the virtues or vices of this nonconformist approach. I only argue that in Bombay, of all cities, where a Congress Government came to power, it was bound to lead to many anomalies and much frustration. Drinking, gambling and the race-course have all been attacked by these champions of the straight and narrow path. The custodians of public morality presented their crusade as the "will of the people". The hollowness of the claim has been ably exposed in a book *Betrayal in India*, by D. F. Karaka.[1]

But more serious than sermons on how to behave is the inevitable clash between such an approach and industrial development. If the Bombay Province could have been content with an economy of cottage industries, then at least the encroachment of the machine might have been harnessed to the will of the people. Inevitably, however, the Province developed towards big industries through its resources and natural conditions, with the result that the Congress advocates of nationalisation came into deep conflict with the great industrialists. The outcome was to create that era of ambiguous accommodation between members of the Indian National Congress and the industrialists which has also come in for Mr. Karaka's effective ridicule. It is a sad situation, for it represents something more profound than the clash of mere material interests. It is the conflict of two systems, and as such assumes a philosophical aspect. If the disciples of Gandhi could all claim the inner conviction of their former Chief Minister, Dr. Kher, then I for one could not have begrudged Congressmen their success. But in falling from that high standard we could wish that they might the more honestly have admitted defeat and made a frank surrender to the vitality of the Bombay industrialists. For it is their genius which in past generations built up this great city from the island villages which King Charles II once passed over to the East India Company for £10 a year.

I have mentioned D. F. Karaka, and I could not regard my diary of Bombay as complete if I were to dismiss this somewhat controversial

---

[1] Published by Gollancz, Ltd., 1950.

E

figure with only a passing reference. From the staff of the *Bombay Chronicle* he had moved on to the management of his own affairs, and in 1948 his new weekly paper *March* appeared on the streets. His latest weekly, the *Current*, has a circulation of some 14,000 copies and enjoys a reputation for discovering the more sensational episodes of contemporary social and political life and exploiting them to the full. You will hear Karaka dismissed as a skilful satirist by Bombay's intelligentsia. Certainly his particular approach is one which in England would not be taken seriously by readers of either the *Spectator* or the *New Statesman*; and yet in independent India, in its first flush of Congress triumph, I find something of value in a paper which quite fearlessly hits out at those who have hitherto enjoyed immunity. I doubt if Karaka's best friends would claim modesty as one of his attributes. Yet if his critics find in him irritating symptoms of a personal arrogance, it is his modesty of approach as an Indian criticising India which should eventually win for him something more than a reputation of just another adventurer in journalism. I have stressed this personal impression, since for an Englishman soaked in the associations of the past it is sometimes refreshing to encounter public recognition of the British contribution to the country supported by an honesty in facing up to certain national characteristics which are a brake on progress. Karaka is at least not afraid of giving the national conscience a jolt, though his particular method will not necessarily win approval from those who are accustomed to an orthodox delicacy in political criticism. His weakness is that he is entirely destructive. He himself admitted that he cared not whom he attacked or to what lengths a campaign led him. The end justified the means. But I confess I was left in some doubt as to what exactly the end was. Here was a case of an agile intellect seeking expression and finding it only in debunking a whole mass of political and social superstition in his country for which others either lacked the ability or the inclination. The motto of his newspaper is " Independent always : neutral never ". It is a brave claim. But even independence must merit our greater respect for the degree of its active suggestion and construction in public life. If the *Current* can avoid the attentions of the police for the next two or three years, I for one hope that it may emerge as an independent political force presenting something more to the public than some good fun at the expense of the Bombay Ministers.

Should Karaka ever drift away from his present method, there are undoubtedly others who will sustain the attack. Two papers in particular were certainly for the lower tastes in polemics. The difference, as it seemed to me, was that whereas an incident recorded in the *Current* was usually true, in the case of these lesser imitators the foundations of a story would be the imagination of the reporter. Under the mere cover of " authoritative sources ", apparently, you can more or less say what you like. Elsewhere I have discussed the status of the Press in both India and Pakistan. In so far as my brief return to Bombay was concerned, I should record that the *Times of India*, under Frank Moraes, maintains its high standard of objective reporting and criticism. With a circulation of 100,000, it exerts a steadying influence of sanity on a public which is only too ready to be led along the easy and emotional paths of nationalism. When the paper passed under the financial control of an extremely wealthy Jain industrialist, many Europeans wondered if the Bombay public were to be re-educated on principles of religious and vegetarian extravagance. In fact Seth Dalmia appears to remain much in the background. In 1950 he startled the Editor by addressing the Hindu Mahasabha without previous warning, but apart from figuring on the Board of Directors and paying a sum of two crores for the purchase of the paper, he seems content with remote control and occasional opportunities to express sincere but obscure opinions of idealism.[1] India's greatest of idealists has passed on, and the world is the poorer. But, in the absence of a leader who can interpret the Gandhian ideal in the example of his daily life, it were better that India should be guided by men of strictly practical ability.

Among the most practical of India's countless and varied religious communities are the Parsees. Over the centuries this small brotherhood have maintained rigidly their separate identity and thrived in comparative isolation. The reason is to be found not only in their greater commercial aptitude, but also in the manner in which they attend to their own social welfare. The Parsees are not all rich. They have to take their chance in shops, offices and factories with the rest of Bombay. But wealthy families do make it their duty to look after their poorer folk, and the result is a number of settlements, under a Board of Trustees, where Parsees of limited means can live a life of humble sufficiency and security. Here they can be certain of medical care, of education for their children and of a home at a rent according to their means. There is no doubt that the Parsees have freed themselves from the devastating poverty of great areas of the city. I think the lesson is not only that of determined planning by a community of enterprise and ability; rather is it that the condition of their poor is dependent on the initiative and charity of their wealthy leaders. It is to Sir Cowasjee and Lady Jehangir, to Sir Shapoorjee Billimoria and others that the Parsees owe their immunity from slums and squalor. The creation of wealth in one section of the community is justified only if the wealthy are actively conscious of their great responsibility. If, however, they then realise their opportunity, it has always been my inclination to believe that here lies the justification of the *laissez-faire* interpretation of economics. To elaborate the matter is to be involved in nothing less than the clash of the rival systems of Marx and Keynes. That is not my intention! Here I am only concerned to suggest that in the past a great city such as Bombay has thrived on the bounty and benevolence of a few captains of

---

[1] The *Times of India* is now published from Bombay, Delhi and Calcutta. It claims to be the most widely read paper in India.

industry and commerce; and in the new India, hesitating between experiments in Socialism and the free exploitation of private capital and enterprise, the Socialists will win the last round if the capitalists fail to take heed of the plight of their millions. Let the Birlas and Dalmias leave their mark on the land with practical evidence here and there of a few thousand human souls removed from hovels and put into homes of self-respect. It is through such service and example that the people will thrive, rather than by the promotion of any number of newspapers to make or destroy passing political reputations.

Before leaving the Bombay Province I passed a few hours at Anand in Gujerat, some 200 miles north of Bombay. In twenty-four years I had never set foot in Gujerat, the traditional stronghold of the Congress and home of the great fraternity of Patels. I therefore readily accepted the kind invitation of Dr. and Mrs. Rutherford of the Irish Presbyterian Mission Hospital at Anand. Here was evidence, all too convincing, of the scope of work at hand for those seeking to serve their motherland. There are hundreds of Anands in India, and to walk their fouled and muddied alleys between hovels masquerading as homes is to soak one's soul in depths of bitter and profitless despair; so that the spirit of service and construction round the Anand Mission Hospital was as water in the desert. It is usually the local missionary who knows more of the people and their troubles than can ever be learnt from the textbooks. What is his future in India? Dr. Rutherford was certainly in no doubt. In 1947 there was a tendency in the Bombay State to regard Missions as alien institutions. Particularly was there suspicion of their schools. But the mood quickly passed. Dr. Kher had himself been a pupil in the Wilson College, and was the last person to wish to close Mission schools. At a Missionary conference in Mussoorie in 1951 representatives of over thirty Missions assembled. They are needed and welcomed. It is, however, apparent that whereas formerly Missions looked to the Western world for their staffs and maintenance, more and more must they now develop their own resources in India. Dr. Rutherford regarded the systematic Indianisation of Mission work as a solemn obligation on all Missions, with the assistance and encouragement of the public in Western countries.

The slender resources of the Presbyterian Mission Hospital did not permit the supply of food being provided for each patient. The patient brought his family with him, and the housewife squatted in a hovel outside the ward and produced the meal. It was all rough and ready; but it represented a little care and attention for women in childbirth, for old people and children, which they could not receive in the bazaar. An unruffled Scots matron who for many years had met all difficulties with a dry humour lent the place confidence, while Dr. Rutherford and his young wife went quietly about their daily round of mercy with a touch more valuable to the people of Anand than all the skill in Harley Street. My last recollection of the place was of an evening rehearsal for the coming Christmas entertainment, with a chorus of girls chanting a rhythm in that high nasal, melodic line which only the East can understand. It was a modest effort, with a rough curtain rigged up on the hospital veranda, and the audience sitting by candlelight below in the compound. But it was to be a great occasion for the hospital; and so in the spirit of the coming Christmas I took my leave of a small pocket of Christian charity. Long may the Missions of India pursue their great purpose of mercy.

CHAPTER FOUR

DIARY OF THE NORTH

TWENTY minutes out of Delhi the evening mail from Bombay passes through Faridabad, now a home for many thousands of refugees. Here is the first evidence of those tragic days of 1947; and yet the form is hardly suggestive of tragedy. For the night-glare of the new factories lights up the skyline; and we are suddenly conscious that perhaps out of the unhappiness of millions are emerging the will and opportunity to make a fresh start. I never saw the long convoys of suffering on the march, the thousands that fell by the wayside, women torn from children and men hacked to pieces in front of their women. But I saw the astonishing fortitude with which refugees accepted their fate and the vigour with which both Governments set about integrating their new citizens into the national life. In Delhi, from the Imperial Hotel down to Connaught Place, the refugees had set up their booths, not with any appearance of despair, but with an animation obviously born of a new hope.

For many in England, Delhi means memories of battles in the Assembly, the splendour of Durbars and Viceroys' receptions, the stimulation of the fastest polo in the world, the rigid routine of official entertainment, and the contrast of Princely extravagance with the squalor of the bazaars. Of course there was change; but not of the nature we might expect. Some would have looked for a general slowing down of life, whether in the conduct of government or in the social round of our successors in those hundreds of pleasant white bungalows. So far from a slowing down, the tempo of life appeared to be stepped up.

I do not know exactly what I expected to find when my host took me along to the New Year's Eve dance at the Delhi Gymkhana Club. But the traditional revelry was there, and the only visible evidence of change was that *saris* had replaced evening dresses, and tail-coats had given way to the black *achkan*. Well, we had left something behind; for the manners and modes of English social life, for better or worse, were still there, not thrust reluctantly on Indian society, but sought out and applied sometimes with a greater attention to detail than in the old days. In six weeks in India and Pakistan I wore my dinner-jacket as many times as I had in the previous six years!

As I stood in the crowded ballroom I could not avoid the reflection that the Army was really responsible! Mess life has a way of handing on its social pattern to the families around it; and how pleasant it was to see once again familiar uniforms, to step back for a few moments to a life which seems so far away.

70

But nationhood has wrought one great change in the pattern of Delhi's social round. In past years Ministers and Government Secretaries, Generals and lesser Staff officers entertained in the proud seclusion of their homes. The dinner-party was the accepted focus of social give and take. It was all rather formal, and organised according to an accepted code of precedence. Conversation seldom ranged very far from the capital and its gossip. Cultural life had to be sought out, and it was left to a handful of enthusiasts to stage a play or organise a concert. But it was all very friendly and extremely efficient. Inevitably I found myself comparing the past with new methods and standards which have arrived with the emergence of a formidable Diplomatic Corps. I suppose there is some prestige in appointing and receiving a Foreign Embassy. A sudden sense of importance attaches both to those who give and to those who take. Up goes the new flag, and for a brief year or so His Excellency the Ambassador is the proud representative of an obscure community a few thousand miles away who may or may not recognise the Indian sub-Continent on the map. Still less will they be aware that they support their spokesman to the extent of quite a considerable salary and budget. Perhaps it is all very encouraging in the search for international co-operation. But I could not help wondering what useful purpose an elaborate representation of Mexico could serve in Delhi.

With an international community has come the technique of the cocktail party. The old methods may have given us a lot to smile at. But I am not so sure that they were not preferable to those of today. The same circle meet and say the same things to each other in the same overcrowded atmosphere. For an Englishman it was particularly irritating to realise that most of them knew so little of India and the past.

It was at the American Embassy that a young Secretary asked me if I had seen the impressive changing of the Guard on Monday mornings in front of the Secretariat. Those splendid men in scarlet uniform on fine horses with their lance pennons; had they been there in my time? I could have reminded him that my father had commanded them in the 1880s, but it was one of those occasions when words failed me! [1] If and when one can hear or make oneself heard in these social contests, there are sometimes opportunities to pick up a useful personal comment. On this particular occasion I had only a couple of minutes with the American Ambassador, who expressed the opinion that the Kashmir question could best be settled by avoiding the Security Council and leaving it all to Dr. Graham. I wonder if he still thinks so!

The Russians, of course, surrounded themselves with the usual mystery. It would have been too much to have expected them to employ the normal staff of Indian servants, and they filled their premises with their own people. It was the habit to laugh off their isolation. In fact there can be little doubt that the Embassies of both the Soviet and their friends

[1] The former Viceroy's Bodyguard, now the President's Bodyguard, was raised at Benares in September 1773 by Captain S. Toone.

are centres for furthering their purpose by any means, fair or foul, in such a country as India. A Russian Art Exhibition may look quite innocuous. It certainly was accepted as such by Maulana Azad, the Education Minister, when it arrived in New Delhi in March 1952. When, however, it is accompanied by Russians who have taken the trouble to master the intricacies of traditional Indian dances, and who can enact the Ramayana and Mahabharata in Russian, it is time to realise that there is a bit more than culture behind the surface of artistic interest as sponsored by the All-India Arts and Crafts Society. The fact that Indian students have found their way in numbers to such institutions as Prague University is not due to mere passing curiosity on the part of the students. Someone in Delhi works to send them there.[1]

One can forgive much Diplomatic futility if at least it provides efficient entertainment. The Italian Ambassador, Signor Ricotti, and his charming wife set a standard of taste and pleasant company without ostentation which was difficult for others to imitate. Nor was the more obvious hospitality of the Egyptian Ambassador at Maiden's Hotel less effective. Something of the spirit of the Khedive Ismail must have been passed down to this most overwhelming of hosts!

To many Indians of a Congress Government the effort to accept the pattern of Western ways must irritate. The President himself, installed in the superlative magnificence of Rashtrapati Bhavan and surrounded by a staff of hundreds, must sometimes look nostalgically to the simplicity of his former social detachment as a President of the Congress. He has had to master a whole range of matters of etiquette and procedure. There have been many experts from former days to advise him. But we give him credit for having absorbed the dignity befitting his office without having lost his charm of simplicity.

Just about a year after my return to Delhi I was in Washington, a city distinguished for its spacious beauty. For myself I find many features common to both Delhi and Washington; and of the two it is Delhi which I regard as having a more enduring quality. If you ride up the tan track on the Kingsway of an evening as the sun is catching the white and pink stones of the Secretariat, you are aware of the ennobling character of a great architectural conception, a worthy successor to the dignity of the ruins of seven cities scattered around the central vista.

---

[1] I have with me many copies of a publication *Czechoslovak Life*, a monthly journal printed in Czechoslovakia which finds its way to England through the Anglo-Czech Friendship Society. The March 1953 issue carried a short article " Aid for India ". The opening paragraph reads: " Condemned for decades to supplying raw materials for the spinning wheels of England, India was forced to import textiles. With plenty of cotton and manpower, she is today seeking to build up her own textile industry—and getting little encouragement and assistance from imperialist countries."

The occasion for the article was the visit of an Indian trade delegation to Czechoslovakia. Four photographs depict the delegation happily lapping up the usual fare provided on visits to factories and textile mills on such occasions.

But it was with a more personal excitement that I drove to the entrance gates of my father's old house. The Prime Minister has made it his home. On arrival in Delhi I registered my desire to meet him, for I had a whole range of political matters to discuss if he could have found the time to see me. But he was far too preoccupied with the elections, and so my nearest approach to the house which my father had built, and in which I had spent happy days on leave, was a glimpse of the veranda on which my parents used to have breakfast, from the distance of the front entrance.

The comfort of General Cariappa's hospitality at "White Gates" would have been an antidote to any irritation. Here it was that old family servants of the 1920s sought me out; and their simple joy at being able to revive memories of Snowdon and the Commander-in-Chief's house was touching.[1] Some of them had made the journey from distant homes; and as they could hardly be sent away without their rail fares and a useful present, at one time it seemed that the revival of old memories was going to be an expensive experience! The Imperial Hotel employs a number of Moslem servants. Some of them would come up to me and open up conversation in hushed whispers with comments on the deterioration of life and the oppression of an alien administration. They were mostly of that loyal stock of bearers and *khidmatgars* from U.P. which formerly provided many Europeans with such good service. But my sympathy was slightly qualified, in that they appeared at least to have suffered no persecution, and went about their work with a confidence supported, I imagine, by an adequate salary.

I passed on to that most bewildering of experiences for Englishmen who knew former conditions: the crossing of the frontier at Wagah. No passenger trains were running between Lahore and Amritsar, and one goods train a day was the extent of the rail traffic. A few lorries, I believe, were negotiating the frontier post on the Grand Trunk Road, otherwise the two Customs officers at the post appeared to have the least exacting of assignments in the world.

The Indian and Pakistani posts side by side just off the road presented a very impressive picture of polish and new paint. The two sentries had evolved a drill which managed to dispense with the awkward question of one sentry giving a command to the other. With precision they could together step forward and back, slope arms and salute in solemn silence. Facing them was a strip of no-man's-land about five yards wide, where relations from both sides could meet and have a chat: five yards of sanity in a world of mistrust! I managed to create a precedent by persuading the Pakistan Customs officer to come over to the Indian side of the wire for a cup of tea. So far as I was concerned both officials

[1] "Snowdon" was the former residence of Commanders-in-Chief in Simla. The "Commander-in-Chief's House" in Delhi was built to replace a previous residence which my father as Commander-in-Chief was reluctant to occupy and which was purchased by the Maharaja of Kashmir. The building of the present residence was watched by my family with close interest, and my mother was delighted to be able to give advice in the furnishing and interior decoration.

were as friendly and helpful as possible. I cannot speak for the general public, because there was no one on the move.

I was, however, soon to realise the difficulties of Pakistan in establishing her public services, Customs and the like on an efficient basis. At the frontier it appeared I should have entered on a form the amount of currency brought into the country. The order for the form had gone out two months before. The Customs officer knew nothing of it. The result was that I had to chase the form in Lahore to get any money, and my entry into the country had to be verified from Wagah. Having procured the form, it then took an hour of some aggression to cash a traveller's cheque at the Bank. I had at least escaped the whole business of queueing at the local High Commissioner's office for a permit to cross from one country to the other, and, thanks to the kindness of Lieut.-General Kalwant Singh in Jullundur and Mr. Tom Keeble of the British High Commissioner's office in Lahore, the crossing had caused none of the headaches which the ordinary traveller experiences.[1] But I learnt as I travelled in Pakistan of the difficulties which that country faced when all Hindus fled from it in 1947. Banks, civic control, passing goods across the counter or clearing them through the port of Karachi: all these move at a slow pace in Pakistan. It was to be expected, and the Pakistanis recognise it. So long as there is recognition it will be only a matter of time before such limitations are remedied.

Once again I took the familiar train that winds its way round the hills west of Jhelum. The Pakistanis have painted their railway carriages the ubiquitous vivid green which they have adopted as the national colour. The paint disguises many carriages of the old North-Western Railway on their last legs; and the replacement of rolling-stock is now being treated as a priority. Diesel engines are creeping in, and a fine modern Diesel express is promised for the run between Lahore and Karachi. If only the search for oil could be rewarded we might live to see the day when not only the railways are no longer dependent on imported coal, but also the industrial expansion of the country.[2]

In my hotel at Lahore I experienced the first real sense of contrast. In pre-war times the place had been a hive of activity. Christmas week

---

[1] Permits have since yielded to the more permanent imposition of passports.

[2] There are indications of an oilfield at Chak Naurang, near Chakwal in West Pakistan. Pakistan Petroleum, Ltd., a new subsidiary of the Burmah Oil Company, conducts operations. Gas has been discovered in Baluchistan and oil-prospecting proceeds near Chittagong in East Pakistan.

In the first half of 1952 coal was produced in the following quantities:

Baluchistan	.	.	.	200,620 tons
Punjab	.	.	.	108,670 ,,
N.W.F.P.	.	.	.	9,000 ,,
Sind	.	.	.	3,640 ,,

In the same period the Attock Oil Company produced 550,000 barrels. Pakistan Petroleum, Ltd., produced 126,800 barrels, a total increase of 18·25 per cent over the similar period in the previous year.

had always brought in numbers of old friends, and one could be certain of a good company and good food. Those days had certainly gone: not only that, but for the privilege of staying there I was charged a rate higher than I had paid recently in an excellent hotel in New York fitted with every modern aid to comfort. The tourists, of course, will never face these conditions. It is no great hardship for those who know the country and its difficulties. But the newcomers judge these matters by their own standards.

The West Punjab Assembly was in session, and there was considerable animation around the open space where Queen Victoria's solemn detachment in marble used to watch over the taxi-drivers and *tonga-wallahs*. I have followed the fortunes of Punjab polemics with a distant interest since the days when, as a Civil Liaison Officer, I had been fortunate enough in my work to contact men of the stature of the late Sir Sikander Hayat and Sir Chhotu Ram. On the day of partition Sir Evan Jenkins handed over his responsibilities as the last Governor of the old Punjab to Sir Francis Mudie in the West and Mr. Trivedi in the East. Mudie assumed office as a servant of the Pakistan Government and Constitutional Governor of the Western Province, with the Nawab of Mamdot as his Chief Minister. The reasons which subsequently compelled the Governor-General to dismiss the Nawab and his Ministry are perhaps best left in some obscurity. Rival factions led by Mamdot and his Finance Minister, Mian Mumtaz Daultana, had for months introduced a most unsavoury atmosphere, and responsible public opinion was genuinely becoming exasperated. It appears that the Prime Minister wrote to the Governor-General recommending immediate action under Section 92A.[1] Orders were passed, and Sir Francis Mudie assumed direct control over the Province in January 1949.

The decision was greeted with general approval, for the administrative machine was on the point of collapse. But there were many difficulties. While it was fortunate that the machinery of the old Government of India Act was still available in the application of 92A, it was equally unfortunate that a British Governor should have the task of its implementation. For Mudie soon became the target of nationalistic elements out to exploit a useful election point, namely the employment of foreign nationals as incompatible with the dignity of a sovereign State. The proclamation under Section 92A took place on 24th January. By 4th February the *Pakistan Times* had elaborated the issue to a demand for the withdrawal of British officers from the Army.

Nevertheless at a Press Conference the Governor was able to meet and

---

[1] Under Section 93, Government of India Act 1935, the Governor was responsible to the Governor-General *in his discretion*. Under Section 92A, the Governor functioned *on behalf of* the Governor-General, and therefore interpreted not his own orders but those of the Central Government, the members of both the Central and local Assemblies retaining the right to question action. Section 92A could thus be regarded as less drastic than Section 93, a point which the Governor was able to make at his Press Conference, at the time.

defeat criticism. It was understood that elections were to be held at the earliest possible date, and for a time the Administration were allowed to tackle the tasks of government. But not for long. As the price of accepting Section 92A government, the provincial Moslem League demanded the appointment of five advisers to sit at the Governor's elbow. Their powers and functions were thus defined :—

> "The advisers to the Governor . . . while having the powers to function as Ministers will in effect have the authority to take final decisions only when the Governor is in agreement with them. . . ."

Differences of opinion were to be referred to the Central Government. It was a dangerous arrangement, and Mudie not unnaturally objected. Advisers with political power but without responsibility were not likely to be of assistance in the day-to-day responsibilities of administration. The subsequent negotiations must again best be left for conjecture. Liaquat Ali Khan had previously insisted on the introduction of 92A rule, risking its unpopularity. It would seem that Sir Francis Mudie's resignation in July 1949 could only have been to save the Central Government further embarrassment. Mudie went, and was succeeded by Sardar Abdur Rab Nishtar, who duly accepted his five advisers.[1] The compromise then continued until the promised provincial elections held in March and April 1951, when Mian Mumtaz Daultana was returned on 5th April as leader of a provincial Moslem League Ministry. In the meanwhile the Nawab of Mamdot with some of his colleagues had to face a tribunal inquiry into their conduct during their brief period of power. Among other matters the obscure fate of large sums of money raised by the Mamdot administration as a "Kashmir Fund" was subjected to criticism. After a lengthy examination the case was dropped; but not before public opinion had swung away from Mamdot in favour of Daultana. That was in the summer of 1950. Mamdot then sought consolation in the formation of his own "Jinnah Awami League". But he has failed to find a following outside Lahore and the Frontier Province.

And yet inside the Assembly when I visited it in February 1952 there was no hint of this stormy background. Daultana's suave control of proceedings was impressive. The opposition was ineffective; and indeed a complaint of reformers was that leaders in Government and Opposition have an understanding with each other behind the scenes which makes a mockery of reform. That was certainly the charge of Mazhar Ali, the new Editor of the *Pakistan Times*.[2] It was his view that not until a real Socialist Party had emerged would there be progress. As to which individual assumed leadership and effected change, that was not important. The point was that change should be effected. In a sense,

---

[1] Sardar Abdur Rab Nishtar was succeeded by Mr. I. I. Chundrigar on 6th November 1951.

[2] Mazhar Ali succeeded Mr. Faiz in 1951 when the latter was arrested in connection with the Rawalpindi conspiracy case.

Mazhar Ali's assessment was not without some justification. A year later Daultana resigned. The provincial Moslem League Assembly Party endorsed his resignation, and Malik Firoz Khan Noon was recalled from the Governorship of East Bengal to lead the party. He had always been a candidate for leadership. But the change is one of name rather than of policy. Personalities and the factions they command continue to govern polemics, and the emergence of a healthy opposition on a doctrinal basis would be a useful injection into the political life of the Province.

A year later I sat in another Legislative Assembly on the other side of the world; and I found myself comparing the evident pandemonium of proceedings within the semi-circular arena of Little Rock, Arkansas, with the comparative order and sense of responsibility in a building of the same size and design in Lahore. Not a little credit must go to the speaker, Dr. Khalifa Shujja-ud-Din, whose firm, impartial handling of debate had won him the respect of all sides of the House.

A hasty visit to the Peshawar valley and a talk with the Chief Minister vividly brought back the by-gone years. I think it is fair to say that the problem of the tribes is far less evident than in the days of British India. Early in 1949 the Pakistan Government initiated an interesting experiment in settling tribesmen, mostly Mahsuds, on the banks of the Indus in the Dera Ismail Khan District. The immediate aim was to distribute about 5,000 acres as soon as the land could be regarded as fit for cultivation. In the battle for the loyalties of the tribesmen as between the Pakistanis and Afghanistan the Afghans have definitely lost the first round. It was therefore puzzling to note the continued nuisance value of that perennial irritant, the Faqir of Ipi. He is obviously thoroughly discredited. But in view of the fact that as long ago as 1937 he was making life uncomfortable for many of us it seems curious that he cannot be apprehended. In the war he received funds and arms through the Axis Embassies in Kabul, and in July 1949 the Afghan Governor of Gardez received him with some show of ceremony. But his chances of acceptance as a leader on the Pakistan side of the border can be completely discounted.

I believe the view has been expressed that at the time of partition the Frontier tribes were in identically the same constitutional position as the Indian Princes. They should therefore have been offered the same kind of choice. They could then have thrown in their fortunes with Afghanistan or chosen a crude independence. It is a view which disregards realities, and so long as Pakistan can offer material advantages which are beyond Afghan competition the tribesmen will look to Peshawar for a traditional understanding of their psychology and their needs.

I passed on to Karachi. The penetrating dust from the Sind desert in a second-class carriage has just to be ignored; and I arrived at the other end looking like a snow-man, a condition which somehow seems reserved for the European traveller.

One day Karachi may be a capital worthy of the name. For several years it can, however, only present the appearance of complete unsettlement, even upheaval. Wealth has arrived, and at the same time, through quite another set of circumstances, about a million refugees have sought shelter in the city. For them, Karachi became the symbol of security and the end of fear; and they poured in for a time in uncontrollable numbers, to present a picture of life at its lowest and most horrifying level. Petrol tins and sacking passed for their housing. Yet by heroic efforts somehow disease was kept under control; and the amazing patience and resignation of these mass sufferers have alone enabled the Government to plan their future with some promise of hope. One condition has helped to preserve that hope and resist political exploitation of the lot of refugees. Until 1952 the Government could boast that with the great food resources of the countryside available no refugee need starve.

His Highness the Aga Khan had just arrived at the new Metropole Hotel, which is now the pride of the capital. Around the entrance I paused to watch the obeisance of an army of secretaries, managers, hall porters and the like. Two minutes later, outside the Sind Club, on the grass just off the main road, I nearly stepped on the prostrate figure of an old man writhing in the agonies of an unknown affliction; for he was beyond any coherent speech. Yet pedestrians had passed him by and accepted him as a matter of daily routine. The two situations had no direct connection. But to pass from one to the other so abruptly could only bring reflection for a moment on the mountains of human injustice which remain to be removed over great areas of the world.

If people are indifferent to human suffering how can they ever be expected to react to the misery of an animal? Up the long slope which carries the road out of Karachi to Clifton over the railway lines, I watched a donkey being flogged, with its human load of six grown men behind it squeezed into a *tonga*. I take no credit for dashing to its rescue and pulling the startled passengers off their perches. There was no alternative. But their reaction was hardly one of anger or protest, for the simple proposition that the donkey was physically incapable of pulling them up the slope was one they could appreciate. Could they follow the further suggestion, that to inflict suffering on a donkey was a transgression of divine law as much as any of the normal condemnations of the prophet? I doubt it.

So often we fail to see that a lack of education is really the explanation. A cat playing with a mouse is unconscious of its cruelty. A man of the jungle who kills his rival in combat is unconscious of crime. One day the gap between ignorance and understanding will be filled; and the time to condemn will be if, when that day arrives, men and women are still barren of that extra sensitivity which is the manifestation of a higher stratum of civilisation. We all know people who keep dogs in cotton wool and who are yet indifferent to human suffering. They prove nothing and can, I suggest, be accepted as the penalties, the freaks, of progress.

But I wander from my diary. An old man dying by the roadside, an affray with a *tonga* driver, an address to the Pakistan branch of the movement for Federal World Government and a walk home after dinner across the flats from Clifton were just those insignificant moments which one always manages to remember at the expense of the more important episodes of the normal routine when one travels. Federal World Government is a brave movement which I attempt to support in London. In Karachi it afforded me the privilege of meeting a few young men of a serious and responsible approach to life who could escape the obsessions of local politics and talk in terms of universal problems. I recall my walk home from Clifton only because of frequent delays to obey the whistles of an army of police along the main road. The Prime Minister was driving out to dinner. There had been cause enough to avoid complacency, but the administration seemed suddenly to have become obsessed with the protection of its public servants, and by the time I had dodged the zeal of policemen and their whistling I had walked a long way off the straight road home to Karachi. There are also the unpredictable whims of thousands of inexperienced drivers to threaten the innocent pedestrian. I saw more accidents in a few days in Karachi than I had seen in years before.

Karachi now boasts the status of a separate unit within the Constitution, though it remains the capital of Sind. I spent a pleasant hour with the Governor of the Province, Mr. Din Mohammed, who at the time was shouldering the burden of executive administration. The Sindis seem quite incapable of running their Province without the stimulus of personal intrigue. Way back in 1943 the Governor had been confronted with a situation in which one of his Ministers, Mohammed Ayub Khuro, faced his trial for murder. The Province has never really settled down, and in 1948 Mr. Khuro, back now as Chief Minister, was once again facing a charge of breach of trust and being in possession of stolen property. He was then removed from office by Mr. Jinnah, but continued to retain the leadership of the provincial branch of the Moslem League. There followed a succession of Ministries until Mr. Din Mohammed finally took over the direct administration of the Province on 29th December 1951. As a result of the political acrobatics of Mr. Khuro, special legislation was introduced in the form of the Public Representation Offices Disqualification Act (PRODA). It is under this Act that Mr. Khuro and his associates are now debarred from accepting office. The further step of removing him from the leadership of the Sind branch of the Moslem League produced a trial of strength with the Prime Minister and has proved more intractable. Elections promised in 1953 are regarded as the opportunity for a fresh start. But until the leopard can change his spots I doubt if Sind can enjoy the blessings of democracy.

Mr. Din Mohammed has a reputation second to none of long and faithful service in the legal profession, and I imagine the conduct of Sind's

administration was far safer in his care than in the hands of Ministers of
doubtful political morality, however capable.   He was a Moslem gentle-
man of the old school, and his wife observed *purdah*.[1]   In the days of
British India the Governor's wife had a part to play.   But it will be some
time before the social life of "Government House" in the Provinces of
a Moslem country pivots around the Governor and his wife.   As I was
leaving the house my eye caught the ubiquitous photograph of the *Quaid-
i-Azam*, this time startlingly produced with that three-dimensional effect
which is coming into fashion in the advertising world in England and
America.   For generations the homes of Pakistan will revere the sharp,
arresting features of the creator of the State.   The high cheekbones and
deep-set eyes contrast so vividly with the robust contour of his great
colleague, the late Liaquat Ali Khan.   As often as not the photographs
of the two appear together.   Some day there will be scope for an author
to write the story of these two men and the teamwork in their joint
colossal enterprise.   Mr. Hector Bolitho was in fact in Karachi last year
attempting to gather material for a biography of Mr. Jinnah.   But there
seemed to be some doubt as to the co-operation which he should have
received if he was to have access to all the relevant data.

In this book I have not attempted a chronological history of India or
Pakistan.   But I must appropriately here record the death of Pakistan's
great Prime Minister, for months later, when I was in Karachi, the sense
of loss had not abated.   On 16th October 1951 Liaquat Ali Khan rose to
address an open-air meeting at Rawalpindi, when two shots fired at only
a few yards' range entered his body, and he died almost immediately,
with a Moslem's blessing on his country on his lips.   The assassin was
promptly lynched by the crowd.   He proved to be a certain Said Akbar,
an Afghan from Khost.   In view of Pakistan's strained relations with
both India and Afghanistan, it was as well that subsequent investigations
revealed no suggestion of any sources of initiation in those countries.
Indeed, a criticism of the appointed Tribunal was that after months of
inquiry they were unable in August 1952 to report any definite conclusions as to motive or outside influence.   Said Akbar was known as a
religious fanatic, and at the time was confined to Abbottabad under a
warrant of 1947; which explains the preoccupation of the police with
efforts to clear themselves of subsequent charges of inefficiency.   Said
Akbar left a widow, but he alone, had he lived, could have provided the
missing evidence.

The loss to Pakistan could not be measured in terms of the passing of a
Prime Minister.   At that critical stage the country needed above all
others one of cool judgment and cautious yet firm action.   Liaquat Ali
Khan filled this need.

Messages of condolence from many countries came in tribute to a
statesman who had won international respect.   If I may borrow an
analogy from across the Pakistan border, Jinnah was the creator and

[1] The wife of the Prime Minister, Khwaja Nazimuddin, is also in *purdah*.

Liaquat the preserver; and of the two contributions it is possible that the latter called for the greater exercise of wisdom and restraint.

The sub-Continent is generous in immortalising the memory of its heroes. Everything I have said of hero-worship applies equally to Gandhi and Nehru. Whether it be a mud hut or the luxury of the most modern home, invariably is to be found the familiar silhouette of that fragile figure in *khaddar*, leaning on his staff, his eyes twinkling from behind his spectacles in a merriment which for me who never knew him was his most endearing quality.

I always think that the most enchanting aspect of travel is the unpredictable nature of human contacts, of sudden friendships resulting in equally sudden plans and decisions. How much more exciting and how much less exacting than the precise, highly organised schedule of detailed planning. If it had not been for Sir Gilbert Laithwaite's hospitality I might not have met Mr. Shaffi at lunch, who promptly planned to put me on a B.I. cargo-ship leaving for the Persian Gulf. Mr. Shaffi is the delightful brother of that active personality in the social and political life of the country, the Begum Shah Nawaz. Years ago she had helped me in my work in the Civil Liaison Office at Jullundur; and now her brother in Gray Mackinnon and Co. was to offer his welcome assistance in finding a cargo-ship ready to take me to Basrah. So my last impression of the sub-Continent was of the little ships of the Royal Pakistan Navy as we sailed down the channel to Manora Point. I trust they may never be used in anger. Nevertheless, for reasons far removed from aggressive intention, I rejoiced to see them.

I had left India in 1944 with a sense of inevitability. I believed I should never return. But I was wrong; and one repercussion from a brief acquaintance is that I believe the stage is now set for us all to visit and revisit each other as often as we like. A holiday trip to India or Pakistan will, we hope, become as common an experience as a Mediterranean cruise. In the reverse direction, too, they are certainly anxious to come over and see what we have to offer. I have before me a letter written a few days ago from Jammu.

" Being an old soldier I have an immense desire to witness the Coronation celebrations in London. Could not a way be found of making it possible? How I wish for wings to fly round to you on that occasion ! "

Thus writes an old pensioner. Others may have less reason to express such simple sentiment. Yet it will be enough if they come. Whether from the comfort of the new Students' Hostel in Fitzroy Square [1] or the less sheltered atmosphere of an Earl's Court landlady, I trust that those who make the journey will receive from the British public that same friendship which these two peoples invariably offer an English visitor when he steps ashore at Karachi or Bombay. In such small ways that strange association, the British Commonwealth, will endure.

[1] Opened by Mr. B. G. Kher, Indian High Commissioner, in an impressive ceremony on 24th March 1953.

F

CHAPTER FIVE

FOR THE SOLDIER [1]

EVER since the introduction of the Montagu–Chelmsford reforms it
had been realised that steps to give India her own army under the
command of Indians must proceed side by side with political
developments. First a plan to Indianise certain units was introduced.
There followed a policy to create a complete Indian division. One
principle was to govern all progress. British officers on retirement
would be replaced by Indians, but an Indian, in his own interests and in
those of the Army in which he served, was to undergo the same periods
of service for promotion as British officers.

Before the Second World War some 2,500 British officers served in
the Indian Army. With them 500 Indian regular officers held the King's
Commission. On the outbreak of war there followed a vast expansion,
the Indian element increasing its numbers by seventeen times, the British
by five times.[2] As early as October 1944 the Commander-in-Chief
announced the cessation of recruitment of British officers in anticipation
of a post-war indigenous Indian Army. Those holding permanent
commissions would be required to stay, but all future vacancies were to
go to Indians, supplemented by the secondment of officers from the
British service so long as was necessary. As the rock on which a new
structure would rise, India's war memorial took the form of a vast new
Academy planned to house 2,500 cadets for all three Defence Services,
with an annual turnover of 500 cadets. Alas, it was conceived in the
belief that a united India assuming Dominion status deserved the finest
training establishment which military ingenuity could devise.

In the autumn of 1946 it was known that an indigenous army would
be set up by 1948. Of the 8,500 Indian officers available, about 8,000
were war-time officers with less than six years' service. So far from the
new army emerging as a natural growth with Indians undergoing the
same length of service as British officers, it was obvious that Indians would
receive greatly accelerated promotion. The nature of the problem will
best be illustrated by quoting Sir Claude Auchinleck's own words.[3]

" The task of planning the replacement of British officers by Indian
officers with such meagre resources on which to draw was difficult

---

[1] Throughout this chapter reference to Appendix III will assist the reader.
[2] Twenty-two thousand officers (13,500 British, 8,500 Indian). I am indebted to
an address by Field-Marshal Sir Claude Auchinleck before the Royal Institution
(March 1950) for these figures and for other valuable material.
[3] Ibid.

and complex enough in itself and the prospect of complete ' nationalisation ' by 1948 could hardly be viewed with complacency by myself
as Commander-in-Chief, or by my principal commanders and staff
officers. Then came the decision to divide India and thus almost
instantaneously our whole problem was changed. Our carefully
worked out plans for ' nationalisation ' by 1948 became completely
obsolete. We had now, in the course of a few short months, to
disintegrate completely an organisation which it had taken nearly
two hundred years to build up and perfect."

No Commander could ever have faced such a problem. Certain data
were known. Thus " class " units—Dogras, Mahrattas and Sikhs—
could immediately be allotted to India, since they were all composed of
Hindu clans. But Punjab infantry regiments and all the cavalry contained companies and squadrons of Hindus, Sikhs and Moslems. Even
more intricate was the problem of splitting the various Corps and
ancillary services. Engineer and Signal units, the Army Service Corps,
Medical, Ordnance and Pay, were all services in which Moslems and
Hindus had to be separated out and dispatched to new units, new homes
and new loyalties. Yet the administration and maintenance of the Army
had to continue. Moreover, this vast game of general post had to be
undertaken over a countryside which was torn with communal strife and
in which for a time the law of the jungle prevailed.

Some weeks before partition Sir Claude Auchinleck had realised that
special machinery would be needed to effect the division. He therefore
proposed that a Supreme Command be established at Delhi which would
retain certain central functions during a period of transition, Auchinleck
himself assuming the appointment of Supreme Commander. The most
exacting function of his command was the movement control of innumerable sub-units in transit between the two new Dominions. Since troops
moving by land across the Punjab frontier were inevitably involved in the
chaos of slaughter, the sea-route between Karachi and Bombay was
taxed to capacity. To effect the actual division of units a committee of
serving Indians with the King's Commission was appointed. It included
an equal number of Hindus and Mohammedans and was presided over
by a senior British officer. The committee started to function before
partition, and completed its task without encountering acrimony or
controversy. As an example of the method, in the case of my own
regiment, stationed at Hyderabad, Deccan, the Mohammedan squadron
proceeded to Lahore, where it was joined by Mohammedan squadrons
from other units. Our Hindu and Sikh squadrons went off to the Deccan
Horse, which became a unit of India's Army.[1] There were thus innumerable sub-units of the old Indian Army moving to and fro throughout July and August, at the one time when troops under firm control

[1] For clarification the two Armies were designated " the Army of India " and
" the Army of Pakistan ".

were needed to deal with the vast communal wave of primitive passion which was gathering force. Where units as large as squadrons or companies could move complete with their arms there was little danger of them suffering in transit, since they could defend themselves. Indeed, some of them were to constitute an additional threat to the countryside. But many small parties of administrative units on the move failed to reach their destination.

On 1st July 1947 it was announced that each Dominion would have operational control over its armed forces by 15th August, but that administrative control would continue under the Supreme Command until the two Governments were in a position to control and maintain their own forces. The date contemplated was 1st April 1948. Sir Claude Auchinleck in his new role had therefore no operational control over any unit except those moving from one Dominion to the other, and he had no control over these once they had come under their new Command. But there was, however, a time lag while the new Dominion administrations were forming, and in this transitional period the troops had to be fed, clothed and paid. These were the functions of the Supreme Command. [In addition, complete responsibility for the discipline and administration of all British officers in either Army who had elected to serve on after the 15th August remained with the Supreme Commander, as did also the control of units of the British Army. In turn the Supreme Commander in these responsibilities had to answer to and take his orders from the British Government.

In London the Government had ruled that in no circumstances were British troops to be placed under the orders of the Governments of India or Pakistan, and in general terms the policy was to send the troops home as quickly as possible.[1] It has been suggested that if British troops in large numbers could have been available for the creation of a Boundary Force on the critical frontier which was to sever the Punjab in two the subsequent slaughter might have been obviated. Instead the force under Major-General T. W. Rees which attempted the task was asked to control a situation beyond its capacity.

Early in July a Joint Defence Council was formed which was the political counterpart of the Supreme Command, and on 11th July Lord Mountbatten by mutual agreement became its Chairman. Both Dominions were equally represented on the Council, which included Sir Claude Auchinleck as a member. Not the least of the responsibilities of this central machinery was the task of dividing the material assets between the two Dominion armies. The vast accumulations of war lay in ordnance depots scattered about the country, the greater number being within Indian territory. It was Pakistan's bitter complaint that though the Defence Council might allocate stores and supplies to her Army, in fact orders were never translated into action. To this day

[1] Mr. Attlee spoke of British troops being out of the country by December 1947 (Second reading, Indian Independence Bill, 10th July 1947).

Pakistan claims that it has received less than justice in the division of
military material. For this reason the Pakistanis viewed the decision to
close down the Supreme Command in November with dismay. They
had not received their fair share, and with the abolition of a central
independent authority they saw no prospect of ever doing so. Nor was
the dissolution in accordance with the views of the Supreme Commander. We are reluctantly forced to the conclusion that at this stage
a certain lack of co-operation on the part of India was gradually under-
mining the effective functioning of the machinery.

We cannot study this aspect of partition without astonishment at the
complexity and confliction of loyalties which were imposed on British
officers. The situation had no precedent. A Supreme Commander
took his orders from London in one aspect of his responsibilities, yet was
responsible to Lord Mountbatten and Mr. Jinnah for the organisation and
administration of two new Armies. In turn, two British Commanders-
in-Chief took orders from two new Governments in operational matters
and questions of policy, but were responsible to Sir Claude Auchinleck
for all administrative matters arising out of the partition. It is not
difficult to imagine situations of bewilderment and confusion with nerves
and tempers tested to the extreme. Auchinleck not only carried responsibilities for dividing the Army which he had served and loved, but the
Royal Indian Navy and the Royal Indian Air Force also came under his
command. In 1946 he had made it clear that whatever the future held,
in his view any constitutional development which envisaged the break-up
of the Indian Army would be disastrous. Yet he was now faced with the
task of implementing the destruction of a unity which he and generations of British leadership had created. He himself was unravelling his
life's work. It was not an enviable task. The wonder is that in the circumstances first of communal slaughter and secondly of the Kashmir
problem, the division of the old Indian Army went through as smoothly
as it did.

Much criticism has been levelled at the Punjab Boundary Force,[1]
which was created in July and which, under Major-General Rees, took
its orders direct from the Joint Defence Council. The force was a mixed
one designed to deal with minor disturbances in villages, and as such it
carried out its task. But even those Englishmen who had worked nearest
to the communal life of the country failed to foresee the scope of the
destruction which would sweep the Punjab in August and September.
A few days previous to 15th August men who had lived long on the
Continent would not have believed the sights which were to revolt the
conscience of those Indians who could retain sanity. Little wonder that
the Boundary Force proved inadequate to the demand and that good
Indian sepoys themselves succumbed under the overwhelming visible

[1] The Force was, in effect, 4th Indian Division moved up from Poona. Its
commander, Major-General T. W. Rees, C.B., C.S.I., D.S.O., M.C. (known as
" Pete "), had made his name in the Burma campaign.

evidence of assassination, arson and destruction. It was therefore not surprising that on 29th August the Defence Council, meeting in Lahore, decided that the Boundary Force should be abolished as from 1st September, since its task had " grown out of all proportion to its responsibilities ". Responsibility thereupon devolved on the two Governments.

On 12th November it was announced in Delhi that the Supreme Command would be dissolved on 30th November, since the absence of a spirit of goodwill and co-operation between the two Dominions had made it impossible for Auchinleck and his staff to discharge their duties.[1] Thereafter the two British Commanders-in-Chief took complete control. In fact the back of the problem had been broken, though there were still many scattered groups of men searching out their new homes.

Throughout these critical weeks there had been many scenes of sad farewell as famous regiments speeded their comrades to the other side. Even when surrounded by every temptation of the common communal curse, fine units under the strict eye of British commanders kept their balance. Not the least moving of experiences for Englishmen were the frequent encounters among refugee columns with old pensioners who had previously served with them. A tragic, bewildered figure would step out from the crowd, draw himself up to a smart salute, and remind a harassed company commander that he had served in his battalion for many years and fought with it in the African desert or the jungles of Burma. Could he and his family, then, be rescued from the hell which surrounded them? As a typical example we should note the movements of the 1/12th Frontier Force Regiment in September, which arrived in the Gurdaspur District from Razmak complete in its old composition. The civil administration had broken down. All over the area misguided patriotism had led to the indiscriminate dismissal of Hindu officials by Moslem superiors and of Moslems by Hindus. The troops had to watch convoys involving their own co-religionists attacked by the police who had been posted to guard them. From Gurdaspur the battalion moved to Llyallpur, where they were split up into small uncontrollable packets in circumstances of sufficient provocation for any sepoy to lose his head. Mixed guards were formed. On the due date the Sikh and Dogra companies left for India, but not before the regiment had given them a *bara khana* and British officers had seen them up to the frontier at Wagah. With iron discipline the best units survived until the last moment. Less fortunate were scattered squadrons and companies. Here is a story of the Sikh squadron of a famous cavalry regiment which was subjected to an exacting but typical test. From the south of India the Sikhs were sent off to return their tanks to Kirkee Arsenal with their subsequent fate in indecision. It was decided that they should await orders in Delhi and be used to restore morale. Billets were taken up in huts outside the

[1] A skeleton British H.Q. continued until 30th December in order to deal with all British officers who remained in the country under the British Government after partition.

Fort, the tanks being lined up facing the main road. Inside the Fort 30,000 refugees living in appalling conditions regarded a Sikh squadron of tanks as their one symbol of confidence. Many terrified and homeless Sikhs sought shelter with the squadron, and the troops set up a special kitchen for hungry refugees. As the days went by the troops gradually absorbed the tales of carnage and destruction which demented refugees poured into their receptive ears. A routine of physical training, maintenance and games was not sufficient to take their minds off the stories of terrible events which engulfed their homes a few hundred miles away. The squadron commander asked to be allowed to move his men farther south, away from the turmoil, but his request was refused. A small party dispatched to report on conditions in the men's homes returned after having contacted as many families as possible, and were thus able for a few days to reassure their comrades, who were now growing extremely restive.

Very soon the squadron commander noticed a distinct change in the tone and attitude of his V.C.O.s [1] and men. He asked his senior Indian officer for an explanation, and received the reply, " Times are changing, Sahib, and they realise that soon they will be their own masters ".

Since the squadron had orders to be constantly ready for action, all ammunition was kept in the tanks. Tanks were locked at night, tank commanders keeping the keys. Early one morning the squadron commander was woken up with the news that a tank commander, the sentry on the quarter guard and the line sentry guarding the vehicles had all disappeared. They had driven off a truck, taking with them their tank grenades, two Sten guns, a Browning machine-gun, 30,000 rounds of ammunition and the rifles and ammunition of both sentries. They were never heard of again.

A report was immediately submitted. A high-ranking Sikh officer arrived to talk to the men. He asked if he might see them alone. He then sat them down under a tree and gave them some innocuous fatherly advice. The squadron commander, who had expected hard, straight talk, was anxious and puzzled. Discipline subsequently deteriorated, and he attempted to deal firmly with the growing tension. But it was too late, and the senior Indian officer, fearing for his commander's safety, placed a reliable guard on his room at night. Finally, after further representation to higher authority, the squadron handed over their tanks to another unit for whom they were destined and the men moved by train back to Jhansi. A week later a Sikh officer arrived and took over from the British commander. The latter set off for England, being dispatched with the usual tea-party. At the station in traditional manner they smothered him in garlands. But these last-minute tributes could not disguise the sad deterioration in a small unit of a fine Regiment which a few months previously would have been regarded as completely fool-proof.

[1] Viceroy's Commissioned Officer. A rank for which there is no equivalent in the British Army, the nearest status being that of a Senior Warrant Officer.

In Delhi officers at Army Headquarters entertained each other at a cocktail party before the large Pakistan detachment left for Karachi. Many promises of eternal friendship were exchanged. Alas, they were not to withstand the fierce impact of communal politics over the months which followed. Officers went their several ways and put the past behind them.   Here and there, in the neutralising atmosphere of England, they can meet, and for a time the bonds of the past are re-established. In London Generals Cariappa and Ayub Khan have been happy enough to remember that they were friends in days gone by. They possibly feel, too, that left to their own devices they could settle the Kashmir issue! Yet the soldier is the servant of policy, and has always to remember that simple condition of service. Indeed, it is surely a legacy of British stewardship that those upheavals in the Middle East which time and again have led to passing military dictatorships will never be repeated on the Indian sub-Continent. Gradually the two Armies assumed cohesion. In the case of India the general administrative problem was perhaps less acute, in that a greater number of units merely underwent a process of subtraction.   There was thus less destruction and less demand for new construction.   India, however, suffered severely in one respect. In the past the main concentration of troops had been in the north-west, which therefore contained the greater number of cantonments. Pakistan's new army found ample barrack accommodation, whereas India's immediate problem of housing her army became acute.   Nevertheless it was Pakistan's Army which was inevitably to feel that the circumstances of partition were weighted against them. As an example of the kind of difficulty which Pakistan experienced it may be noted that General Messervy in command had immediately to release his popular Chief of Staff, Lieutenant-General Kalwant Singh. There had been talk of the latter's acceptance of service in Pakistan. Had he remained he would certainly not have been alive today.

In Pakistan, it was on General Gracey, commanding the 1st Corps in Karachi, that much of the immediate burden of anxiety was to fall. The desperate speed at which partition had to be conducted resulted in conditions of administrative chaos for the new Government. Office staffs arrived without accommodation. When a roof over their heads had been found they had to search for furniture. Typewriters, stationery, files, the entire range of office equipment, were missing. Many of the trains bringing in Government personnel had been attacked, and the condition of those who completed the journey was pitiful. No attempt at a previous estimate of numbers or accommodation could be made. So the new Government of a nation in embryo had somehow to muddle its way into office trusting to Allah and the spirit of its people. It received encouragement from an unexpected quarter. I doubt if Pakistanis had anticipated that perhaps the displaced British would co-operate. Gracey took the view that he was now a responsible servant of Pakistan and it was therefore up to him to place the weight of his knowledge and ability at the country's disposal. His troops were ordered to surrender barrack accommodation and the resources of the Army were generally made available to the harassed Government. Such consideration coming from a British officer had its profound effect. Here was no soured and embittered critic, no sarcasm or complaint, but merely willing and efficient co-operation.

On partition General Gracey became Chief of Staff, General Messervy holding the chief command until 11th February 1948, after which Gracey assumed command, which he held until 19th January 1951. He then left Pakistan for well-earned retirement, being the last of a long line of British officers of the old Indian Army to hold the senior command of at least the Moslem portion of many of its finest and most experienced officers and men. On his shoulders had fallen the main task of constructing Pakistan's Army. His difficulties will be appreciated if it be understood that in October 1947 there was hardly a single formed unit in Pakistan. Several units still had Hindu and Sikh commanding officers, and Hindus held appointments at Pakistan General Headquarters. A Madrassi and a Gurkha unit were in Pakistan as late as the middle of December, and smaller sub-units were still in Kohat and Bannu in the beginning of 1948.

In such circumstances talk of the deployment of large regular formations in or near Kashmir was sheer nonsense. At this point we should note a major decision of policy which is of intense interest for many Englishmen with memories of the old perennial Frontier problem. The Hindu units which had left Pakistan had mostly been stationed in distant Wana and Razmak. Their departure left the Frontier posts weakened. Simultaneously Pakistan's Army had to be created under the shadow of a distant national emergency. At that stage the Kashmir situation for Pakistan had hardly developed as a threat of urgency. Nevertheless it was regarded as a potential danger for the future. There was only one thing to be done if a Pakistan Army was to be created. The Frontier commitments must be abandoned. As Chief of the Staff, Gracey had already worked on a scheme which would have completed withdrawal by March 1948. But the rapid Indian advance in Kashmir indicated an earlier date; so it was decided to effect the evacuation of all Frontier posts in which regular garrisons had been maintained by December 1947. The troops accordingly came away from north and south Waziristan without a casualty. The decision eventually to evacuate Razmak and Wana had in fact been taken months previously by Sir Claude Auchinleck as Commander-in-Chief in consultation with the Viceroy and the Political Department in the days before partition became a possibility. Pakistan was therefore implementing a policy which had already been contemplated by British authority.

In the middle of December, Razmak, for twenty-five years the costly symbol of British policy on the Indian frontier, was abandoned. In spite of its reputation as "India's white elephant", the place had always held the affections of those whose fate it was to be stationed in isolation

in the heart of Waziristan.   The garrison of 4,700 wound their way back
for the last time along the road which led down to Tank and the Indus
plain beyond, leaving behind them the little church and graveyard of
120 British dead.   In the gardens the chrysanthemums were blooming.
Chimneys were smoking out their last fires and the cinema stood empty,
advertising in irony, "In Which We Serve".   While Major General
R. E. le Fleming and Brigadier R. S. Steed were leading their men away
and closing a stage of history with all the care and precaution which had
characterised a hundred such operations in past years, a few miles away
the political agent for south Waziristan, Mr. Patrick Duncan, was busy
trying to restrain the Mahsuds from their advance on to the prize around
which for years they had played their own particular form of hide and
seek.   Thus "Operation Curzon", which heralded a return to the policy
of non-commitment of regular troops, was executed for the new Pakistan
by a British commander in the field, while a young British political
officer supported by half a dozen *khassadars* held the attack on the political
front.[1]

The troops had fully expected the tribesmen in their exuberance to
harass the final retreat.   But whether through tribal preoccupations
farther afield in Kashmir, or whether in recognition of a new era of
comparative freedom, the Razmak garrison escaped unscathed.   One
ponders on the reactions of the followers of Ipi when in bewilderment
they noted the high-heeled footprints in soft cement of the six Ensa girls
who had enlivened the garrison on a night in June 1944![2]

That Pakistan's decision has been fully justified would seem to be borne
out by subsequent tendencies.   So far from the new policy leading to an
extension of Afghan influence in tribal territory, the effect has been almost
to drive a wedge in between the tribesmen and the solicitous attentions
of Kabul.

Thus the seal was set on a policy which for many years had wavered
between a full political commitment up to the Durand line and a withdrawal to the boundary between the tribal areas and British India.
The compromise had cost us lives, money and wasted energy without
producing any return in the form of social or economic advancement
within tribal territory.   A phase was ended.   But it was not, as has been
generally accepted, the result of an enlightened political decision of the
moment, although, as indicated, it had already received full consideration.   In December 1947 it proved a military necessity.   With the with-

---

[1] Lord Curzon, who created the N.W.F.P. in 1908, always favoured a limited
policy of extension into tribal territory from the administered Districts, the various
Militias and Scouts being considered sufficient to exercise tribal control.
[2] These were the only women who ever visited Razmak, though one young lady
once made an enterprising attempt disguised as a man.   The withdrawal from
Razmak was graphically described by Douglas Brown in the *Daily Telegraph*,
19th December 1947.
The Faqir of Ipi, who lives on the Waziristan border, has for long years been a
thorn in the flesh of British and Pakistan authority.

drawal of the troops, the Pakistan Army was immediately created on a basis of fighting Divisions. The reader should understand that the old Army-in-India in times of peace was based on a system of districts according to geographical and administrative convenience. Fighting formations were then formed which allowed for an " internal security " component to be left on the ground in the event of mobilisation. Pakistan's reorganisation cut out all such considerations and took account of the need for organisation on an immediate war footing. In this respect her Army had some advantage over that of India, which was still harnessed to a normal peace-time distribution. Pakistan's Army was in effect nationalised from the front back, and not created from training-centres in conventional deliberation. In implementation of these changes it was not difficult to enlist the tribes of the Frontier who previously had been regarded as tough but unreliable fighting material. Thus it is that Mahsuds have found their way into the Frontier Regiment, and a new unit, the Pathan Regiment, is gradually developing.

We will pass over the years, and we come to 1951. To an Englishman crossing the frontier at Wagah on the Grand Trunk Road, halfway between Amritsar and Lahore, the fact of two armies was aggressively evident. From Jullundur General Kalwant Singh kindly placed a car at my disposal, and I was able to negotiate the frontier in comfort with every assistance. A haze lay over the flat Punjab countryside, but here and there one could see the camps and paraphernalia of an army under operational conditions. In Pakistan I made enquiries for my own Regiment. In Lahore I was discreetly told that I should enquire of higher authority. Eventually in Rawalpindi I heard that they were hidden away in a *bagh* near Gujranwallah; and there I found them with their tanks under the mango trees, their Mess dug neatly into the ground and officers and men looking as if they had never really put aside the way of life of Burma in 1945.

It is perhaps appropriate here to pay tribute to the manner in which both Armies loyally maintain the standards of the past. As I talked to the young Pakistani officers in whose hands lay the future of an institution in which I had spent the greater part of my life, my heart warmed to a realisation that they jealously guarded and retained those many small symbols of tradition with which we of another generation had grown old. It may only have been manifested as anxiety to know if the Mess *khidmatgars* were correctly dressed. But the feeling that we spoke the same language was there, and was to return on many occasions both in India and Pakistan.

India's Army is perhaps in some doubt as to the manner in which old associations are to be retained. India is a Republic, and certain units of her Army can hardly continue to regard themselves as " Royal " or retain titles linking them to the British Royal Family. And yet, wisely, there is little rigid insistence on the abandonment of past titles, and the present generation of Indian commanders would be reluctant to see them entirely forgotten. Certainly the Royal Bombay Sappers and Miners under the command of Colonel Bhagat Singh, V.C.,[1] will keep their Royal title and continue to wear a crown in their berets for many months to come. There is a story of a well-known cavalry regiment in Pakistan which had fought at the Battle of Tel-el-Kebir. At the time the centre page of the *Illustrated London News* reproduced a picture of their Sikh squadron setting on Arabi Pasha's Moslem Army with their lances. This, how-ever, in no way deterred the officers of the regiment a short while ago from tracing old copies of the paper and ordering them for the Mess.

I sometimes wonder if the people of Britain realise the significance of Her Majesty's health being drunk in an isolated Pakistani Mess in an obscure station of the Punjab. Loyalty is a two-way traffic, and if it comes to us from overseas we should return it with all the gratitude of which we are capable.

An appendix sets out the division of the old Army. Within the text of a chapter I therefore confine myself to a general comment. It will be seen that the two Armies have not yet considered renumbering their units consecutively on to new lists. In England it is pleasant still to be able to identify the units we knew by their numbers. But the time will come when the old numbers must give way to a new sequence in the interests of creating a sense of unity within the two Armies. If there was ever a remote prospect of a happy reunion, the old numbers could remain. But reunion is now a phantasy, so that one day we must expect our favourite numbers to disappear, as indeed they have frequently done throughout the past 200 years.

In India the authorities have cut right away from previous patterns and have retained the system providing joint basic training for the Army, Navy and Air Force under one roof at the National Defence Academy, which is the new name of the establishment at Dhera Dun. The original scheme for a combined Services Academy to which I have referred was Sir Claude Auchinleck's legacy to the Indian Army, though it was intended to cover an undivided continent. Two years' basic training is now provided for all three services in the "Joint Services Wing", cadets being given a broad education in which a way of life is developed rather than technical knowledge. Drill, discipline, equitation, sport, *shikar*, drama and music are included in the first two years, involving the employment of some fifty academic teachers. The age of cadets on joining varies from fifteen to seventeen, and the figures (1,600 applicants for 160 vacancies each term) indicate that there is no shortage of material. Candidates, who must have reached the matriculation standard,[2] come up

---

[1] This officer was the first Indian to receive the Victoria Cross—in 1940, in Abyssinia.
[2] Involves the school-leaving Certificate from a Secondary School.

before a united Public Services Commission and a Services Selection Board, stating at the time the Service which they prefer.

After two years Army Cadets continue at Dehra Dun to complete four years, passing from the Military Wing into the Technical Wing. It is, however, the intention to move the Technical Wing by 1954 to Kharakvasala, near Poona, which was the original site chosen by Auchinleck. Here cadets will continue their training in touch with existing establishments, such as the Artillery School and the College of Military Engineering. After four years of concentrated study a cadet should certainly be well qualified for a commission and the great day of posting to his unit.

From Dehra Dun naval cadets are posted first to Cochin, after which they pass on to Dartmouth and Chatham, where excellent reports have testified to the high standard of selection and basic training which they have already received in India. Air Force cadets pass on to Jodhpur and Secunderabad to complete their technical training. While at the Academy cadets receive pay at the rate of Rs. 30 a month, which may be increased to Rs. 40 if the income of the parent is certified by a magistrate as under Rs. 400 a month.

It could be argued that the Defence Academy at Dehra Dun and the standard and type of training which it provides is one of the most important factors in the future development and welfare of India's Forces. These were certainly my reflections as I watched the passing-out parade of the Military Wing in December 1951. The parade reproduced the identical precision which one expects at Sandhurst. But more significant perhaps was the intense interest and pride displayed by a large gathering of parents and relations. Mothers and sisters who in a previous generation would have been safely behind the latticed windows of the *zenana* watched their young hopefuls on the parade-ground with a critical eye and incidentally heard some practical advice from India's Commander-in-Chief on the dangers for young officers of early matrimony and extravagance. Nothing to which we who are familiar with Sandhurst procedure are accustomed had been omitted, even to the Adjutant's final exit on his horse up the steps of the main building.

After parade we dispersed to wander round the buildings. The great Academy Hall now houses the former King's Colours of all battalions of India's Army. They had been handed in for custody the previous year in a ceremonial parade which is still the talk of all those who were lucky enough to see it. It is reported that Congress Ministers not given to an interest in military ceremonial were deeply moved at the sight of these symbols of great traditions carried in public for the last time to their final home. My memory is of a happy day rounded off in the desultory English atmosphere of cricket, leaving the conviction that the foundations for the training of India's officers have been firmly laid and the net spread wide to draw in young men from many strata of life hitherto not included in the search for military talent.

Apart from the competition for Dehra Dun, a National Cadet Corps based on the Universities receives encouragement, and a small percentage of its members find their way into the military wing of the N.D.A., while for others outside the Universities the Territorial Army, based on the larger towns, is available.

What of the Indian Sepoy and his welfare? It will be seen from the appendix that India retained units—Sikhs, Dogras, Mahrattas—which were based on a class composition. But the general tendency is gradually to break down the class segregation, which under British officers most certainly drew out the finest qualities that each separate community could contribute. The new Brigade of Guards is the first manifestation of the mixing of classes and a revival of conditions which were discarded after 1857. It may well be that a step to overcome prejudices which would have been subject to suspicion if initiated under British authority will be accepted and successfully developed under Indian leadership. If so, there will follow repercussions in a social sphere outside the Army.

General Cariappa's Guards—for they are his particular interest and creation—will become a feature of the busy scene around Sir Edwin Lutyens' great legacy to the President of India. Eventually they will comprise a self-contained formation of four battalions, the training-centre and one battalion being in Delhi for ceremonial purposes, while the other three battalions are in circulation. So far as one could judge from a pleasant morning spent at their training-centre in Delhi, classes and castes, not excluding a few Moslems, had adopted non-communal messes and kitchens without difficulty. Imitation, one presumes, is some flattery, and the Indians are adopting many details of organisation, dress and equipment from the customs of our own Brigade of Guards. Even the grouping of buttons on tunics finds its counterpart in Delhi.

Outside the Guards, a start is being made in pooling castes and classes in the technical arms. Sikhs and Madrassis serve together in the Signal Corps, and Bengalis are enlisted as gunners. The eventual intention is to mix classes within all sub-units. The difficulties of overcoming certain customs and habits regarding food are formidable. A Madrassi has to be persuaded to like *chappattees*. A Sikh must develop a taste for rice. There are difficulties of language. Yet, if India is to retain her political unity, the greater uniformity that can be achieved within the Army as between the many communities, the greater will be the impact for a common loyalty in the countryside.

The Indian soldier now serves for seven years with the colours and eight years in the reserve.[1] He receives basic pay, and his promotion is linked closely to his educational standard and professional ability. He remains the patient, willing and simple servant of his country, which won the respect and affection of thousands of British officers. The officers who lead him take intense pride in the new Army. They not unnaturally

[1] In the case of the Signal Corps, Colour service is twelve years, with eight years in the Reserve.

wish to create new traditions. But in doing so they adhere closely to old methods.[1] In accordance with declared principles of policy, they insist that the Army is open to Moslem and Hindu alike.[2] As before, recruiting is controlled by training-centres, but regimental recruiting parties on a quota system are given a fairly free hand. There is no shortage of recruits for an Army which receives skilful advertisement and a good Press. It is, indeed, something of a paradox to note the natural antipathy of politicians for military associations and the popularity of the Army in the countryside. Not a little of the credit for the soldier's status must go to General Cariappa, who would be the first to acknowledge the character of the great brotherhood which India inherited from the past. The spirit of Clive is preserved and lives on.

India's Army is still assisted by over a hundred British military advisers in various senior appointments. They include Lieut.-General Sir Dudley Russell in his capacity as Chief Military Adviser. As in America, command of all India's Defence Forces is vested in the President. President Rajendra Prasad shared with his colleagues that shy approach to the Army to which I have drawn attention. Encouraged by the sympathetic advice and instruction of senior officers, he has overcome his difficulties and willingly and successfully accepted his somewhat symbolic position.

It is appropriate to leave India's Army with a record of a tribute recently paid to the small Indian Field Ambulance which represents her contribution to the Commonwealth Division in Korea. A senior British Commander from Korea, speaking recently in England, expressed the view that had the Indian personnel had their way, they would have left their ambulances and stretchers and trained as parachutists ready for any emergency to which he might direct them.

Everything that has been said of the present Indian Army is equally true of the Army of Pakistan. How could it be otherwise, with such wonderful material at the country's disposal as the rugged Punjabi Moslem clans; Gakhar, Janjuha, Awan, Tiwana and many others? The officers of the Army are drawn from a wider geographical and social sphere than the rank and file. Many of them came over from India, leaving homes in Uttar Pradesh (United Provinces).[3]

Pakistan is perhaps more conscious of her Army and its needs than is India. She has no great iron and steel plants round which to build up an ordnance and munition industry; and so a vast new township is taking shape on the sheltered plain between Taxilla and Hassanabdal. For about five miles on either side of the Grand Trunk Road factories, godowns, living quarters and offices are transforming the peaceful

[1] As an example old medal-ribbons are retained. But new medals have been struck for " Kashmir " and " Independence Day "; and new " gallantry " medals have replaced the V.C., D.S.O., and M.C.

[2] India's Quarter-master General is a Moslem—Major-General Anis Ahmed Khan.

[3] Pakistan's Adjutant-General, Major-General Sher Ali, is a brother of the late popular Nawab of Pataudi, with his home only a few miles from Delhi.

landscape into a great military centre. It is not for me to say whether the ultimate object is to be self-contained in the supply of all modern weapons and fighting vehicles. But obviously munitions and the less complex requirements of a mechanised army will in a few years be manufactured on Pakistan soil.

An observant visitor to Pakistan might well detect something of Prussian exaltation in so far as pride in the Army and its status is concerned. Yet it would be misleading to regard the country's aptitude for soldiering as dangerous. The Rawalpindi conspiracy case drew attention to the ambitions of less responsible leaders. Had the conspiracy been successful, Pakistan might have drifted into an era of military dictatorship from which she would have extricated herself with difficulty. But the mood has passed, not without its repercussions. The Pakistan sepoy was one who would blindly face certain death if ordered to do so by his officers. Obedience was his second nature. For a time the example of a number of senior officers under trial for conspiring to overthrow the State was not without its noticeable effect in the ranks of the Army. Whether a drawn-out trial and delayed verdict have had an unsettling effect of any permanency is less certain. To an observer in 1951 the Pakistan Army under General Ayub Khan appeared to be the fine disciplined fighting machine which we would have expected.[1]

Pakistan seems determined to enhance, if it were possible, the social status of her officers. This is reflected in the generous scale of allowances which officers receive, particularly when they serve abroad. Thus no officer stationed in London or coming to the United Kingdom for a course suffers through any lack of either an initial outfit or a subsequent maintenance allowance.[2] I think it is generally agreed that officers of

---

[1] (a) General Ayub Khan, a Pathan, received his commission at Sandhurst in 1928, and served a year with the Royal Fusiliers. He commanded a battalion of 14th Punjab Regiment in Burma and a brigade on the North-West Frontier.

(b) Verdicts in the Rawalpindi conspiracy case were finally made known on 5th January, 1953. They ranged from transportation for a term of twelve years under Section 121A of the Pakistan Penal Code, awarded to Major-General Akbar Khan, to four years' rigorous imprisonment to a group of seven.

Briefly the facts are that on 9th March, 1951, Major-General Akbar Khan, his wife, Begum Nasim, Brigadier Latif and Mr. Faiz Mohammed Faiz, editor of the *Pakistan Times*, were arrested on charges of conspiring to overthrow the State, involving liaison with foreign agencies. Subsequently Group-Captain M. K. Janjua and others were arrested. A special Tribunal of three judges was set up. It then took nearly a year to examine the 208 witnesses for the prosecution, after which the prosecution Counsel argued the case for forty-two days, to be followed by a further seventy-three days occupied by the defence.

Only one of the accused—the Begum Nasim Akbar Khan—was acquitted.

[2] An officer receives basic pay of Rs. 750 p.m. Staff pay is Rs. 75 p.m. A Field Officer on service abroad receives an allowance of £75 p.m. All officers, on first commission, receive an outfit allowance of Rs. 500 p.m., with a monthly kit allowance of Rs. 25.

On permanent posting to a Mission abroad an officer receives an outfit allowance of Rs. 3,000.

both Pakistan and India in their appearance and deportment in England reflect just those high standards which we hope to find in young leaders of our own Defence forces.

Wisely the authorities discourage early marriage in the Army. A small marriage allowance is paid after an officer reaches twenty-six years of age, before which the Government view matrimony " with disfavour ".

Pakistan's military contacts with the United Kingdom are close and very cordial. Some 200 British officers were still in Pakistan service in 1952. About eighty of their officers are under continuous technical training in England, and many apprentices train at Cranwell for the Royal Pakistan Air Force.

The Royal Pakistan Military Academy is at Kakul. Cadets for the Navy and Air Force train at Karachi and Risalpur. But to assist boys to reach the necessary educational standard a pre-cadet training-school is established at Quetta on a joint-Services basis.[1]

Being very conscious of potential external threat, the Pakistan Army appreciates its need for arrangements covering a rapid expansion in time of a national emergency. An officers' training-school is established at Kohat at which nine months' training is given to young men who come before a competitive Selection Board. They then receive an " emergency " commission. There is no shortage of candidates. In addition, a Pakistan National Guard on a voluntary basis, which in effect is a Territorial Force, receives popular support. It is commanded and trained by seconded Regular officers and N.C.O.s, and it includes an active women's branch.

It is impossible to view the scope of all these very comprehensive plans without mixed feelings. They go forward with a noticeable degree of British professional support and advice. For Pakistan they represent an even greater demand on the Central Budget than does the similar commitment in India; and while that demand continues, expensive plans to develop and industrialise the country must obviously suffer.[2] In contradiction to such obvious logic, I find myself among those who believe, in all sincerity, that for countries who launch into the world in political independence, the greatest nation-building agency they can inherit from the previous dispensation is a disciplined, well-led Army. An Army, and less frequently a Navy and an Air Force, become the focus of so much that is solid and progressive in the national life. Within this context I like to recall a conversation I once had with General Cariappa. He had been telling me of a battalion in camp in the Meerut district which, finding time on its hands, decided to help a few local

---

[1] A similar need for boys proposing to enter the ranks is met by the well-known King George's Royal Indian Military schools, which continue both in India and Pakistan.

[2] When the " Collective Measures " proposals were recently being debated by the United Nations General Assembly, Pakistan informed the United Nations that she was unable to contribute units so long as she was faced with the Kashmir problem.

G

villages with a little rural reconstruction.   They accordingly settled down
to digging manure-pits and village drains, not without some suspicion
from the civil authorities!   The talk drifted into speculation on armies
and their future.   Would they disappear in a Utopian world in which
confidence and peace had been restored?   Could not armies and their
great potential for national service be utilised for progress and construction?   After all, in England at times we had turned to the Army for
help both in dealing with dock strikes and in merciful assistance to a
seaside town devastated and partially swept into the sea by the caprices of
Nature.

I do not know what the attitude of Trade Unions in England would be
to national battalions of construction under discipline, operating as
adult Boy Scouts, with official recognition.   But on the great sub-
Continent I can certainly think of no more constructive kind of evolution
for military forces than their eventual use as national Labour in the
worthy and honourable task of physical construction and development.

CHAPTER SIX

INDIA AT THE POLLS

O N a fresh January morning in 1952 I set out from Jullundur for Nakodar. Nakodar is just a typical *tehsil* centre of the Punjab lying to the south of Kartarpur, off the Grand Trunk Road. The houses, haphazardly thrown together round the village pond and a large peepul tree, have never quite decided whether to be built of brick or mud. The school, the police *thana* and a few of the more opulent *zemindars* and *baniyas* boast double-storied brick mansions with elaborate pictures of playful gods, tigers and elephants painted in bright colours round the doors. But the greater number of its modest inhabitants are content within their mud walls sharing a cheerful squalor with the usual farm-yard family of buffaloes, hens and the inevitable mongrel staking his preference for a home rather than being a welcome member of the family.

On this particular morning Nakodar was busy making Indian history with thousands of other *tehsils* up and down the land. For the school was on holiday, and the classrooms had been adapted to the rough-and-ready requirements of the country's first full election. Long before the " slumbering millions ", in ignorance of the blessings of democracy, had shocked the late Mr. Edwin Montagu, the process of an election had been understood in its application to the indigenous *panchayat* system of the country. As a result of the Montagu-Chelmsford reforms a limited electorate of some 9 millions first went to the polls. In the next venture in 1937, following on the report of the Lothian franchise commission of 1932, a total of 36 millions voted. At the time this represented an average of 27·6 per cent of the population, and the advance was considered revolutionary.[1] Most certainly without Lord Lothian's careful enquiry those who planned the elections of 1952 could not have recorded the gratifying success which they were able to claim. The interesting feature of the Lothian Commission's recommendations was the fact that it was possible to classify and restrict an electorate according to an educational limitation. Whereas for women a simple literacy qualification was imposed, men were required to have reached the Upper Primary school standard.

The decision of Independent India to extend complete suffrage to all adults, male and female, over twenty-one years of age, was inherent

---

[1] The electorate of the 1935 Government of India Act represented 43 per cent of males and 10 per cent of females in British India. The high percentage of the male franchise is often overlooked.

in the circumstances by which the nation hastened eagerly to confirm its new status. For the India of 1946 and 1947 there could be no niggardly deliberate process, no modest creeping into nationhood unnoticed. Nothing less than a vote for every man and women could suffice for a sovereign independent Republic based on a constitution of 395 clauses and eight schedules! We will return to consider the wisdom of this decision; but we should first be clear on the facts of the election. By what method was it conducted and who were the competitors? What parties did they represent, and were those parties representative of definite political convictions, or were they the result of personal aspirations to leadership?

To us who are accustomed to the completion of our voting in one breathless period of twelve hours, the Indian system of staggered elections over three months is full of anomalies.[1] It was necessitated by the fact that there was no surplus trained staff to conduct elections. The civil administration responsible for day-to-day government was the only available machinery, and in order that they could carry on the business of legislation and revenue, of law and order and public service, staffs had to be moved from one district to another. Perhaps the hardest pressed of a willing army of officials was the Sub-Divisional Officer, who acted as Returning Officer and generally carried out the important but unspectacular arrangements at the polling-stations.[2]

No understanding of the elections would be complete without some knowledge of the structure and constitution of the new India; and the reader is therefore asked to accept a description which, though not light reading, is important, not only as explaining the elections, but as lifting our knowledge a little beyond the superficial.

The Union of India today comprises twenty-eight States.[3] They divide into three categories, known as Part "A", Part "B" and Part "C" States. For practical purposes Part "A" States are the old Governors' Provinces, and are nine in number. There are eight Part "B" States, and they cover most of the territory which was formerly the India of the Princes. Lastly there are eleven Part "C" States, such as Delhi, Coorg and Ajmer, administrative enclaves too small to justify full legislative machinery and administered by Chief Commissioners directly under the Central Government.[4]

[1] Polling started in the hill districts (Himachal Pradesh) on 25th October 1951 and was completed in India on 21st February 1952.

[2] The S.D.O. is an officer, subordinate to the Deputy Commissioner of a District, who may have a variety of responsibilities thrust upon him of a judicial, revenue or administrative nature. If he is conscientious he cannot escape being overworked.

[3] The word "State", formerly used to define only the territories of Princes, is now used to describe all the main administrative units of India. The term "Province" has disappeared. By the time this is in print the State of Andhradesa will have been added, to complete twenty-nine States. See the map facing p. 132.

[4] Three Part "C" States have Legislatures—namely, Vindya Pradesh, Himachal Pradesh and Bhopal. It is understood that in these cases the status of Chief Commissioner will be raised to Lieutenant-Governor.

The Central Parliament of India consists of two Houses : the Council of States (216) and the House of the People (496), the latter, with control of the purse, enjoying the greater power. Within the States the majority of legislatures consist of one House, but seven States have two Houses, known respectively as the " Legislative Council " and the " Legislative Assembly ".[1] In order to save time, cost and administrative staffs, the elections to the States' Legislatures and the Centre were carried through in a single simultaneous process, the voter recording one vote for his State member and another for his representative in the House of the People in Delhi. By an ingenious device the strength of the State Assemblies was fixed as an exact multiple of the number of representatives of the State in the House of the People. Thus Uttar Pradesh, with eighty-six members in the House of the People, has 430 members in its own Legislative Assembly. This simple arrangement was adopted to facilitate the delimitation of constituencies. In the case of Uttar Pradesh the Central constituencies each contained exactly five local constituencies.

The direct system of election by the single non-transferable vote was adopted for the Lower Houses. But in the case of the Council of States and the seven local Upper Houses the indirect method was chosen, the elected members of Lower Houses forming electoral colleges for the purpose. In all cases, however, in the Upper Houses a number of nominated seats are reserved to provide for the representation of particular interests. Thus the Council of States includes twelve members nominated by the President for the special contribution they can make in literature, art, science and the social services.

It is India's claim that the pattern of communalism which was stamped across the land in the establishment of separate electorates for Moslems and others has been removed by their abolition in the new constitution. For a period of ten years, however, special representation has been preserved for the Scheduled Castes and Scheduled Tribes, more easily recognised by the public outside India as the untouchables and aboriginals. In certain areas double-member constituencies were therefore created, each voter registering not only a vote each for candidates for the House of the People and his State Assembly, but a third and fourth vote for a candidate for the two corresponding reserved seats. The object of the whole electorate voting in the " reserved seat " category was to obviate the sense of isolation of a community and the encouragement of communalism which would result if reserved seats were to be of interest only for their own communities.

Constituencies were so deliminated as to provide for one member to represent between 500,000 and 700,000 of the population in the case of the Central Parliament, and about 100,000 in the case of the State. Every citizen who had attained the age of twenty-one on 1st March 1950 and who had resided at least 180 days in his constituency between certain specified dates was entitled to vote; and so an electorate of 176 millions

---

[1] Bihar, Bombay, Madras, Punjab, U.P., West Bengal, Mysore.

was registered, of whom about half exercised their right to vote. For those who enjoy figures it can be recorded that some 6,520 million ballot-papers were prepared. There were totals of 18,300 candidates, 224,000 polling-booths, 3,293 constituencies, and the President of the Union for his own amusement calculated that if the electoral roll was printed with forty names to a foolscap-size page the pages bound together would cover about 200 yards!

How was such an operation conducted for a community with perhaps a 15 per cent literacy? The system of placing a cross against a candidate's name on the ballot-paper would obviously be ineffective, since the voter could usually not read the name of the candidate: nor could a cross be recorded against a symbol, since this would involve the printing of ballot-papers carrying a dozen or so pictures, and in confusion the voter's cross might well find its way into the wrong column. The only foolproof system was to provide one ballot-box for each candidate in the constituency and to decorate the outside of the box with the Party symbol. Yet another necessary precaution was the marking of the forefinger of every voter with indelible ink before supplying the ballot-paper. The mark was calculated to last ten days, so that within that period the voter could not return for a second chance!

The reader must imagine the corner of a schoolroom screened off by a crude curtain of sacking. Behind the screen is a table on which is a row of large tin boxes. Outside the screen a policeman controls the constant stream of villagers who have come in from the surrounding country. The women, huddled together, chatter excitedly at the mysteries of so novel an occasion. Today they are provided with a separate polling-booth. Perhaps in a few years' time it will be different. One by one the people are admitted to the secret sanctuary, where they hurriedly search the row of boxes for the picture of their choice. I watched an old man as he found himself in some bewilderment alone facing a dozen boxes.[1] He glanced suspiciously at me, as if suspecting a detective ready to apprehend him in a crime. At last he discovered the familiar picture of the two Congress bullocks, and thrust in his paper. And so by these rough-and-ready methods, operated with a high sense of duty by a devoted staff, was recorded India's verdict. There were mistakes. In a constituency of Madhya Pradesh about 11,000 votes out of 76,000 had to be declared invalid owing to a failure to instruct the electorate in procedure. There were frequent brawls outside polling-stations. But the machine worked, in spite of the fact that the entire electorate in Part "B" and Part "C" States were exercising their right to vote for the first time.

One feature of the local arrangements seemed open to abuse. The Government had prepared the electoral rolls in books which could be

[1] Ballot-boxes for the House of the People were green, those for Legislative Assemblies were brown. A Bombay firm, Godres and Company, secured the contract for their construction.

purchased by the public. The voter on arrival at the polling-station could thus be checked up by the various party representatives who had taken the trouble to purchase the local rolls. He would then present himself to the Returning Officer with his name and number on a slip of paper, receiving his ballot-paper in return. It appeared to be an in-genious method of making the Party staffs do the work of the under-staffed Government machinery. But when I saw the various Party agents, each with their flag and emblem flying proudly on their par-ticular plot staked out on the Grand Trunk Road outside Kartarpur polling-station, and as I noted the country-folk arriving and wondering under which flag to register their arrival, I could not avoid the reflection that here were the circumstances for some obvious exploitation of an illiterate electorate.[1]

In Delhi Mr. Sukumar Sen, the hard-working election Commissioner, had proudly displayed his election boxes to me. They had certainly met with fair success in defying the many efforts at sabotage. But to provide one box for every Party at every polling-booth proved an expensive business: for each box cost five rupees, and polling-booths were pro-vided on a scale of one for every thousand voters. At this rate I calcu-lated that the cost of boxes and their dispatch to polling-stations for Nakodar alone, which is comparable to a large English village, must have been about £100![2] Frequently one saw railway-trucks laden with ballot-boxes shunting about in the sidings at stations, and altogether boxes and their movement and protection seemed to occupy no small amount of the time and labour of the administration.

As to the symbols, the countryside soon became familiar with a dozen or so emblems of topical interest. The Congress chose a pair of bullocks, the Socialists adopted a banyan tree. The Communists retained the sickle, but replaced the hammer with a less aggressive ear of corn. In-deed, the Government stipulated that symbols should be innocuous and unlikely to excite communal or political passions. At the height of election fever, posters and emblems were profuse everywhere—on walls, at street corners, even decorating the statues in New Delhi and defying the dignity of a former generation of Viceroys. A certain amount of mild fun was had by the Socialists at the expense of the Congress. What was the use of a couple of bullocks yoked together without a driver? How would they know where to go? They might even want to go in different directions! Compare them with the Socialist banyan tree, which could at least offer shade to the people and good timber for the

[1] Since all Parties had purchased copies of the electoral rolls, any individual could register his arrival at any Party Agent and have his name and number checked.
[2] The liberal scale of polling-booths was to obviate the necessity of country people travelling long distances, thus both avoiding the use of mechanical transport and encouraging polling.
The total cost of the election was £5,250,000.
Early in 1953 the election commissioner, Mr. Sen, was appointed to lead the Commission which is to superintend the Sudan elections.

practical use of men! In such ways the vast electorate were humoured
into exercising the right to listen to their candidates and decide whom to
support with a minimum of bad behaviour. Some measure of the
success of the great experiment was due to an inherent sense for a public
occasion. The Indian loves a *tamasha*. Declare a holiday and stage a
village fair and the peasantry will flock in from far and wide. Something of this spirit obviously found its way into the elections.

Polling was highest in areas of greatest education. Thus about 70 per
cent of the electorate recorded their vote in Travancore-Cochin, while
in contrast only 20 per cent voted in Rajasthan. Tradition in Rajasthan
dies hard, and it will be many years before the peasants of Jodhpur and
Jaipur, of Kotah, Bundi and a dozen other former strongholds of feudal
splendour come to exercise their choice according to a reasoned conclusion of their own. Thus, when, to the surprise of the Indian public,
many of the Princely order decided to enter politics and stand as candidates in the elections, it was only natural that their subjects followed
them. The result was that at one time it seemed as if the Princes and
Jagirdars in Rajasthan, standing as Independents, might have been in a
position to form a coalition Government with the many smaller groups.
The final result, however, gave the Congress a majority of two over all
parties.[1] The Princes, had they been able to form a Ministry, would
have first needed to formulate a policy; and since a loose collection of
Independents are hardly likely to survive, this may still be their need.
But they are not all firm in a belief in the wisdom of Princely interest in
politics. When Princes such as the Maharaja of Jodhpur decided to
enter the contest, Pandit Nehru expressed his strong disapproval of the
movement. It might have seemed more logical had symptoms of public
interest been welcomed in those who had formerly lived in exclusive
isolation. But this was not the case, and in the face of official disapproval
some of the Princes were unwilling to take any action which might be
regarded as jeopardising their privy purses; for these rest as much on
the goodwill of a Congress Ministry as on any formal statutory arrangement. A reluctance to offend is therefore not unnatural. Others,
such as the Maharaja of Dholpur, would in honesty regard political
interference as unbecoming to the dignity of those who have for generations looked upon their position as beyond the reach of representative
institutions. But whatever the attitude of the former Ruler, the general
tempo of election fever in Rajasthan was slower than elsewhere. So it
seemed to me as I watched a *tonga* gaily festooned with pictures of the
lamp of the Jan Sangh, edge its way slowly through the main bazaar of
Bundi city. A few curious street urchins, attracted by the raucous
chanting of an ancient gramophone, followed its progress; and that
seemed the sum total of political enthusiasm in the city of Bundi. In
contrast, in Jaipur, the seat of the Government of Rajasthan, where the

[1] In a House of 160, the Congress secured eighty-one seats, the Independents being
second with thirty-five.

election atmosphere was more stimulating, candidates managed to whip up the public to some sense of the occasion by staging colourful processions. A few days before polling, Jaipur city was treated to a Congress display of fifty pairs of bullocks with the usual attendant noises of drums and slogans. Not to be outdone, the next day an Independent candidate who had adopted a camel as his symbol paraded through the streets with fifty camels.

I have referred to Rajasthan, but in Orissa and Madhya Pradesh there was equal support for the Princes; and in all about twenty-four former Rulers were elected. Particularly unreal in Rajasthan was the effort to induce in women any concern for their political destiny; and those who know the circumstances of the *zenana* in a typical Rajput family will appreciate the point. Not only were many women known merely as the wife or daughter of a male, but where they were recognised by their own names they were frequently reluctant to give them. In Jaipur some 50 per cent of the women were disfranchised for this reason.

In a vast country with a shortage of trained staffs it was inevitable that the elections should throw a great strain on the civil administration. We who register our vote without recognising any of the efficient gentlemen who preside at the polling-station find it difficult to comprehend that in India the administration which conducts the elections is an all-powerful bureaucracy, the members of which are personally known to the electorate and who are feared or respected, according to the personal reputation of the official involved. The Deputy Commissioner in the District and the Sub-Divisional Officer in the *tehsil* are still the focus of the many day-to-day problems of life. It was therefore inevitable that when this father and mother of the people took over the operation of elections, there should arise many situations involving abuse and opportunities for malpractice. The Government of the day could, if it chose, smooth its own particular path; and undoubtedly it sometimes did so. There was some conscientious legislation concerning a limit on funds spent by candidates for election purposes and a check on the use of transport. But there was sufficient evasion to provoke a lot of criticism. It started with some concern at the Prime Minister's use of a military aeroplane for his hurricane election campaign. It ended in an unlimited number of ways and means by which a Congress Minister could oil the machinery of administration for a Congress candidate. Nevertheless, exploitation at no time developed to the extent which had been anticipated; and the overall results represent the people's verdict through a free and fair election.

That the great majority of voters were ignorant of the issues is hardly the point. At Kartarpur in the Punjab, where I roamed about among the villagers outside the polling-station, the reasons given for support of the Congress were the haziest. One *zemindar* said that he had held a family conference and they had unanimously decided that it would be unwise to vote against the Government! Personalities rather than policies mattered; nor is this necessarily an ineffective gauge among a peasant community who have a shrewd facility for judging character. In any case, the profusion of mushroom parties emerging, some of them only a week or so before polling day, was sufficient excuse for the bewilderment of the public.[1] Not a few of those who sponsored obscure parties were disappointed candidates who had been refused the Congress ticket, but who were quite willing to fight the accepted Congress candidate for the sake of a vague hope of political power. The result of this scramble for candidature was to ensure a prolific number of objections. The Government then gave a curious ruling that rejected cases, which in effect amounted to all objections, would be decided by special tribunals after the elections. Tribunals were to consist of a High Court Judge and a District Judge sitting together. Accordingly, Mr. Sen's office prepared lists of suitable Judges in anticipation of the demand. They were not disappointed, for some 400 appeals awaited a hearing after the elections. By August the tribunals had not made a start on their inquiries.

I think it is generally accepted that it would have been wiser to have established some agency for scrutinising appeals at the time they were made; and it is probable that in future Summary Appeal Courts may be given certain powers.

We will turn from the people and their adventures at the polls to the policies which their leaders claimed to pursue. Some seventy Parties put up candidates, of which about a dozen could claim an All-India complexion. It was only to be anticipated that the Party whose organisation had been firmly established for many years would reap the benefit of experience; and so the Congress capture of 362 of the 496 seats in the House of the People fairly represented the position of a Party which had lost the glamour of its championship of the cause of freedom, but which had not yet been challenged by any rival with a comparable organisation or definition of policy. The effective rivals might be regarded as the Socialists, the Kisan Mazdur Praja Party, the Jan Sangh and the Communists. The innumerable small groups which sprang up all over the country were invariably of a communal nature combined with local interests.

The Congress success derived from no spectacular presentation of an ambitious programme. It came as much from the mistakes of its opponents as from its own appeal. The personal contribution of its leader also played its effective part. In the countryside many thousands of illiterate voters registered their vote not for their candidate, but for Pandit Nehru. Certainly a Prime Minister who addressed an average of a dozen meetings a day over a period of about three months deserved his success.

Nehru had little difficulty in disposing of the communal Parties. They made such elementary mistakes! Dr. Syama Prasad Mukerjee, the

[1] In Appendix IV, an attempt is made to define the main parties and their programmes.

President of the Jan Sangh, for example, for a time insisted that India had concluded a secret pact with Pakistan to betray Kashmir. He then turned to attack the economy of India, an aspect of the country's administration for which he himself, as Minister for Industry and Supply, had held some responsibility. Acharya Kripalani, formerly of the Congress Working Committee and now leader of the Kisan Mazdur Praja Party, talked wildly of " bloody revolution " if the Congress returned to power. Such tactical errors and unintelligent exaggerations were quickly noted by the Prime Minister and equally quickly ridiculed at the first subsequent public opportunity.

Dr. Mukerjee's Jan Sangh found it difficult to disclaim the intensely communal background which it had inherited from its deceased parent, the Hindu Mahasabha. Bravely its leader spoke of reuniting greater India, knowing well that it would be quite impossible to force reunion on an unwilling Pakistan. The Jan Sangh is communal in that it is anti-Moslem. But it would not claim to champion orthodoxy, since it does not support the rigid manifestations of caste. Its eclipse is best appreciated in noting that in Bengal, where millions of refugees from East Pakistan might have supported a communal policy, it won only nine seats.[1]

No more fortunate were the Ram Rajya Parishad, a party pledged to Hindu orthodoxy, opposing divorce, cow-slaughter and anything in the nature of change. To the layman its programme was difficult to distinguish from that of the Jan Sangh. Indeed, in Uttar Pradesh the two parties came to an accommodation with each other, uniting in opposition to the Congress.

The Kisan Mazdur Praja Party (Peasants', Workers', and Peoples') attempted to exploit the name of Gandhi and the Gandhian ideal. It had little else to offer save a righteous condemnation of Congress corruption. Its leader, Acharya Kripalani, a former President of the Indian National Congress, quarrelled with the Congress in May 1951 when he came to the conclusion that the great organisation had succumbed to the influence of patronage and the power of the purse. At the time there were those who held the view that the Prime Minister was driving his friends into opposition at the expense of those whose methods he himself detested. But it is difficult to see how the parent body could have achieved any purpose by liquidating itself. If it was to remain, the only logical development was an attempt to cleanse both its ranks and its policy under the leadership of Mr. Nehru. Emerging first as " the Democratic Front ", the K.M.P.P. was bound to suffer from a situation in which the play of personal feelings and the memory of past loyalties could be exploited.

Less simple to explain was the poor showing of the Socialists. Their

[1] Pandit Nehru described the Jan Sangh as the illegitimate child of the Rashtriya Swayam Sevak Sangh (RSSS). This organisation will be remembered as the militant arm of the Hindu Mahasabha in the days of British-Indian administration.

leader, Jaya Prakash Narayan, had never been really interested in the technique of non-violence. He learnt his Socialism during eight years in America, where he passed through five Universities on the proceeds of some hard work put in on fruit-farms in California. On return to India he was placed in charge of the Labour Research Department of the Congress, where he found scope for his faculty for work and devotion to the cause of Left-wing Socialism. But the programme he offered was too academic. It was related to Western thought and university audiences rather than the needs of rural India. The promises were too sweeping in scope ever to be translated into practical results. The abolition of *zemindari* without compensation, the nationalisation of industries and foreign capital, and the creation of a third power bloc in world affairs, with India as its focus, were attractive vehicles for passionate oratory but a bit beyond the villagers of India. Nevertheless, the Socialists in fact polled the greatest number of votes after the Congress. But they suffered from a dispersion of effort which accounted for the fact that the Communists and allied parties, who were able to concentrate their forces, with fewer votes, obtained more than twice the number of seats in the House of the People.[1]

Late in August 1952 we heard that the Socialists and K.M.P.P. had decided to amalgamate to form a new group, the Praja-Socialists. Their programmes were certainly close enough to each other to make distinctions meaningless to the less-educated elements of the electorate. In the House of the People the new party is able to present a voting strength of twenty-two, which is sufficient to challenge the Communists (without their allies) in a claim to represent the largest party in opposition.

The eclipse of the Scheduled Castes Federation was sad in that it saw the downfall of that faithful servant of his community, Dr. B. R. Ambedkar. The arrangement by which the entire electorate within a constituency voted for candidates competing for the special seats reserved for the Scheduled Castes resulted in nominees of the Congress Party competing for the reserved seats and naturally carrying the Congress votes with them. The result was that out of a total of some 550 seats reserved for Scheduled Castes in the various Legislatures, only sixteen were returned on the S.C.F. ticket. It could be argued that this small number alone truly represented the interests of untouchability; and that just as African interests in South Africa are protected by European members in the South African Parliament, so in India are the interests of the untouchables in the hands of alien representation. If, however, the social stigma attaching to untouchables which has lasted for 4,000 years can in fact as well as in theory be eliminated within ten years, then the present compromise in representation will certainly have been justified.

Of the many local parties sprinkled over the land, my interest was mainly in the fortunes of the Akali Sikhs, with whom I had had close

[1] The Socialist total poll of 10 million votes was nearly twice that of the Communists.

associations in the past. The Sikh community are today concerned with two States, the Punjab and PEPSU.[1] In the two Assemblies the Akalis contested ninety-nine of the total of 186 seats and succeeded in winning thirty-two, which provided them with four members in the House of the People. It is hardly appropriate here to recall the past history of the Akali movement. Suffice it that it be understood that the Akalis under their leader, Master Tara Singh, have always stood for the rights of militant Sikh nationalism, a policy which in 1945 had hardened into a demand for a Sikh State. The bisection of a great Province in 1947 not only destroyed a fine administrative unit, it carved the proud Sikh community into two. Friends of the Sikhs will find it difficult ever to forgive Tara Singh for the blind folly and bigoted leadership of his flock in 1947. Nevertheless the utter frustration of the Sikhs in their situation after partition merits much sympathy, and the limited success of the Akalis reflects the last desperate efforts of men such as Master Tara Singh and Giani Kartar Singh to rescue something from the political disintegration of a community which would like to regard itself as a nation rather than a religion. At the elections the Akalis attempted an accommodation with the Jan Sangh. They protested that the *Panth* was in danger. Finally, urged on by Giani Kartar Singh,[2] they again claimed their State based on a linguistic formula by which Punjabi would be the accepted language and foundation.

All this was the kind of talk which Nehru was well able to punish. If the Akalis were really concerned to protect and preserve the *Panth*, they would hardly hope to do so in accommodation with an organisation such as the Jan Sangh, seeking to establish the Akhand Bharat of ancient Hindu tradition. Such liaisons were mere political opportunism. Communalism was doomed throughout the length and breadth of India; nor could he support any movement which would further weaken and divide the country. Since Nehru addressed some 300,000 people of PEPSU in nine meetings in one day, his personal oratory and appeal were able in no small measure to influence election results in North-West India. But he was up against sterner and more formidable enemies when he turned his attention to the South.

It was natural that the one aspect of the Indian elections which really held the attention of the British public was the comparative success of the Communists in Southern India. I have discussed the movement more conveniently in Chapter Nine. Here we are concerned only with the

[1] The term " East Punjab " for that portion of the old Punjab Province which comes now within India has been dropped. The new State is referred to as " Punjab (I) " or merely " Punjab ". PEPSU stands for " Patiala and East Punjab States Union ".

[2] Giani Kartar Singh has for long been the skilful politician in the Akali Party, in contrast to Tara Singh, the apostle of doctrine. After partition he left the Party for the Congress. But he recently returned to the fold. In pressing for a separate State, the Akalis were able to quote the recognition of the principle of the linguistic State in the case of Andhra.

manner in which this new element in Indian polemics established itself. The scope of success has been greatly exaggerated. In the North of India they had negligible support in Uttar Pradesh and they commanded less than 5 per cent of the votes cast in PEPSU and the Punjab.

Their success was mainly confined to Travancore-Cochin, Madras and three districts in Hyderabad. In the first two States the Congress lost their overall majority, though they remained the largest single Party. In Travancore-Cochin for a time the Communists were banned. They were able to obviate the effect of the ban by assuming new titles, such as " United Front of Leftists " and " The People's Democratic Front ". In West Bengal they won twenty-eight seats in the House of the People against fifty-seven seats won by the Congress. On the other hand, the Socialists won not a single seat, and the indication is that Calcutta will prove a fertile breeding ground for an increase in the Communist poll. Certainly the tradition of the city is such as to encourage those who thrive on underground planning and the logic of the bomb.

The truth is, first, that the Indian National Congress had not taken the South of India very seriously, and secondly, that in the case of West Bengal, where the community retains its highly individual character, they represent the only area more concerned with local loyalties than with the personal appeal of Pandit Nehru. Lastly, Nehru's own approach to the Communists was one more of pained surprise than of anger. So often had he felt himself in sympathy with their *ideals*— and who among us has not?—that he seemed unable to appreciate the tough nature of the challenge required if they were to be fought and held decisively within their own small cells of intrigue.

There remained only to elect the membership of the Council of States, and then for members of all the Parliaments to elect the President. On 27th March the 216 members of the Council of States had been elected and nominated, the Upper House naturally reflecting the Parties represented in the House of the People in the same proportions.[1] The subsequent election of the President by one electoral College took place early in May, and on 6th May Dr. Rajendra Prasad was declared elected.[2] The result was a foregone conclusion, Dr. Prasad securing 507,000 votes, the runner up being Professor K. T. Shah with 92,000. His rival, who represented Left-wing interests, really competed as a matter of party prestige. Dr. Prasad has been a respected figure in political life for many

[1] Two hundred elected by members of the Legislative Assemblies of States.
Twelve nominated by the President under Article 80 of the Constitution to represent special interests.
Four representatives from Kashmir State.
Polling was by personal ballot at the capital of each State.
[2] The system of election in this case is Proportional Representation by the single transferable vote and the secret ballot. The method of determining the number of votes of each member of the central Parliament and the Legislative Assemblies is complicated and need not concern us. The evaluation of votes ensured parity between Parliament and the States.

years, and his sincerity and integrity were well recognised in the days of Congress hostility to the British Government in India. In his hands the dignity of the office of President is safe.

Let us turn to weigh up the meaning of these results. I think a dominating reflection is that the people of India have at last spoken their mind in no uncertain terms. The task and obligation of Mahatma Gandhi to place the Indian peasant and his 750,000 villages on the map have been fulfilled. Secondly, at last an effective opposition has been created as the necessary condition for the growth of democratic Parliamentary procedure. Thirdly, the champions of close communal conservatism have lost heavily, which in turn connotes that the Opposition will develop on the logic of its political programme rather than on the barren appeal of preserving worn-out caste conceptions and religious prejudices. Pandit Nehru can fairly claim to have set the stage for the secular State.

Speculation on the future is left for a later chapter. It remains to record that this great experiment should not be judged by either the rough-and-ready operation of its machinery or the comparative ignorance of the electorate. It is as an educational process in the business of learning democracy that we should regard the Indian elections. Once a new Constitution had decided the pattern for the future, and responsibility for electing their own Government had passed to the mass of the people, then the sooner the lessons of free elections were learnt the better. It is to their credit that by returning the Congress Party to power they have endorsed a middle-of-the-road policy of sanity and have not been led astray by wild promises from Right or Left. The Congress in turn have been placed on their mettle. Twenty-eight of their Ministers have lost their seats, and they face an opposition which is quite capable of ferreting out the more scandalous processes of policy which in the past have characterised Congress polemics when beyond the reach of their highly scrupulous and conscientious leader.

Looking back over the pattern of the emergence of parties we are reminded of an analogy in the history of Egyptian development, where a great central organisation, the Wafd, dedicated to achieve freedom from foreign domination, from time to time threw off splinter groups each claiming to be the only true interpreter of the message of the late Zaghlul Pasha. The Socialists and the K.M.P.P. were splinters, and there may be more to follow. But at least for five years the first party in the land has the opportunity to fulfil a programme of mild ambition and clear definition. The Hindu Code Bill, the extension of land reform, the spread of education, increased food production and all the ramifications of a five-year plan await its attention. I drew an Egyptian analogy. But it was not completely accurate; for whereas the process by which the Wafd climbed to power and subsequently maintained its position could not stand up to impartial investigation, in India the Congress, in spite of some obvious anomalies, can claim to continue in office as the result of elections carried out in a spirit of integrity not unlike that which we ourselves have come to accept as the normal standard of progressive democracy. India may well take pride in her first elections; and there is little doubt that when the time comes Pakistan will record the same success. Benefiting from the Indian experience, she may be able to avoid some of the limitations of the first attempt.

CHAPTER SEVEN

IMPRESSIONS, DEPRESSIONS, SOCIAL AND ECONOMIC. THE FACTS

IN this chapter I attempt a survey of the economic and social problems of the sub-Continent in contrast to its political evolution. I am no economist; yet there is comfort for the layman in the approach which is often associated with the doctrine of the late Lord Keynes—namely, that economic policies and their results are finally subject to the minds of the men who handle them. Nevertheless, in so far as the nature of economic planning dictates progress, India and Pakistan present a challenging study for those who are interested in the development of lands we speak of as " under-developed ".

The fashion for plans was presumably set by the Soviet, with its two ambitious Five-Year Plans between the wars. In India as long ago as October 1938 the Indian National Congress set up a National Planning Committee under the chairmanship of Pandit Nehru. But the war came, and Congress leaders went into isolation. Nevertheless, the idea of national planning had taken root. On the Government side a Reconstruction Committee of the Viceroy's Council was appointed with six sub-committees to cover the post-war programme of reconstruction. A more tangible expression of the views of those associated with big business interests came from some Bombay industrialists who in 1944 published a Fifteen-Year Economic Plan covering an expenditure of Rs. 10,000 crores.[1] The sum was considered ambitious at the time; yet their figures do not appear to be so wide of subsequent estimates when we note that the accepted Five-Year Plan for India over the more limited period from 1951 to 1956 provides for a capital outlay of Rs. 20,690 million. Bearing in mind the fact that the Bombay Plan included the territory which is now Pakistan, the authors apparently contemplated expenditure on a scale which is now accepted as essential.

But there is one striking difference in their approach. The Bombay Plan placed industry at the top of the list with Rs. 4,480 crores, allotting only Rs. 1,240 crores to agriculture and a mere Rs. 490 crores to education. The allotments were defended on the premise that the agriculturist would be the first to benefit from a greater availability of consumer goods,

[1]			*India.*	*Pakistan.*
	12 Pies	= 1 Anna	—	—
	16 Annas	= 1 Rupee	(= 1s. 6d.)	(= 2s. 2d.)
	Rs. 100,000	= 1 Lakh	(= £7,520)	(= £10,840)
	Rs. 100 Lakhs	= 1 crore	(= £752,000)	(= £1,084,000)

and that therefore it was not so much capital expenditure on agriculture as the defence of the peasant's purchasing power which was required.

In March 1950 a Planning Commission was established with the Prime Minister as chairman. It was asked to survey the material, capital, and human resources of the country, to fix priorities, formulate a plan and report on its implementation. After fifteen months a draft plan was produced in July 1951. While concerned primarily with a problem of economic planning, the Commission opened its report with a broad statement of objectives, boldly covering the more abstract and idealistic aspects in planning. They claimed that their objectives derived from " the Directive Principles of State policy " written into the Constitution. In doing so they appeared somewhat to confuse the political conditions against which the plan should develop with the promotion of those same conditions as part of the actual objective. They were at pains to work to a compromise between totalitarianism which " brings in its train violence, conflict, regimentation and the suppression of the individual ", and concessions to private enterprise. Much thought went into this initial statement.[1] The claim was developed that real democratic planning must bring private enterprise into co-operation with the public sector, " for the common good of the people under the broad direction of the State ". The State is " to assist and direct private enterprise. The private sector will thus continue to play a significant part in both production and distribution. But it will have to visualise for itself a new role and accept in the larger interests of the country a new code of discipline."

This looks rather like an attempt to have the best of both possible worlds. Progressive enterprise regards the fetters of control as brakes in progress. Nevertheless the reader is impressed by the sincerity of the initial chapter of theory, even though a little surprise may be caused by the emphasis on the political aspect of " economic democracy " and the need to iron out all inequalities.

A year later, on 15th December 1952, in introducing the plan to the House of the People, Pandit Nehru seemed to go beyond the qualified idealism of the Commission. The objective, he said, was to bring about economic democracy. " In other words, we have to put an end gradually to various classes and ultimately develop in India a classless society." On a recent occasion the President endorsed this intention in precisely the same terms. Indian Communists may well have been gratified at such direct approval of Marxist doctrine.

There is thus a definite classification of industrial expansion into two sectors, public and private, the former including both Central and State projects.[2]

[1] Chapter II. *Approach to Planning, The Five-Year Plan. A Short Introduction.* Ministry of Information, Government of India. December 1951.

[2] Estimated expenditure in the public and private sectors is Rs. 940 million and Rs. 2,330 million, respectively. Expenditure under the two Sectors, together with Rs. 1,500 million estimated for replacement and modernisation of plant, complete a total of Rs. 4,770 million.

Between the initial publication of the draft plan and its final presenta-tion to Parliament jealous demands for increases came from various sectors of the national life. The final plan was therefore considerably more ambitious than the draft, the total contemplated expenditure rising from £1,120 million to £1,551 million. The most noticeable adjust-ment was an increase to agriculture, which at £270 million claimed 17 per cent of the total.[1] Within the public sector the Central Govern-ment sponsored such vital enterprises as the great Sindri Fertiliser Factory [2] and lesser though important projects, such as factories to produce penicillin, D.D.T., locomotives and machine-tools. The State projects included paper-mills in Madhya Pradesh and an expansion of the Mysore iron and steel works.

Expansion within the private sector covers forty-two industries. Practically every aspect of industry appears to have been remembered.[3] Diesel engines and radio sets, electric transformers and hurricane lanterns; while included within the chemical group are 4,515,000 tons of cement and 16,000 tons of bangles!

The largest allotment (27·2 per cent) is reserved for Irrigation and Power. It is under this heading that those tremendous schemes are included: the Bhakra-Nangal project in the Sutlej Valley, the Damodar Valley project and the Hirakud Dam scheme in Orissa.[4] The Bhakra-

[1] *Allotments under the Five-Year Plan.*

	Revised Expen-diture 1951–56 (£ million).	Percentage of Total.
Agriculture and Community Development	270·3	17·4
Irrigation, Power	421·1	27·2
Transport, Communications . . .	372·8	24·0
Industry	129·8	8·4
Social Services	254·9	16·4
Rehabilitation	63·8	4·1
Miscellaneous	39·0	2·5
Total	1,551·6	100·0

[2] Completed in October 1951, and planned to produce 350,000 tons of ammonium sulphate per annum by 1955–6. The factory is on the banks of the Damodar River in Bihar. Its development will lead to the emergence of a number of subsidiary industries, and a modern township will in turn prosper from cheap electric power as the Damodar Valley multi-purpose project progresses. The local production of fertilisers is calculated to save the country Rs. 100 million of foreign exchange a year. The factory is the largest of its kind in Asia. When in full production it will require to take in about 12 million gallons of water per day, for which purpose a barrage (the Gowai Barrage) has been built to produce the necessary catchment area. An American firm designed the factory and supervised its construction. A British firm acted as agents in the procurement and supply of plant. The engineers operating the factory will be Indian, but will include at least one Englishman, a German and a Japanese.

[3] In March 1953 the Planning Commission published a separate volume to the Five-Year Plan giving details of industrial development and showing under each industry the expansion contemplated and the cost.

[4] The main multi-purpose schemes, together with many other aspects of the Five-

Nangal scheme was conceived many years ago, but progress was held up through the resistance of Bilaspur State, in spite of the great economic advantages which were to accrue to the State administration. During the five-year period most of the estimated capital expenditure will be absorbed in the completion of these schemes, and new schemes, of which at least five are in the drafting stage, must wait for the end of the first period before they can be launched.

The experts estimate that every year about 94 per cent of the waters of India flow to waste into the sea. Yet of India's total area under cultivation only one-fifth is under irrigation. The rest is subject to the hazards of the monsoon. The Five-Year Plan aims at adding another 8,800,000 acres to the 48 million acres now under irrigation.

Of the many aspects of communities in development, the multi-purpose scheme, in which great rivers are harnessed to produce power and irrigate barren wastes, is that which appeals immediately to the imagination. In India the spectacular results of the great Tennessee Valley scheme undoubtedly attracted the planners, and T.V.A. became the central focus and example for planning. The Damodar Valley Corporation is a direct legacy of T.V.A.[1] It was recently my good fortune to see something of the T.V.A. achievement on the spot; and I was impressed not so much by its technical excellence as by the manner in which results in the social sphere of community planning had been obtained. It should be realised that irrigation plays no part in T.V.A. A great river is controlled where formerly its unpredictable behaviour spelt insecurity and often disaster for many thousands. At the same time cheap power is provided for all. But the real achievement is the development of a community spirit of progress through co-operation. The people of the valley have not been spoon-fed so much as made to feel that the central authority is a friend to offer advice and assistance to those who are prepared to help themselves. It will be years before we can know if this aspect of the Indian development schemes has been understood and operated for the advancement of millions who will receive at least the initial benefits of careful settlement.

It is clear that the planners regard the new irrigation and power projects

---

Year Plan, are also named as objectives in the Colombo Plan. (See *New Horizons in the East*, the Colombo Plan, H.M. Stationery Office, 1950, which contains details of the Damodar Valley scheme.) There thus appears to be some overlap of planning. The Five-Year Plan has been described as " dovetailing " into the Colombo Plan. The Colombo Plan may be regarded as the overall blueprint for planning in Southeast Asia within which the Indian Plan is an integral part. In so far as the Colombo Plan envisages finance being available to India from resources such as sterling balances and other means, those resources may be regarded as placed at the disposal of the Government of India to assist in the financing of the Five-Year Plan.

[1] The Damodar project includes eight multi-purpose storage dams and an irrigation barrage with a network of canals and a power-plant to produce 200,000 kilowatts. The cost is shared by the Centre and the Bihar and West Bengal Governments.

as the main contribution to a higher standard of life over the country as a whole. The example of planning will be infectious, and those who promote lesser State and local schemes will catch the infection. A higher standard for the peasant will bring with it the demand for the amenities of life and encouragement for local industries.

In another chapter I hope to show that the true progress of any community, whether it be under-developed or over-developed, rich or poor, is a matter of relating education very closely to the raising of economic standards, the two elements being harnessed together so that one is never predominant at the expense of the other. The problem is perhaps simpler where we can start from scratch and the entire community can be regarded as illiterate. The great Gezira cotton scheme in the Sudan is the perfect example of ordered progress from primitive beginnings. But when the gap between leadership and those who are led is wide, the problems of education are less simple. If one were therefore to search for points of criticism in the Indian Five-Year Plan it would be in the comparatively unequal allotment of funds as between material need and education.

In a bold and imaginative plan for progress 16·4 per cent of the total expenditure is allotted to Social Services, of which about half is to be spent on education. Thus education receives about 8 per cent of the total, as compared with 17·4 per cent for agriculture and rural development, and 27·2 per cent for irrigation and power. The allotments are not unreasonable, but funds for education could well have been on a more liberal scale.

In Chapter X of the Government's official publication setting out the plan their view is stated in the following terms :—

"The Commission recognises the vital role of education in nation building. In order of importance, however, the strengthening of the country's economic foundations comes first, so that in later years the nation's resources can be increasingly spent on education and other social services."

It is difficult to accept this. Brains surely produce wealth just as much as wealth can create facilities for education. My mind goes back to many hundreds of villages scattered over the sub-Continent where life could be happier, healthier and cleaner in a very few months without one rupee of Government expenditure or one dollar of aid from outside. Merely the will of the people themselves, assisted by a little education of a practical nature, and of course a little leadership, could be sufficient to change those conditions which are the despair of sensitive Indians and Pakistanis. Pandit Nehru has himself supported this view. "The people should remember that no nation can progress merely through foreign aid. Ultimately it is the work of its own people which sets the country on the path of prosperity." These were his words as he dug the first clods of earth to initiate the contribution of Alipore village to the Community Projects Programme; and they seem to confirm the principle that self-help is the one permanent and effective element in the progress of under-developed communities.

Education in India is a State subject, the centre confining its interest to co-ordination and the definition of principles.   Of 123 crores of rupees for education in the Five-Year Plan, 91 crores are provided in the States and 32 crores by the Centre.   If there be some logic in the principles we have noted, it will be appreciated that to divert time and money to teaching many millions a new language is hardly going to be of immediate value in the great task of building a happy, healthy nation.

It is surely vital that these matters should be understood by a British public which is still concerned with the welfare of some 60 million colonial citizens thirsting for education.   We planned education in India, but we planned it late; and in the meanwhile the gap between some of the finest brains in the world and aboriginal illiteracy widened. In the past I was always astonished by the tremendous range of educational development in between those who governed and those who were subject to government.   The distinguished gentlemen who came and went through the Viceroy's Council seemed separated by worlds from the village life of the country.   Equally unrepresentative of the masses by educational standards were the famous leaders in political isolation, many of whom are today in ministerial office.   It is in the educational field that I believe lay our most evident failure.   Yet it is hardly fair to blame many worthy disciples of progress whose work only lacked the co-ordination of a great central plan resting on foundations which should have been laid in the village school.   In lectures at home I referred frequently to the economic and educational levels, with a bare reference to figures.   I explained that 17 per cent of the men and 5 per cent of the women could read and write, giving an average literacy of 12 per cent over the country as a whole.   How was it, I was then asked, that after nearly 100 years of official British government so little had been achieved? The answer was not easy.   We left behind the Report of Sir John Sargent, which was to make the entire Continent literate within forty years.   The present Indian Government believe they can improve on this, and by ordering adults to school a period of sixteen years is spoken of as the target.   I do not believe it can be done, since to break down illiteracy on such a scale a million or so teachers would have first to be trained.   It therefore takes two generations to achieve full literacy.   But the point I wish to make is that our very conscientious endeavours in the past resulted mainly in a vertical system of education which gave the opportunity of excellence to the few rather than a little useful knowledge to the many.   In short, primary education should have been given preference over the facilities for clever students to take degrees.   The Constitution now directs the provision of free and compulsory education for all children up to the age of fourteen.   Here is the chance to sow the seeds of true citizenship from which will grow the future India.

Principles look logical enough on paper, but to implement them needs a vast amount of courage; for immediately the great union of inter-national intellectualism is called into opposition, interpreting our motives as a western capitalist device to keep under-developed countries in political and economic bondage. It will certainly take longer for the many to learn the elements of good citizenship than for the few to take their degrees. But it will ensure that our future structures of self-govern-ing nations are built on foundations of rock rather than on shifting sand.

Nor is it sufficient to be satisfied with a comprehensive primary educa-tion covering the land, without further inquiry as to the form it will take. As on the Indian sub-Continent, so in the Colonial Empire, 80 per cent of the inhabitants are agricultural people, with their lives bound up in the problems of cotton-seed, terracing rice-fields, fighting soil erosion and canal seepage; and the greatest service which these people can receive is an education closely related to their immediate needs. Village economy, village planning, simple hygiene, animal husbandry, the justice of the locally elected Council sitting in open court: these are the foundations of their society. Let them seek their progress from such foundations. That India herself realises the value of these principles is evident from the bold experiments she has initiated in the development of the *panchayat* system, and in a vast new Community Projects pro-gramme launched in October 1952, and which may be regarded as supplementary to the Five-Year Plan. We could do worse than insist on the local equivalent being applied throughout the Colonial Empire; nor would it be logical for India to criticise when we attempt to apply those methods elsewhere which we believe she herself accepts as the foundations of progress.

I would not wish to imply that in any way talent and ambition should be stifled. But the difficulty to be surmounted is that when an intelligent young man is removed mentally from his environment through educa-tional facilities in English Universities, he is subsequently seldom satisfied merely to apply his learning to the local assistance of the village of his birth. Either the Government must find him an appointment, or a Court of Justice is the whetstone for his intellectual agility, or he must seek his outlet in journalism. There are seldom enough Government jobs to go round, and usually it is to the latter that he turns, seeking to satisfy frustration in opposition to the constitutional Government of the day, whether it be good or bad. That was the pattern of development in India, and it is evident in many corners of the Colonial Empire. Nor has it faded from the sub-Continent with the passing of power.

I drew attention to the great Community Projects scheme inaugurated by the Indian President on 2nd October 1952 on the occasion of the eighty-third birthday anniversary of Mahatma Gandhi. Fifty-five separate projects covering 18,464 villages are to constitute an experiment, which will be watched with close interest by planners all over the world. The projects are sprinkled over the countryside all the way from the Punjab down to Travancore-Cochin, each area averaging about 200,000 people. The total cost is estimated at Rs. 380 million, of which the United States have contributed Rs. 40 million under the Indo–U.S. Technical Co-operation Agreement of January 1952.[1] It was this agreement, negotiated on the American side by Mr. Chester Bowles, which at the time played its part in improving India's relations with the United States.

All over the country on 2nd October Ministers were busy turning clods of earth to initiate rural projects. School-children enacted plays. Baby-shows and folk-dancing enlivened the ceremonies. Up in Kashmir Sheikh Abdullah and his Ministers took to their shovels and turned the first earth for the construction of a new road near Srinagar. Undoubtedly the great concept caught the imagination of the people; and if after the first flush of enthusiasm relays of voluntary villagers still continue to press forward laying roads, reclaiming land and building schools, India may well claim a national social renaissance which could mean the end of stagnation and the initiation of a new standard of life and security for millions. It is just this kind of approach, this conception of placing the responsibility for the foundations of the structure in millions of modest homes of mud walls and kerosene *battis*, that will give Englishmen who know India confidence in her future.

So much of comment on India's progress must apply equally to conditions in Pakistan. The Government in Karachi have not produced the blue-print of a plan in formal terms, such as is the case in India. Instead they have been content to formulate certain development schemes, regarding them, if it be necessary to talk in concise terms of planning, as falling within the scope of the Colombo Plan.[2]

Under the Colombo Plan a six-year programme for Pakistan was prepared, costing approximately £250 million, which included £145 million of outside aid in the form of extra imports. The money to meet the outside assistance was to be found by loans, gifts, private investment and, not the least, by drawing on the sterling assets built up in London during the war.[3] But the first estimate which had been hurriedly prepared in May 1950 proved quite inadequate. By the summer of 1952 the expenditure for power development had already

[1] Certain undertakings, such as training-centres for staffs, are joint projects of the T.C.A. and the Government of India. Others are assisted by the Ford Foundation.

[2] See note 4, p. 115.

[3] Under the Colombo Plan, Pakistan has received gifts of £2 million from Australia, £250,000 from New Zealand, $10 million from Canada and a Railway Loan of $27·2 million from the International Bank. Against the Canadian offer the expenses of a contract with the Photographic Survey Corporation, Ltd., of Toronto, are to be met over the next four years. This organisation is undertaking a photographic survey of the whole country to assist in the collection of all data necessary for a " resources inventory ".

In March 1951 the Pakistan Prime Minister expressed his disappointment with the scope of the Colombo Plan. In his view " small measures of technical assistance " were inadequate to meet the needs of under-development as encountered throughout South-east Asia.

absorbed a major portion of the provision made for it under the Plan. At the same time Pakistan's whole financial position underwent a transition, and four years of prosperity turned suddenly to adversity. So far as the early fulfilment of contemplated development schemes are concerned, it would therefore seem that Pakistan may have to think again.

The schemes which are already under way include several which British engineers and administrators had hoped to see initiated. Thirty years ago, as an officer attached to the Frontier Constabulary, I had once a week to ride along the wire which then separated tribal territory from the Peshawar District between Shabkadar and the point at Warsak where the Kabul River flows out of the hills into the Peshawar Plain. I used to look at the swollen waters from Afghanistan pushing their way through the gorge at Warsak and wonder if the day would come when so obvious an opportunity to produce power would be accepted by the Frontier Administration. The possibilities were of course fully realised, but in those days the Frontier was a deficit province turning to Delhi for an annual subvention; and it needed an indigenous Pakistan Government to translate this and other schemes into action.[1] In a country which has little coal, the more power which can be produced by harnessing water the better; and it seems clear that the Peshawar valley, set in the midst of a junction of minor mountain systems, is destined to enjoy an expansion of industry within a decade through the great opportunities to produce cheap electric power.

Yet another hydro-electric project of great scope is the Mianwali scheme on the Indus River, with a power-station and headworks at Kalabagh. Together the power from Mianwali and Warsak will in time supply the needs of an area enclosing Peshawar in the north, Lahore in the east and Multan in the south. Thus the Punjab will at last receive service in kind from a province which was too long regarded only as a drain on the resources of British India. It seems strange to think of the harsh, uninviting landscape around Kalabagh as the source of a modern electrical system of power and potential progress.

But Pakistan can boast at least one scheme which amounts to more than the mere production of power for industrial expansion. It is only natural to think of projects which are mainly agricultural as representing the greater contribution to the welfare and progress of the community in such a country as Pakistan. The Lower Sind Barrage scheme, which will open up 1·6 million acres for cultivation, is one. But the scheme which must appeal to the imagination, and which I therefore feel should be appreciated in some detail, is the Thal project. In the north-west Punjab, where the River Indus leaves the low, rocky hills south of Attock,

[1] The Warsak project is calculated to produce 150,000 kilowatts. The detailed examination of this and two other large schemes—Mianwali and Karnafuli—is being undertaken. The Warsak and Mianwali schemes are scheduled for completion within five years of work being started. Electricity will eventually be available at the cheap rate of half an anna ($\frac{1}{2}d$.) a unit. Other projects in part completed are the Malakand (extension) scheme, Rasul and Dargai projects.

the new Jinnah Barrage feeds the main canals which take off to irrigate land on either side of the river. The scheme had been conceived many years before partition, and was at first regarded as a means of rewarding and settling many men returning to the land from the Forces after the war. A problem of some 8 million refugees in the months following partition speeded up the plans, and priority has been given to 250,000 refugees to be settled on 900,000 acres. Once again the T.V.A. example appears to have been prominent in the minds of the West Punjab Government, and the Thal Development Authority bears a resemblance to the American scheme. In fact, I find a closer analogy in the Sudan Gezira scheme.

The Thal desert is a sandy waste covering some 4 million acres. A million and a half acres east of the Indus are now coming under irrigation from the main canal, and colonisation is proceeding at a vigorous pace. Consider what this means in terms of the busy humanity which seeks to wrest a new and better life from this most forbidding soil. A thousand villages and 38,000 houses will cover the land.[1] Over 600 miles of metalled roads will knit them into one distinct community. In the old days it was a matter of handing out squares of land to the individual settler, who then relied on his own resources to make good. Today on the Indus as a block of land becomes ready for sowing the Development Authority brings in a batch of selected settlers, puts them each in possession of 15 acres and a house, and provides them with implements, bullocks, seeds and the necessities of life. The settler's debt to the Government is recovered from him by easy instalments over a number of years.

I have referred to the change in the fortunes of Pakistan which has overtaken her after initial years of comparative prosperity. The outbreak of war in Korea in 1950 created a demand for raw materials in Asia which in turn produced a favourable balance of trade in many Asian countries. Pakistan was quick to profit from the situation. Her exports of her two indispensable cash crops, cotton and jute, continued to rise, improving her balance of payments and enabling her to spend freely on internal development. The Government set up a Planning Commission, and it seemed that nothing could prevent a rapid expansion of industry with the promise of comparative prosperity. But within Pakistan all was not well. The channelling of all imports through Karachi gave the city a monopoly of foreign trade, and in the process huge profits were made. Meanwhile the same goods outside in the country secured little profit and the small markets stagnated. Imports accumulated at Karachi. Then came the change. World trading conditions slumped with a diminishing Korean demand. At the same time Pakistan traders were attempting to maintain artificially high prices for exports, particularly

[1] The standard type of house costs Rs. 600. A type of brick made of cement and local sand has proved both cheap and suitable for the climate. (" Thal " is the Punjabi word for " desert ".)

of jute. Yet the importers continued to pile up stocks in Karachi. Finally, after the big importers had taken their profits, the local traders were forced to face losses on the clearance of goods. The story was the same on the export side. Before 1951 huge profit margins were being taken in Karachi on exports. The Government promptly imposed heavy export duties. These were retained after the slump, with a crippling effect on the export trade. For the first time Pakistan, which had hitherto been regarded as a welcome source of food, had suddenly to import wheat to meet requirements.[1]

The psychological effect of these trends has been considerable. There was undoubtedly a general loss of confidence, particularly in up-country markets. The Karachi market and the mill-owners appealed to the Government to maintain prices. But action was not taken, since it was felt that until confidence was restored the goods in the countryside would not find their way to the consumers.

The situation seems to be that of a phase representing the penalty to be paid when an agricultural country sets about industrialisation. Pakistan's industries are at present in no position to compete with a foreign product. The creation of industries in contrast to their development must connote a shortage of trained labour and a low standard of efficiency. Many ambitious projects have been set up only at high cost, so that in turn the fruits of industry when handed on are in no position to attract the foreign markets. It amounts to the purchase of the local product at a higher price than the better article from abroad. Once industry can turn the corner and learn how to produce goods of quality which can be marketed abroad without delay, confidence will return to the country. But measures to control the speculative and monopolising influences of the powerful Karachi market would appear to be necessary if a healthy background for the export trade is to be created.

We would like to think that Britain could play her part in helping Pakistan through these difficult teething troubles. If, for instance, British firms of experience could participate fully in the new industrial drive, we believe that we could lend that confidence and stability to the country's development which are at present lacking. The heart of Pakistan is sound, and her fresh youthful enthusiasm for a rich future of industrial expansion commands our whole-hearted admiration. Not unnaturally, she has been suspicious of our intentions. Restrictions were placed on movements of British capital. A certain proportion of Pakistani capital had to be introduced into British business, and such enterprise was very difficult to find. To *risk* capital is a new experience, and quite foreign to the Pakistani nature.[2] British firms, too, were

---

[1] In 1951–2 wheat production dropped from 3,950,000 tons to 3,060,000 tons.

[2] In view of the tendency to exaggerated caution, much interest attached to a recent issue of capital by Glaxo Laboratories (Pakistan), Ltd. Rs. 18 lakhs of shares were reserved for Pakistan subscribers. The result was encouraging in that the offer was closed after four days, applications for twice the amount having been received.

slow to realise their opportunity, while an over-conscientious bureaucrat, the Controller of Capital Issues, was ready enough to discourage enterprise. Maybe that the example of Iran in 1951 was not without its effect on British industry at home. There were also cases which were hardly such as to induce in British traders a confidence in their future security.[1] On the banking side Pakistan appeared to be prepared to take full advantage of British banks, yet placed restrictions on the opening of new branches.

With the experience of the years, many of the doubts and difficulties of today must pass. The present level of efficiency of a great army of clerical workers in commerce and industry is naturally low. This results in staffs, both British and Pakistani, who should be engaged on policy and planning having to spend much time on normal matters of routine and instruction. The hope of British trading-houses, in the face not only of internal Pakistani restrictions but also of determined competition from foreign countries must be in a very thorough appreciation of the quality of British workmanship.[2]

The threat to British markets is certainly not a mere matter of Pakistan's restrictions. Throughout the sub-Continent import licensing to save foreign exchange and protective tariffs are together punishing British imports. Once again the remedy would seem to be in British manufacturers going into the sub-Continent to produce consumer goods; and in India they have been more successful in pursuing this policy than in Pakistan. Since 1947 some £8 million of British money in association with Indian capital and Indian employees have been invested in the country to produce cars, telephones, bicycles and chemicals. Inevitably the Japanese, with their traditional ability to copy and produce the Western product at half the price, constitute a most formidable challenge. Nor are the Germans behind the Japanese. Both have lost their pre-war Chinese market and both are determined to capture the Indian and Pakistani markets in substitution. As an example of German methods I quote the Delhi correspondent of *The Times*. In his article of 23rd December 1952 he related the case of a German firm which, hearing that teleprinters were in demand, immediately flew out technicians with four teleprinters prepared to demonstrate their machines to Government officials, leave them in the country and supply the balance required in a far shorter time than could be guaranteed by any British firm in competi-

---

[1] The Bevan-Petman case, in which a coal-mine, formerly the property of a well-known English family in the Punjab, passed to Pakistan ownership, is an example. The case of the British Metal Box Company is an example of British enterprise which has not allowed itself to be discouraged. The Company calculated that it would pay them to send out their staff from England. But the Pakistan Government insisted on local employment and a local allotment of 30 per cent of the capital.

[2] Japan is now Pakistan's biggest customer for cotton, and in return has greatly increased her sales of textiles. The loss has been as equally sustained by India as by Britain.

tion. It is hardly reasonable to suppose that Commonwealth ties of
sentiment will be sufficient to withstand the temptation to accept the
fruits of such enterprising persuasion. It would almost seem that in
the field of markets for consumer goods Great Britain has lost the lead
and is unable to recapture her position. But in the demand for capital
goods there is still time to make good. As an example, India is busy
with the development of a great new port, Kandla, on the Kathiawar
coast, to relieve the congestion at Bombay. A whole range of capital
equipment, including cranes which will cost not less than £1,500,000,
will be in demand. Too often British firms are inclined to dismiss lost
opportunities as the penalty of a monopolising defence programme at
home. It is for the British Government to bear in mind the factors
which could limit British trade with the sub-Continent and weigh the
significance, economic and political, of lost trade against the demands of
defence.

In the case of Pakistan her troubles are the more prominent because
of the circumstances, for which there can be no precedent, by which two
territories separated by 1,000 miles regard themselves as one political
unit. Whatever may be the factors, ethnographical and otherwise, at
work to separate the two Pakistans, economic conditions will continue
to operate to hold them together. In spite of trade between Karachi
and Dacca having to traverse 3,000 miles of sea, the fact is that so long as
East Pakistan grows 70 per cent of the world's raw jute and West
Pakistan has wheat and cotton to export, each limb will continue to wish
to profit from the export trade of the other. It is inevitable that in this
situation a continuation of the cold war between India and Pakistan must
serve to reinforce Pakistan's solidarity. Solve the problem of the Indo-
Pakistani relationship, and I doubt if East and West Pakistan would
continue for many years to present a united front.

In so far as the jute trade was concerned, on partition in 1947 East
Bengal immediately realised her shortage of mills and her lack of facilities
to get the jute away to the markets of the world. In consequence, we
witnessed the paradox of confusion in the jute trade resulting in a rapid
expansion of industrial activity in East Pakistan, with an urgency born of
necessity attached to the development programme. The immediate
needs were to construct an adequate port and build up its inland communications—needs which were manifested in the development of East
Bengal waterways, improvement to the harbourage at Chalna and a
rapid expansion of the port of Chittagong.

East Bengal is a land of quiet canals threading their way through jute-
fields and steamy marshes. For years some 2,000 miles of channels have
formed a haphazard grid of communications for local trade. This is
now to be expanded to over 4,000 miles, at an expenditure of about
£19 million. The scheme deserves attention, since it affords an excellent
example of international co-operation in assistance and advice from the
" haves " to the " have-nots ". A party of twelve experts from the

United Nations Technical Assistance Administration recently visited East Bengal under the leadership of a naval architect of the Netherlands. They were mainly concerned with experiments in new forms of barges and river-craft. Thirty-six dredgers were ordered from abroad, and in April 1950 the Government started to build their own flotilla. Meanwhile Chittagong, which before the war handled 500,000 tons of cargo annually, is being developed to deal with 2,500,000 tons by 1954. There should result a rapid and efficient movement of jute to Chittagong from riverine points in East Bengal and a quick clearance at port.

The improvement in the facilities to move jute should logically go forward with the recovery of the trade itself. The chaos of the post-partition days is being slowly sorted out with India feverishly growing raw jute and Pakistan with equal determination constructing mills for processing. The heavy duties which Pakistan at first imposed on the export of jute had the effect of throwing the Indian mills into unemployment. The result was an accumulation of the raw material in Pakistan. When Pakistan decided not to devalue the rupee on the devaluation of the pound in 1949, the price of raw jute soared. In the following year the Korean crisis stepped up the demand. The result was that such processed jute as India was able to export was heavily taxed by the Government of India; and the United States, who were the chief importers, increasingly turned to substitutes.

Meanwhile Pakistan mill-owners have realised the dangers of demanding excessive profits, and jute policy is being reorientated to reinstate India as the first customer.[1] Although the present policy is one of State assistance and a measure of control, owners have always to bear in mind the possibility of nationalisation and its attractions for a Government which needs all the resources at its command for an ambitious programme of expansion. At present the ownership of raw jute is with about a million cultivators in Bengal, each owning a small plot of land. The few mills are owned by the big companies and industrialists. But four new mills under construction are projects of the Pakistan Government.

Whatever may be the final pattern of the Pakistan jute industry, the general tendency of the trade as a whole can only be towards a highly competitive situation between Pakistan and India. Within a few years both countries will have the means to export the finished material, and the one which can undersell the other will hold the world's market.

---

[1] Jute quotas are laid down from year to year (July–June) for each country.

In the twelve months ending June 1952 India purchased jute worth Rs. 37 crores, total jute exports being valued at Rs. 116 crores (an increase of Rs. 30 crores over the previous year).

In January 1952 Mr. Nurul Amin, Chief Minister of East Bengal, addressed members of the Pakistan Jute Association and appealed to them to observe Islamic principles and display " magnanimity ". He presumably had policy in regard to the Indian market in mind. In March 1953, as a result of a new trade agreement, India indicated that she would need 1·8 million bales a year for three years from 1st July 1953. Pakistan is prepared to facilitate export up to 2·5 million bales a year.

fear in this case has been that the development of the Hariki scheme and the great Bhakra Dam project on the Sutlej in its upper reaches would endanger the availability of water for Bahawalpur and the south-west Punjab. The Bhakra Dam is specifically to provide water for the Hissar and Karnal Districts in India, which for various reasons of altitude and topography have hitherto not been fully developed.

There were therefore logical reasons for Pakistan to be apprehensive of her future water-supply, and in some spirit of pessimism, elaborate plans were prepared to secure water for Lahore in the event of the River Ravi running dry. A triple project involved water being brought south from the Upper Chenab Canal and syphoned under the Ravi to feed the Lahore District. Water from the Upper Jhelum Canal would then be brought down to the Chenab to compensate for the water taken off.

Pakistan's water consciousness was undoubtedly encouraged by the award of the Gurdaspur District to India and the consequent passing of the control of the River Ravi,[1] and it was to lend some stability to a very uncertain situation that on 4th May 1948 the two countries reached a temporary agreement.[2] In it Pakistan recognised the principle that India was entitled gradually to draw more water from the River Ravi for the development of land which was inferior to her own irrigated territories, provided that the process was sufficiently slow to enable Pakistan to develop alternative sources. In addition, Pakistan agreed to pay certain charges for water supplied and the upkeep of the headworks. Time passed with little action towards a permanent settlement until February 1952. It was then wisely suggested that agreement might be achieved with outside assistance in combination with a complete survey of the basin of the River Indus and the possibility of a fuller utilisation of its resources. For example, could it not be harnessed above Attock in a manner to secure Pakistan's complete independence of any future irrigation developments which India might wish to undertake? If the Indus basin was properly used was there not ample water for both?

But first a complete technical survey had to be undertaken. Accordingly, in February 1952 Mr. Eugene Black of the International Bank visited India and Pakistan, and at his suggestion representatives of both countries went to Washington in June. Subsequently, in the winter of 1952, General Wheeler visited the two countries, toured West Pakistan and held conferences with representative engineers from Delhi and Karachi. Unfortunately, in the meanwhile an extremely weak monsoon had resulted in a drought both in Pakistan and India.

To what extent Nature or the alleged machinations of India are responsible for a water shortage in Pakistan it is impossible to say without a full impartial inquiry. But the manner of Pakistan's registration of her complaint was hardly such as to convince us completely of the validity

[1] See Chapter One, p. 35.
[2] Registered (by India) with the United Nations as Treaty 794 on 10th May 1950.

of her case.   There was apparently no official appeal to the Government
of India.   Instead Pakistan preferred to register her objections in the
form of a statement made before the United Nations Secretariat in
terms vehement enough to create a suspicion that the allegations were
framed with some sense of their propaganda potential.   The accusation
of *Dawn*, that Pakistan was facing " starvation and economic ruin by a
process of slow strangulation at the hands of India ", was certainly an
over-statement.   International engineers were at the time touring
Pakistan, and it would not have been unnatural to exaggerate the charges
for their consumption.   Pandit Nehru met the allegations convincingly.
There was not, nor had there ever been, any intention or desire to deprive
Pakistan of her dues.   The truth was that both East and West Punjab
had experienced a severe drought; and, incidentally, Pakistan had not
paid the amounts due from her under the 1948 agreement.

A curious feature of the situation at the moment is that the two countries
have declared their readiness to take the dispute to international arbitration.[1]   Nor are there the conditions for prevarication which govern the
Kashmir situation.   Just as in the economic sphere alternative markets
are eventually discovered to restore a belated equilibrium, so also as time
passes, and the multi-purpose schemes of both India and Pakistan come
into operation, the quarrel must surely settle itself.   I cannot myself see
what is to prevent the appointment of Pakistani officials at the headworks
of disputed systems in the same manner of settlement as pertains in the
case of the River Nile.

Herodotus tells a story of the Greeks and the Galatians who were led
before the Persian King, Darius.   Darius asked the Greeks the price at
which they would consent to eat their fathers when they died.   In horror
they declared that for no price could they do so.   To burn the dead was
the only civilised method.   The King then summoned the Galatians
and asked them also the price at which they would consent to consume by
fire the bodies of their fathers at death: and with equal disgust and
amazement they cried aloud, saying that they could only consider eating
their dead!   In short, although two communities accused each other of
barbarism, they did in fact both reveal identically the same mental
approach to the particular problem of the disposal of the dead.   The
pattern of thought in contrast to the physical method was the same.

In noting conditions on the sub-Continent we watch a situation which
has some analogy to the story of the Greeks and the Galatians; for when
we have finished with all the traditional and very obvious observations on
divergencies of culture, religion and custom which separate the Mohammedan and the Hindu, are we not left with a common denominator,

---

[1] At the end of March 1953 the position was that representatives from both
countries were to meet experts from the World Bank in Washington in September to
draw up a plan.   Meanwhile the World Bank was looking into Pakistan's complaints.
(Statement by Sardar Rab Nishtar, Pakistan's Minister of Industries at the time,
25th March 1953.)

which, if only it can be recognised, would provide the foundations of agreement? The symptoms are there. India finally accepted the Pakistan rupee at its old par rate. A trade agreement *was* concluded. "Minority" ministers and commissions were set up in East and West Bengal; and in April 1950, when the Liaquat–Nehru pact was signed, the leading actors in the drama displayed considerable understanding and an ability to see "the other point of view". In the two Assemblies each Prime Minister readily declared his belief in the good faith of the other—and that at no little risk of a certain degree of local unpopularity. When leaders in both countries are prepared once again to meet, preferably in isolation, to yield ground to each other, and to come away determined to stand or fall by the acceptance of fresh terms, however unpopular in their own countries, then will the soil be fertile for a fresh understanding.[1]

[1] Much of the material in this chapter was the subject of an address to the East India Association on 18th October 1951, and is reproduced by the courtesy of the Editor, the *Asiatic Review*, from the issue of January 1952.

CHAPTER EIGHT

IMPRESSIONS, DEPRESSIONS, SOCIAL AND ECONOMIC. THE THEORIES

I HAVE attempted to isolate some of the salient features of planning in India and Pakistan. It remains to comment on certain conditions which, since they applied to the sub-Continent we knew before partition, remain as characteristic of both India and Pakistan today. It would be dishonest to speak in glowing terms of results expected from vast plans driven forward with the energy of idealism and disregard the problem of population, which may well absorb all the utopian gifts of planning. The 1951 census showed the population of India as 357 million, an increase of nearly four million a year since 1941. The same rate applies to Pakistan. A wise dispensation can open up the desert and clear the jungles. Soil erosion can be controlled and millions of unproductive acres turned to account. But unless the communities which are settled on to new land can control their numbers, the only result within a decade will be to produce a few more million mouths to feed. A realistic approach is now evident which was hardly possible in the days of British India. The fact that an Indian Prime Minister gives the matter his serious personal attention is significant. Government centres are available for advice. A Family Planning Association was formed three years ago, and in 1951 held its first All-India Conference. The Planning Commission subsequently invited the Association to give their views to the Health and Social Welfare Panels of the Commission. A small sum of Rs. 25 lakhs was then allotted for a Family Planning Service, and the result was the establishment of centres mainly in existing maternity hospitals. This is no substitute for the scientific education of the population, but it is a beginning.

I have heard it said by those who have studied the matter that the most practical approach is to teach the extension of certain simple primitive methods which are already understood in the Indian countryside. The ways and means which are available to Western civilisation are certainly beyond the purse of the average rural family in India or Pakistan. Nor is there apparently any prospect of such doubtful expedients as " rhythm " methods being effectively adopted. In 1952 a World Health Organisation expert, Dr. Stone, visited India on the invitation of the Government to advise on this particular method. From the views he expressed it was apparent that he himself was by no means confident of its success. Subsequently Dr. Marie Stopes poured scorn on its problematical nature. It would certainly seem ineffective in a land in which so many women

theless nothing can hold up the advance of the disciples of progress, and Dr. Ambedkar will live to see the recognition of his labours.

What is it exactly that is involved? Hindu law and custom covers marriage, divorce, inheritance, the status of widows, the seclusion of caste and a hundred other matters. Lord William Bentinck successfully assailed it in 1829 with his enactment to abolish *suttee*.[1] But over the years Englishmen were scrupulously cautious in avoiding the charge of interference in indigenous religious practice.

In every case custom and convention operated to undermine the freedom of women. Refusal of the right to own property, widows forbidden to remarry, restrictions on a daughter in inheritance—these were some of the anachronisms which circumscribed the lives of millions of Hindu women. Practice differed from one area to another. In the south succession was often matriarchal. Much conscientious legislation had been introduced within the last fifty years,[2] and it was to standardise and codify these measures that the Hindu Code Bill was introduced. Such opposition as delayed its implementation can only be regarded as in complete conflict with the spirit of the Constitution in its zealous protection of human rights.

I have elaborated the issue of Moslem and Hindu womanhood because it bears so forcibly on the wider and momentous problem of population. My feeling is that conditions will never really be ripe for an assault on the expansion of the population until women have emerged from the obscurity of the *zenana*.

It is in relation to the frightening race between food and population that we must view the whole problem of the challenge of industry in a land of agriculture. In the first flush of independence, industrialisation was regarded as symbolic of a new unleashed creative spirit and a matter of prestige. Nor can we ever expect such natural desires to abate. " Multan is growing into an industrial town, and as such I am sure it will revive its ancient glory." So said the Pakistan Prime Minister in March 1952 as he opened a new generating plant for the local electric supply company. The two new nations were, I think, at first suspicious that Western advice, which always took the form of advocating priority for agricultural interests, was conditioned by the desire, conscious or subconscious, to perpetuate Western industrial supremacy. If that mood existed, it has passed; and it is now generally accepted both in India and Pakistan that food and its production constitute an honourable and vital contribution to the welfare of the world. In more practical terms

[1] The burning of Hindu widows on the funeral pyres of their husbands; not to be challenged by the widow, and accepted as inevitable. Orthodox opinion resisted it at the time. But the great Hindu reformer, Raja Ram Mohan Roy, who was then in England gave it his full support.

[2] Examples are the Brahmo Marriage Act, the Gains of Learning Act and two Acts of 1937 and 1938 to permit women to own property. The *Sarda* Act of 1928 to prevent the marriage of young children was not limited to Hindus. But : lenient penalties and haphazard application rendered it comparatively ineffective.

Pakistan, with a succession of balanced budgets, reflects the fundamental strength of an agricultural economy. The position is recognised in both the Indian and Colombo Plans.

But the view is often expressed that only in a process of industrialisation will the surplus millions be absorbed. In a Continent in which 75 per cent of the population work on the land, for much of the year a large section of productive humanity is idle. The function of industry is then not so much to create prosperity as to absorb a seasonal community of unemployed. Yet the very nature of industry is always to seek the means by which fewer can be employed to produce more; the paradox of Shaw's " dangerous consequences of efficiency ". If industry in the two countries can be directed not so much to the search for labour-saving devices as to assist employment and assure a higher standard of life for labour, then it will serve its purpose. A diversified development of small industries is surely indicated. Yet how difficult to achieve, for it is contrary to every instinct of imaginative planning in its search to create and control on the vast scale.[1] Nor can we regard an industrial drive to mechanise agriculture as a necessary contribution. That the mechanisation of agriculture must increase agricultural production is not denied. But it can also only throw more men out of employment in the villages. We return to the dictum, commonplace yet profound, that the villages themselves provide the way out of this dilemma. If village industries are developed side by side with the production of capital goods, the peasant will find that there is still useful employment for him near his home in the days when power-pumps replace his Persian wheel and twenty pairs of bullocks give way to one tractor plough.

There is another qualification to this application of science. It is that in the present conditions of land tenure mechanical assistance to produce more food is often quite unpractical. The fragmentation of land through its division equally among sons of a deceased landowner results in the *patwari*'s map of the land surrounding a village looking like a patchwork quilt.

It is here perhaps appropriate to pause and take stock of the general position in regard to land and its administration. I appreciate the dangers of generalisation. Yet there are certain common conditions which can be regarded as applying to the sub-Continent as a whole and which have grown as much from the soil itself as from the follies of man-made systems.

On the sub-Continent the pattern is ancient. It passes as the *batai* system, which in different forms covers so many countries east of Suez. Its evolution came about as a process of nature from an ignorance and suspicion of cash transactions and the mysteries of keeping accounts. The land is owned by the landlord, and the tenant is a share-cropper.

[1] A brilliant exposition of this thesis is to be found in an address by Sir Alagappa Chettiar, LL.D., to the East India Association. (See the *Asiatic Review* of October 1951.)

He is allotted land which he tends and tills, trading his labour for a
surrender of a half-share of the crops and the use of a pair of bullocks.
He pays no cash rent, no lease-money and no water rates.   But he is
under one severe restriction, in that his tenancy is subject to a yearly
agreement with his employer and can be terminated by either party at the
end of the crop season.   It is this insecurity of tenancy, together with the
fifty-fifty percentage of division, which has been assailed by the Left-
wing Press and ardent reformers, particularly in the West Punjab of
Pakistan.

Despite its obvious anomalies, the *batai* system has by no means been
unacceptable to the peasant share-cropper.   At the time of crop division
both parties view each other's motives with some suspicion.   But
throughout the year relations are generally based on a mutual trust which
withstands attempts to persuade the peasant that he is the miserable victim
of exploitation.   Nor is the status of a landless labourer necessarily to be
despised.   It offers a social standing somewhere in between that of a
peasant proprietor and a wage labourer which is not unattractive, while
it affords the opportunity to indulge in some semi-independent farming
of his own.   Those who have not seen conditions are apt on hearsay to
believe that landlords are recognised by their absence from the land.   Yet
there could be no finer manifestation of the strength and good common
sense of the rugged Punjabi peasantry than the great clan leaders of the
Punjab.[1]   Among them we should not forget a few Englishmen who
have produced astonishing results in the colonisation areas south of
Lahore.[2]

On 9th January 1952 the West Punjab Assembly passed the Punjab
Tenancy Amendment Bill, thereby amending an Act which had governed
tenancy conditions ever since 1887.   A few days later, on 12th January,
the Assembly unanimously passed the Punjab Abolition of *Jagirs* Bill.
Thus, on paper at least, the local Government in three days swept aside
much of traditional practice which had governed the relations of landlord and tenant since the days of the Moghuls.   The former Act ruled
that occupancy tenants should become owners of the land for which they
paid no rent.   The latter gave the Government power to resume all
jagirs except awards for military service and religious or charitable endowments.   Yet another measure—the Punjab Auqaf Bill—sought to ensure

[1] I have seen no better description of land conditions in West Pakistan (with
particular reference to Sind) than the excellent Report of the Government Hari
Inquiry Committee (1947–8) appointed by the Government of Sind under the
chairmanship of Sir Roger Thomas, C.I.E.   The chairman for several years served
as Agricultural Adviser to the Sind Government.   He farms a large acreage of land
in the Province, and is accepted by the Pakistan Government as an outstanding
authority on all questions concerned with agriculture.

[2] An example is the farm of some 3,500 acres owned by Lieut.-Colonel Leo
Conville in the Montgomery District of West Punjab.   Twenty-five years of
careful progressive management have served to produce the finest crops in the
country.

that income from religious endowments was placed "to the most progressive and healthy use and to ensure that endowments cater for the purposes for which they were originally dedicated". The measure was opposed by Chaudhri Mohammed Shafiq of the Jinnah Awami League, on the grounds that the Government might conceivably abuse its powers and use confiscated funds for party purposes.

The zeal for reform was the direct legacy of a manifesto of the Punjab Moslem League drafted in 1950; and to the casual observer it would seem to have gone far enough for the moment in the simple process of taking from the "haves" and giving to the "have-nots". In theory it involves the reduction of holdings to a limit of 100 acres and the reduction of the landlord's share of produce to 40 per cent. Nevertheless the new legislation was attacked by the *Pakistan Times* as inadequate. For example, land classified as *khud-kasht*—which is land personally cultivated by the owner—was exempt from the new provisions. "Large tracts of land will be shown as *khud-kasht* and tenants ejected or reduced to the status of landless labourers", was their comment. They would have swept away the "iniquitous *batai* system" with one sweep of the broom. The Jinnah Awami League attacked the measures for different reasons, claiming that they had not gone far enough in support of *shariat* principles. In general terms, criticism amounted to the charge that there was much scope for evasion, that the long delay in the preparation of the Bills had given landlords time to farm out their properties to relatives, and that landlords and tenants would take their disputes to Court, and the dice was heavily loaded against the tenant. This remains to be seen. It remains, too, for the peasant proprietor to realise that he will now be taxed for his land and his water, and that in the process the agent who weighed out the crop has only been replaced by an equally unresponsive Government official.

In conclusion I turn aside to more speculative considerations. Each time we return to the sub-Continent we look around the bazaars and note those manifestations which chill the heart of any sensitive observer, whether from the West or East. It starts with a realisation of the travesty of life for dogs and donkeys and *tonga* ponies. It embraces the squalor of drainless alleys and hovels which pass for homes. On my visit last year I found myself wondering if in my lifetime there would ever be recorded an advance on such conditions—conditions which drive unsuspecting frustrated youths to Communism. I have said enough to indicate that my personal belief is that men can by their own free will overcome much of those conditions which degrade. In Gujerat they speak of a *patel* who daily swept the public streets for three hours as his duty to the community; which is a fair enough example of the conquest of degradation.

Yet the more we search for the pattern of a formula for progress, the more inescapable is the conclusion that we are really wrestling with immutable conditions of geography and climate. Always they seem to have the last word. I put this not as a dogma, but in some spirit of inquiry: that politics and policies can effect temporary changes, but they leave no enduring result? The character of a people is conditioned by its climate and environment. The attitude of its neighbours, the length and formation of its frontiers; all play their part. The soil from which a people spring will therefore take any ideology—Socialism, feudalism, monarchy or republic, Fascism or Communism—and eventually mould it to its own purpose. We give our systems labels. Yet monarchy in Britain will always be something different from monarchy in Egypt; and by the same token a hypothetical Communism in Britain would finally assume a different shape from that we recognise in Russia. If there be logic in the principle, maybe then a dose of Communism might even be the right corrective for certain nations in certain conditions, though the process of correction would be long and unpleasant. The hand of Nature seems not content to rest at fashioning the men and women who live on the soil. It must even undermine the fruits of their labours. With immense effort we covered the Punjab with some of the finest canals in the world. Today thousands of acres of irrigated land on either side of the canals are turning to waste through water-logging. The level of the subsoil water has risen through constant irrigation, producing a snow-like salinity on the surface which renders the land useless.[1] The peasants who live on the western fringe of Rajasthan have a greater enemy than Communism to overcome. It is the ceaseless encroachment of the desert. The west winds blow the sands from Sind and the Rann of Kutch over their fields; and it remains to be seen if the expenditure of millions of rupees on afforestation will resist the relentless hand of Nature. Once again geography defies even the modest legitimate ambitions of Homo sapiens. Against such an approach of fatalism we see bribery and corruption, nepotism in high places, and sloth and apathy in public administration as the inescapable penalties of conditions over which mere men have no control! If we accept some element of logic in the conclusion, we do not necessarily recognise it as " the whole truth and nothing but the truth ".

Yet, as the facilities for travel increase and the world shrinks, in so far as East and West meet and identities are lost in the cauldron of ideas, the effects of geography are overcome. Let us apply the supposition to the sub-Continent. Consider, for example, the large injections of foreign capital which are made available for economic assistance. Is the effect a mere temporary matter of passing prosperity for a generation, or does some intangible element of permanency take root? Both India and Pakistan are now thoroughly persuaded of the need for foreign capital.

[1] In 1952 some 10 per cent of the land under irrigation in West Punjab and Sind was thus affected. In the Thal project the walls of the canals and subsidiary channels are being laboriously bricked and cemented. Several theories are advanced for the prevention of water-logging, including pumping the water back into the main canal. But no satisfactory remedy has yet been evolved.

Within the past three years the two Prime Ministers, without admitting
that such assistance is indispensable, have stressed the part it can play.[1]
Should the political tendency therefore be a drift towards Marxist
ideology, this would be one of the first matters on which we could expect
a clash.   Once you admit the validity of the capitalist system you have
further to recognise that a poor nation cannot possibly develop the
ability to save, invest and build up its own capital strength without large
healthy injections from outside.   An Indian economist has put the
situation with clarity :

> " Unfortunately capital accumulation is a sphere where the first
> few steps are the most difficult.   It is extremely hard for a poor
> nation, as for a poor man, to save a large part of its income; the
> little increases in income that it manages to obtain are more likely
> to be spent on consumption, however urgent the need for more
> capital and however productive investment may be.   Foreign
> capital provides the one way out of this dilemma." [2]

think we might justifiably conclude that on the economic plane the
wise application of Western assistance can help to raise the standard of
life : not only that, but in the process a new economic strength *can* be
grafted on to the community, which can then in honesty be regarded as
indigenous.

Are we to be sure of a similar sort of operation when we turn from
economic implications to the realm of human relationship?   It is hardly
a question for an author who knew British-India to attempt to answer.
For there must first be admitted that the West—and we are now speaking
of men, not machines—has still something to offer to the East which is
not available within Eastern frontiers.   It is a claim that would come
better from someone with a less traditional background than myself.
But, risking the accusation of a smug Western respectability, is it not fair
to assert that if the world and the 2,500 million who live on it had decided
never to progress in Western terms, but to turn for its development

---

[1] " Indian capital needs to be supplemented by foreign capital, not only because
our nation's savings will not be enough for a rapid development of the country on
the scale we wish, but also because scientific, technical and industrial knowledge and
capital equality can best be secured with the help of foreign capital." (Pandit
Nehru, in Parliament, September 1951.)

" Although the Government's policy designed to encourage the participation of
foreign capital with indigenous capital in the country's industrial development was
generally well received by investors abroad, and the response has been encouraging
in respect of some industries, the amount of foreign capital that has so far entered the
country has not been large enough to step up appreciably the pace of industrial
development as a whole. . . . There is no doubt that if enterprising organisations
possessing the necessary resources and technical knowledge will participate with
domestic capital in exploiting Pakistan's vast natural resources, much benefit will
accrue to them and to the country." (Khwaja Nazimuddin, Address to the Royal
India, Pakistan and Burma Association, 11th December 1953.)

[2] *International Aspects of Indian Economic Development*, by Professor D. T. Lakdawala,
Reader in Economics, Bombay University.

to the introspective tranquillity of Eastern philosophies, then indeed there would be nothing more to say? Yet the world has not chosen that way. The East itself has confirmed the pattern of its own development; and we surely have no other choice than an acceptance of a long era, perhaps of centuries, in which men from the West will go into Eastern lands and, for better or worse, give their services in the confidence that at least they can offer technical knowledge weighed as a kind of commercial commodity. What worries me is that, with the new winds that blow through international conference halls, the days of the long-term administrator, the man who was prepared to go into foreign lands and identify his life with those of the people, are over. Instead we are faced with the short-term bureaucrat, operating under a temporary halo of Point Four aid or the sanctity of a United Nations welfare organisation; and too often does the latter prove to be an international spiv, happy enough to accept an inflated salary for passing employment. It is in the acceptance once again of the long-term expert that I see a more secure pattern for progress in the East, a compromise which, while retaining all that was best in old conceptions of colonialism, would in no way represent a challenge to sovereign independence.

With certain qualifications we can therefore accept the proposition that injections of Western assistance, in the form of the influence in addition to the knowledge of good men, can play their part as much as tangible economic aid. By the same token I suggest that some element of permanency remains in the process. Let the traffic in ideas be a two-way affair. The more Indians and Pakistanis that can be welcomed within our shores the better. So often when East and West meet each gives to the other the less attractive qualities of mind and purpose. Contacts are based only on commercial relationship. In the case of the sub-Continent a background of a century of association is surely the firm foundation which puts our mutual relations beyond the limited scope of normal commercial exchange. It is with such thoughts in mind that we are conscious that over the years those limitations of the national character which sometimes defy the most careful planning will be ironed out in the mellowing process of experience.

As one who believes vehemently in the international purpose of the British Commonwealth, I would claim that if Britain can continue her close associations with India and Pakistan, securing from them a priority of demand for her talent among the nations of the West, the Commonwealth example may then come to be accepted as worthy of imitation among others less happy in their mutual relations.

CHAPTER NINE

THINGS TO COME

THE time has come to weigh the events of the past five years against the relentless processes of time and to speculate on the shape of future tendencies. So often when a man looks into the future and predicts development contrary to the aspirations of the day he is answered in indignation and ridicule. So the wise writer avoids prophecy. All he attempts—and to this much he is entitled—is to say what might or may happen in the light of logic and experience. Even in this cautious approach as often as not he comes to be regarded as wanting to see history work to the pattern of his prediction. This is a misconception. If I argue that India may in certain circumstances disintegrate, that is no reason whatsoever for supposing that I desire to see disintegration. On the contrary, no one in his senses could wish for any process but further unification.

In another chapter I have suggested that 100 years ago some statesman with second sight might conceivably have saved us all a lot of trouble if he could have anticipated and established a separate administration in the North-West. Be that as it may, no Solomon could ever have foreseen that one day Pakistan would take the form of an eastern territory, with its concentrated population of Mongol-Dravidian stock in political alignment with the Aryans of the West Punjab. If in 1939 we had asked a Moslem of Dacca if he felt himself to be one nation with the Janjuha or Awan of Jhelum and the Salt Range 1,000 miles away, he might have thought us mildly simple for asking the question. To assert this is in no way to deny the reality of today. It is merely to suggest that while there is no prospect whatsoever of West Pakistan and India abolishing their mutual frontier in recognition of a wistful Indian desire in some quarters to recreate the greater Bharat, it would not be unnatural if one day the eastern limb of Pakistan decided to cut itself adrift from control from Karachi. Whether that step would ever be followed by its subsequent absorption by India is doubtful. Such a development would certainly solve some administrative headaches for India in view of the present ridiculous situation of Assam, by which tortuous communications with West Bengal have had to be laboriously constructed through the slender mountainous corridor which skirts round the northern frontier of East Pakistan.

If there was one area on the sub-Continent where previously a provincial loyalty might have been said to take precedence over religious sentiment, it was Bengal. Lord Curzon discovered this many years ago in a short-lived attempt to divide the Province.

In February 1952 there were riots in East Bengal. The immediate cause of the trouble was the legislation by which Urdu is accepted as the national language for Pakistan. The District Magistrate of Dacca promulgated an order forbidding the assembly of six or more persons. It was disregarded by the local students. A general strike to protest against the language regulations was called. The result was a brawl in which eight persons were killed and about 100 injured. In a public statement on 28th February the Commissioner of Dacca sought to convince the public that the riots were inspired by the Communists. That was less than half the truth. Communism is sometimes a convenient alibi, as the Union Government in South Africa and the French in North Africa have discovered. But in East Bengal the fact was that the attempt to impose an alien language on the people, and particularly on the literate elements, was extremely unpopular, and quite naturally the Communists were quick to take advantage of the situation.

In April the Prime Minister of Pakistan made a statement which, while acknowledging the reality and causes of unrest, seemed to avoid facing the only effective remedy; which is to regard Bengali as the first language in Bengal.[1] The issue was national. It might threaten the unity of the two portions of Pakistan. Therefore it should not be dragged into party politics. There is surely a flaw in the argument. If there is a grievance of national importance, a normal and constitutional method by which it can receive attention is in Parliamentary debate through the representatives of the people. To resist publicity is to drive a natural movement to more desperate methods.

The link between the two Pakistans is essentially economic. With surplus wheat in the West and a monopoly of the world's jute in the East Pakistan should be able to show surplus budgets for many years; and it therefore becomes a matter of practical policy for her leaders to foster ties of sentiment which are sufficiently artificial to fade to insignificance if neglected. It was for this reason that a statesman from Dacca was chosen first for the office of Governor-General and subsequently to follow the late Liaquat Ali Khan as Prime Minister. I record these conditions with no intention of suggesting an immediate crisis. But the relationships of the two Pakistans with India and with each other puzzle the British public, and it is useful to set out the conditions. It will be remembered that the late Mr. Mohammed Ali Jinnah for many years

---

[1] " It is an issue which I believe may create a strong difference of opinion between the two wings of Pakistan. And if this difference is allowed to grow, it might lead to disunity among ourselves. . . . I claim and maintain that this language issue is of great national importance, and I can reasonably and justifiably ask you to keep it outside the sphere of party politics. While East Bengal does not contest the claim that Urdu has been the language of the Moslems, feeling there in favour of the Bengali language has been equally strong. A hurried decision on a question where opinion is likely to be sharply divided cannot be in consonance with real national interests. . . ." (Prime Minister of Pakistan—Press Conference, Karachi, 13th April 1952.)

K

refused to define the geographical boundaries of Pakistan. Throughout
that period I always felt that if the demands were confined to the West,
there was a basis for their fulfilment by the logic of ethnographical and
racial conditions. Even so, the firm Unionist tradition which had been
built up by men such as Sir Fazul-i-Hussein, Sir Sikander Hayat and
Malik Sir Khizar Hayat Khan would first have to be overthrown. But
the further demand for an eastern State I found difficult to defend.[1]
The lesson is surely that when the pandits have finished with defining
race, and when politicians have exploited the weaknesses of nationalism,
language is after all not such a bad gauge of a people's sense of unity.
It would therefore be a natural process of evolution if one day the two units
which now form one State should discover that the political relationship could no longer be maintained. I have mentioned the effect of
an improvement in Indo–Pakistan relations, and it is interesting to
speculate on the results of the free passage of trade across India between
the two Pakistans. Might it not be that such conditions would herald
a trade revival between the two countries which would result in the
economic interdependence of East and West Pakistan becoming far less
prominent?

The one aspect of future development which can always be depended
on to arouse interest in Britain is the position of Communism on the sub-
Continent; and though the results of the Indian elections tended to focus
our attention on Communism in India, the tendencies in Pakistan are no
less important for the greater subtlety of a more obscure relationship.

At a time in 1949 when Pakistan was particularly sensitive to the
greater attention which India appeared to command in Commonwealth
negotiations, the impulse of the moment was manifest in an invitation
to the late Liaquat Ali Khan to visit Moscow. It was accepted, but never
fulfilled. A formidable Soviet trade commission arrived in Karachi,
and for a time were fêted and offered tea-parties. They refused the
tea-parties—which offended their hosts—and, with the exception of a
small Soviet cotton-purchasing agency which continues, this aspect of
co-operation with the Soviet has lapsed. But though we hear less of
official contacts, there is much interest displayed by a restless intelligentsia; and we should analyse the tendency with some care, for it
carries the potentiality of important international repercussions.

We are apt to think of the sub-Continent—a vast human complexity
of peasant poverty—as the perfect breeding-ground for Communist
expansion. In so far as resistance to Communism is concerned, we pin
our faith to the age-old beliefs and restrictions of religion. We need
to revise this optimism. Wherever organised religion can be identified
closely with a narrow but flourishing nationalism, there also is the

[1] With the support of Hindus such as the late Sir Chhotu Ram, the Punjab Unionist
Party from 1937 to 1945 represented the peak of Provincial statesmanship in British
India. An account of the Unionist Ministry and the work is to be found in *A
Continent Experiments*.

hunting ground of the Communist. It would therefore in no way be surprising if one day we were to discover a temporary understanding between the Hindu Mahasabha and the Indian Communists. But it is among the followers of the Prophet that the tendency is most marked. All over the world there are examples, not so much of Islam openly co-operating with Communism, as affording it a mild toleration which is equally effective for the latter's purpose; and the medium of contact is the frustrated nationalist. In Indonesia we note Dar-al-Islam and the Communist, in Egypt the Moslem Brotherhood and the Communist, and in Persia Fedayan Islam and the Tudeh Party. But for us the lesser but more significant case is in Pakistan, where the Chief of the General Staff, the officer in charge of Air Force Personnel, and the Editor of the *Pakistan Times* faced their trial for conspiracy with an outside Power—a Communist Power.[1] Islam—the religion of the one God revealed to men through his Prophet Mohammed—is therefore no deterrent to many who think they can see in Communism a background to their own confusion of ideals. I do not doubt that most of those concerned with the conspiracy would regard themselves as good Moslems, answering the call to prayer along with the faithful; and we need to examine the reason for these curious loyalties more carefully to find out the truth.

Those who are attracted by the Communist ideal are activated by a variety of motives. In the security of British democracy the point is difficult to appreciate. But in a dozen countries in the Orient the issue is constantly in evidence. At one end of the scale is the complete political opportunist activated by nothing more than the love of power and capable of any intrigue to attain it. At the other extreme is the idealist, disgusted with the futility in public life which he sees around him. His contacts with the West have taught him to recognise nepotism, graft and corruption, and they lend him strength to fight them fearlessly when encountered. The struggle may need to take refuge underground. But the motive is much more than the familiar fascination and search for power which play such a part in oriental politics. Faiz Mohammed Faiz, who was accused in the Rawalpindi case, was a conscientious and efficient member of a Government Directorate which was set up after the war to maintain the morale of the Army. The times needed special measures, and the Directorate of Morale was the result. A senior British officer has testified to his integrity and honesty of purpose, though he took no steps to hide his Communist sympathies. Major-General Mohammed Akbar Khan was a gallant leader suffering from an obsession of frustrated ambition. He had tasted blood in the Kashmir campaign, and he considered the Kashmir policy of his Government, and in particular the direction of Pakistan forces by a British Commander-in-Chief, as restrictive and timid. In December 1947 he may well have visualised himself at the head of a Pakistan Army committed to a militant crusade in Kashmir and the enhancement of his country's reputation in

[1] See Chapter Five, footnote 1 (*b*), p. 96.

the world outside. He was married to a lady of ambition and ability. He and his colleagues spoke openly of turning to Russia if they received no support from Britain. It was the kind of wild talk that came out freely over a drink or round a dinner-table. But it had little to do with the Communist dialectic or the experience and convictions of the true Marxist. Sooner or later these men would have been disillusioned. But in the meanwhile they clearly thought that they were about to rid their country of all that seemed rotten and unworthy of preservation. The sad reflection is that both they and others such as the late Liaquat Ali Khan were fighting the same enemy. The Constitutional Government of the day may well contain many parasites. It was so in the past, and it will be so in the future. Nevertheless the leaders are certainly the best men available, and it behoves true patriots to rise above their immediate reactions to maladministration in day-to-day government and recognise the value of the leadership beyond.

That the Pakistan Prime Minister himself is seriously concerned about the undercurrent of subversive activity in his country is clear from his public statements. Addressing a meeting on Pakistan Day in Karachi, he devoted several minutes to the theme: [1] " Certain elements in our country are fomenting hatred between rich and poor. Most of the people at the back of this propaganda are Communists, who have no faith in Islam nor any belief in God. . . ." Rumour-mongers, fomenters of dissatisfaction, preachers of class hatred, and certain sections of the Press, all received his censure. There is no doubt that the assassination in 1951 of Mr. Liaquat Ali Khan had thoroughly alarmed the Government, and on this particular occasion elaborate precautions were taken for the Prime Minister's protection. Nevertheless it gave the public confidence to realise that the authorities were alive to the methods of those who for ever plan in secret. My own belief is that Pakistan will accept the path of evolutionary development and avoid the spectacular but sinister attractions of revolution.

There are certain principles of common application to the two countries concerning Communism: and for the better understanding of what is happening in Southern India it is as well to set them out.

So often is the problem of holding Communism at arm's length regarded as a mere matter of raising the standard of living. The vast scope of the Colombo Plan, though it purports to represent an act of post-war reconstruction which would in any case have been initiated, also takes incidental pride in the belief that by removing hunger and want it defeats Communist expansion in South-East Asia. I suggest that this is only half the truth. All true social progress is surely a matter of balancing educational and economic advance. A man may be poor, but he remains perfectly happy so long as he is unaware of his poverty. Give him an education beyond that compatible with his economic condition, and the seeds of unrest immediately take root. Reverse the process

[1] 14th August 1952. (India celebrates " Independence Day " on 15th August.)

and offer him plenty before he is ready for it, and results are equally disastrous. The toys of civilisation arrive before he understands their use. So often the wealth never finds its way down to the level of those whom it should benefit. Instead it is frittered away through many fingers in many devious processes between the Government treasury and the peasantry.

As often as not, the two processes operate simultaneously within the same country through conditions which have their foundations back in the dawn of man's history; and the systems of thousands of years die hard. True progress, then, is a matter of educational and economic progress going forward side by side, never the one being allowed to race ahead of the other; and the result of the elections in Southern India was fundamentally a manifestation of educational advance having outdistanced economic conditions as represented by an outworn system of land tenure. In Travancore-Cochin, where the Communists captured thirty-two seats in the State Assembly against the Congress score of forty-four, the standard of literacy is the highest in India, and about two-thirds of the electorate went to the polls.

It is sometimes said that in Southern India the Communist vote was given not so much for Communism as against the Congress. It is only a half-truth. The few Communist gatherings which I saw in the north of India were travesties of political convictions. Any wild-eyed firebrand waving a red flag and shouting slogans down the bazaar alleys appeared to be able to collect a few urchins, but there was certainly more to ridicule than to impress. That is always the way it starts. But in lands where mouths are hungry and shouted slogans are simple of comprehension as compared with the laborious business of reading, it is easy for the infection here and there to find its willing victim. The student with his Left-wing textbooks does the reading. He shouts the slogans, and those with the hungry mouths are his ready audience. It gives him the first taste of the most alluring and dangerous of all motives, the love of power.

I do not suppose for a moment that in Travancore-Cochin or Madras there are more than a handful of men who can argue about the principles of dialectical materialism. But that hardly matters. The important point is that there are many ready listeners, and enough of the trained Communists about to form the cells and impose the normal technique of propagation. It is something of a paradox that the system becomes of more importance than the ideology for which it professes to be the vehicle.

For India, the overall result was to return twenty-seven Communists and fellow-travellers to the House of the People—less than 6 per cent of the membership. But already the Government benches are experiencing their first taste of the methods of those who seek the limelight in a manner out of all proportion to their small numbers. The Communist leader, Mr. Gopalan, has the usual resources of a soap-box demagogue at his command. British imperialism, germ warfare, American spies, rich

landlords and *jagirdars*, are all scourged in the same monotonous bombast
for the benefit of a much larger audience than India's Lower House.
Supporting Mr. Gopalan is a team of obedient imitators varying from
Mr. Hiren Mukherjee, whose ability in debate covers the mistakes of his
leader, to Mr. Bhupesh Gupta from West Bengal, who calls for the
confiscation of all British assets in India.   Hitherto the climax to many
swift exchanges and abuse has been the first demand on the Marshal of
the House to eject a Communist for insulting the chair.[1]   But before
five years have passed there will most certainly be many lively episodes.

The immediate effect of this new technique in opposition is to give the
Congress Government all the appearance of a Tory stronghold patiently
defending the tenets of tradition.   It seemed suddenly to produce a latent
sense of bad taste in the House.   The Government were able to discover
an effective opponent of Communism within their ranks in a certain
Dr. S. N. Sinha from Bihar, who had served in the Russian Army,
and had studied his Communism under Maxim Gorki.   Claiming a
personal knowledge of the Cominform organisation, he accused the
Indian Communists of being in direct touch with Moscow and of
reporting their progress to an agency in Leipzig.   He supported his
accusations with documentary proof.

It would seem that as time passes two distinct processes will emerge in
India.   On the one hand the Government and its supporters will come
more and more to appreciate the nature of that aggression which has
daily taxed the patience of the Security Council, Allied control in Berlin
and Vienna, and the Government and police of Western Europe for the
last five years.   This may prove just the medicine needed to prevent
stagnation and secure an alert and conscientious awareness of the problems
of government.   It is possible that the Prime Minister's generous but
lukewarm inclination to condemn Communism's method while up-
holding its principle will receive the jolt necessary to awaken the country
to its real danger.

On the other hand, if the Communists can consolidate their gains and
the Congress prove unable to offer the country a healthier, happier future,
the movement which has taken root in the south may spread to infect
the north.   The next elections might then well see the defeat of the
Congress, which might be the first step in disintegration.

These grim reflections are not made lightly.   The past failures of the
Indian National Congress are frankly acknowledged by men such as
Pandit Nehru.   There has been a tendency to regard the Party as a closed
shop with little scope for young students who knew not the days of the
significance of the Gandhi cap.   Congress leaders who have spent their
lives in opposition have found it difficult to grasp the correct relationship
between a Minister and the Civil Servants with whom he must work.
The need to find many hundreds of candidates to contest the elections

[1] 18th July 1952.   Debate on the Preventive Detention Bill, when the Communist
Mr. Nambiar, was forcibly removed.

resulted in large numbers of extremely indifferent individuals competing for power, and not a few have been successful. Representation in the Upper House, based on the greater selectivity of the indirect vote, is noticeably of a higher quality. But the position of the Party generally is one of a future of blood, sweat and tears. Against this assailable opponent the Opposition may have cards to play. But the most obvious opening at the moment is an attack on the unity of India.

It is no accident that in one important aspect the nature of the Communist's opportunity in India is identical with that of the conditions offered him in Pakistan. Reduced to its simplest definition it is the preaching of disintegration conveniently disguised as self-determination on a basis of the freedom of language. The movement received expression in a debate in the House of the People on 7th July 1952, when the Communist, Mr. Tushar Chatterjee, moved a resolution advocating nothing less than the complete revision of the map of India on a linguistic basis. Mr. Frank Anthony [1] for the Government pointed out that if the thesis that cultural autonomy required administrative autonomy was accepted, they might just as well at the same time accept the principle of fragmentation. Mr. Nehru's firm handling of the debate made nonsense of this particular attempt. But the whole question of languages is not so easily disposed of, and since it is vital in the future fortunes of the country, it is as well to review it dispassionately, if we are to be forewarned of the dangers.

The particular areas selected by the Communists are Hyderabad, Andhra, Karnataka, Maharashtra and a demand for the enlargement of West Bengal at the expense of Bihar. In addition, the Naga tribesmen in Assam are quite ready to push their own claims for an independent Naga State, and in March 1952 they sent a delegation to Delhi to plead their cause. By far the most important area is the strip of country to the north of Madras from the coast inland to Hyderabad. Here the Telugu-speaking community have for long cherished the conception of their own separate identity. In the pre-war constitution of the Indian National Congress, Andhra was one of the twenty Provinces for purposes of Provincial Committees, and there are some grounds for the local complaint that the Congress have failed to honour a pledge. But the significant feature here is that for several years Andhra has been associated with the more militant aspect of political unrest. In 1942, when the Indian National Congress, in obedience to the Working Committee, called into operation a campaign which purported to be "non-violent", the Madras Government unearthed a document drafted by the Andhra Committee which elaborated plans of a revolutionary nature to paralyse the administration in successive stages. [2] It has therefore been a not unnatural development to watch the tendency to violence find its level

[1] Mr. Frank Anthony is the representative of the Anglo-Indian Community.
[2] *Report on the Constitutional Problem in India*, Part II, Prof. R. Coupland, Ch. XXII, p. 303.

in the appeal of Communism, and in a separate Andhra State the Communists will at this moment command a majority.

I had recorded so much when, on 19th December 1952, the Prime Minister of India announced the Government's decision to create the separate State of Andhradesa. Throughout the autumn the All-Party Convention of Telugu-speaking people had increased their pressure. Eventually their leader, Mr. Potti Siramalu, resorted to a " fast unto death " which in fact was seen through to its conclusion. On 16th December the death of Mr. Siramalu was the signal for an outbreak of rioting and hooliganism at the cost of some Rs. 50 lakhs of damage. The Government then relented, and Andhradesa is to receive its full status on 1st October 1953. Thus all the problems which faced the central Government of British India in 1947 will on a smaller stage confront the present Congress Government. A Boundary Commission must now settle the fate of the doubtful Districts of Bellary and Chittoor. Financial assistance must come to the new State from outside. There is even the analogy of an irrigation project (the Tungabadhra) which, since it is to feed both Andhra and Mysore, must now receive special treatment. On one point the Government have been firm : that the city of Madras can neither be included in the new State nor regarded as the temporary capital pending its establishment. It is all rather ominous, and many former champions of Andhra are none too happy at the prospect of becoming citizens of India's first Communist-governed State.

But when we have examined the opportunities for subversive exploitation of the Indian Government's difficulties in resisting extravagant claims, we are still faced with a fundamental problem of language which, whether we like it or not, is there, and which has nothing to do with the hopes of those who seek to exploit it. The trouble began when Hindi was accepted as the official language under the Constitution, although English can be used as an alternative until 1965. In effect this means the continued use of English in official speech and correspondence. A long time ago, when I was working for an Urdu examination, I developed the habit of always reading the names of railway stations first in the Urdu script before noting the confirmation in English. It remained with me for some twenty-five years. Alas, when I returned in 1952 gone was the familiar flourish of the Persian and Arabic characters, and in their place were the square-cut symbols of the Hindi script, which I regret I had never mastered. More significant, I reflected, was the fact that at least half the people who travelled on the Bombay Mail with me were as ignorant as I was. The spirit of nationalism is in its most hysterical manifestation when the question of language is concerned; and the enforcement of Hindi has become an obsession in certain quarters not unlike the ridiculous revival of Erse for at least a million Irishmen born to speak and write English. In May the newly appointed Minister of Railways, Lal Bahadur Shastri, replied to the railway budget debate in

Hindi. Under the Constitution he was perfectly entitled to do so. The President had himself in his Parliamentary inauguration speech spoken first in English and then in Hindi. Shastri was dutifully applauded, but many who had protested were not prepared to waste time listening to something they could not understand, and they left the Chamber. To the Prime Minister, who has been educated and immersed in the English language, this solicitude for an All-India mother tongue must sometimes appear a mountain of nonsense. The Ministry of Education have now not only to rewrite a mass of textbooks, but also to invent a complete range of scientific terms to cover physics, chemistry and mathematics. At considerable expense a Board of Scientific Terminology is established, while a committee of philologists with technical staff advisers is formed and dictionaries are laboriously prepared. For myself I find some interest in wondering by what process a new language will be absorbed by many officers of the Indian Army who have learnt their soldiering from English textbooks and issue all orders, whether on the parade-ground or the battlefield, in English.

And so I submit, in no spirit of false pride but as a matter of practical necessity, that the English language remains as a common denominator for unity free from local controversy.[1] To preserve it will be a simpler process than teaching a new language to many millions. To abandon it may encourage a fragmentation which might prove disastrous. Great schemes of development and progress; canal systems and controlled water-power, take no heed of boundaries erected by narrow nationalism. A Five-Year Plan becomes meaningless in a fragmented India. Maybe there was an initial failure to see into the future as the whole fabric of British India came gradually to be knit together in administrative unity. One hundred and fifty years ago India was a country of twelve major languages and 220 dialects, and it remains so today. But that is no reason for throwing aside such unity as has been achieved. Let Indians take heed of a lesson from the Middle East. In 1914 the Arab world was stagnant. Under the old Ottoman Empire education, health, culture and social welfare looked after themselves. But there was one aspect of life in those bad old days which the Arab nostalgically contemplates. In those times he could travel from the Gulf to Cairo and from Aleppo to the south Arabian coast without a passport or a customs inspection or a currency restriction. Nations have been created, but a price has been paid; and for India if this movement were to get out of hand the penalty would be the same. For such reasons the events in Andhra must be

[1] In the debate quoted Mr. Frank Anthony, the Anglo-Indian Leader, referred to English as the one cementing factor that had maintained the unity of India. In September 1952, twenty-six leading Indian educationalists and scientists addressed a strong letter to the Government of India deploring the deterioration in a knowledge of English among students. While in no way resisting the official displacement of English by 1965, they stressed that the tendency to hasten the process was quite impractical and there would be certain needs which always could only be met by the English language.

regarded ominously as an unfortunate example for future similar aspirations.

I have left a final doubt of the future for a matter of personalities. Men and their character govern policies. In Pakistan there is an even level of public service in the top strata of administration. But there is now no outstanding leader to make or mar events. In contrast, one's mind naturally turns to the Indian Prime Minister in contemplating events to come. No man is infallible, and we know Mr. Nehru's limitations. Yet when he disappears from the scene one wonders who can step into his place as the focus for unity. The occasion may produce the leader. He will certainly be needed.

In another chapter I have recorded the relations of these two members of the Commonwealth with a Britain solicitous for their welfare. But I was then concerned with the present. In looking into the future, it seems that countless ties of sentiment and a thousand happy memories of past associations must fade into the twilight of history. The judgment of the world has confirmed that 15th August 1947 may be regarded as a landmark in man's political evolution. Power surrendered and freedom gained were the symbols of a great stewardship. What is less realised is that the happy result could never have been achieved without every day of the previous 150 years at the disposal of a British Government in India. It hurt and irritated many at the time. But the reward has been in foundations which are firm: one wonders, therefore, how long memory will serve? A new generation of Englishmen will arise who never knew the Indian Civil Service. A new generation may arise on the sub-Continent more interested in the Universities of Peking or Cairo than in Oxford and Cambridge. What will then emerge? Perhaps it is profitless to speculate. Let the future take care of itself so long as the will to serve rather than exploit governs those who profess to love their country. In that spirit of service Sir Walter Scott's patriot lives; not as a symbol of outmoded Victorian jingoism, but as a true servant of the State to honour and respect in an era of confused loyalties.[1]

[1] See the opening quotation, p. vii.

PART II

EXTERNAL PROBLEMS

CHAPTER TEN

INDIA, PAKISTAN AND THE COMMONWEALTH

It was natural that the events of 15th August 1947 should be regarded as of momentous significance in relation to the peoples on the sub-Continent. It is not every day that two nations, old in culture but with their whole political existence before them, take the stage of world relationship; and when it happened, and because of the way it happened, it was *their* welfare and *their* problems with which we were mainly concerned. Yet if this great experiment is now a precedent available for imitation in the future, the logical conclusion is that one day the choice which was recently that of Pakistan and India will be before many other peoples of the Empire and Commonwealth. We must then inevitably reach the end of a phase in our Constitutional existence at the moment when we discover that the family has grown to a rich maturity of some fifteen or sixteen partners, equal in status, independent and interdependent, bound together only by that loose formula round which the Statute of Westminster was conceived in 1931. It is in relation to this inspiring conception that I wish to consider India and Pakistan. This, for us, is surely the vital aspect of 15th August 1947 for our future cognisance.

When on 9th December 1946 the Indian Constituent Assembly declared their goal to be a Sovereign Independent Republic, they were but interpreting the mood of the Indian National Congress as the climax to a generation of struggle. It was, however, an interpretation which took little thought for the morrow. The impulse of the moment had to be satisfied. The future could look after itself. This is such a common experience in the daily management of our own individual affairs that it would be hypocritical and unreal to attack its manifestation in the Indian decision of 1946. We can but deplore it, for it gave to the future evolution of our relationships with both India and Pakistan a confusion for which there was no precedent. Much of this complexity is reflected in the personality of Nehru himself, who was responsible for the original resolution. In 1946 the memories of past years of political confinement, of hopes and frustration, of the strength and loyalty of the Congress in adversity, were fresh and vital. But as the months passed and the years of bitter strife were superseded by the urgency of sudden overwhelming responsibilities, the mood changed. A background of Harrow and Cambridge, of a science degree and a thirst for English literature, played its part in the personal transformation. The result, so far as Nehru is concerned, seems to lie in a hope for the best of both possible worlds; and that quite natural desire is reflected in the whole content of the country's political thought and evolution.   On the one hand they seek to retain not only the very practical advantages of membership of the British Commonwealth, but they also appreciate the value of the best that Britain can offer in experience of government and interpretation of democracy.   That which we call the British way of life is of real and permanent significance.   On the other hand, the title of a Republic is a talisman which truly interprets the fulfilment of all past hope and aspiration.   Honour and prestige are satisfied.   Dominion status has been defined as " Independence plus ".   In the case of India it may well have become " Independence plus two " !

Each one of us will interpret this situation according to his own background and inclination.   You may feel, as did the late General Smuts, that the terms of " the Statute of Westminster have been whittled down to become meaningless "; or you may agree with Mr. Attlee, that with greater flexibility there has been achieved a " greater unity of purpose ".   Certainly the silken cords which Burke described as binding closer than iron chains were strained to the point of snapping, and time alone will show whether the elasticity is such as to take the additional weight.   Kashmir is perhaps as exacting a test as could be imposed.

Had it been possible to launch two new nations in mutual harmony, the effect of the Indian decision to assume a Republican status might not have been noticed.   But the events of 1947 were too fresh in the memory, and in the event Pakistan suffered from a sense of injustice from which she has never quite recovered.   The feeling that India had acquired something which she had missed was noticeable, and a sense of penalty was prevalent. I regard it as the solemn responsibility of all who can make or mar policies to break down this unfortunate reaction.   Certainly if it were justified it would represent a situation which the British public would deplore.   Unfortunately, the Government of the day in Britain gave the impression that they were obsessed with the need to satisfy Indian policies and sentiment in view of India's rising power and prestige in Asia. It seemed almost that an assessment of India's greater physical size had influenced the British Government, and Pakistan was quick to react to any justification for this belief which existed.   If India, being a Republic, could receive such appeasement, where was the advantage of a strict adherence to the Statute of Westminster?   From this stage, it was only a short step to an open accusation of British partiality for India in all the differences which separate India and Pakistan.   In an address to the East India Association on 16th December 1949 Mr. Altaf Hussain, the Editor of *Dawn*, criticised the British for failure to intervene on Pakistan's behalf in the dark days of partition, and particularly in the Kashmir dispute.   In developing the argument he accused British elements of interference in affairs of Pakistan's domestic concern.   Englishmen circulated stories of " internal intrigues ", though with what conceivable motive he did not say.   The fact of internal intrigue is, I think, acknowledged by all honest Pakistanis, and is referred to elsewhere.   Here it is only my intention to differentiate between the justified grievances of a new Dominion in the unhappy manner of its entry into full partnership and the obsession of certain elements of the Pakistan Press that Britain is responsible for all the disabilities from which their country has suffered since partition. Such lack of foresight as Britain displayed in the handling of the transfer of power was equally shared by the leaders of both the Moslem League and the Indian National Congress. I have yet to discover the Indian or Pakistani who would ever claim to have foreseen a communal *débâcle* or a war in Kashmir, let alone suggesting the measures which Britain could or should have taken in the event. To have given one country or the other physical assistance against its neighbour in the pangs of birth would have been fatal. It might even have driven the partner without favour into the arms of Moscow. This, however, does not exclude a frank statement of opinion now that the first anguish of those unhappy days is in the background. Indeed, an honest expression of opinion in all our inter-Commonwealth relations is surely the symbol of a general acceptance of a high standard of tolerance and intelligence in our leaders. To be able to give and take freely of criticism is an accepted attribute of true democracy; and a healthy understanding of the process is yet hardly evident in the Press of either India or Pakistan.

In contrast to some irresponsible criticism of Britain, I found that the work of British officers who remain in employment in the two countries is highly appreciated. A very effective process of natural selection resulted in those officers who were eager to stay on and assist in the task of nation-building finding their opportunity; and their work went far to repair the damage caused by loose, irresponsible talk in the clubs of London and the bazaars of the sub-Continent. The pity is that those with a background of years of experience, and with their roots in the land, are now passing on, to be replaced by the " short-term " man from England with little more than his own interest in mind. This is apparently the penalty, inevitable, but sad for those with sensitive memories.

The British family of nations for so many years existed in the tradition of a self-governing portion of Dominions and a governed Colonial Empire that when, in the case of the Indian sub-Continent, the day of transition arrived it took us all by surprise. The result was that men who were only dimly aware of each other's existence and who should have been in previous consultation met for the first time at the Prime Minister's Conference in January 1951. It is this firmly established conception of a structure that exists in two separate sealed compartments, which must be broken down in the interests of our future evolution. If within a period of time—it may be twenty, thirty or forty years—Jamaica, Malaya, the Gold Coast and others are to advance to the point of the great choice, then the sooner we can all get to know something of the leaders in these countries, and their problems, the better. There is, so far as I am aware, no knowledge of or interest in the affairs of Lagos in Ottawa. There is no exchange of students between Singapore and Sydney. There is little desire to invest Canadian or Australian capital in Africa. The borrowing powers of the Colonial Development Corporation up to £100 million are on the British Treasury, and the British Treasury only. These are matters which, if we are to profit from the Indian experience, can be considered now; for only by their timely contemplation can we go far to foster that true desire for unity which is infinitely more enduring than a mere matter of economic convenience.

There is another lesson to be learnt from our long association with the sub-Continent. We have so often been accused of dividing to rule. In fact our greater sin of omission has been to encourage a unity where little foundation for it existed. It might seem a heresy to quote the case of the Sudan, which, through a failure in 1899 to look into the future, was initiated as that freak in administration, a Condominium. A lot of damage was done when, in picturesque language, it was recorded that the Egyptian and British flags should always fly together in the Sudan. But the point to which I here draw attention is that whether or not there is now regret for the Egyptian association, whether or not that regret is justified, an artificial unity in the Sudan has been encouraged over the years which will result in trouble for someone in ten years' time. Nubian and pagan south have as much in common with Arab and Moslem north as have Tamils with the Punjabi Moslems on the Indian sub-Continent.

When in the 1850s we found ourselves in haphazard control of a great portion of North-West India through a drift into war with the Sikhs, there was a chance, if the man of vision could have been found, to have created a separate administrative unit owing no allegiance to Delhi whatsoever. Hindus and Sikhs were, it is true, sprinkled over the Punjab as if out of a pepper-pot. The natural direction of expansion was from a secure centre to an insecure North-West. Yet there was sufficient evidence of conditions to indicate that the people of this area— a rugged, agricultural community of Turko-Aryan stock—might more naturally develop to political and economic maturity if their administration had been centred on Lahore or Karachi.

As a matter of administrative convenience the old Indian sub-Continent was always an excessively large unit; while Karachi, the natural port for North-West India, could never come into its own so long as Bombay was regarded as the main port of a united India. We would then never have known the tragedy of 1947, for the minorities would have merged into the social structure of the majorities without realising the process, and the transition to Dominion status would in each case have been effected with the wisdom and goodwill which characterised the event in Ceylon.

Let us turn from the lessons of the past to the problems of today. In my recent return to the sub-Continent a feature of Pakistan's development which was constantly in evidence was that of duality. Two

Pakistans are emerging: the one in the tradition of the Indian Civil Service, cautious, sane but conservative, certainly appreciative of the Commonwealth association for reasons of both sentiment and practical advantage, yet completely loyal to Islam; the other, impatient in its desire to assert Pakistan's individuality more aggressively in world affairs than is attempted by the present Government, seeking to cut adrift from past associations, free in external policy to lead Islam away from the West, and, in internal affairs, determined to sweep away the rule of landlords and set up the social-welfare State.

Yet these two distinct pressures had one element in common. Both shared a belief that in the gap which separates India from Pakistan, Britain was on the side of the nation whose physical size and power carried most weight in international negotiation. This is a very serious charge, arising from the manner in which Kashmir negotiations have developed; and if in the past British policy has in fact lent encouragement to the belief—and I incline to the view that such is the case—it is now our sober responsibility to do all that is possible to regain lost confidence. The issues are discussed in the chapters on Kashmir, to which I would here only add that if and when a final international decision on Kashmir is given, and if that decision is in any way favourable to Pakistan but impossible of implementation, Pakistan will then with justice blame the United Nations and with less justice blame Britain. Within this context it is not unusual to hear Pakistanis of responsibility and position speak of cutting the Commonwealth connection. Furthermore, it is sad to find that those who fully appreciate the meaning of the Commonwealth are quite unable to advocate the strengthening of such bonds as now exist. Yet this is the nation whose powerful Foreign Minister on a memorable occasion once spoke of his " duty to King and Country ".[1] Today Sir Zafrullah Khan is probably more mindful of the Commonwealth association than most. In a long and heated debate on foreign policy in Parliament at Karachi on 27th March 1952 he came as near to its spirited defence as he deemed possible. Pakistan's extremely popular High Commissioner in London [2] had apparently spoken innocuously of an identity of ideals with the Commonwealth, and the Foreign Minister had been called to account for the lapse. " My attention was drawn to the fact that our High Commissioner in London had stated that we shared many ideals with the Commonwealth. Well, that is true; we do. We share ideals with them, but we also differ with regard to the method of achieving those ideals." If one may hazard a conjecture, I would say that so long as a Moslem League administration governs in Pakistan, the

---

[1] 4th September 1939. Sir Zafrullah Khan (Law Member, Viceroy's Executive Council and Leader of the Legislative Assembly), " I am certain everyone of us here fully realises the gravity of the crisis and is determined to do his duty to King and Country."

[2] In February 1952 Mr. M. A. H. Ispahani succeeded Mr. Rahimtulla Khan as High Commissioner in London, the latter moving to the Embassy in Paris.

L

country will remain within the Commonwealth. The further deduction that the Government will be able to resist pressure for a Commonwealth-Republic of the same pattern as India, is by no means certain.

In my belief two elements of controversy continue to prevent the consolidation of the Commonwealth ideal: in the case of Pakistan, the Kashmir issue; and in the case of India, the South African policy of *apartheid*. Though Pakistan's foreign policy may not at all times be in accordance with the views of Her Majesty's Government, there is no reason whatsoever why disagreement should not represent a healthy respect for the views of a friend. Recently our representative on the Security Council was instructed to oppose the presentation of the case of Tunisian nationalism to the Council in direct conflict with the attempt of Pakistan to achieve its hearing. Yet so far as we are aware no damage to Commonwealth relations resulted, and we agreed to differ in that spirit of compromise which we hope will govern all inter-Commonwealth negotiations.

We return to the conclusion that it is the mutual relations of India and Pakistan, rather than any inherent differences between Britain and either of the two partners, which hinders the Commonwealth in its ever-constant search for constructive progress. Those relations received emphasis from a curious alignment of loyalties which has developed since 1949 in the North-West. Whether by accident or design, Pakistan's relations with Afghanistan throw into relief a situation in which that country has turned increasingly to India for encouragement and moral support. To what extent, if any, Indian initiative was behind the development it is impossible to say. But the evident symptoms cannot be ignored. Afghan students who formerly went to Lahore now travel to Delhi. In the autumn of 1951 the Afghan Ambassador in Delhi entertained the Indian Prime Minister, when some heavily charged and rather meaningless platitudes were exchanged. I will return to this situation in a later chapter. I only use it here to draw attention to a general tendency in the Pakistan Press to exploit such occasions for the further confusion of relations both with India and Britain: nor has it prevented the Pakistan newspapers from suggesting extravagant remedies, such as the need to come to an understanding with Soviet Russia. Pakistan's differences with Afghanistan were at the time the means of a firm reaffirmation of Commonwealth solidarity by the Secretary for Commonwealth Relations. On 30th June 1949 Mr. Noel-Baker, in lending the Government's full support to the principle of Pakistan's inheritance of the rights of the former Government of India, was asked a question concerning the measure of our own commitments in the event of hostilities on the Afghan frontier. While giving no pledges in advance about hypothetical situations, it was made clear that the Commonwealth was to be regarded as a " bastion against aggression ". Our interpretation is surely that Britain would never stand idly aside to watch Pakistan fight her own battles where real aggression against her soil was involved.

The flexible nature of new Commonwealth loyalties was recently aptly demonstrated in neighbouring Ceylon at the time of the Ceylon elections.   The Indian Tamil community in Ceylon, employed mainly on the tea and rubber plantations, number over 800,000.   But they represent imported labour; so that when the time came to prepare electoral registers, few of them bothered to apply for Ceylon citizenship. The Ceylon Indian Congress, which watched their interests, seemed to disdain the offer of citizenship outside India.   Suddenly, however, when they became aware of the imminence of elections, they changed their view, and applications to register poured in at a rate with which the authorities were unable to cope.   Thus the Indian community, which had previously sent seven Congress members to the Ceylon Parliament, now lost their representation.   They replied with a *satyagraha* campaign of non-violence in the Gandhian tradition which fully taxed the resources of the Ceylon police.   Protests came from the Government of India, in spite of the fact that their representations were for the support of a renunciation of Indian citizenship.

Less welcome were protests from a group known as the Travancore-Cochin Trotskyist Party.   In spite of many hours spent by two Indian leaders squatting on the veranda of the Senate buildings near the Ceylon Prime Minister's office, the situation was allowed to lapse, and has now lost its immediate significance.

Soon after these events a New Zealand cruiser put in at Colombo, with a message of greeting for the Ceylon Prime Minister from the Prime Minister of New Zealand: "As the two smallest countries in the Commonwealth, we have much wider traditions in common, in that both our peoples prefer the democratic way of life, and we are both prepared to defend those ideals."   With these words the Captain of the cruiser *Bellona* handed over Mr. Holland's message; and one dwells on the two episodes, the one important, the other trivial, since they seem to indicate that the relationships established have really little to do with a colour consciousness of which events in South Africa continually remind us, but that they possess a transcending reality which other nations find difficult to understand.

I referred to a logical development by which one day this great partnership may discover that its evolution has resulted in a family of fifteen or sixteen members, each sharing in and contributing to the common welfare of the whole.   That being so, an interest and understanding of the Colonial Empire by us all will help to smooth the process of this consummation of our hopes and ambitions.   The pity is that the solicitude which is expected for an African colony seeking its independence is confined only to the goal.   The ways and means of its achievement, the administrative and economic problems to be solved and the immediate welfare of colonial peoples are of little interest to the self-governing component of Empire and Commonwealth.   This is true whether it be Australia or India, Canada or Pakistan that we consider.   Though India and to a lesser extent Pakistan watch carefully the welfare and progress of the African Bantu, it is with his status as an African rather than with the method of advancement of that status that they are concerned.   And since it is on the great African continent that the battles of Commonwealth evolution will be fought, I shall attempt to set out the issue particularly as it affects India and Dr. Malan's policy in South Africa.

More and more as facilities to present the case of frustrated African nationalism before the United Nations increase, will the complexity of inter-Commonwealth associations become apparent.   More and more will the effects of unequal education be evident.   In the General Assembly of the United Nations it counts for little that the representative of a country, through his personal polish and distinction, might conceivably be the only citizen capable of guarding his country's interests.   Some-times, as in the case of Yemen, he may even not be an inhabitant of the State he is sent to represent.[1]   Thus will the voice of political leadership in the African Colonies increasingly find ready international support, and in so far as India and Pakistan are concerned, the Union of South Africa becomes a common denominator for opposition in a mutual understanding.

In embracing the scope and complexity of the normal colour bar, this colossus of Africa harbours also a subsidiary problem, by reason of a small and powerful Indian community of 280,000 who are continually reminding India of her obligation to champion their local rights in South Africa.   Though within the Union they remain of their own free will in complete segregation from nine million Africans, in distant India the two communities represent the one common issue of human rights. Here is the gravest threat of all to the unity of the British Commonwealth.

The inhabitants of India and Pakistan comprise a great range and variety of the human race.   They speak twelve different languages and about 200 dialects.   But the Bantu of Africa enjoys a crude unity which draws the miners of the Rand to the cocoa-farmers of the Gold Coast.   The kind of argument which will become increasingly familiar is presented in the following way.   If a West African Nationalist was in conversation with an Englishman, this is how his case might sound.   "You assure us that our eventual goal will be reached when we arrive at that point of decision as to whether we are to become a Dominion of the British Commonwealth or strike out on our own.   We accept your assurance. But we find it very difficult to reconcile with your tacit acceptance in the Union of South Africa of a policy which cuts right across such worthy intentions.   We do not know whether you agree or disagree with Dr. Malan's policy.   You do not say : and in the absence of a clear statement we must assume that your fear of offending Dr. Malan is greater than any regard for our susceptibilities in the matter.   That being so, I doubt

---

[1] The Yemen is represented by Najib-Izzuddin, a Jebel Druze, who subsequently became a citizen of the Lebanon.

if there is a place for us in the future British Commonwealth." The argument does of course ignore the fact that relations between the European and African in West Africa are very different from those which exist in the South. Yet in that sentence, I think, lies Britain's dilemma.

I spoke of the identification of the Indian and the African in the eyes of the Indian sub-Continent as a simple issue of colour prejudice. In his Presidential Address to the Indian Assembly on 6th August 1951 Dr. Rajendra Prasad made this comment:

"I regret that the Union of South Africa has rejected a resolution passed by the General Assembly of the United Nations in regard to Indians in South Africa. This question does not affect India only. It is vital and affects the future of the world; because on the right solution of it depends the peace or conflict between great races. Only on the basis of equality and equal treatment of different races and peoples can there be peace in this world."

The claim that the matter was international sought its fulfilment a year later, when, in August 1952, the Government of India decided to raise the question of the passive resistance campaign in South Africa before the United Nations General Assembly, not in connection with their own quarrel with South Africa, which has confronted the United Nations for the last six years, but as a matter affecting peace in the African Continent, with international repercussions.[1]

In the year 1855 a letter was dispatched to the Government of India by the Governor of the forty-one-year-old British colony known as the Cape of Good Hope. It requested permission for the emigration of Indian labourers to assist colonists in the development of the sugar industry in Natal, which, twelve years previously, had been annexed to the Cape Colony from the Zulu kingdom of T'Chaka. Long before 1855 the coasts of Africa had known Indian traders. They had come in with the Portuguese in their early search and expansion to the East. But it was the imported labour from 1860 onwards which provided the great flow from India.

The European farmers who saw quick wealth in the growth and development of sugar all down the Natal coast had soon discovered that the local African natives, with their easy-going ideas of short-term engagement, were unreliable material on which to build the new agricultural industry; and so the Indians came, lending force in these later years to India's claim that her countrymen, now denied the normal rights of human relationship, were originally brought into South Africa by the forebears of those responsible for the denial. The claim may be somewhat over-simplified from the point of view of historical precision, but it has reason.

The newcomers were drawn from the poorest of the vast Indian

[1] The South African–Indian issue was high up on the agenda for the United Nations General Assembly in October 1952.

peasantry. Moreover, because their needs were simple they attracted to South Africa an equally humble trading community prepared to satisfy their modest domestic demands. Had the circumstances been such as to encourage higher-caste Indians to emigrate, the subsequent racial entanglement might have been more adaptable to a rational settlement. As it was, the Natal Government failed to foresee that a community who had so little to lose by leaving their homes might wish to remain in the land of their temporary adoption and there sow the seeds of a future full of hope and comparative prosperity.

The Indians remained. They acquired small holdings of land. They took to market-gardening and domestic service. But, above all, they drifted into Durban and took to trade, and their traders were prepared to undersell the Europeans and work harder for less profit. It was not until 1877 that Natal, which had become a separate Colony twenty-one years previously, awoke to the fact that there was now a large Indian community in the country which had no intention of leaving. The Natal Government hurriedly attempted to procure the prevention of further Indian immigration. Legislation to hamper and restrict Indians crept in, and by 1911 was sufficiently oppressive to invite the strong protests of a British Government of India. In the meanwhile Mr. Gandhi had arrived in Durban in 1893, and was to make his name in the championship of the Indian cause in South Africa. After 1927 the Indian Government and Union co-operated in schemes to encourage Indians in South Africa to return to their motherland. Free passages, a £20 bonus and an allowance of £10 for a child were the inducements. By 1947 some 94,000 Indians had returned, and it was realised that the limits of persuasion had been reached. The fact is that however irritating and oppressive may be the restrictions, Indians in Natal still prefer to think of Africa as their home, and they regard their African way of life as comparing favourably with the conditions they would enjoy in the land of their origin. The majority of those Indians who now form the subject of controversy have never seen India. Born and bred in South Africa, their status is not unlike that of the persecuted Jews of Europe, without, however, the appeal of a national home to offer them shelter from their persecution.

In 1946 the tension between the South African Government and the British Government of India increased when the Asiatic Land Tenure and Indian Representation Bills were presented in the Union Parliament. These Bills were designed mainly to prevent Indians from acquiring property in European areas, and at the same time they were given a limited measure of franchise. Once again a British Government of India protested. In December 1946, before the end of the British Raj, the Indian case was presented to the United Nations.

General Smuts, who took the view that the matter was one for domestic settlement, was nevertheless prepared to submit it to the International Court. Latterly, however, the view of those in South Africa who hold that international interest represents outside interference in a domestic matter has prevailed, which explains South Africa's complete indifference to subsequent resolutions on the welfare of Indians passed at Lake Success with monotonous regularity, and to similar expressions of international opinion on the status of South-West Africa.

In the winter of 1946 India withdrew her High Commissioner, leaving only a Secretary to conduct her affairs until November 1951, when he, too, was withdrawn from the contest. Trade sanctions were imposed with full effect by India, but less vigorously by Pakistan. Indeed, at a time when Pakistan was denied coal from India, she turned to South Africa to make good the shortage.[1]

Early in 1950 delegates from both India and Pakistan met the Minister of the Interior in Cape Town, and efforts were made to set up a conference of the three countries. But in the meanwhile in June 1950 the South African Parliament passed the Group Areas Bill, which successfully destroyed all prospect of negotiation, and in spite of some relaxation of tension between South Africa and Pakistan, the deadlock continues. Today it merits the classification of a crisis in embryo in Commonwealth affairs.

The specific proposal which recently afforded the background for controversy was a suggestion, sponsored by India, Indonesia, Burma, Iraq and Persia, for a three-nation committee. One member would be nominated by South Africa, one by India and Pakistan, and the third by the first two nominees in consultation.[2] Anticipating failure to reach agreement on the appointment of the third member, the proposals allowed for the further appointment of an individual arbitrator by the Secretary General of the General Assembly of the United Nations after sixty days, should the committee fail to start its enquiry.

By the spring of 1952 the Indian and African communities in the Union, never very happy together in their day-to-day domestic life, had been politically fused in a determination to fight the Government's policy. Already Mr. Manilal Gandhi had set the pattern for an imitation of his father's method and had courted arrest in protest against the new legislation.[3] On 31st May representatives of the African National

[1] Less than 30 per cent of those concerned are Moslems. The original immigrants were mostly Tamil and Hindi-speaking Indians. The case before the United Nations has undoubtedly suffered through the absence of a united Indian–Pakistani presentation.

[2] On 5th January 1952, the proposal was passed in the special (ad hoc) Political Committee: forty-one for; two against (Australia and South Africa) with thirteen abstentions. The Soviet supported the proposal. On 12th January the General Assembly confirmed the proposal by forty-four votes to nil. South Africa took no part in any of the proceedings. A further proposal in the Political Committee by Israel was that the Secretary-General, Mr. Trygve Lie, should personally intervene to bring about a resumption of negotiations.

[3] On 21st September 1951 Mr. Gandhi walked into the Durban municipal library reserved for Europeans. He then moved on to a suburban railway station and sat on a bench marked " Reserved for Europeans ". The authorities ignored him, but

Congress and South African Indian Congress met at Port Elizabeth and decided on a national campaign of passive resistance. An order was served on Dr. Y. M. Dadoo, the President of the Indian Congress, to resign his appointment. The order was defied, and Dr. Dadoo was later arrested at Johannesburg for attending meetings despite a ban imposed under the new "Suppression of Communism Act.". Throughout the summer of 1952 the passive resistance campaign gathered force, with Indians and Africans offering themselves for mass arrest in Durban, Johannesburg and Port Elizabeth. In August for the first time Indian women joined in the campaign. It was against this familiar background of martyrdom that the Indian Government announced their intention to bring the passive resistance movement before the United Nations; and in doing so they had the support of countries as far apart as Indonesia and the nations of the Arab League.

In India itself 24th August was celebrated as "South Africa Day". From the many reports of enthusiastic meetings one comment seemed of particular significance. Speaking in Madras, Mr. Jagjivan Ram, the Minister for Communications, sounded a mild warning. Dealing with the help they could offer their brothers in South Africa he added these words: "But in sending our moral support we should not give the impression that India would come to their aid if *satyagraha* should fail".

As the months went by the situation deteriorated. The latest development which it is possible to record is the introduction in February 1953 of two measures which were challenged not only by the coloured communities, but also by many elements of the European population. These were the Public Safety Bill and the Criminal Law (Amendment) Bill, introduced by the Minister of Justice, Mr. Swart. Both these measures sought to arm the Government with the most drastic powers, and since one of them appears to be permanent, there is every justification for the belief that the Government have encroached on the normal and legitimate rights of the citizen. A law which makes it an offence to attempt to repeal, modify or vary existing laws is certainly something outside the operation of normal democracy. Of more definite application to the Indian community is the proposed Bill to prevent entry into the Union of the wives and children of Indians domiciled in South Africa, a direct refutation of a previous measure in 1932—the Cape Town Agreement—which at the time was regarded as promising a new relationship between India and South Africa. The Torch Commando movement, many advocates, and members of the Church, including the Bishop of Johannesburg, have condemned a policy of despair. It remains to be seen if the verdict of those who have the vote will follow their lead in the coming elections.

These are the bare bones of a story which, if given substance of flesh and blood, would tell of human cruelty on a scale irreconcilable with the

---

eventually he repeated the same process at Durban main station and a summons was issued.

aspirations of a world now conscious of its obligations to its less fortunate citizens. The conditions are those which enabled the representative from Burma to quote the case of a South African in Durban forced to see his Burman wife into a separate lift when they find their way up to their top-floor apartment, which apparently they share on precarious terms outside the law. To the outsider the astonishing feature of this spectre of social deformity is that it presses on to its unknown destination waving the scales of justice in one hand and the Bible, if not actually the New Testament, in the other!

So far as India is concerned, it is hardly relevant to argue that a community is involved which might be considered to have lost its Indian loyalties. India regards them as her children, and her sentiments cannot be ignored.

This is no place to raise the great moral issue of the clash of colours as it occurs here on its most concentrated of battle-grounds. But, as citizens of the British Commonwealth, we have a duty to think out at least an intelligent approach to the future. In so far as the late General Smuts bequeathed a racial policy to the United Party in South Africa, it might be defined as the acceptance of the inevitability of a gradual assimilation of the colours in a process spread out, not over the years, but over a century. Such a policy should logically recognise the need for European leadership, and at the same time allow talent and integrity to find expression from any quarter, whatever the colour, for the common welfare and progress. No man, judged worthy by the highest standards of moral conduct and ability, should be denied the fruits of his labour or the opportunity to make his contribution.

But for our purposes the immediate interest lies in the effect of the South African policy on Commonwealth relations, with particular reference to a situation by which an Indian Republic and a South African Union on the brink of republican status continue as partners within the same great enterprise. An examination of Mr. Nehru's many expressions of indignation at the policy of Dr. Malan reveals the significant feature that never once has he regarded the situation as to be exploited for the purpose of a move to leave the Commonwealth. Indeed, on at least one occasion he has referred to events in South Africa as a reason for remaining within the fold, claiming that thereby he was in a better position to influence policy and its direction.[1]

The question arises—and for us this is the core of the matter—as to what should be the attitude of a British Government if and when that unhappy situation should result in which Britain is placed in the position of arbitrator between these two contending members of the family.[2]

[1] Debate on an Opposition motion to reduce the financial appropriation for the Foreign Ministry, Delhi, 12th June, 1952.

[2] On 2 January 1952, in the ad hoc Political Committee, United Nations General Assembly, Mr. Tambe, the representative of Liberia, bluntly asked the question as to how long South Africa and India could remain together within the Commonwealth.

In which direction should we lend the weight of our opinion and authority? I can only contribute the personal reaction of a mild student of these issues. It will have been noticed how previously a British Government in India was quite prepared to fight India's battles in South Africa, so that there would be nothing inconsistent in a readiness to support the Indian point of view, even though apparently another member of the Commonwealth, Australia, associates itself with South Africa.[1] In a subsequent chapter is developed the conception that India may one day effectively interpret Britain throughout Asia. At this stage I would only suggest that if we deem the maintenance of our position in Asia to be of more importance than the defence of the South African Union in an effort to secure its continued adherence to the Commonwealth, we should be unwise not to shape our policy accordingly. That is the practical point of view; and in recording it we ask ourselves wherein lies the value of attempting to retain countries in partnership once they have decided that their destiny is better served by severing the last link of acceptance of the Crown. Is not the quality of the family relationship more important than its size? If South Africa should decide to cut the painter, serious issues concerning our obligations to three Protectorates would arise. There would be economic and strategic problems to be solved, and no one can pretend the loss would be welcome. But the position would be one of even greater tragedy if India and Pakistan were to desert us on an issue which could be interpreted as an abandonment of principle. Therein lies the key to all policy. Great principles of human rights must be upheld, even though the immediate loss may loom ominously ahead. The maintenance of justice will one day reap its reward.

There is yet one more factor in this maze of racial controversy. We all regard the prospect of Communist encroachment in India with fear and horror. Recently the Indian Communists have been able to score many points at the expense of other political groups by claiming that they, and they alone, are in the van in fighting Asia's battles on African soil. That is one legacy—and an important one—of South Africa's anti-Communist legislation.

Amidst these great controversies—matters for despair when one pauses to think out the possible course of future fortunes within the Commonwealth—we search for any signs of hope and encouragement; and we find them in those messages of sentiment which from time to time are exchanged between Britain and India, Britain and Pakistan, and India and Pakistan. Do words really mean what they say? Or are they mere gestures of conventional diplomacy? The President of India greets Her Majesty the Queen on her official birthday. The Prime Minister of Pakistan on the same occasion supplements his official message with a glowing tribute not only to the Monarchy as an institution, but also to the Commonwealth in all its failures and hopes for a contribution

[1] See footnote 2, p. 167.

to the progress of mankind.[1] When it came to messages on the great
Day of Independence, the exchanges between India and Pakistan were
shorter and more formal.   Nevertheless the sense of a desire for friendship was there, and while the courtesies of language continue we should
never abandon our faith in the future.   Let us then be thankful for the
outward and visible signs, for the acceptance of an invitation to Jawaharlal
Nehru to attend the Coronation, for the presentation of an Ispahan rug
by Pakistan's High Commissioner to the Royal Air Force College at
Cranwell.   So long as good manners govern our day-to-day relations,
it will be the more difficult to stoop to that cheap abuse which would
inevitably precede any retrograde process of deserting the Commonwealth.   Nor are the statements in internal political controversy such
as would suggest that there is any lingering resentment at the Commonwealth association in the mind of Mr. Nehru.   In a speech in the House
of the People on 12th June 1952 which ranged over every aspect of foreign
policy, Nehru defended India's position in the Commonwealth in terms
which were significant for the practical advantages which were stressed.
India found it easier to get the goods and services she required from Britain
and the United States rather than from any other country.   For him the
Commonwealth meant, "meeting together once or twice yearly,
occasional consultation or reference to each other, and certain advantages
which I get by being able to influence larger policies, aside from the
normal method of doing so.   In other respects it does not get in my way
at all.   If I admit the right of the Commonwealth to interfere in the
affairs of a member, then I cease to be in the Commonwealth."   Such
was the approach in face of criticism, and it was the politician who was
speaking.   But when it comes to a direct message to the British people
on the fifth anniversary of Independence the language and emphasis are
different; for then it is that the man speaks from the breadth and
generosity of his heart :—

   "We remember the trials and difficulties of these five years, our
   achievements and our lack of achievements. We remember above
   all that day, five years ago, when the United Kingdom and India
   set an example of peaceful and co-operative settlement of a difficult
   and complicated problem which had previously given rise to long
   and continued conflict and all the unhappiness and bitterness that
   came in its train, and yet by a stroke of statesmanlike wisdom that
   conflict was ended without bitterness and in friendship. . . . On

[1] "The Commonwealth of Nations of which Her Majesty is the head is a unique
institution in the present-day world.   It has an elasticity and adaptability to changing
circumstances which is its own peculiar characteristic.   The Commonwealth is
based on the willing assent and voluntary co-operation of a number of free and
sovereign nations whom historical circumstances have brought together. . . . The
monarchy too has shown an admirable capacity to keep abreast of the times and
hence it retains its place and esteem. . . . Her Majesty Queen Elizabeth has been
nurtured in the fine traditions of constitutional monarchy, fostered by her illustrious
ancestors. . . ." (Prime Minister of Pakistan, 5th June 1952.)

this day I send my greetings to our countrymen abroad and to the people of the United Kingdom, who have come nearer to us since the old enforced bonds were broken." [1]

Here surely is the key to our relations with the sub-Continent; and while the present direction of affairs both in India and Pakistan continues in that spirit of understanding, we need not worry overmuch at such diversions as protests at the flying of the Union Jack or the inadvertent playing of " God Save the Queen ".[2]   Neither must we expect too much of those who, as nations in the political sense, are still in the infancy of experience.   An old adage which comes out of the East says that " he who seeketh the perfect friend remains friendless ".   In returning such wisdom to the East, our ship of Commonwealth may yet weather the storms of international jealousy and false ambitions which are always ready enough to carry her on to the rocks of disintegration.

If we place the post-war international tendencies in their perspective, we see that one movement as formidable almost as that of the issues of rival ideologies is the tendency to blocs both of power and numbers.   It is no accident that the new Arab–Asian bloc cuts into international negotiation to create a regional loyalty comparable to the unity of Europe or the Americas.   Yet it is surely wrong that nations should continue to cling to regional integrations, particularly when the regions so clearly separate out into groups of brown and white.   Across these divisions the British Commonwealth still stands for a unity which cuts through the grouping of colour.   Long may it continue to exert its mellowing influence, even though within its family membership the stresses and strains of *apartheid* create their own domestic tension.

Tolerance, to be effective, must be a two-way traffic.   We ask the new States to forgive many of the errors of ignorance in the British public; for they are patently obvious when one starts to cross-examine the people of Britain about the lives of 400 million citizens of the Commonwealth. We ask ourselves, too, if there are any measures left untaken which could give our relationships with India and Pakistan life and reality.   If, as I believe, the Royal Family have won for themselves a status beyond the petty controversies of local politics, what happier manifestation of the quality of our Commonwealth could there be than an invitation from Delhi and Karachi to the greatest of all Commonwealth Ambassadors? [3]

[1] Mr. Nehru is also responsible for one of the most British of definitions of the Commonwealth. In a speech greeting Mr. Menzies from Australia in Delhi on 27th December 1950 he described it as " that rather strange and old collection of nations which seems to prosper most in adversity ".

[2] On the Queen's birthday in 1952 the flying of the Union Jack over the Indian Parliament building led to some heated exchanges in the House of the People.   About the same time it was reported that a village band in South India had played the British national anthem on a festival occasion because they knew of no other tune to play.

[3] Some of the material in this chapter was the subject of an address to the Royal Empire Society on 20th November 1952 and is reproduced with the kind consent of the Editor, *United Empire*, from the January–February 1953 issue.

CHAPTER ELEVEN

PAKISTAN AND HER NEIGHBOURS
(THE MIDDLE EAST)

I F the British Commonwealth was comparatively unaware of the
nature of the great transition in 1947, the world at large was completely ignorant. The event was hailed rightly as the greatest
experiment in progress to nationhood in history and as a matter for
mutual pride in Britain, India and Pakistan. The subsequent focus of
attention was confined to such obvious matters as the relations of Pakistan
and India, the problem of Kashmir and the operation of the new Indian
Constitution. The fact that policy over a very large area of the globe
from North Africa to the China Seas had overnight received an entirely
fresh orientation escaped notice. To take but one example, a trail of
events which ended in the abandonment of the Persian oil-fields and a
refinery worth £300 million in no small measure derived from circumstances by which troops from India were no longer available to protect
our interests in Khuzistan. To say this is in no way either to support or
condemn policy in Persia at the time. It is merely to state a fact. In
these chapters I hope to examine some of the implications in this new
direction of international affairs.

We could perhaps feel happier over the future if we could record that
the emergence of Pakistan and India had resulted in cohesion and consistency in a new purpose. But those same conditions which from the
turn of the century had gradually accumulated to force the events of 1947
have lingered on to bequeath their legacy of divergent interests in the
international field today. Inevitably Pakistan turns to the Moslem world
of the Middle East, while India is drawn to China and South-East Asia.
An Englishman might be forgiven if he could hope that in this way
Britain's policy might receive more successful interpretation to the
countries of the East through the medium of two members of the
Commonwealth family than has hitherto been possible through the
normal channels of diplomacy. It is too soon to say: but it is at least
certain that we are fully justified in generally regarding both Pakistan
and India as cushioning influences of moderation for the promotion of
harmony as between East and West, rather than as elements which might
in certain circumstances further estrange some rather doubtful relationships. Unfortunately this somewhat natural reaction of Englishmen is
often interpreted as a desire merely to perpetuate domination in the East
through the medium of a pair of Governments maintained by local
stooges of Britain.

We will deal first with the aspect which is geographically nearer home. Pakistan's position in relation to the Middle East is in a sense comparable to that of Britain in relation to Europe. As a vital influence in the fate of Europe, and as the focus of a great Empire and Commonwealth, Britain experiences some difficulty in reconciling loyalties which could be considered as in conflict. In exactly the same way, Pakistan feels a tug in one direction—to Britain—and in another to the Moslem world of the Middle East. The first is based on practical considerations of material advantage no less than on the associations of the past. It would be very strange if a country whose whole corporative life and civil administration derived from British thought and method should decide to sever the links of so much friendship built up in the process.

The second tug—towards Islam—is no less real for the fact that it is an emotional rather than a practical appeal. But in recording this it should be borne in mind that Pakistan's problem in living up to the demands of a new loyalty is by no means a simple one. Sir Zafrullah Khan has frequently emphasised that his country in no way seeks the leadership of the Moslem world; yet it could hardly be unnatural if this largest and most powerful of Moslem nations should gradually draw the following of a number of countries in the Middle East, and greatness thus be thrust upon not unwilling shoulders. Pakistan's advocacy of the cases of both Libya and Tunisia should be placed no higher or lower than that. In these and other situations the forensic skill both of Sir Zafrullah Khan and Mr. A. S. Bokhari, and a desire to exploit their talent have been a considerable factor.

But there are voices within Pakistan which would go far beyond this logical approach. In March this year a Convention in Karachi was summoned with the object of setting up Anjuman-i-Shabal-Muslimeen (Moslem People's Organisation). It drew up an eight-point programme the main purpose of which was to work for the creation of " Islamistan " not as a mere matter of common cultural or religious interests, but as a practical force, with all the qualities of a " bloc " pledged to defend mutual interests against alleged attack. Its sponsor, Chaudhri Khaliquzzaman, defined the objective as a " free and independent Islamistan ". His eighth point was a demand for Arabic to be recognised as the *lingua franca* of the Moslem world, a proposal hardly to the taste of East Bengal, or, for that matter, anywhere in South-East Asia. One wonders exactly how the people of East Pakistan will accept his recent appointment to their Governership if his views on the language issue remain so emphatic.[1] In his insistence on the scrupulous observance of non-violence, Chaudhri Khaliquzzaman may have had Mahatma Gandhi in mind, and there was also a hint of the Indian example in the desire " to escape being drawn into the vortex of power politics ". Nevertheless it was to be a bloc, not in rivalry, but in co-operation to similar Islamic institutions.

In presenting his programme in Karachi in January 1952, he informed

[1] See Appendix IV, Pakistan (c).

the public that in reply to an inquiry from Al Haj Amin el Husseini [1] he had requested him to inform Allama Kashani, the Persian leader of Fedayen Islam, that he and other friends would be only too glad to attend an inter-Islamic Conference to be convened in Teheran. Kashani enjoys the reputation of harbouring more concentrated hate for European associations than any leader in the Middle East, and the Chaudhri would certainly find his principles of non-violence under fire should he ever make the journey to Teheran.

In January a Pakistan Branch of the Akhwan-ul-Muslimeen [2] was formed in Karachi under the leadership of Mr. Sharafat Hussein. Again its purpose was Islamic renaissance. I once had the opportunity of a long talk with Sheikh Hassan-el-Banna, the first leader of the parent Egyptian organisation. The brotherhood was then regarded by British officials as a highly explosive institution, and when its headquarters were raided in December 1948, enough arms and ammunition were discovered to have disrupted the normal life of Egypt. Nevertheless, I was impressed with the leader's frank appreciation of the futility of Egyptian public life at the time, and a passionate desire to clean it up as a matter of religious obligation. His dislike of Englishmen, it seemed, was only part of his bitter hatred of all foreigners. It was therefore no surprise to read that on 25th January a Punjab branch of the organisation had met in Lahore under Maulana Abdus Sattar Khan Niazi when the speaker had advocated an economic boycott of British goods and material help to the Egyptians, "against the British tyranny". Exactly the same approach was taken by another organisation, the Jinnah Awami Moslem League. In this case the motive is more definitely an exploitation of the theme of Western imperialism than the pursuit of an Islamic purpose, for the J.A.M. League has thwarted ambitions at home, and personal jealousies as the background to its policy. On 13th January in Karachi Mr. H. S. Suhrawardy, an Awami leader from East Bengal, called on the Pakistan Government to support "our brethren in Iran and Egypt, where British Imperialists are trampling down the national aspirations of two Moslem countries". The attack was simultaneously being pursued in the Press, and on 17th January the *Pakistan Times* published a leading article, which is reproduced as an Appendix. It is given to the reader in full, since it sums up forcefully and ruthlessly the sentiment typical of a restless community of intellectuals whose views have for a year or so been prominent in the English and Urdu Press.

These examples, chosen at random from many similar statements, were the kind of items of news which confronted the citizens of Pakistan in January 1952 over the brief period when I was again in the country; and there is no reason to suppose that the same attitude does not continue.

---

[1] More familiarly known as "the Mufti of Jerusalem".
[2] The Moslem Brotherhood. The founder, Sheikh el Banna, was assassinated in Cairo in February 1949. Previously the Brotherhood had been dissolved in December 1948.

In meeting such attacks what is in the mind of the Government of the day? Are these the views of those in office, and if not how does the Government attempt to answer those who, for different reasons, would wish to see their country in the van of a march of united Islam? It is doubtful if men such as Mr. Shaukat Hayat and Mian Iftikharuddin have really thought out the final results of the policies they advocate [1] and the irresponsibility of many who enjoy the stimulating sound of slogans appears to be an infection from polemics in the Middle East.

The official record of Pakistan in international relations has hardly been one of negativism. The cases of Libya, Eritrea, Somaliland, Morocco and Tunisia all at times received the Pakistan Foreign Minister's advocacy. Indeed, in the case of Libya, Sir Zafrullah Khan has claimed that had it not been for Pakistan, Libya would today consist of three States under the trusteeships of three European Powers. It so happens that this particular case is regarded by many serious students of the international scene as the greatest folly yet perpetrated by the United Nations: a Government in one capital, a monarch in another greeted by a bomb on the only occasion on which he has visited his western city, and a new nation initiated without a single indigenous qualified doctor throughout its territory. But that should in no way deter us from understanding and admiring the sincere determination of Sir Zafrullah to help the plight of honest patriots in countries where they are still deprived of their final right of self-government. It must be exasperating for educated Tunisians to watch Libyan nationhood receiving international encouragement when Tunisia, with its far higher standard of education and economic viability, has still to watch and wait.

"Whenever there is a question of liberty and independence from imperialism or of opposing colonialism, of pushing forward a march towards freedom, Pakistan is always second to none. Whether it be the cause of the country that is awaiting its independence, we have always supported it." In these familiar terms Sir Zafrullah Khan bravely defended his policy,[2] and though we sometimes tire of hearing the selfless labour of countless fine missionaries of progress invariably dismissed as crude and selfish exploitation, in the particular case of the official Pakistan policy there is much to invite our sympathy in appreciating the manner in which Sir Zafrullah manages to temper the inevitable emotional and popular approach with a sane appreciation of truth.

---

[1] In the last week in March 1952 these two gentlemen attacked Sir Zafrullah Khan, describing him as " an agent of British Imperialism ". Iftikaruddin's own reactions to British policy in Egypt and Iran were summed up in the words, " We are tied to the chariot-wheels of the United States and the United Kingdom ". Shaukat Hayat is the son of the late Sir Sikander Hayat Khan, Premier of the Punjab, and much-respected leader of the Punjab Unionist Party during the Second World War. His son held a commission in Skinner's Horse. Mr. Iftikaruddin is the wealthy owner of the *Pakistan Times*, whose Left-wing sympathies seem difficult to reconcile with the somewhat affluent nature of his social background.

[2] Pakistan Assembly, 27th March 1952.

Truth in the Middle East is often no friend of those who aspire to power on the short cut to patriotism which thrives on hating the British; and it is clear that Sir Zafrullah Khan is well aware of the need for a spirit of critical self-examination throughout the Arab world as the true foundation for negotiations with the West. " It is devoutly to be hoped that, in the first instance, law and order in all Middle East territories, in which Pakistan is also included, will be impartially, firmly and, if necessary, even ruthlessly maintained." This was his comment on the disturbing picture of bewilderment which the Arab world has for months presented. Of Persia and Egypt in June he observed : " Our sympathy with them is very deep, but it does not mean that on account of these factors, if any of these countries were in the wrong and we thought that they were in the wrong, we would nevertheless support them simply because they are neighbours or Moslem States or Asiatic States ".[1] Such caution and the refusal to be pushed into a more spectacular support of Egypt were to be fully justified by the course of events in that country; and many of those who had shown such vocal bravery in the advocacy of active measures had subsequently to nurse their disillusionment, conscious of the poverty of their own failure to think clearly.

When, however, General Neguib came to power, Egypt's relations with Pakistan revived under a new stimulation. A Press delegation from Cairo arrived in Karachi in March 1953, and verbal bouquets were exchanged. Simultaneously Sir Zafrullah Khan spoke of the mutual relations of the two countries in lavish terms at the Officers' Club in Cairo. At the time Mr. Tayyeb Hussein, Chargé d'Affaires for Pakistan, had just been appointed as temporary Chairman of the new Governor-General's commission in the Sudan; an event which lent some point to Egyptian effusive professions of sentiment and unswerving friendship.[2] It is in such situations that the claims of the Commonwealth to a more enduring if less assertive relationship are tested.

So long, then, as the present direction of policy is allowed to continue we will see a dual purpose in operation. Just as India's foreign policy derives from the intensely international outlook of one man, so, too, does Pakistan's policy draw its vitality from a single mind. Sir Zafrullah Khan experiences both the elation of a crusade and the logic of a need to temper that crusade with a full appreciation of truth. Britain is not an evil octopus seeking the strangulation of weak Arab countries. Those who have shouted loudest for the unity of the Nile Valley are not all martyrs in a crusade of service for their country. Israel and the Arab world must settle their differences. The countries of the Middle East must co-operate among themselves and with Israel for the general economic advancement of the Arab world. As to Persia, the Persians were entirely within their rights to nationalise their own oil, and such

[1] Press Conference, 2nd June 1952.
[2] " It would suffice for public opinion in Egypt to know that love and regard for Egypt in Pakistan have reached a stage of adoration." *Al Misri*, 2nd March 1953.

M

action was in keeping with the example set by a British Government within its own country. But the method of execution would require mutual give and take. The analogy of the British Government's nationalisation policy is always tempting in discussing the Persian oil case, though in fact the circumstances are very different. For our purposes we should note that the official support for Doctor Moussadeq is again guarded and cautious. Not a few good Pakistani technicians of the Anglo-Iranian Oil Company have reason to curse the folly which in 1951 drove the Persian Government relentlessly on to destroy their greatest single economic asset. Meanwhile events in Egypt may have caused irresponsible critics in Pakistan to pause and reconsider the principles involved in Persia. For the fundamental issues of West and East in relationship are the same in both cases.

I have indicated that Pakistan's official direction of foreign policy follows a different course from that which certain very vocal elements in the country would pursue. One exception came to my notice and, I confess, shocked me at the time. Throughout January 1952, Raja Ghazanfar Ali, the Pakistan Ambassador in Teheran, was busy in the West Punjab expressing his personal views on the Persian oil case to the Press and to any audience which would offer him a hearing. I draw attention to one incident from among several which were reported in the *Pakistan Times*. Under the auspices of the Punjab University Historical Society, Ghazanfar Ali addressed students and staff, using a whole battery of *clichés* to elaborate his picture of a Persia groaning under unscrupulous foreign exploitation. The familiar theme was coupled with some thickly spread sentiment concerning the personality of Doctor Moussadeq in particular, and the virtues of Persia in general. Sometimes the speaker sank to utter banality, as when addressing the Punjab Olympic Association. " In Iran the Government helped sports organisations in every possible manner. Even the Shah of Iran himself takes an interest in sport! " It so happened that I was able to challenge Raja Ghazanfar Ali in Karachi on his views. He took my heated assault with good grace; but it was interesting to note that we quickly collected a few silent young men around us who listened with rapt attention. I apologised later for my manners on a purely social occasion, but they replied that, as they had never heard the British point of view, they were only too glad to listen to what I had to say. The motive which actuates a man of distinction so to abuse his official position has something to do with a weakness for notoriety. But from the British point of view the very damaging effect of his misrepresentations might well have merited some official protest.

It would be wrong to assume that the official direction of Pakistan's policy necessarily eschews the popular appeal. On 6th July 1951, addressing a huge congregation after Id ul Fitr prayers, the late Liaquat Ali Khan spoke forcefully of the need for all Moslem countries to get together and proclaim their ideology and code of life. But the emphasis was on the contribution which Islam in general and Pakistan in particular could make to the common good; which is a very different approach from the sulky, defensive attitude of those who would believe their way of life to be in constant danger of attack from the West.

The public attacks which were recently directed at the Pakistan Foreign Minister were unfortunately based not on the pros and cons of foreign policy, but on purely personal issues. Sir Zafrullah Khan has for some time been the most prominent member of a sect of Moslems, the Ahmadiyyas, whose views are not quite in accord with orthodox Islamic doctrine and belief. In the third week in May 1951 a mob of hooligans attempted to break up the annual meeting of the Ahmadiyya Association in Karachi. This was followed by a demand that the Ahmadiyyas should be declared a minority community and the Foreign Minister should be dismissed.[1] Sir Zafrullah has withstood the assault, and the episode is closed, but not necessarily forgotten. Whatever his enemies may feel about his beliefs, there is general appreciation of the power and skill of his oratory. Sometimes the most subtle of the legal profession fail to convey a sense of their own conviction and urgency. Yet Sir Zafrullah is able to impress his listener with the sincerity of his heart no less than the process of his mind. If there be a fault, it lies in a tendency to over-statement and the aggressive confirmation of a point by stating it in every possible way. Reading his speeches I am reminded of a Mahler symphony! Sometimes, too, we are puzzled by a sudden hint of frustration, the slash of the whip in a bitter moment of oratory. "Our emotions are to-day held in greater bondage to the West than before independence. We are sinking deeper and deeper into intellectual slavery." Here is strong sentiment not to be easily interpreted. Nevertheless it will be a long time before a new State entering the rough-and-tumble of international negotiation will be able to claim the services of so impressive an advocate; and it may have been with this in mind that the Prime Minister of Pakistan requested him to accept an invitation from the Foreign Minister of Turkey to undertake a tour of the Middle East in the spring of 1951. It was this tour which was subsequently represented as being staged in the interests of the United States and the United Kingdom, "for purposes of bringing Middle East countries into the fold ".

I have stressed the individual qualities of Pakistan's Foreign Minister because so much of the welcome assistance afforded to the Middle East is due to an appreciation of the personal contribution he can make. Beyond this, there is at present no tangible movement amounting to a reorientation of loyalties. In the Persian Gulf, in Bahrein and Kuwait, I

---

[1] See Appendix IV, Pakistan (f).
The demand came from a West Punjab political group, the Ahrars. The Ahrar movement was founded in 1934, and was at first in close sympathy with the Indian Congress, combining religious zeal with rural economic improvement. Instructions have since been issued to the effect that Ministers must not exploit their position for purposes of promoting their religious beliefs.

found that the old Bombay trade associations were of more interest than any links with Karachi. The Arab Press in Iraq gives no particular prominence to news from Pakistan, nor am I aware of any movement such as long-term plans to exchange students which might have been expected. The links are confined to the highest diplomatic levels. More definite perhaps are the indications of an understanding with Turkey, where the greater solidarity of Turkish administration has attractions of a practical nature to offer.

The position might be modified if and when Pakistan can provide armed forces for defensive purposes outside her territory. Early in July 1952 the Pakistan Government informed the United Nations that they could furnish no troops for the purposes of the General Assembly's January resolution on collective measures, since troops could not be spared so long as the Kashmir problem remained unsolved. Thus the only two local forces of consequence in the Middle East—the Arab Legion and the Pakistan Army—are both tied down to watching with suspicion the moves of their immediate neighbours, when we could wish they were available for integration in a wider system of defence against a far more formidable enemy. The availability of a Pakistan Division either in a Middle East system deriving from Western patronage or in the existing Arab Security Pact might well connote a new sense of vitality in the hitherto rather cautious development of Pakistan's Arab associations. That these associations have yet to be consolidated is indicated by such features as a conference of Prime Ministers recently convened in Karachi but never held.[1]

In our reflections on Pakistan's position in Middle East strategy there is one development which has recently been prominent to confuse our thinking. Western talk of harnessing Pakistan forces into a Middle East defence organisation will, it seems, be unpalatable to India. In January 1953 stories were spread around that Pakistan had been invited by Britain and the United States to join a Middle East defence system. The Indian National Congress, which at the time was sitting in annual session at Hyderabad, reacted violently. Accepting the rumours as accomplished fact, the Anglophobes of Congress spoke of India leaving the Commonwealth.

What is the objective truth? Pandit Nehru, with logic, still regards the sub-Continent as one from the aspect of strategy. If Pakistan were to be drawn into a major defensive system, then in war a threat to Pakistan becomes equally a threat to India. At this moment inevitably a situation in which Pakistan might be committed to active measures to support the West, while India remained neutral, could only tend still further to separate the two countries. From this stage it is but a short step to the suggestion which would obviously come from Congress

[1] The Conference which had been suggested in April 1952 was postponed until after the Ramzan, when it was again indefinitely postponed owing to " pressing domestic difficulties in some of the countries concerned ".

extremists, that Pakistan was being armed by the West for a war against India. Sir Alexander Clutterbuck, Britain's High Commissioner in India, denied that any overtures had been made to Pakistan, since when the matter has receded into the background. But it is only natural to believe that it might well return in the form of a definite and practical proposition. Meanwhile India's emphasis on the value and purpose of an Arab–Asian bloc in international affairs can be interpreted as a move to draw the attention of the East away from developments of a pan-Islamic nature and focus thought on the wider aspect of Arab and Asian support for Eastern peoples allegedly suffering under Western Colonial domination. In such a policy India naturally has in mind the effect of pan-Islamic talk of a political complexion, on her own large Moslem minority.

On the economic side, it will be recalled that the first Islamic economic conference was staged in Karachi in November 1949. The second conference moved to Teheran, but Mr. Ghulam Mohammed, the present Governor-General of Pakistan, presided. We are promised a third conference in Damascus; and it is in the promotion of economic co-operation that Pakistan can make its most useful contribution. For the country is in just that stage of development which is able to display an agricultural people eager to press forward with a limited programme of industrialisation with outside assistance.[1] There are Pakistani realists of sufficient experience who could perhaps help such a lame duck as Persia, now surrounded in its own defensive ring of national pride. If Pakistan's diplomacy could further prevail on the Arab world and Israel to co-operate for their mutual economic advancement, her leaders could indeed take pride in a contribution to international peace and progress such as no Western Power has yet been near to achieving.

Such is the measure of Pakistan's encroachment in the Middle East, and much of the nature of future development will depend on the tendencies at work in her own internal situation in its constant state of evolution. On the one hand are the Mullahs and their followers, seeking ever to advance the cause of Islamistan. In contrast are a group of practical capable administrators trained in the traditions of the old Indian Civil Service. If the former are able to influence policy, we shall see such movements as Fedayan Islam and the Akhwan-ul-Muslimeen receiving support and encouragement abroad and a corresponding relaxation of Western associations. If the latter can keep control, it will be with the more progressive elements in the Middle East that Pakistan's interest will lie: with countries such as Turkey and Syria. If that is to be the pattern for the future, the more conservative pockets of Arab stagnation may follow the lead. The danger of Pakistan sinking to the level of statesmanship

---

[1] In October 1950 a training-centre was inaugurated in Lahore for students drawn from all over Asia. The first course was attended by parties from eleven countries. The project was sponsored by the World Food and Agricultural Organisation, the Pakistan Government, the International Bank and other international agencies.

which for years has governed Middle East polemics will have been obviated.

That the appeal of Islamistan is by no means infallible is apparent when we note the confused relations between Pakistan and her immediate neighbours, the Afghans. We have lately not heard quite so much of the movement encouraged from Kabul known as " Pathanistan ". But in 1949 relations with Afghanistan had so deteriorated that the prospect of war was by no means fantastic. Here was a gap in the solidarity of Islam which led us to wonder what exactly is the nature of sentiment to which appeal is made.

In April 1949 Shah Mahmud, the Afghan Prime Minister, was at work initiating a campaign which would have had his country believe that the frontier tribes inhabiting the wild stretch of country along the mutual frontier with Pakistan were in fact Afghans. There was talk of rescuing " our Afghan brothers beyond the Durand line ". The tribes themselves, whose territory had for years constituted a formidable playground for the old Indian Army, were quick to renounce this solicitude, and at a tribal *jirgah* of the Khyber Agency a resolution was passed resenting Afghan interference and confirming loyalty to Pakistan. Later in June the British Government supported the Pakistan protests, maintaining that Pakistan had inherited the treaty made with a British Government of India which had recognised " the Durand Line " as the frontier in 1882. On 4th August 1949 the Afghan Ambassador in London stated that his Government regarded treaties with a previous dispensation as invalid and did not now accept the Durand Line. " We shall never allow *seven million* of our own flesh and blood to be absorbed into Pakistan," he said.[1] He concluded with a threat to take the case to the United Nations. His Government have, however, never cared to put their claims to the test; and so it looks as if the conception of Pathanistan—a State of doubtful autonomy under Afghan patronage, conceived with the motive of internal Afghan political interest in view—will never see the light of day. But for the student of international relations the interesting feature of the episode is that a country—Afghanistan— steeped in the traditions of the power of the Mullahs was apparently unable to register any response from corresponding religious elements in Pakistan. Furthermore, the Afghan–Pakistani relationship does seem to indicate that the solidarity of the Islamic front is subject to the normal stresses and strains of nationalism, and that loyalties within Islam are at least as inconstant as they are in Europe.

I began with the suggestion that an Englishman might hope for the day when the British point of view could be sympathetically interpreted through the medium of two members of the Commonwealth : India

---

[1] The 1941 census estimated the population of the tribal areas as 2,331,000. Relations with Afghanistan were not improved by the inadvertent bombing of an Afghan village, Moghalgai, on 12th June 1949. As the result of a joint inquiry the Pakistan Government were wise enough to admit a mistake.

and Pakistan.   Here was to be the bridge between East and West.   In watching the development of a foreign policy in both countries I have sometimes wondered what would be the effect if men such as Sir Zafrullah Khan, when charged in the Press or in debate with submissively following the lead of Britain, would freely acknowledge the nature of the sentiment and interest which is still the link in a chain of so many years of association.   Would not thousands in the countryside welcome a frank and fearless admission?   Why need the British associations be a matter for apology?   And if presented instead as a matter of pride would there be no response from that sturdy Punjab peasantry we once served with some measure of acceptance?   From our side there is nothing to be ashamed of whatsoever in a frank avowal of the hope that Pakistan can and will use her position both to promote our policies when they are wise and resist them when they are foolish.   Such is the method of true construction and friendship.

CHAPTER TWELVE

INDIA AND HER NEIGHBOURS
(CHINA AND NEPAL)

WE have noted Pakistan's difficulties in reconciling conflicting loyalties, and it might be supposed that for this reason her policy would be the more difficult for observers to comprehend who watch from a distance. Yet whether it be through the simpler direct approach of the Moslem mind, which reduces problems to straightforward decisions and choices, or whether because of the vast range and complexity of Far Eastern problems, it is in India that we find the pattern of policy more obscure. One feature stands out in clear relief. The men who stepped into power in 1947 were those who for years had regarded themselves as the only true pilgrims in a search for freedom. They had fought, suffered and won. How natural, therefore, that this same sense of freedom through strife should now dominate policy in relation to their neighbours. In no individual was the new elation of a mission more restive than in Pandit Nehru, who assumed the office of Foreign Affairs; and in no aspect was the resulting reorientation of policy more prominent than in the relationship with China. The approach to China, therefore, derives not from a guarded admiration of the achievements of Communism in a country which was in any case ripe for change; but from a common sense of sharing in the capture of the same freedom. We should remember that Nehru claimed an association if not a friendship with Generalissimo Chiang Kai-shek long before Mao Tse-tung swept into power.

The Indo-Chinese relationship may be regarded as the corner-stone of India's foreign policy, compared with which exchanges with Burma, Indonesia, Afghanistan and others appear as mere diplomatic platitudes. Nevertheless, from a new sense of unity with China in the achievement of freedom it was only a step to an obsession concerning the mission of playing the brave part of protector of millions throughout Asia against alleged Western exploitation, and it is within this context that we should appreciate the understanding with Peking. Exactly how powerful that understanding could be in governing Asian thought and development will be appreciated when we recall that the two countries speak for nearly a third of the population of the world. Nevertheless, at this stage we could regard their mutual relations as undergoing a process of test and reconnaissance rather than consolidation, and it is with such a process in mind that I turn to examine the circumstances in more detail.

In January 1951 I sought out Sardar K. M. Panikkar, who was then India's Ambassador at Peking and was in Delhi on a holiday. I had long regarded him as a key man in international affairs. Believing as I did that the similar approach of China and India to "colonialism" might betoken the power of Indian persuasion to influence the Chinese, I further argued that India could form the common denominator by which British policy and intention might be interpreted to China more effectively than through our own diplomatic representation in Peking. The time had passed when we could hope for psychological warfare waged across the Iron Curtain in Europe to be effective. A visit to Czechoslovakia in the summer of 1951 had convinced me that the Western barriers dividing the minds of men were clear-cut and seemingly impregnable. Perhaps in China India could provide the bridge. At the time Mr. Panikkar was certainly the only diplomat with one foot in the Western camp who had also ready access to Mao Tse-tung. It seemed a conception worthy of the highest statesmanship.

The Indian Ambassador's comments were not quite what I had expected. India was a poor country, he said. She could never throw her weight effectively into the scales so long as her policy could not be backed by both economic and physical power. If she led Britain to believe that an Indian contribution of armies could in any way play its effective part in a Third World War, she would be leading Britain down the garden path. It would be ten years before India's active assistance in war could be an asset. Without a much greater concentration of force than was possible, India, by inviting attack, would be only a liability. All this was true enough but it was certainly a new aspect of what has been described as "dynamic neutrality".

While in Delhi I supplemented my talk with Mr. Panikkar in an interview with Sir Girja Shankar Bajpai, who was then Secretary of the Ministry for External Affairs. The conversation served to confirm the Indian approach to world problems. But there were some new debating points. The United States had used the argument that she could not recognise the Communist Government of China until Chinese forces withdrew from Korea. To retreat on this point would be to submit to blackmail. But the Chinese had not intervened in Korea until October 1950, and the North Korean attack was launched four months earlier, in June. The non-recognition of China by the United States during that period had undoubtedly been exploited by the Soviet to encourage Chinese intervention in Korea. India now felt that merely to meddle would be to be misunderstood by both sides. Mao Tse-tung might conceivably have been able to make acceptable proposals. But the crossing of the thirty-eighth parallel and the neutralisation of Formosa had prevented him from doing so. So far as Moscow was concerned, relations with India were no more intimate than with any other country.

What is the truth of the present relationship with China? It started with a common interest in a common freedom achieved. But I am not sure that it is not developing into something less emotional.   In spite of brave words, it has certainly lost some of its initial appeal.   In 1951 a Chinese cultural mission visited Delhi, and in 1952 the compliment was returned.   If the public exchange of verbal bouquets could be an accurate gauge of future relations, then certainly India and China are destined for years of uninterrupted harmony.   But the mere consistency—even monotony—of platitude leads us to wonder if an artificial note has not crept into this outward display of unity among millions.   It was with these doubts that I followed the movements and reports of the Indian cultural mission in Peking in 1952.

The mission of sixteen delegates headed by the Prime Minister's sister, Mrs. Vijayalakshmi Pandit, landed at Canton on 7th April, and spent some five weeks in China, which allowed time for their hosts to display not only the new China but also to throw in some melodramatic stories about germ warfare.   The mission travelled 6,000 miles, journeying to Peking, Mukden, Tientsin, Nanking and Shanghai.   They visited universities, science institutes, sanatoria, hospitals and clubs for workers. They roamed round factories and went down mines.   Occasionally their hosts remembered that they were entertaining a cultural mission.   There was, after all, Miss Shanta Rao, who on return offered the dancer's testimony.   "Encouragement is given in China to both classical and modern Chinese operas," was her illuminating comment, and apart from a note to the effect that her performances of Indian classical dancing were greatly appreciated, for the public there was little else to indicate that art or culture received any more attention than cooking.   The highlight of a programme carried through with a satisfying stimulation of mutual admiration appears to have been the functions at the Peking People's University.   These, with a dinner-party for 200 guests given by Mr. Panikkar and a reception at the People's Institute for Foreign Affairs, provided ample scope for the comforting oratory of good hospitality offered and accepted.

Perhaps I am prejudiced.   I have been once myself on a conducted visit to a satellite country, and I know the form.   It matters not whether you are the guests of Czech trade unionists in Marianske Lazne or of the Chinese Government in Peking.   The technique is the same.   I read that the delegation met and talked with Tien-hsu, leading actress in the "famous" Chinese film "White-haired Girl".   They showed us " White-haired Girl " in Czechoslovakia, and a more poisonous piece of diabolical propaganda I never wish to see.

On returning to India the delegation spoke of the deep impression that the great Chinese experiment had made on their minds.   That was to be expected.   Without passing judgment on the ethics of Communism in China or the final destiny of the country, it is obvious that a movement of dynamic vitality has gripped the Chinese to rescue them in some measure from the chaos and corruption of centuries.   Whether the price paid will prove to be merely a consolidation of tyranny remains to be seen. But for the moment the Indians could only expect to be impressed. For a balanced view I turned to a member of the mission, Mr. Frank Moraes, Editor of the *Times of India*. He replied promptly to my inquiry, and this is what he said :

"This was my second visit to China, my last being in 1944-45 when Chiang Kai-shek was in power. Although the cultural delegation's itinerary covered a different lie of country it was possible to make some comparisons and observations. Chiang's regime was, of course, the last thing on earth. It reeked with corruption, certainly in its final phases, and stank to high heaven. Any other regime succeeding it could not but be an improvement. There is no doubt that the Communists have achieved a fair deal in the three years in which they have been in power. Certainly they have been able to control their currency and the prices of basic commodities.

Since 80 to 85 per cent of the Chinese people belong to the have-nots, the overall impression is inevitably one of support for the regime. Over the past six months the Communists have carried out a great anti-corruption drive both against party members and officials as also against commercial classes. The result is that the administration and business community have been terrorised into honesty. Youth has pride of place in the new China and the Communists, as elsewhere, are concentrating on them. . . ."

There followed a description of the itinerary and a conclusion :

"If you judge China by the ends or results the Communist achievements are not unimpressive although on the industrial side their progress is far less than they would have the world believe—they are certainly behind India in this respect. If you judge China by the means you begin to ask whether the results were worth the methods employed—regimentation of the people, mass trials, executions, the imposition of a set pattern of thought and life. So far as I personally am concerned I do not think the results are worth the means. This was the first Communist country I have been to and I never realised before so strongly the value of intellectual and individual freedom. This was particularly obvious when meeting professors, scientists and other intellectuals. There was an intellectual timidity, a mental furtiveness about them which I found degrading. As you know, the Chinese are among the most nimble thinkers and the liveliest of conversationalists. Today they talk one set language—and that very guardedly. We used to say even in the old India that though the British might imprison the body of a man behind iron bars, nobody could imprison his mind. In China one realises for the first time what the imprisonment of the mind means."

The reader may have wondered why I have bothered to quote at length an opinion on China in a chapter on India. The views expressed are, after all, what we either already know or could guess. The main interest is, however, in the true Indian reaction. While the opinions of Mr. Moraes will not necessarily be identical with those of other members of the delegation, they could not be in direct conflict with a general impression, and it was for this reason that I was hardly surprised to read a report which threw a new light on individual Indian reaction. Students of East Europe will be aware of a weekly publication, *East Europe and Soviet Russia*, in which Lady Listowel, with the perseverance of one who has reason to appreciate Communist persecution, relentlessly attacks the Iron Curtain with resources not normally at the disposal of the British Press. On 26th June 1952 her editorial was headed " Mrs. Pandit's Revelations ". There followed an account of a report which Mrs. Pandit was said to have sent to the Chairman of the United Nations Committee on Forced Labour. The Committee was presided over by Sir Ramaswami Mudaliar, an Indian with a long record of fine service for his country. Mrs. Pandit was reported to have told the Committee that she had been disconcerted to discover that two million Chinese men and women had been conscripted out of the fields to work without pay on the Huai River Dam project. The source of these reports was Mr. Robert Trumbull, the Delhi correspondent of the *New York Times*, and the general picture he presented in his messages was certainly very different from the delegation's unqualified approval as described in the Indian Press. But for me the feature of this episode which seemed most disturbing was the alacrity with which the Press office at India House hotly denied Mr. Trumbull's story when I questioned them on the telephone. Back came a sheaf of cuttings, mostly from the *Hindu*, reproducing the various extravagant expressions of gratitude to their Chinese hosts in which members of the delegation had indulged on their return. As to Mrs. Pandit's allegation, I was referred to her own refutation in New Delhi on 26th June.

> " My attention has been drawn to publication given by some newspapers in India and abroad to statements alleged to have been made by some members of the Indian Cultural Mission. Many of the statements which are often made anonymously, *as published*, are incorrect and very misleading. . . ."

Someone had apparently complained of the complete control of the party by interpreters. This, too, was open to misunderstanding. Interpreters were obviously essential. Chinese hospitality was proverbial, and was extended to the mission in the fullest measure. Mrs. Pandit continued :

> " So far as we know, there was no question of forced labour. It is a well-known fact that the Huai River Dam was built through the

willing co-operation of about two million peasants who were paid in catties of rice (which is the usual form of payment) for work done by them. . . . Conditions in China are obviously different from what many people have been used to elsewhere. Each person reacts to them according to his own temperament. The overall impression of the mission was one of admiration for the enthusiasm, discipline and energy with which the people of China are tackling the difficult tasks that face them, and for the measure of success they had obtained."

Whatever public denial is made of having spoken unkind words about China, we cannot shed our doubts in this matter. Mr. Trumbull is a respected journalist of the highest reputation, and the *New York Times* is not given to reproducing idle gossip. A fair deduction would be that the delegation, having accepted concentrated hospitality, could hardly turn on their hosts and criticise them immediately on their return to India. Least of all could the leader of the delegation have admitted the whole affair to be a flop. The mission set out with an intention of good-will, and that intention had to be preserved. But that India House should have corrected my interpretation with such emphasis and concern seemed unnecessary, to put it mildly. It almost seemed as if the Press Office sensed a slur on their country's reputation in the indecent sugges-tion that the mission could have discovered any element of doubt in the united purpose of India and the new China.

I would not wish this assessment in any way to reflect on the high intention of Mrs. Pandit, whom I have never met. One can admire the leader of a delegation for her energy, enthusiasm and leadership without necessarily accepting her political judgment. It is easy also to allow that judgment to be conditioned by the particular Chinese official with whom for the moment you are concerned. If he irritates, then that irritation is reflected in the subsequent evaluation of his country. If he pleases, then everything in the Chinese garden is roses. It is some such process as this that I suspect governed the reactions of the leader of the Indian delegation.

In international diplomacy the habit of saying one thing and thinking another is as old as time. But where the issue is so great, India will need to beware of many traps which lie hidden behind the approach of "proverbial hospitality". It is very pleasant to indulge in soothing platitudes about "the exchange of cultural heritages which have lasted over centuries". Members of a delegation can exercise their imagina-tion, while to the Indian peasant working in his fields China remains but a name, even if his education has permitted him to know of its existence. In the practical way of a practical world I doubt if such words as "ancient friendship born of a common cultural heritage" have any meaning at all. Nevertheless they oil the machine of diplomacy, and our only fear is that they may oil it too thoroughly. As a result of the recent exchanges, a China–India Friendship Association [1] has been formed. My own experience of " friendship " associations is that they exist, at least for one of the partners, for a single purpose only ; and that purpose has little to do with friendship for constitutional government.

A less sentimental view of India's great neighbour may have been in the mind of the Indian Prime Minister as he watched events develop recently nearer home in the border kingdom of Nepal. For it was obvious that in dealing with Nepal the Indian Government were very conscious of the dangers if conditions in that country should so deteriorate as to invite the attention of the Chinese Communists knocking at the door along the Tibetan frontier.

For many in Britain, Nepal is but the home of tough little Gurkha soldiers from a Ruritanian kingdom in the East. In view of its new importance, I will record the mere outline of the past. In 1867 King Surendra, on behalf of himself and his descendants, renounced all temporal power ; since when the King and the ruling Rana family have functioned on parallel lines, in much the same way as King Victor Emanuel was permitted a titular status alongside Mussolini's dictatorship. We need only to note that for years relations between the palace and an all-powerful Maharaja, combining the functions of Commander-in-Chief and Prime Minister, were unhappy.[2] Three years ago matters came to a head.

On the afternoon of 7th November 1950 His Majesty King Tribhuvana Bir Bikram Jung Bahadur Shah was out for one of his rare drives through his capital, Katmandu, when quite suddenly his carriage turned in through the gates of the Indian Embassy ; and there the King remained to take shelter from his alleged enemies. A few days later the Indian Government dispatched two planes, and the King, accompanied by his eldest son and a small party of relations and courtiers, were flown to safety in Delhi. Once before he had managed to slip away to India, and had discovered that an incognito life in Calcutta had its attractions. The routine of a monarch preserved mainly for religious ceremonial and regarded as a reincarnation of Vishnu was not exactly exhilarating. Yet requests to visit India for medical treatment had always been refused as contrary to convention. For the moment, however, the refusal was due more to the Maharaja's belief that the King would use his time to plot against the Rana Government and work for its overthrow.

King Tribhuvana's appeal to the Indian Government for protection placed the latter in a very awkward position. They had recently concluded a treaty of trade and friendship with Maharaja Sir Mohun Shum-

---

[1] The Association was inaugurated on 16th May, 1952, in the Peking People's Institute of Foreign Affairs. Dr. Ting Hsi-lin, Vice-Minister of Cultural Affairs, who led the Chinese Mission to India in 1951, is President of the Association. On this occasion the vocal exchanges concerning common cultural heritages were thick and fast.

[2] The titles of Maharaja, Commander-in-Chief and Prime Minister were reserved for the head of the Rana family. They were hereditary, passing always to the oldest brother or nearest cousin.

shere Jung Bahadur. Yet they could hardly approve his somewhat feudal and uncompromising dictatorship. There was also the reflection that if they openly encouraged interference in Nepal by Nepalese Congressmen sheltering in India, it would hardly be logical simultaneously to protest at Chinese interference in Tibet. Though this point may seem academic now that the Chinese grasp on Tibet is complete, at the time it was of real significance. Early in October 1950 the Nepalese Government had unearthed a plot to assassinate the Maharaja and leading members of the Government. The conspiracy was believed to be the work of the Nepalese National Congress, an organisation which had received help and encouragement from the Indian National Congress and which sought to remove the Maharaja and his prolific ruling family, claiming also that in their aspirations they had the support of the King.

The King, whose flight was accomplished only after obtaining the permission of the Maharaja, was received in Delhi by a guard of honour of the Fifth Gurkha Rifles,[1] and representatives of the heads of the services. His somewhat dishevelled appearance was hardly likely to inspire confidence in those who received him. However good his intentions, his life had not been such as to develop any capacity for either politics or administration, and it was fair to deduce that the Nepalese National Congress were really out to exploit his position for their own purposes. On 11th November, the day of his arrival in Delhi, irregular bodies of men raided into Nepal at several points along the Indian–Nepalese border. In the centre they captured an important town—Birganj—where they proceeded to set up a parallel government. Simultaneously the Rana Government were demanding in India that the King should not return and that his three-year-old grandson, Gyanendra, should be recognised as the new King, with the appointment of a Council of Regency. If the Indian Government were to yield to the Rana regime they would obviously antagonise many of their own Congress supporters. If, on the other hand, they were to ignore the Ranas and openly encourage the armed revolt rapidly developing under the banner of the Nepalese Congress, the result could only be the collapse of ordered government in Nepal for the benefit of the Communists in Tibet. In the circumstances the subsequent rapid achievement of a compromise agreement was a triumph of diplomacy as gratifying to Pandit Nehru and the Indian Ministry for External Affairs as it was unexpected. Throughout negotiations the British position had not been easy. We had a long history of friendship and co-operation with the Rana family and their Government to remember. At the same time there could be no question of active interference in a problem which mainly concerned another member of the Commonwealth.

[1] This fine regiment was formerly the 5th Royal Gurkha Rifles, F.F., and some surprise was felt when, on the division of the Gurkha battalions between India and Britain, a Royal Regiment and unit of the old Punjab Frontier Force was allotted to the Indian Republic.

The settlement took the familiar form of the establishment of an Interim Government composed of an equal number of representatives of the Ranas and the Nepalese Congress Party on a basis of joint responsibility. Within two years elections on a basis of complete manhood suffrage were to be held, and the resulting Constituent Assembly was then to evolve a new Constitution. But the treatment was, alas, to prove too rapid and superficial for a people so isolated from the world of modern democracy. Exactly why a Maharaja and Prime Minister who had everything to lose, not only for himself but also for his large family, completely reversed his decision concerning recognition of the boy prince, Gyanendra, and signed away his future so conveniently to all concerned is at present a mystery. But it is to be admitted that in doing so he showed a readiness to co-operate which was not expected and which was in fact to lead to his own eclipse.[1] Perhaps on sober reflection he and his Government realised that a feudal kingdom shut in between a Communist Tibet and a republican India on which Nepal was entirely dependent, could hardly afford the luxury of choice.

On 15th February 1951 King Tribhuvana returned in triumph to his capital, accompanied by an escort of two queens, three princes, daughters-in-law, grandsons and retainers, to be welcomed by the Maharaja, Cabinet Ministers and cheering crowds.

In the meanwhile the Nepal Assembly of Notables had ratified the terms of the Government of India, and in a Cabinet of ten, five of the old order of Ranas, including the Maharaja, retained their posts, and were joined by five new nominees of the Nepal National Congress. The stage was thus set for an initial dose of the blessings of democracy; and all because of the acceptance of India's " friendly advice ". To mark the occasion, under an amnesty all political prisoners were set free. But there were signs that the initiation was far from healthy. Although the Nepalese Congress revolt had officially been called off, in the distant foothill districts of the Nepal Terai [2] the more excitable elements were refusing to recognise so tepid a compromise in government. The town of Biratnagar in the east of the State was particularly the scene of chaos. Here, Nepalese Congress volunteers continued to make the most of their opportunities. The levying of contributions and requisition of cars were the outward manifestations of a control which was rapidly deteriorating to terrorism. Communist hand-bills appeared. In the north an organisation—the Gurkha Dal—under the leadership of young members of the Ranas [3] was making a futile bid to restore the family fortunes. Meanwhile their elders were busy quarrelling over the method

---

[1] The decision was officially taken in the name of the Bharadari (Assembly of Notables).

[2] The Terai is a strip of territory on the edge of the foothills of Nepal, where the thick jungle has for long been a State reserve for shooting tiger.

[3] The revolt was led by Bharat Shumshere Rana, a grandson of General Babar Shumshere, the Defence Minister, who had already left the State for Bombay.

of selection of their Cabinet representatives. By the middle of April, dyarchy, as a transitional experiment in government, was collapsing, and the Maharaja was forced to surrender his hereditary title of Commander-in-Chief, which was promptly assumed by the King. Thus within five months were the traditional roles of King and Prime Minister completely reversed. From then on it was only a matter of time before the final eclipse of Maharaja Mohun Shumshere Jung and his retirement into private life in India. It is true that in May he paid a visit to Delhi, accompanied by Mr. B. P. Koirala, the President of the Nepalese Congress, where Mr. Nehru succeeded in extracting a promise to work in harmony. But it was a very precarious truce, and by November coalition government had broken down and the Maharaja then faded from the political scene.[1]

But who was there to step effectively into the vacuum caused by the collapse of Rana rule? The leaders of the Nepal National Congress, vociferous enough in political campaigning, had no practical experience whatsoever of government. They had been exiled in India, and could hardly claim a knowledge of conditions in their own country. In the circumstances India sent up two or three experienced administrators. In particular Mr. Srinigesh, Commissioner of a Division in East Punjab and a trustworthy servant of the old Indian Civil Service, was able to restore some confidence to a very insecure administration.[2] Even so, the foundations for government were too shallow, and one ministerial crisis followed another. Intrigue and dissension now entered the ranks of the Nepal Congress, taking the form of a simple, rather sordid brawl between two brothers, Mr. B. P. Koirala, the President of the Nepal Congress, and his elder brother, Mr. M. P. Koirala, who had assumed the office of Prime Minister. The quarrel appears to have been a matter of the latter's refusal to accept certain names for the Ministry which had been submitted by the Nepal Congress Working Committee; an issue of personalities and not politics. At the end of July 1952 it had culminated in the expulsion of the Prime Minister and two of his Ministers from the party for three years. These events, ironically enough, took place within a few days of the King's inauguration of a new Advisory Assembly in which he spoke of " another big step towards democracy "! Almost in the same breath the King asked his audience to believe that the cordiality between Nepal and her northern neighbour Tibet had not been

[1] On 16th November, 1951, a new Cabinet of twelve included eight Nepalese Congress Ministers and four Independents, of whom only two represented the Ranas.

[2] The Indian decisive handling of Nepal at this stage was reflected on a miniature scale in the small neighbouring hill State of Sikkim. In June 1949 the Government of India assumed responsibility for the administration of the State after disturbances staged by the Sikkim State Congress, and an Indian official became Dewan at the head of an interim Government. In December 1950 a new Treaty with the Maharaja of Sikkim provided for the status of a Protectorate under India with internal autonomy.

N

affected by the presence of the Chinese. I have quoted from the report of *The Times* correspondent on 6th July. Yet only a month later, on 3rd August, the same observer had to report that on 30th July fourteen Nepalese Communists had been arrested in a north-west border district of Nepal, and that they had had contact with the Chinese! Finally in August 1952 Mr. M. P. Koirala submitted his Government's resignation to the King. On 4th September the King dissolved the advisory Assembly and hurried to Delhi, nominally for medical treatment, but more certainly to take counsel of Mr. Nehru.

Where will this turbulent and childish quarrel of political greed lead the Nepalese? The happiest development would have been for the King to rule through the best advisers which India could provide, and leave experiments in " popular " government for at least a decade. Instead he has taken the administration into his own hands, and has chosen five councillors to help him. Three are members of the outgoing Ministry without party ties, while the other two are a retired general and a retired judge. These are regarded as " interim " measures pending elections in 1954. Since the State at present enjoys a standard of 95 per cent illiteracy it would seem that the longer the *interim* the better! We can only hope that India, having with every justification established the precedent for interference, will not be shy of grasping a situation which if allowed to drift would prove so disastrous for her own interests. There was talk of fresh injections of Indian assistance, and Mr. Panikkar was mentioned as an envoy. Mr. Panikkar is a man of many parts. He has been able to reconcile working with great ability on behalf of the old feudal order of princes with a modern understanding of Communism in Chinese clothing, to which at one time were added outspoken attacks on British Imperialism.[1] But he would hardly seem the man to rescue Nepal. Would not a less political and more practical contribution be the medicine from which a country steeped in intrigue can benefit? It makes us wonder if, after all, the Rana dictatorship was not the more secure basis for the future evolution of the country. In the years when the world outside was accusing Nepal as representing a pocket of stagnation in the midst of progress, the difficulty was to rouse the interest of the people, particularly of the Gurkhas, in anything approximating to representative government. It became the fashion to speak of a clamour for reform from numbers of returning soldiers who had seen and envied the public services which function in Western democracies. Naturally enough, Gurkha officers who returned to a country without an effective postal service asked questions. But the greater number of Gurkhas were quite content to remain politically unconscious and render unto the

[1] On 26th January 1951, in the " Republic Day " commemoration number of *India News* Sardar Panikkar contributed an article entitled " Political Forces in India ", in which the whole range of the British association with the sub-Continent was attacked. The basis of the theme was the economic strangulation of a continent, which otherwise could have flourished as an industrial exporter in world markets.

Ranas what they believed belonged to them.   That being so, it is possible
that the Government of India could have achieved a greater stability
through a Regency Council, leaving some power with the Maharaja
and recognising the King's twenty-two-year-old son as Regent.   Meanwhile, for better or worse a modern search for progress is abroad.   In
August 1952 for the first time in history a Queen of Nepal spoke at a
public function!   For the first time, too, a national budget has been
published.   At last a road to link Katmandu with the Indian border is
being constructed by the Indian Army.   Indeed, if only a wealth of
goodwill and outside technical assistance were needed, then the country
could be regarded as safe.   Alas, I cannot subscribe to the view that the
generous allotment of $320,000 to Nepal under Point Four Aid from
America is of any permanent value.   The availability of firm leadership
by men of integrity would be a more practical gift: and it is this element
which India can now supply.

Throughout these negotiations the British Government watched the
situation anxiously.   There was an understanding of India's difficulty
and an appreciation of her readiness to exercise only the minimum degree
of interference.   But there was also anxiety for the eight fine battalions of
Gurkha troops which now form part of the British Imperial Forces and
are fighting our battles in Malaya.   How would they react to so much
rumour and uncertainty at home?   Nor can we be certain that, with the
new winds which blow from Nepal, the Nepalese Government will wish
to perpetuate an arrangement by which Gurkha soldiers are available to
support distant British interests in Malaya.   We can but hope that
they may continue to regard the situation as offering considerable
advantages to the few troops affected and less tangible assets to their
country in general.[1]

Paradoxically Nepal, which for years produced such magnificent
battalions for the Indian Army, has maintained only an inefficient
indigenous force of some 25,000 retainers without training or modern
equipment for its own defence.   Years ago in Katmandu I watched their
primitive artillery file past the saluting base on the backs of scores of
ponderous elephants.   I sat also in a glittering throne room while the
King and his Court heard my father announce the appointment of
Maharaja Sir Bhim Shumshere Jung as a Major-General in the British
Army and Colonel of the Fourth Gurkhas.   On that occasion the robust
figures of generals and officials in their scarlet and gold, with their
jewelled head-dresses surmounted by bird-of-paradise plumes, betokened
almost a Habsburg splendour, with an added gay touch of operatic

[1] This issue is distinct from that of the facilities to recruit Gurkhas and hold them
in three depots on Indian soil pending their despatch to Malaya.   Questions have
been asked in the Indian Parliament, and Mr. Nehru has been forced into a declaration
to the effect that facilities cannot be afforded indefinitely.   Under the tripartite agreement of 1947 between Britain, India and Nepal, the Government of India agreed to
give transit facilities through India to Gurkha troops serving with Britain's Gurkha
battalions.

unreality. Outside in the crowded bazaar the poverty was obvious.
But somehow it was not the aggressive poverty of despair. For these
people were happy. In our search for an elusive freedom and the will of
men to control their own destiny I sometimes wonder if we do not
neglect their right also to a happiness which is not to be despised. More
important, however, for India than hypothetical speculation is the
immediate practical issue as to whether Nepal in her present chaotic
condition can protect herself politically or physically from the new and
powerful influences in Tibet. For this reason I suggest that the Indian
military mission in the country is as useful as any academic advice. A
few strong administrators with executive power supported by some
good professional soldiers would be the most practical contribution
which India could offer both in her own interests and those of Nepal.

The Nepal Communist Party is now definitely in touch with the
Tibetan Communists. Officially the Katmandu Government have
closed the Tibetan frontier, but one might as well attempt to demolish a
swarm of locusts with a shot-gun as try to hold back Communist infiltration if it really means to penetrate Nepal. It would seem that a new
more vigorous intervention from Delhi will be required if the Indian
Government are effectively to safeguard their northern frontier from
future movements, whether of military force or political revolution.

CHAPTER THIRTEEN

INDIA AND HER NEIGHBOURS
(JAPAN, AMERICA, KOREA, THE SOVIET)

W E have been considering India's relations with China and Nepal. In the former case we could conclude that there was a desire to believe the best, in the latter case there was a reluctant readiness to face the worst. But what of relations with the source of all controversy? Are we entirely to discount the value of India's possible intervention if and when those who direct policy in Moscow ever abandon their will to control the world? If, in contrast, they press their intentions to the point when a third World War is precipitated, can India's part as a mediator be effective? Those who have made a long study of the theory of Communism and who know Russia will tell us that one might as well negotiate with a stone wall as hope for a change of heart in the U.S.S.R. Others who seek for any sign or gesture which might indicate a desire to make a fresh start say that the Russians may have worked themselves into a position from which they cannot now retreat without loss of face. That being so, they would welcome some gesture from the West, such as the reversal of a policy to rearm Western Germany, as the excuse to extricate themselves from the impossible position in which they are situated. They would be prepared even to reconstitute the frontiers east of the Oder–Neisse line in return for the opportunity to be able to do it with a reason which could be conveniently dressed up for the millions under their control.

It is a theory which will take some digesting. But its improbable nature is hardly the point. For our purpose the significance is that when a British delegation recently attended the Moscow economic mission, these views were seriously put to them by Sarvepalli Radhakrishnan, the India Ambassador in Moscow.[1] It so happened that one of our own delegates was deeply interested in a movement with which I have some association: the movement to encourage the conception of

[1] Sir S. Radhakrishnan, M.A., born Madras 1888. Fellow of All Souls College, Oxford. Vice-Chancellor, Benares University. Professor of Eastern Religions and Ethics, Oxford, since 1936, known now as " Shri Radhakrishnan ". Leader of the Indian delegation to UNESCO, 1946. Contributed on Indian Philosophy in the *Encyclopaedia Britannica*, 14th Edition. One of India's most erudite and distinguished of international figures. He was relieved in Moscow in July 1952 by Mr. K. P. S. Menon, and returned to India to assume the Vice-Presidency of the Indian Union. He took his leave of Marshal Stalin on 6th April, 1952. In his new post his knowledge and experience of international affairs will be readily available to the Indian Prime Minister.

World Federal Government.[1] He wished to discover if the Russians could in any way be approached through the presentation of our ideas for a federal world; and for his purpose he immediately sought out the Indian Ambassador. The story goes that Shri Radhakrishnan, after his arrival in Moscow, shut himself up for weeks and studied his books on philosophy, rather than plunge into the eddying currents of political controversy. This new approach so astonished the Russians that they gave him their confidence in a manner not offered to anyone else. When Shri Radhakrishnan handed over his office in Moscow in April 1952 he was received by Mr. Stalin in an interview which lasted half an hour. He was the first foreign diplomat for two years to receive this attention. So I return to the first and last aspect which concerns us; which is the degree to which India can effectively play the role of mediator. In the particular case quoted Radhakrishnan apparently got nowhere. But in general terms I believe that it would be only right to bear in mind always the main feature of a situation which allows one Power in the world at least access to leadership on both sides. A bridge, to be effective, must reach to both banks. Whether India as a bridge really reaches the other bank we do not know. Yet if we abandon all hope in her ability to do so we only advance the process of division. It is in the possibility of success rather than in the probability of failure that we should judge the purpose of India's neutrality. The quality of hope as the third and most obscure of the three virtues is so often neglected; and in so far as India offers us the chance to recapture a forgotten confidence, we should never lose sight of the vague circumstances which might conceivably give history an unexpected twist and restore sanity in the fullness of time. For such reasons we cannot dismiss Indian neutrality which could be vital to the world, as mere diplomatic weakness.

Nor is the desire to remain without commitment contrary to the natural interests of the country. If foregoing the luxury of expensive armies in any way contributes to improve the lot of millions who live at subsistence level, we should welcome the economy. But there is sometimes a suspicion that independence of action and decision is based not so much on the logic of neutrality as on a desire to impress the world with the power to choose. Was it really necessary to adopt that very individual attitude in the matter of signing a separate treaty with Japan? [2] Need every opportunity be seized to emphasise alleged examples of domination and exploitation of East by West?

The Indian objections to attending the San Francisco meeting in 1951

[1] World Federal Government is a movement which in Britain has developed on a non-party basis. A British Parliamentary Group under the Presidency of Lord Boyd Orr have taken the lead in stimulating international interest.

[2] The Indo–Japanese Treaty was signed in Tokyo on 9th June 1952. It was ratified by both countries on 27th August 1952. It covers " most-favoured nation " treatment in imports and exports, the return of confiscated property and the waiving of all reparation claims.

to sign the Japanese Treaty were based mainly on two contentions. First, it was claimed that the treaty denied to Japan an honourable position of equality among nations. Secondly, it was said that the terms did not allow other countries especially interested in a stable peace in the Far East, to subscribe sooner or later to the treaty. In so far as any reaction to its own fate coming from a defeated nation after the war has value, the Japanese reaction itself supplied the answer to the first point. Japan in fact fully acknowledged the adequacy of her return to an honourable international status. The United States answered the second point in the following terms. The Treaty made full provision for multilateral signature, in that it " obligates Japan to conclude similar treaties with all countries not now signatory who are party to the United Nations' declaration of 1st January 1942 ". This was the declaration by which twenty-six nations pledged themselves to use their united military and economic resources against the enemy and not to make separate armistice or peace terms. The second clause stated : " The foregoing declaration may be adhered to by other nations which are or which may be rendering material assistance and contribution in the struggle for victory over Hitlerism."

An interesting situation at the time arose in that Burma, which can be regarded as an inexperienced but usually obedient younger brother, on this occasion also opposed the Japanese Treaty, though for very different reasons. Burma had suffered cruelly and wanted her pound of flesh. Here was an occasion when the Indian gesture of waiving reparations received no response. Here, too, was an indication that though Asia, under Indian leadership, may in certain circumstances speak with one voice, we may when matters of purely Asian interest are concerned, expect the normal rough and tumble of less lofty negotiation.

More logical was the Indian attitude to the complete by-passing of Communist China in the Japanese settlement. But in elaborating the Indian view the measures which Nehru would have preferred could only have deprived the United Nations of all effective military defence of the Western Pacific, and thrown this vital responsibility on to the shoulders of a defenceless Japan.[1] It was the implication of the abandonment of responsibility for the physical defence of the Far East by the United States that was the real cause of some American resentment at India's isolated attitude to the Japanese Treaty.

As time passes, one has the impression that the Prime Minister's approach has mellowed. Gone are the passionate declamations to which we were subjected in 1946 and 1947. Instead there is a saner, more practical approach, tempered naturally by the desire to protect those

[1] India would have advocated the return of Formosa to Communist China and the return of the Kurile and Ryuku Islands to Japan. The latter measures would have been contrary to the terms of the Potsdam Agreement, which India had not questioned during the five and a half years she had served on the Far Eastern Commission (Washington Correspondent of *The Times*, 26th August 1951).

whose voices are not yet articulate in international negotiation.   Not a little of this new caution can be attributed to a growing sense of identity of interest with Britain and the Commonwealth.   For example, we can well imagine a very different attitude to such matters as the controversy over Persian oil or the dispute with Egypt had they been prominent a few years ago.   Instead we find in the case of the former no effort made to purchase Persian oil and the refusal to be drawn into the controversy, while in the latter case, at least in so far as the Sudan is concerned, the support of freedom of choice for the Sudanese is identical with our own declared policy.[1]

Thus it would seem that increasingly as the ties with Britain are strengthened, so is moderation more conspicuous in foreign policy. Former obsessions are turning to natural reactions, and each case tends now to be considered on its merits rather than governed by the previous inflexible will to act as a focus for the championship of Asian nationalism. In so far as Nehru experiences an irritation at United Nations impotency, he will merit the sympathy of many in the West who are increasingly conscious of the misuse of the UNO machinery.   Pandit Nehru has generally seemed inclined to leave the advocacy of under-developed territories in the Middle East to Pakistan.   Yet in the particular case of Tunisia he could not resist the temptation to emphasise his disapproval at the failure of the Arab–Asian bloc to achieve a hearing of the case.[2] I would not attempt to inquire into a problem which is so fraught with doubt and difficulty as the part the United Nations should play in balancing up the mutual relations of great Powers and their colonial territories.   We in Britain might claim that the effect of international interference is but to substitute the rule of many novices for that of a single agency with generations of experience; and so, if we agree that the machinery of UNO needs an overhaul, it would be for somewhat different reasons from those of Mr. Nehru.   Nevertheless, in so far as there have been occasions when the facilities of UNO have been abused by Western Powers,[3] the Prime Minister of India will be understood when he hints that the day might come when Asian Powers would have to consider their whole position in relation to their ability to be heard effectively in such conditions as obtained in the Tunisian dispute.

Closely in accord with suspicion of the United Nations is the fear of encroachment by the United States.   Where the French and the Dutch are regarded as maintaining political domination, the American guilt is in

---

[1] Statement by the Prime Minister at his Press Conference, New Delhi, 20th July 1952.

[2] This was one of the rare occasions of Mr. Nehru's active interest in Middle East polemics.   In January 1951 when passing through Paris Mr. Nehru held a long conversation with M. Habib Bourgiba, the son of the leader of the Tunisian Nationalist Party " Neo-Dastour ".

[3] An outstanding example of such abuse was the manipulation of the General Assembly vote by the United States in November 1947, to obtain a two-thirds majority vote on the partition of Palestine.

economic aggression. Yet here, too, we note a tendency to soften the
sharp edge of previous accusation. As late as October 1950, at the conference of the Institute of Pacific Relations held at Lucknow, Indian
opposition to American policy was unambiguous and intense; nor were
the Americans inclined to take criticism without hitting back. At the
time India's attitude to the crossing of the 38th Parallel had been declared,
and while at the conference India accused the United States of using the
United Nations for her own purpose, the United States retaliated with
the charge that Indian neutrality and her support of the Peking Government were an abandonment of obligations to the United Nations. One
of the Americans summed up with the reasonable contention that
American confidence in the integrity of Indian neutrality would be
reinforced if India could show that she really understood the dangers of
Communism as we know them in the West. Indian public opinion is
now receiving its education. But in 1950 there was certainly little to
show that the country had any idea of the manners and method of Communists once they get into their stride. It was with an appreciation of
alleged Indian indifference to Western fears that until recently there was
resentment in America at the thought of economic aid to India. Why
waste money on fellow-travellers? was the crude reaction. But with
the arrival of Mr. Chester Bowles as Ambassador in Delhi there was an
abatement of former tension, and the signing of the Indo–American Aid
Agreement in the spring of 1952 was the outward manifestation of the
new spirit.

I think it is true to assert that in India and Pakistan, indeed throughout
the East, the trend of policy receives its direction more from the play of
personalities than from the will of Governments. Certainly in so far as
India is concerned her status and influence in international affairs derive
from the Prime Minister. That foreign policy is his exclusive interest
was emphasised during the elections when relations with countries
outside India, whether within or without the Commonwealth, hardly
featured as issues for the consideration of the electorate. The process is
one of two-way traffic, and in the case of relations with America, where
there has recently been some adjustment, it was due as much to the
personal reactions of Mr. Chester Bowles as to any fundamental change
in national sentiment.

Mr. Bowles' enthusiasm will not entirely commend itself to Englishmen
who claim to understand India and her problems. Maybe we are too
shy of flattery and the sentimental approach. Here is an example of the
American Ambassador's opinions: [1]

"First of all we are interested in India because we have watched
for many years India's struggle for freedom. We also were a

[1] Address to Project Executive Officers; Nilokeri, 1st August 1952, in the presence
of prominent officers of the U.S. Technical Administration. Mr. Bowles's term of
office came to an end in March 1953.

colonial country. One hundred and seventy-five years ago we got rid of the British and remained their friends. You have also got rid of British rule five years ago, and continue to be their friends. Secondly, we admire the people who work to help themselves. I doubt whether there is another country in the world, which, with such slender resources, has done so much in five years as you have done."

There followed a list of achievements: the integration of the States, the drafting of the Constitution, the peaceful conduct of elections and the solution of the refugee problem. Mr. Bowles continued:

" Three hundred and sixty million people, who had lived a miserable life under Colonial rule are now awakened and are marching on their own strides. This has an important significance to the world of to-day torn with conflict and strife."

Some impeccable observations about international peace achieved only by the freedom of mankind, concluded heroically.

" The people of the world are on the march. They are determined to go forward to get rid of feudalism, to live a better life."

I fear that whenever I hear of millions " on the march ", I am suspicious. It is the kind of *cliché* that has become the stock-in-trade of all those who thrive on mass applause. I should have liked, too, to draw the attention of the American Ambassador to the circumstances which allow a man trained in the misery of that Colonial rule to draft the new Constitution, which Mr. Bowles so admired.[1] But there is little profit in bitterness; and if Mr. Bowles's fertile oratory in any way furthers the opportunity for India to accept American economic aid or conclude satisfactory trade agreements, all luck to his eloquence.

In turning again to the Indian side of the direction of policy, we should note that though the Prime Minister is at the helm, he is certainly served by some able navigators. Men such as Bajpai and Benegal Rao have interpreted India to the world with a skill and persuasion which have won her many friends at times when her policy seemed out of step with the West. Particularly did the influence of Benegal Rao convey a sense of urgency in the part India chose to play in the Korean War; and since Korea continues to dominate the international situation, an analysis of the Indian attitude will help our better understanding of a very entangled web of controversy.

Late in June 1950, after four days of hesitation, India accepted the two United Nations resolutions by which action was taken to halt aggression

---

[1] The new Constitution was very largely the work of Dr. Ambedkar, who for many years was an able and much-respected member of the Viceroy's Executive Council.

in Korea.   The acceptance was the more welcome because it had been
wisely made, after the receipt of a report from Mr. C. Kondappi, the
Indian delegate on the United Nations Commission for Korea, whose
sympathies were known to be by no means with the Southern Korean
administration.   The Indian attitude was therefore governed solely by
the firm conviction that the North Koreans had committed an act of
aggression, and Nehru felt that the weight of his country's moral conviction should be lent to the cause of the United Nations.   " Where freedom is menaced or justice threatened, or aggression takes place, we cannot and shall not be neutral," Nehru had said in Washington in 1949;
and his bold assertion was now to be tested.   Its interpretation—and
I say it in no spirit of criticism—has taken the form of the contribution of
one Field Ambulance.   It would have been a happy symbol of India's
interest if an Indian Minister, or even a delegation, could have found time,
after cultural exchanges with China, to have visited Korea, and seen the
fine work of their small unit.   Nevertheless, the Indian Field Ambulance
is a manifestation of a consistent Korean policy, which was defined at the
Prime Minister's Press Conference in Delhi on 7th July 1950.   Nehru
stressed that his country had had no previous associations with either
North or South Korea.   Being, however, convinced of the guilt of the
North Koreans, his Government very forcefully condemned it.   But
support of the United Nations resolutions in no way involved any further
acceptance of expanding obligations arising out of the initial action,
which was confined to aggression in Korea.

Behind the Indian approach lay the full weight of their sympathies
with the Peoples' Government of China and their disapproval of the
non-recognition of that Government by the United Nations.   There
followed the Soviet withdrawal from the Security Council in January
1950;   and it was Nehru's view that subsequently a progressive deterioration of conditions in the East had set in.

It was in this spirit that later in July Nehru penned his identical appeals
to Marshal Stalin and Mr. Acheson.   His object, he said, was to localise
the conflict, and then win peace through an end to the *impasse* in the
Security Council.   The People's Government of China must take their
place in the Council, so that the Soviet could return.   All could then find
the basis for a settlement.   Stalin was asked to use his influence to this
end.[1]   It was a sincere bid to rescue the international situation, but it
could never have had a chance, for the conditions of aggression which
had brought about India's condemnation were never acknowledged by
Stalin.   On 3rd August, in the Security Council, Mr. Malik declared
that the conflict had started with an unprovoked attack from the South,
with the help of U.S. military advisers.   Over two years later, in August
1952, Stalin was wishing the North Koreans success in their battle against

---

[1] This approach was further emphasised, together with an insistence on the
complete independence of India from " blocs ", in an address to an emergency
meeting of the Indian Parliament on 31st July 1950.

the United Nations, and talking of the "heroic Korean people in their struggle for the freedom and independence of their homeland."[1]

Stalin's reply to Nehru was therefore merely an amiable confirmation of Nehru's suggestions. Mr. Acheson, in contrast, set out the American objections in some detail. His main contention was that the question of the Chinese representation at the United Nations should be decided on its merits by the United Nations themselves, and should not be dictated to them by North Korean aggression amounting to blackmail. Nor did he believe that the termination of hostilities in Korea could in any way be contingent upon the determination of other questions, which were concurrently before the United Nations. To this Nehru replied that the question of the recognition of the Peking Government by the United Nations had been advocated by the Government of India ever since Indian recognition of the Communist regime in December 1949. His present appeal was made only with the object of creating a suitable atmosphere for a peaceful solution.

The argument served the purpose of throwing into clear relief the deep and fundamental cleavage which separates the champions of rival ideologies; and in so far as we, too, have afforded official recognition to Mao Tse-tung's China, we can appreciate the sincerity of the Indian point of view. That view was soon to be subject to stresses and strains in which the feeling of a dilemma was apparent. On 1st August the Soviet representative, Mr. Malik, returned to the Security Council to occupy the seat as Chairman. There were those who thought that he was better out than in, for he promptly pressed a resolution to the effect that all forces should withdraw from Korea, thereby leaving the North Koreans free to achieve their original intention.

It was at this stage that Sir Benegal Rao seemed to be in some doubt as to how to interpret his country's intentions. Where the majority of the Council were quick to turn down Mr. Malik's proposals, Sir Benegal took the view that it was better to argue than fight. The Soviet proposals were "complex", and rather than renounce them out of hand, he would first consult his Government. On 19th August, as an alternative, he put forward the practical suggestion that the Korean crisis should be handed over to a sub-committee of the six non-permanent members, who could be regarded as neutral. This appeared to have the merit that it could have provided the Soviet with a face-saving device to withdraw, and there will be many who will regret that it was not adopted. But when we have given the Indian representative's diplomacy the fair and full consideration which it fully deserves, when we have taken note of subsidiary matters, such as the Indian fear of the effect of America's isolation of Formosa, when we have finished weighing the justice of Nehru's broad indictment that Western Powers take decisions affecting

[1] Telegram to North Korean Premier on the occasion of the North Korean national holiday. Reproduced in all Moscow newspapers. A.P. message 15th August 1952.

vast areas of Asia without understanding the needs and minds of the people, we are still left with a grave contradiction, which requires to be explained. That is the simple fact that while fully acknowledging the evil intent and nature of North Korean aggression, it does not ever seem to have occurred to Sir Benegal Rao to question the Soviet denial of North Korean guilt. Some will call this diplomacy, an inevitable evasion through the force of relentless circumstances. Others may crudely regard it as dishonesty. Whatever the verdict, the challenge was never made by the one Power in the world which might have forced the issue into the daylight of open discussion and international exposure. Would that not have represented a service worthy of the highest statesmanship, even though the immediate results might have been to create yet greater tension?

Running through the sincere but sometimes ambiguous Indian approach to the Korean problem is always the theme that the danger to economic progress and political freedom in the East is a revival of Western imperialism, compared with which the subversive influence of Communism is a poor competitor. To Jawaharlal Nehru nationalism is the source of all progress.[1] Therefore where Communism supports Nationalism, it is at least a more welcome agency than Western Colonialism.

It is consequently not surprising to note the personality of the Prime Minister asserting itself in his interpretation of colonialism nearer home, when his sense of impatience at the fact of those few small islands of foreign territory on Indian soil is very evident. How irritating it must be to tolerate those blotches of colour—Goa, Kariakal, Pondicherry and others—which disturb an otherwise consistent unity across the new map of India![2]

In the mystery which surrounded the truce talks in Korea we, the public, remained helpless and bewildered spectators. We read that the resistance to repatriation of some 15,000 Chinese prisoners was a loss of face which the Chinese Communists could not tolerate; and we can well believe it. We read an unconfirmed report that Mr. Panikkar was told by Chou En-lai that the armistice would be signed if the prisoners were returned; and once again we were reminded of the possibilities and hopes of Indian intervention.

Yet the first moves in this direction were not encouraging. In June 1952 the American Government invited India among others to send military observers to investigate conditions in Koje prison camp. Mr. Nehru's reply was qualified and vague. Prison camps were the responsibility of the Red Cross. Germ-warfare investigation was work for

[1] In Mr. Nehru's opening address at the 11th Conference of the Institute of Pacific Relations (3rd October 1950) he stated : " No argument in any Asian country would have weight if it ran counter to the nationalist spirit of that country—communism or no communism."

[2] The present situation in regard to these territories is set out in Appendix VI. They constitute a somewhat separate problem to the normal issues raised by India's foreign relations.

scientists. "We have added that we feel all these matters are really part of the larger and far more important problem of the exchange of war prisoners. . . . If we could help in finding some way out of that we should gladly do so."[1] Of events in Tibet, Mr. Nehru spoke in very subdued terms as compared with the shocked disapproval he had expressed when China first moved her armies across the Tibetan border. The Indian Mission would remain in Lhasa with a somewhat changed character. He did not think there would be any difficulty, "as it is a matter to be negotiated between China and Tibet"! If this was to be the measure of Indian conviction for the future, we could hardly expect any dynamic interference in the international scene by the Indian Government. Is there not in such hesitancy and meek acceptance a suggestion that to risk Chinese and, by implication, Soviet displeasure is at all costs to be avoided? I would therefore close on a plea: that in interpreting her assumed role of help and mediation to powerful and quick-tempered antagonists, India could usefully accept any call on her ability to investigate and offer her solution which may come her way. But let her arbitration be completely objective. If a crime is alleged, we call in not a diplomat, but a detective. Let the detective, then, do his job conscious of his duty to pursue truth, however unpalatable the process may be with its revelations and results. In the years to come fearless mediation will merit international respect and reap its reward. Sir S. Radhakrishnan on the eve of his departure from Moscow after his interview with Marshal Stalin made this statement: "There is no outstanding problem now dividing the world that cannot be settled by discussion and negotiation. It would be unwise to bang the door against every approach and give up the task as impossible. No effort should be wasted, and every effort should be made to get the top people together."

May his message of hope continue to sustain our world of doubts and suspicion. All we ask of his country is the fearless pursuit of truth in its welcome mission of mediation.

I had concluded this chapter on a note of disappointment. A few weeks later I had to confess that Mr. Krishna Menon's adroit handling of his country's new proposals to deal with Korean prisoners of war led me considerably to modify my views. Menon's proposals in November 1952 undoubtedly captured the imagination of some fifty nations at New York. If nothing else was achieved, he managed to set in motion a chain of new international cross-currents. At one moment Britain's relations with the United States were in some danger; at another it almost seemed as if a wedge might be driven between Moscow and Peking! But quite apart from considerations of success or failure, the significant feature of the proposals was surely a claim that they had the support of the whole Asian world. Here for the first time was a proposal by an Asian Power claiming to speak on behalf of Asia, receiving

[1] Press Conference, Delhi, 22nd June 1952.

the full support of Britain, and at least the acquiescence of America. Here for the first time was the prospect of a realignment of loyalties. The Government of Republican China could not have enjoyed the obligation to echo the thin arguments of their Soviet comrades. Nor could the Indian proposals have been put forward without some indication from the Indian Ambassador in Peking that the Chinese would listen to them. Here at last was an example of neutrality exercised convincingly and with sincerity as an agency to help us all in our bewilderment.

Let us close, then, with a clearer conception of Indian neutrality than was possible a few months ago. When Mr. Aneurin Bevan in Delhi in February 1953 advocated the creation of a third bloc in world affairs, he stood rebuked by Mr. Nehru. For it was clear that Mr. Bevan was thinking in terms of force; and in so far as a bloc of any kind is regarded as a solution by Nehru, it is a bloc of thought; a bloc of true pacifism based only on a belief in the evils of armament, and a hatred of war. Paradoxically, while I have always regarded Western rearmament as a duty so long as a challenge to our way of life exists, I equally feel that we can be grateful for a neutrality on which we can depend in all circumstances; a kind of haven of sanity in a world at war. It is this need which I feel Nehru's India could meet, and in doing so provide the catalytic element in a crisis which might be the salvation of a shattered world. In the meanwhile in such dim idealism there is nothing incompatible with a fearless exposure and defence of truth in the contemporary situation of today.

PART III
KASHMIR

CHAPTER FOURTEEN

THE BACKGROUND

ON 19th March 1849 Joseph Cunningham, a lieutenant of Engineers, achieved prominence through the publication of his *History of the Sikhs*, a searching and careful work covering the origin of the Sikh nation and closing with the Sikh Wars.

Cunningham had known the Sikh frontier as a political officer and had been attached to the staffs of both Sir Charles Napier and Sir Hugh Gough. At Sobraon he served with the Governor-General, Sir Henry Hardinge. At the time his services earned him a brevet and an appointment in Bhopal State, where he presumably wrote his History. Much of Cunningham's detailed account of events in 1846 may be summarised as an accusation that the British had an understanding with Raja Gulab Singh of Jammu by which the Sikh Army should be attacked and abandoned in defeat by its own Government. "Under such circumstances of discreet policy and shameless treason was the Battle of Sobraon fought," wrote Cunningham. His frankness cost him his career, and he was removed from political employment by the East India Company and returned to military duty.[1]

The story, as he tells it, relates how in 1846 the Governor-General was able to satisfy Gulab Singh, who had become an embarrassing element in the general post-war settlement with the Sikhs. Kashmir had fallen to the Sikhs in 1819, and in 1820 the small principality of Jammu was granted by the Sikh, Maharaja Ranjit Singh, to Gulab Singh, a petty Dogra hill chief. Gulab Singh has been described as both avaricious and ambitious. The quality which, however, was in evidence from the point of view of British negotiations was his extreme skill in secret diplomacy. In 1841 Gulab Singh was sent by Ranjit Singh to quell a rebellion of Sikh troops in Kashmir, which he did with ruthless efficiency. Thereafter he became virtual master of the Kashmir Valley. In 1845 his intrigues miscarried and, with a Sikh army approaching Jammu, he was forced to hurry to Lahore and submit to a fine and some loss of territory.

After their war with the Sikhs, the British demanded an idemnity of the Sikh Government in Lahore, but since little of it could be taken in money, territory was ceded instead. Kashmir and the Hill States from the Indus to the Beas were accordingly detached from the Punjab and transferred to Raja Gulab Singh as a separate sovereignty for the sum of

---

[1] Cunningham died at Ambala in 1851, and was buried in the cemetery on the Grand Trunk Road near Ferozepore.

£1 million. The final transaction was confirmed in the Treaty of Amritsar of 16th March 1846,[1] and in token of British supremacy under Article 10 of the Treaty, the Rulers of Kashmir until recently presented the British Government each year with one horse, twelve goats and six Kashmir shawls. Exactly who profited from this rather uneven but quite practical generosity I have never discovered.[2]

The reader may have wondered why I have dealt at some length with the distant events of another century. Their significance for our purposes is just this : that the modern Kashmir problem in no small measure derives from an award of doubtful wisdom and integrity made to a Dogra Chief Minister of the young Maharaja Dulip Singh of the Punjab, whose kingdom at the time had been placed under a Council of Regency, and as such it would have been at least satisfactory if a British Government could now have seen the matter through to its conclusion.

The geographical expression, Kashmir, covers 82,258 square miles and includes communities with as little in common with each other as a Scandinavian has with a Spaniard. We are apt to think of an exaggerated homogeneity because of recent years we have been constantly reminded of the fact that of its population of four million, over three million are Mohammedans. The problem is therefore always presented to us as one of a small Dogra tyranny dominating a vast number of Moslems. In fact it is a mountainous country of no roads, whose isolated groups are conscious only of their own existence, and have consequently easily been divided to be ruled by powerful invaders for many centuries. For example, in Eastern Ladakh some 40,000 Buddhists have for centuries lived in complete and serene isolation.

The heart of this beautiful country is the Jhelum Valley, an oval plain, 100 miles in length and 30 miles in breadth, which stretches from east to west, sheltering within the mighty protection of the Karakoram and Pir Panjal ranges, and only a few days' journey from the plains of Pakistan and India. Within this valley dwell the people we know as Kashmiris, distinct from their co-nationals of the distant inaccessible areas, a gentle, friendly people of little stamina who in trouble bark loudly, but who seldom really bite. Little wonder that their pathetic incompetence has been successfully exploited by Scythian Hindu Princes, Moghul Emperors, Duranis of Kabul and Ranjit Singh the Sikh. Finally the award to Gulab Singh handed them as easy prey to a Hindu Dogra dynasty.

We need thoroughly to appreciate this quality of hopeless resignation which permitted exploitation, if we are to appreciate the psychological significance of the presence today of Indian armed forces in the Vale of Kashmir. That great sage of modern Islam, Sir Mohammed Iqbal, himself a Kashmiri, in shame and sorrow wrote of the plight of his people, " The Kashmiri has come to hug slavery to his bosom. . . . A stranger

[1] The Treaty of Amritsar effected the transfer of " all hill country between the Indus and the Ravi for the sum of 75 lakhs of Rupees ".

[2] I am informed that the shawls were annually presented to Queen Victoria.

to the dignity of self, ashamed of his ego." Sir Zafrullah Khan was a little more realistic and less poetic when before the Security Council he said that one soldier armed with no more than a bayonet could drive 4,000 Kashmiris in whatever direction he desired. It is this inherent sense of inferiority which Sheikh Abdullah recently claims to have conquered for the greater dignity and welfare of the Kashmiri.

Maharaja Sir Hari Singh, a grand-nephew of Gulab Singh, remained in aloof indifference to the welfare of his people throughout the twenty-three years of his rule. While his own detachment contributed to the final *débâcle*, we should remember that he inherited a system of taxation and land revenue which allowed the barest margin of subsistence to the Moslem Kashmiri. The production of silk, saffron, paper, tobacco, wine and salt was a State monopoly. An *ad valorem* duty of 85 per cent was levied on all woollen manufacture. The incidence of land taxation was three times that levied in the neighbouring Punjab. Carpenters, boatmen, butchers, bakers, even prostitutes were taxed. Until 1934 the slaughter of a useless cow was a capital offence. The issue of arms licences was limited to Hindus. It is easy to blame the Maharaja in terms of the standards of a Western free democracy. It is not quite so fair to condemn when we assess him along with others of his order, and remember that British policy in general terms allowed Princes to live and let live, and the Indian Political Department stepped in only when events were so obvious that they could not escape publicity. Of the many thousands of Europeans who came and went through Kashmir in the Indian summers not a few were quite prepared to criticise the Ruler and yet accept his hospitality.

My own acquaintance with this beautiful country dates back to an old house in Lincolnshire where my grandfather had smothered the walls with enlarged photographs of family groups depicting the carefree social life of northern India in the 1890s. For many years from Lahore he and his three daughters had set off for Srinagar, covering the 230 miles from Rawalpindi in a jolting *tonga* with the pony teams changing every six miles or so. My mother had stories to tell of three sleepy girls being turned out at five o'clock in the morning to strike camp and take to the road; for my grandfather apparently drove his family on a tight rein. Those were times when a few annas tossed to the boatman produced a basket of vegetables sufficient for the needs of a family living on a house-boat for the next few days. The Kashmir I myself had known had lost the charm of isolation, and every year a few thousand Englishmen and women motored through in the day from Rawalpindi, shot and fished in the valleys, played golf in Gulmarg on the most beautiful of courses and bargained with the cheerful rogues in Srinagar for silks, furs and papier-mâché. Every time I made the journey I found myself turning over in recesses of the imagination the possibilities of this country under Western scientific and conscientious development. Marred the country might be under the impact of the European. But it was fascinating to reflect on the manner of the modern Utopia which might have emerged if that mutilation could have developed under ordered and progressive administration. The potential mineral wealth, the development of local rural industries, the crafts and patient skill of Kashmiri craftsmen, the opening up of the great mountain valleys, an electrified railway and—the greatest of tasks—the clearance of the physical and moral filth which pervaded the hovels in and around Srinagar; [1] all these not unworthy dim reflections could have been the realities of today had it not been for that stupid, unimaginative and opportunist award to Raja Gulab Singh in 1846.

We are, however, now concerned with a practical problem of intense complexity, and it is my purpose only to indicate the past in so far as the present has emerged out of the years of consolidation of an initial mistake. In 1931, after disturbances, a State Legislature was set up and a Moslem agrarian reform party—the Moslem Conference—won sixteen out of twenty-one elected seats.[2] Hitherto the Maharaja had personally displayed no particular manifestations of an anti-Moslem bias. But subsequent to the riots of 1931 his attitude changed. In 1938 a certain Sheikh Abdullah, a prominent member of the Moslem Conference, broke away to form his own " National Conference ". Henceforth there were, therefore, two political organisations in the State, both opposed to the Maharaja's Government, yet also in ambiguous opposition to each other. Years later, when the choice of accession or independence was an issue for the Maharaja's settlement, a sufficiently complicated political entanglement was further obscured by the fact that junior leaders in both these parties were quite conscious of their greater opportunities in an independent Kashmir, as compared with a status of subordination to either India or Pakistan. The National Conference in the war years was able to strengthen its hold on the vale of Srinagar. It welcomed Moslems, Sikhs and Hindus, but its secular appeal in its early days was based more on a common hatred of autocratic government than on any transcending sense of mutual brotherhood. Within the valley its membership was about 50 per cent Moslem. But proportionate to the distance from Srinagar the Moslem support faded into insignificance.

The modern story may be regarded as dating from 1946. In that year Pandit Nehru, on a visit to the State with the object of defending his friend Abdullah, had been arrested and held in custody by the Kashmir

---

[1] For a vivid account of social conditions, the reader is referred to *Tyndale-Biscoe of Kashmir*, an autobiography. Seeley, Service and Co., Ltd. Canon C. E. Tyndale-Biscoe was a well-known figure and reformer who, through the medium of his Mission School, managed in recent years to exert a cleansing influence in the morass of Kashmir public life.

[2] It was the clamour of the Moslem Conference for agrarian reform which precipitated the disturbances. British troops had then to be used. There followed the Glancey Commission, as the result of which certain land reforms were introduced and a Legislature was set up.

authorities. Sheikh Abdullah and his National Conference Party were then at work to rid the State of the rule of Sir Hari Singh, and an aggressive "Quit Kashmir" campaign had been launched. Abdullah was one of that rare community of Moslems devoted to the service of the Indian National Congress. In that capacity he was frequently in and out of prison, and in 1946 the Maharaja held him safely in custody on a long sentence. Some features of the problem are therefore simply explained by the fact of Nehru's intense interest as a Kashmiri Brahman in the home of his ancestors, his personal friendship with Sheikh Abdullah,[1] and an identity of political views, in that Abdullah was also President of the All-India States People's Conference. Thus it was that for many previous years he had been thrown into close contact with the Indian Congress. And so Abdullah's whole background has been one of close sympathies with the Indian Congress, an interest in Left-wing Socialism, nationalism and sincere secularism. He was therefore always quite impervious to the appeal of the Moslem League, particularly as the League was never over-concerned with such matters as the relations of Princes to their subjects. It was equally natural that the Moslem Conference came gradually to assume the aspect of an extension of the League in Kashmir.

In 1947 the Maharaja invited Lord Mountbatten to visit his State. It was not until the third week in June that the latter could accept the invitation. He found his host in a defensive mood, unable to face up to the great problems which sooner or later would inevitably present themselves. It was clear that in isolated independence he would receive the worst of both worlds. Pakistan would be plotting to remove the Hindu dynasty from continuing to rule a Mohammedan people, while the Indian Government, through Sheikh Abdullah, would be seeking his downfall as an enemy of their own neighbouring progressive democracy. And yet, in view of the geographical position of his State, for which there was no precedent in Princely India, his hesitation merits some sympathy. His apology would be that the consequences of a hasty step might prove disastrous, and that his particular problem needed further reflection in the light of experience elsewhere in the India of the Princes. In this there was some truth.

The Maharaja and those around him had always feared encroachment and interference from outside. The mere fact that Kashmir had for many years been accessible to Europeans in a manner which did not apply to other States in India, led the Kashmir Government into a mentality of suspicion of foreign intentions, an outlook which persisted after 15th August 1947, and which was applied equally to Pakistan and India. This jealous concern for their own independence had been reflected for years past in the rigid application of stringent "State subject" laws. Against this background throughout the summer and autumn of 1947 the Maharaja and his Government had to watch events in the neighbouring Punjab which in no way encouraged accession either to

[1] Developments in 1952 appeared to be straining this friendship.

India or Pakistan. Refugees in thousands were pouring across the border into Jammu Province, and a State administration quite inadequate to handle the situation was struggling to arrest the flow and keep the State immune from the consuming communal fires of India. It was in defiant reaction to these more worthy motives that a State policy of persecution of Moslems in certain areas came to be applied. To this I will draw attention later; but in justice to the Maharaja it is fair to believe that for a time his will to independence was not uninfluenced by a desire to save his State from being drawn into the slaughter. It should be recalled that the throne of Kashmir had for four generations rested on the firm support of its Dogra Rajput subjects. In existing conditions in the Punjab an open accession to Pakistan might well have resulted in the massacre and expulsion from the State of its Hindu and Sikh inhabitants. Alternatively, an accession to India meant the signature of the Maharaja's death-warrant so far as his own power was concerned; and so it came about that for a while he and his Prime Minister, Rai Bahadur Ram Chandra Kak, strove for their dream of independence. To the natural and human reactions which sought to retain power were added the more subtle persuasions of the occult, and prophecies of a renascence of Rajput power in India under Kashmir leadership were whispered around. In particular, Her Highness of Kashmir listened attentively to the extravagant imagination of her Swami.

Maharaja Sir Hari Singh is a man of intelligence, as many who served in the State will testify. But in his blind refusal to face reality he was his own enemy. With his State in suppressed turmoil, with his scattered State forces dealing with revolt in Poonch and refugees in Jammu, he yet would not see that he had neither the political support nor the physical means to sustain his country in isolation. The Treaty which for nearly a century had governed Kashmir's relations with the Crown stipulated that the latter would accept responsibility for protection from external aggression, while the State should maintain such forces as were sufficient only for the preservation of internal security. In successive agreements under the Treaty all details of strength, composition and armament were decided, arms and ammunition being obtained on payment from the Government of India. A force of one horsed cavalry regiment and nine battalions of infantry was therefore called on at short notice to deal with internal chaos and external aggression, a situation which the Kashmir Government might be forgiven for regarding as simple and unilateral abrogation of a Treaty.

No one could better appreciate the Maharaja's skill at evasion than his military commander, Brigadier H. L. Scott,[1] who persistently sought to drive home the practical impossibility of the Kashmir army meeting the many demands on its services in sustaining the Maharaja and his Government. Written appreciations and memoranda would either be returned

---

[1] Brigadier Sir Henry Scott, C.B., D.S.O., M.C., formerly of the 1st Battalion P.W.O. Gurkha Rifles, Chief of Staff, Kashmir State Forces, 1936–47.

or filed unread. Definite appointments to discuss the military situation would prove to be gatherings of courtiers and visitors, with servants standing around in open *durbar*. Such was the background to those difficult conversations conducted on long motor rides, in which Mountbatten now urged the Maharaja to abandon the concept of independence and discover the will of his people. Furthermore, he assured him that the newly created States Department under Patel on behalf of the Government of India would not regard a verdict in favour of Pakistan as an unfriendly act. This is important, since the story has frequently been misinterpreted, and we have been asked to believe that Mountbatten and his Government had exercised some kind of previous influence to produce the Maharaja's accession to India. That Mr. Gandhi and Acharya Kripalani would have advocated the Indian case on their visit to Kashmir in the summer is obvious. But that the terms and details of a plot were ever elaborated is, in my belief, a play of the imagination. Alan Campbell Johnson [1] describes how Mountbatten, having previously prepared the Maharaja's mind for the need for a quick decision, then hoped to confirm the latter's general consent in an open discussion with Pandit Kak, George Abell [2] and the British Resident. The Maharaja, however, at the last minute suffered a convenient attack of colic! Later, Lord Ismay on sick leave in Kashmir had hoped to add the weight of his balanced advice, being prepared to advance the claims of Pakistan equally with those of India. He, too, discovered the Maharaja's artistry in avoiding unpleasant discussions, for whenever the conversation looked like approaching politics the Maharaja conveniently diverted it to reminiscences of polo!

Throughout July and on into August, with the time limit for accession running out, the Maharaja remained in indecision. Finally, three days before the transfer of power, the Kashmir Government announced its intention of signing a standstill agreement with both Pakistan and India.

Pakistanis have, I think been apt to exaggerate the significance of the standstill agreement. The agreement was a device which any Prince could sign with one or other of the Dominions in order to ensure that, in cases where the Ruler needed more time to make up his mind, the normal services and economic understandings which hitherto India had provided should continue. It was on this basis that Pakistan continued to operate the small stretch of railway within Kashmir territory which forms a portion of the link between Sialkot and Jammu. In fact no formal agreement was ever signed, and the *status quo* was confirmed only by telegram. Nor at that stage could the need for a formal document have been anticipated, since on 15th August Pakistan did not foresee the subsequent chaos which resulted from a tribal invasion. A telegraphic agreement was therefore regarded by Pakistan as sufficient to

[1] *Mission with Mountbatten*, Ch. 10, p. 120.
[2] Sir George Abell, K.C.I.E., O.B.E., Private Secretary to both Lord Wavell and Lord Mountbatten. Director, Bank of England, since 1952.

ensure that she stepped into the shoes of the former Government of India
in its relations with the State before partition.

India's attitude to a standstill agreement is less certain. She has been
represented as unwilling, and certainly no agreement was signed. Yet,
after some research, my conclusion was that had not the circumstances
arisen to precipitate her war with the tribesmen, an agreement would
probably have been concluded. In these critical days before and after
partition the objective seeker of truth is impressed with the apparent
absence of any higher-level attempt at negotiation with Kashmir on the
part of the Pakistan Government. Had there been merely a negative
absence of inquiry as to the Maharaja's intention, it could have been
regarded as a constitutional and correct attitude in a refusal to exert
pressure. But in fact the evidence is to the effect that in so far as a Pakistan Government then existed it was attempting to force the Maharaja's
hand by economic pressures on the State, which could only have the
effect of damaging her own interests. Chaotic conditions in both India
and Pakistan had in any case killed the Kashmir timber trade, and to this
was now added an embargo on the sale of Kashmir produce in Pakistan
which drove the State well-nigh to bankruptcy. This not very imaginative policy was being pursued at a time when the Prime Minister, Pandit
Kak, while fostering independence, was certainly closer to Pakistan than
to India in an identity of broad policy. Like the Nehrus, the Kaks were
Kashmiri Brahmans, but an old family rivalry had much to do with
sharpening the edge of political relations between the Maharaja's Government and India. With Pandit Kak's dismissal the chances of an understanding between the Kashmir of the Maharaja and Pakistan receded.
Shortly after the new Prime Minister took office, Mr. Jinnah asked permission to come to Kashmir for a holiday. The request was refused,
and with it probably the first and last chance of accession to Pakistan
disappeared, never to return. Some correspondence appears to have
taken place between Mr. Jinnah and Sheikh Abdullah, but pride prevented
both from making the first move towards a personal conversation.

Just over the Jhelum River where it bounds the District of Rawalpindi
was the tiny State of Poonch, a principality within Kashmir, constituting
in itself a secondary similar problem. The Hindu Raja of Poonch owed
loose allegiance to the Maharaja of Kashmir. Yet his subjects were
Moslems.[1] In the spring of 1947 the Moslems in Poonch rebelled
against the extension of Kashmir taxation to their small territory.
Kashmir State troops were accordingly despatched to bring them to
submission. But the Moslems in the State Forces deserted, and there-

[1] Maharaja Ranjit Singh awarded the Poonch *Jagir* to a younger brother of Raja
Gulab Singh. Poonch was therefore not a creation of the family of the Maharaja of
Kashmir. Maharaja Sir Hari Singh's relations with his predecessor and uncle, Sir
Pertab Singh, were never happy; so much so that Pertab Singh, unable to deprive
Hari Singh of the succession, was yet able to establish the Raja of Poonch as his
" spiritual heir ", a move which in turn did not improve relations between Poonch
and Hari Singh when the latter came to power.

after Poonch became a secure base for the movement, known as " Azad Kashmir ", to establish an independent Kashmir government under one Sardar Mohammed Ibrahim. Ibrahim is a citizen of Rawalkot in Poonch, a country which supplied some of the finest fighting-stock of the old Indian Army. These were the men who, returning from a world war, now rallied to a cause which, in the face of the military Dogra dictatorship in their midst, rapidly turned to a fierce faith. Subsequently I shall draw attention to their obvious limitations. But against their defects their physical toughness and intimate knowledge of the country were certainly assets of nuisance value, if not of real military significance. The Azad Government were thus quickly able to raise their own forces, and could soon muster some 30,000 villagers from Poonch and Mirpur.[1] It should be realised that the Azad forces were a body of men quite distinct from the more loosely organised tribesmen. While the latter were seeking to avenge the slaughter of Moslems from whom they were geographically separated, the former were men suffering from a very real sense of personal grievance, and claimed never to have been defeated, in spite of some indiscriminate bombing of their villages. As we shall see, their claims were hardly compatible with the results achieved.

In August an anti-Moslem movement within the State was initiated with all the appearance of a systematic persecution. It started on 26th August at Bagh in Poonch, when Moslems were set on and killed by the State troops for contravening orders which had forbidden the celebration of Pakistan Day on 15th August. It continued and increased in tempo with the infiltration of members of the R.S.S.S., Akali Sikhs and the I.N.A. into Jammu Province in October; and it culminated with the massacre of two crowded convoys of Moslem evacuees who had been promised a safe conduct to Pakistan. On 5th and 6th November the convoys drew up at a village on the Jammu–Kathua road, and were set on by armed bands, their Sikh escorts joining in the slaughter. The overall result of resort to jungle morality was to cause some 500,000 Moslems to flee from their homes, about 400,000 seeking shelter in Azad territory and at least another 100,000 dribbling over into Pakistan. It is hardly surprising that the Moslem Kashmiris accumulating in the western extremities of the State came to think of the fight as for nothing less than survival. The motives of the Kashmir State Government in prosecuting so disgraceful a campaign of persecution are not difficult to divine. A systematic modification of the population in favour of the non-Moslem elements would obviously achieve popular support for an extension of their own precarious term of office. Secondly, it was an old device

---

[1] The British and Indian Press reported these forces as being commanded by a certain " General Tariq ". In fact no such person ever existed. The name was a Pakistani fabrication borrowed from the identity of a famous Moslem leader of the days of the Moorish conquest of Spain. This, and the invention of fictitious formations by both sides, played a part in the war of deception which was carried on with some good humour.

offering a cheap and easy diversion, to beat up a little communal hatred when things went wrong. A Ruler could always obtain a new lease of life simply by fanning the flames. While the State bureaucracy were thus recklessly abandoned in an orgy of slaughter, the obvious legacy of these crimes had taken seed in the distant frontier districts beyond the Indus.

CHAPTER FIFTEEN

THE TRIBAL INVASION

THE Indian Government received no hint of impending events. On the evening of 24th October rumours of tribal movements were circulating in Delhi, and on 25th October, at a meeting of the Defence Committee [1] General Lockhart read out a telegram from Headquarters, Pakistan Army, giving the first official news. Later in September 1948, when the Government of India were holding an inquiry, a certain amount of comment was directed to a letter the Governor of the Frontier Province [2] had written to General Lockhart towards the end of October 1947. General Bucher, in evidence before the United Nations' Commission for India and Pakistan, quoted this letter, and in one way or another it found its way into the Indian Press. One newspaper spoke of " vipers under Nehru's pillow ", and there appeared to be a cheap campaign to discredit British officers and their loyalties to the two Governments. In fact, the letter quoted had never mentioned Kashmir.

On the frontier Sir George Cunningham was engaged in making desperate efforts to dissuade Mohmand Maliks and others from entering Kashmir. But the seed had been sown, and control at that stage was out of the question. This was not surprising in view of the absence of any formed units of the Pakistan Army at the time. It would take long days of research on the spot to determine the degree to which the initial advance of the border tribes was made with the forewarned knowledge of the Pakistan Government. Senior British officers in Pakistan at the time believed that Mr. Jinnah at least was honestly and completely taken by surprise. Another view is expressed that he vaguely heard of the intention and immediately satisfied his conscience by a refusal to ask further questions. Whatever the truth, the many censures on his attitude at this period have been grossly exaggerated. Nevertheless, officers of the Pakistan Forces sensed what was afoot, for I have their own testimony. The tribes had let it be known that whatever attitude the Pakistan Government took, they would not be deterred from moving to the assistance of their brothers in distress. The earliest contacts between Kashmir and the tribes must almost certainly have taken place in August, when ex-servicemen in western Poonch began collecting money to buy arms and ammunition from the Frontier Province factories in tribal

[1] This was a Committee of the Indian Government, not to be confused with the Inter-Dominion Joint Defence Council.
[2] Sir George Cunningham, G.C.I.E., K.C.S.I., a former Secretary to the Viceroy (Lord Irwin). Rector of St. Andrew's University since 1946.

territory. At that time the State troops had established a blockade
along the southern border, destroying the Jhelum River ferries and placing
pickets on the bridges. A few of Ibrahim's men, however, managed to
cross the Jhelum in rafts and were able to make for the frontier and
purchase arms and ammunition with hard cash. It is reasonable to
believe that the plans for tribal action were initiated in these first
contacts.

My own inquiry in Pakistan led to certain conclusions. First, no
British officer, civil or military, had any idea of the plans in preparation.
Indeed, there was a deliberate policy of keeping them in ignorance in
order to save them subsequent embarrassment. Had they known, they
would have been torn between their willing loyalty to Pakistan and their
sense of duty in preventing a situation with such obvious dangers in a
wider political sphere. Secondly, certain senior officials were well aware
of the intention, and discreetly turned the other way. Finally the Chief
Minister of the Frontier Province, who has family connections with
Kashmir, gave it his blessing and unqualified assistance, without which the
operation might not have been possible. He apparently held the rather
simple view that tribal action would force accession to Pakistan on the
Maharaja.

In so far as Pakistan officials were concerned, the wrong ones were
chosen, and at least two officials with no knowledge of the tribes worked
as emissaries. They paid for their folly in the choice of Mahsuds, who
by tradition are the most ungovernable and wildest of a wild community. Contrary to expectation, few Afridis were implicated, and the
balance was completed by Wana Wazirs, Mohmands, Swatis and Buner-
wals. There is evidence that a few of the leading Mohmand Maliks were
secretly interviewed in Rawalpindi as early as 2nd October.

The first news of actual movements reached the Governor on 20th
October, when it was reported that 900 Mahsuds had left Tank in lorries
for Kashmir. He immediately ordered their advance to be blocked at
Kushalgarh, but they were already across the Indus. Simultaneously,
news came from General Ross McCay, who commanded the Peshawar
Division, that tribesmen in lorries were crossing the Attock Bridge.
McCay was then asked by the Governor to take preventive action, but
he was quite unable to do so, since at the time he had no formed units
ready. Moreover, in view of the prevailing political temper, at that
stage Moslem troops ordered to oppose tribesmen bent on a *jehad* in
Kashmir would almost certainly have laughed at their orders and gone
over to join their co-religionists in the adventure. Mr. Grace, the
Inspector-General of Police in Peshawar, appears to have received the
news from Attock simultaneously with General McCay. But the
earliest clue to the movement which came my way was a report of a
message received by the British Deputy Commissioner of Mianwali,
150 miles to the south, who was given orders to lay on rations for 200
refugees passing through. Accordingly he awaited their arrival from the

north. Yet it was from the south that they came, fully armed and hardly looking as if they needed charity!

The general conclusion is that while there was no plan of control by the Pakistan Government at the highest level, there was knowledge and tacit consent; and I believe the Pakistan case would not have suffered by a frank admission of the position. It was in its denial that heated controversy was engendered.

As to the value of the adventure from the point of view of Pakistan, it should be remembered that the tribes were leaderless. An unpleasant character—Kurshid Anwar, a Punjabi who had held a commission in an obscure administrative appointment in the Indian Army—had been prominent in Hazara organising *lashkars* for Kashmir. He it was who was responsible for the foul massacre at Baramulla. He has since met the death he deserved. There were a handful of bogus heroes from the I.N.A., and in the first months of 1948 there was Brigadier Akbar, later involved in the Rawalpindi conspiracy case, a fearless and energetic leader of tribal bands in the fighting east of Muzzaffarabad. But in the absence of real leadership on an effective scale the military value of the tribes was always limited. Later, they found they could successfully blackmail the Pakistan forces into letting them have arms, ammunition and stores, a procedure discovered to be more profitable and less dangerous than slaughtering Hindus. Finally, many of them broke south into the western Punjab and were able successfully to terrorise the population. It could be said that both from the military and political points of view the tribal invasion proved a disaster for Pakistan.

The first movement of tribes has been spoken of as an isolated decision born of nothing more than traditional irresponsibility and love of adventure. It was in fact the accumulated fanaticism of many days of bazaar rumours. Stories of atrocities committed against Moslems in East Punjab, in the Punjab States and the persecution in Jammu and Poonch already related, were magnified and distorted to fan the flames, though indeed the plain truth was sufficiently revolting. In particular, many Sikhs, forced from their lands in West Punjab and without homes in the east, were smouldering in resentment and seeking revenge. There was talk of an armed march on Lahore. And in the meanwhile they hit out brutally and without mercy at any Moslems within their reach. The counter-movement from the frontier was therefore not only an adventure: it was a *jehad*, the kind of reaction which is comprehensible only to a few who have worked for long years among the Mahsuds, Wazirs and Afridis of the frontier.

The first tribal force, which numbered about 2,000, passed through Abbottabad in trucks and entered Kashmir territory on 22nd October, looting and burning Domel and Muzzaffarabad in the process. By 25th October they had advanced up the Jhelum Valley to Uri, with only the timid opposition of the Kashmir State troops to bar their way. As they advanced, all their wild, adventurous savagery was let loose and, with the prospect of the rich Jhelum Valley ahead as the prize, they successfully terrorised the hamlets and villages which cluster along the familiar road to Srinagar. Their outstanding success, however, was to determine the Maharaja's indecision.

Lord Mountbatten had emphatically advised his Government that without the formal accession of Kashmir it would be neither right nor wise to take military action. Accordingly, Mr. V. P. Menon was flown into Srinagar on 25th October and informed the Maharaja of the view of the Government of India. He returned immediately to Delhi with the news that it would not be possible to hold Srinagar from the tribesmen without sending in troops. At that stage arms and ammunition which were owing to the State under a previous agreement had, for various reasons, not been dispatched, and it appears that the Maharaja's first request concerned this claim. On 26th October the Defence Committee decided to prepare to send troops by air the following day and to accept the accession if it was offered. On the same day Mr. Menon flew back again to Srinagar, this time returning with both the signed accession and the request for troops in addition to the arms and ammunition which were due. I stressed that there was no previous plot. But at that late hour the advice which Mr. Menon was prepared to give the Maharaja could only have been to throw in his fortunes with India. Having once acceded, the Maharaja at that stage could hardly be expected to refrain from asking for India's assistance. The decision to fly in troops was therefore an Indian one. It fell to General Sir Dudley Russell to superintend the operation, and Russell was certainly convinced that he was executing an errand of mercy. I had his firm assurance that the operation was entirely spontaneous, without any previous preparation. It is most important that this should be recorded, for there are few Pakistanis who do not believe that so successful an air-borne project could only have been executed with previous detailed planning. There happened to be a number of civilian planes available which were being used in connection with the evacuation of Moslem refugees to Pakistan. Russell and his staff were down on the aerodrome commandeering military and civil planes in as fair a piece of military improvisation as any commander could desire.[1] Here surely is an example of the kind of

---

[1] As a military operation the Indian airlift was an impressive success. The troops arrived only just in time to save Srinagar, going straight into action as they landed on the edge of the airstrip. After finishing this chapter, my attention was drawn to the following statement which was signed by the three officers commanding the three Services in India at the time.

(a) It has been alleged that plans were made for sending Indian forces to Kashmir at some date before 22nd October, on which day the raid on that State from the direction of Abbottabad began.

(b) The following is a true time-table of events . . . [there follows a detailed time-table covering all decisions and action taken between 25th and 27th October].

(c) No plans were made for sending these forces, nor were such plans

suspicion which successfully bedevils the emergence of a new relationship between the two countries.

It has been argued that only swift military action saved the European community in Srinagar from the same fate as the Baramulla convent. Certainly Srinagar, undefended, would have provided a Roman holiday for the tribesmen, in which case the Pakistan Government would have been called on to intervene. Whatever degree of urgency may have seemed to demand the decision in Delhi, it is impossible not to deplore the circumstances by which troops called in to save Srinagar assumed the role of rescuing a vast State in which large sections of the people were unwilling to be rescued! In exoneration of Nehru we are told that he subsequently telegraphed Liaquat Ali Khan and gave him full information. This, alas, was wisdom after the event. If Nehru could have brought himself to the telephone for a talk with Liaquat before his Cabinet took their decision, if the tribal invasion could have been treated as an adventure damaging to both countries and demanding their joint efforts to defeat, the subsequent disastrous trail of events might at that last moment have been obviated. At the time Lord Ismay was flying back to India from London, and we can only regret that his measured judgment was not available to pour oil on troubled waters.

Mr. Jinnah first received news of the Indian action at Lahore on the evening of 27th October. At the time he was the guest of the Governor, Sir Francis Mudie, a host of generosity and infectious geniality. Jinnah immediately rang up General Gracey in Rawalpindi with instructions to dispatch Pakistani troops into the Jhelum Valley. The view has been expressed that had this been done the valley could quickly have been consolidated and Pakistan would today be in possession of most of the territory she now claims. Gracey, however, felt that even if the troops could have been found, he could not give such an order without the knowledge or sanction of Sir Claude Auchinleck, and he begged to be allowed to delay until Auchinleck could arrive in Lahore for a full discussion. Not only was there the need for restraint in order to prevent war between two Dominions, but also the Pakistan Regular Army was still in no position to undertake a campaign. Two or three units rushed into Kashmir might have won Srinagar for Pakistan. They could not have held an Indian direct attack on Pakistan's western Punjab which might well then have developed. On the morning of 28th October Auchinleck and Gracey were able to persuade Jinnah to withdraw his order. For Jinnah it was a hard decision. His sense of frustration was

even considered, before 25th October, three days after the tribal incursions began.

(Sd.) R. M. M. LOCKHART
   General. Commander-in-Chief, Indian Army.
(Sd.) T. W. ELMHIRST,
   Air Marshal Commanding. R.I.A.F.
(Sd.) J. T. S. HALL
   Rear Admiral. F.O.C., R.I.N.

P

complete, for he was being deprived of a country he felt racially and economically to be part of Pakistan. But whether the military or political arguments weighed uppermost in his mind he gave in with a good grace and accepted his defeat with dignity.

It had been the intention to follow up the meeting on 28th October with a full meeting the next day of all concerned in the direction of policy, with the object of thrashing out a settlement. Those expected to arrive were Lord Mountbatten, Pandit Nehru, Liaquat Ali Khan and Maharaja Hari Singh. By an unlucky stroke of chance, it so happened that while Liaquat was indisposed in Lahore, Nehru was also in poor health in Delhi; and so a summons from Lord Mountbatten to Mr. Jinnah to come to Delhi on account of Nehru being in bed was answered by a similar demand for Mountbatten to come to Lahore on account of Liaquat's indisposition! After some delays, Mountbatten came to Lahore without Nehru on 1st November. Although Nehru's condition had genuinely prohibited him from making the journey, the general opposition of the Indian Cabinet to any meeting in Lahore is on record.[1] The Kashmir problem is indeed an example of how the chances of settlement can recede by the refusal of leaders to risk agreement through the mellowing influence of the personal contact.

Meanwhile, within Kashmir Sheikh Abdullah was released on 26th September, and on 31st October was sworn in as head of the State with full powers to meet the emergency. Sheikh Abdullah's release has been represented as the price of accession. In fact a month was to pass before the crisis which forced the Maharaja to make up his mind; and the release was but the logic of relentless circumstances at the time. It had at first been the Maharaja's intention to set up an interim government with Abdullah sharing the powers with his own Prime Minister, Mehr Chand Mahajan, who had succeeded Pandit Kak. But events were too swift, and on 26th October the Maharaja left Srinagar never to return. The Maharaja's accession has always been used as the legal foundation for India's claim to Kashmir. Yet on 20th June 1949 he was to be forced to his final surrender when he left the State for Bombay. Having used the Ruler conveniently to satisfy legal obligations, India lost interest in his fate. He may not have merited State mourning. But his departure does lend the legality of accession a somewhat artificial appearance.

In accepting the accession, once again the Governor-General of India stressed on behalf of his Cabinet that Abdullah's administration was only to be regarded as an interim government. When the threat to peace was removed steps would be taken to ascertain the will of the people. The point was emphasised in a broadcast by Nehru on 2nd November. " We are prepared when peace and law and order have been established to have a referendum in Kashmir under international auspices," said Nehru; and he proceeded to raise doubts as to the good faith of the Pakistan Government, which could not have been ignorant of an opera-

---

[1] *Mission with Mountbatten*, Ch. 19, p. 227.

tion executed by tribal forces with every evidence of considerable preparation.

Possession is nine-tenths of the law, and it is difficult to believe that after a visit by Abdullah to Delhi in October, Nehru and his colleagues ever seriously contemplated any measures which would replace Abdullah's administration. Mountbatten was therefore unwittingly voicing a pious hope rather than an honest decision; and that is the impression which unfortunately has lingered on through subsequent months of bargain and procrastination. On 1st November, after a meeting of the Joint Defence Council, Mr. Jinnah put forward a plan by which both the Governors-General were to issue a joint proclamation calling on all those engaged in fighting to cease fire within forty-eight hours. If the tribesmen did not obey, the two armies were to take collective action against them. Thereafter the administration would be in the hands of the two Governors-General, who would accept responsibility for a plebiscite. A technical difficulty was that whereas Mr. Jinnah had taken unto himself the maximum powers possible under the Indian Independence Act, Mountbatten had been careful since partition to exercise the minimum control. Mountbatten promised to place Jinnah's proposal before his Government. The answer was a flat refusal. Whatever our verdict on the Indian interpretation of their Governor-General's powers, it should be recognised that Jinnah's proposal was a perfectly fair and honest attempt to put forward an effective settlement; and to dismiss it as a prevarication [1] is a complete distortion of truth.

On 30th October the Pakistan Government issued their repudiation of the Maharaja's accession to India, achieved, as they alleged, through fraud and violence. Their repeated efforts to reach an understanding with the Maharaja had either been ignored or rejected. They then developed the argument that as early as 15th October the Maharaja's Government had in fact sought to stage situations which would provide him with the excuse to ask for India's assistance. Poonch was such an example. In this they were obviously drawing on their imagination. Furthermore, in a broadcast on 4th November Liaquat lost his usual caution and hit out with more zeal than discretion. The people of Kashmir were fighting not only for their freedom, but for their very existence. They had been caught in the meshes of a widespread plan for the extermination of Moslems. The plan had succeeded in Alwar, Bharatpur, Patiala, Faridkot and Kaparthala, and all these were States which had acceded to the Indian Union. Thus argued Liaquat. Of Pakistan efforts to negotiate with the Maharaja little is known; and, as I have previously indicated, such efforts as were made to bring Sheikh Abdullah and Mr. Jinnah together failed because both being men conscious of their own position and importance, neither could bring himself to make the first move.

The problem was rapidly slipping away from the prospect of individual statesmanship and negotiation, and was entering the stage when public opinion takes charge and leaders, alas, are compelled to follow.

[1] *Mission with Mountbatten*, Ch. 19, p. 226.

The Pakistan terms for agreement were published on 3rd November, and simultaneously formally rejected by India. They amounted to a complete negation of the existing situation. The State troops were to be immobilised and Abdullah's Government held in abeyance. The only common ground was an agreement to a plebiscite under international supervision. It is this one common denominator which ever since has constituted the hope for a final compromise.

In the meanwhile the Indian forces had gradually got the measure of the opposition. On 7th November Indian troops attacked the rebels within 5 miles of Srinagar and inflicted heavy casualties. On 14th November the Indians reoccupied Uri. This coincided with a formal announcement by General Gracey that the Pakistan Army had issued no weapons to the tribesmen and that no serving officer had played any part in planning or directing the Kashmir operation.

The tribesmen had now shot their bolt. They had stuffed their lorries with loot, and the burning impulse of a *jehad* had rapidly deteriorated into the less lofty motive of a snatch-and-grab raid. There were in fact more coming out than going in, and such as remained constituted a liability rather than an asset to the subsequent Pakistan plans for holding the enemy. Their political value for Pakistan had been to enhance the reputation of Abdullah, while their military value had been limited to deceiving India as to the real strength of the opposition.

With the tribesmen back to their point of entry it was natural that subsequent operations should extend to the south and south-east of Muzzaffarabad. For months now the line has therefore been stabilised at a point west of Uri, taking its shape from the extension of operations which developed from November 1947 onwards.[1] As fresh reinforcements of tribesmen arrived, so they attempted to find a free flank to the south for raids into Kashmir territory. By 14th November they had reached to Mirpur, and a line which ran through Mirpur, Kotli and Poonch became stabilised. Behind it the Kashmir Azad Government spread out its control over the whole of the country which constituted the great spurs and valleys radiating south-west from the Pir-Panjal range. Such of the Maharaja's State forces as were in the area were cut off, the Poonch Moslem sepoys deserting with their arms to join the liberation forces in allegiance to the Azad Government.

With the new year and the gradual entry of Pakistan regular forces into the story, operations came to assume the aspect of a war. It is to this most ambiguous of wars that we now turn, novel in that never before can two armies in opposition have known quite so much about each other, nor really have been more surprised at finding they were expected to put into practice against former colleagues the lessons they had learnt together in the same school.

---

[1] The line, with minor modifications, became the " Cease-fire " line which was accepted by both sides on 27th July 1949.

CHAPTER SIXTEEN

CONTROLLED WARFARE

O N 19th November Indian reinforcements set out to relieve the beleaguered State garrisons, and by 21st November they had succeeded in reaching Poonch. But relief could not be achieved without a full commitment to fight and defeat the Azad forces, and thus, early in the new year, the Army of India found itself entangled in a prospective major campaign with a long vulnerable line of communications stretching through Jammu to Pathankot in India. The Indian extension of the fighting was contrary to the advice of General Bucher, who had urged discretion on his Government. But the zeal of the local Commanders appears to have been beyond the control of Delhi. In any case there was much public support for an aggressive policy to extend the operations. It was in these circumstances that regular units of the Pakistan Army came gradually to assemble behind the Azad forces, a process which was responsible for the whole scope of the Indian accusation of an illegal act of international aggression. The initial Indian advance towards Mirpur had caused very large numbers of Moslems to flee over the Kashmir border into Pakistan. If the Indian Army, sweeping aside the resistance of the irregulars, were allowed to advance and lap up the last corner of token Azad resistance, Pakistan could well expect another half-million refugees to swell the millions which were already the despair of her Government. In the circumstances it was perhaps not unnatural that, with Indian final intentions unknown, the Pakistan Army should increasingly be deployed behind the irregular forces of the Azad Kashmir Administration.

India's intentions were almost certainly quite innocuous. But at that stage a new nation in an emotional state of over-charged nationalism, seeing her neighbour's army posted all the way from Tithwal round to Ferozepore, was hardly able to appreciate the fact. It was thus the combination of a belief in the threat to her security with a great influx of refugees which was the motive behind the intervention of Pakistan's Regular Army.

Once again I draw attention to the obscurity surrounding the first use of Pakistan Regulars in the war. At G.H.Q. in Rawalpindi, in so far as they were prepared to discuss the matter, I was assured that no regular unit was moved before May. Yet a battery of mountain guns with an infantry escort were in action in an unsuccessful attack on Poonch on 17th March,[1] while on the Indian side General Russell believed that

---

[1] Had the doubtful quality of the Azad troops been realised at the time, the attack

r troops were involved in January. He accordingly asked to be
ed of his command. Whereupon on 20th January General
ppa took over.[1] Cariappa was also convinced that at this stage
n was using regular forces. He based his opinion on the fact
that a number of prisoners of regular units had been taken, and he faced
his Pakistan friends with the charge. This he was able to do since an
invitation to the Pakistan Armoured Corps "Week" in Lahore came
through to him from his old friend, Major-General Iftikar,[2] who was
then commanding the 10th Pakistan Division in Lahore. Towards the
end of May, General Cariappa again crossed over to the enemy on a self-
appointed mission of his own initiative. At a party in his honour given
by Major-General Loftus-Tottenham in Rawalpindi he repeated his
charge. This time he was on more certain ground, for May has always
been the month which Pakistanis have admitted as the date of the first
employment of their army. In conversation with Cariappa, Brigadier
Sher Khan, the Pakistan Director of Military Operations, admitted he
was worried about the number of deserters who were dribbling off to
fight in Kashmir.

What is the truth? After discussion with many of those concerned
it was possible to formulate broad conclusions. As early as February it
was clear to the Pakistan Commanders that Azad forces by themselves
could not possibly hold India's Army, which was deployed in considerable strength. It was therefore decided that 7th (P) Division should
occupy firm bases a few miles behind the Azad forces, but that they should
not be directly employed against Indian troops. Their presence would,
at that stage, constitute an insurance against a break-through, but nothing
more.[3] Battalions were therefore deployed within Kashmir but the
Headquarters of Brigades remained on Pakistan soil. Previous to the
moves of 7th (P) Division a process had developed by which generous
leave was granted without much worry as to how or where the applicant
took his holiday. In particular small sub-units, signallers and others,
took their leave together and were of use to the Azad forces. The
sanction of leave, and later the deployment of 7th (P) Division without
its full commitment to action, therefore fairly represents the Pakistan
participation before May 1948. The pity was that though the official

---

would not have taken place. The Pakistan mountain guns had registered accurately,
and in the evening they opened up, taking the Indian garrison completely by surprise.
But the Azad units failed to advance and occupy the vacated positions. The airfield,
however, remained under fire.

[1] In order to restore confidence throughout the demoralised area north of Delhi, a
special military command was set up, and General Russell was appointed to the
"Delhi and East Punjab Command". This command later included responsibility
for Kashmir, and was then assumed by General Cariappa.

[2] This fine officer was killed in a plane accident in December 1949.

[3] Pakistan Headquarters issued orders that no British officers were to participate
in Kashmir operations. I was informed that one or two officers, in their zeal, overlooked the order. General Bucher had issued similar orders in India as early as 29th
October 1947.

intervention in May was admitted, the admission was not made until September. Had a full confession been made at the time, together with a clear statement of the reasons, the path of subsequent negotiation would certainly have been smoother. Where there is so much cause for sad and sober reflection, it is refreshing to note the delightful manner in which India's General responsible for operations was able to cross over and enjoy a cocktail party at the expense of one who, though certainly not an enemy, found himself in duty bound to play the part of opponent.

A glance at the map will reveal India's military predicament. It was soon realised that nothing less than a force of two Divisions would suffice to relieve Poonch. As an increasing number of their troops became involved farther west, so a road had to be constructed behind them from Pathankot to maintain the forward troops. The sequence of events was not unlike many a similar campaign which had developed through thoughtless, haphazard plans and policies down the old Indian Frontier in the past fifty years. The initiative to attack and raid the Indian lines of communication remained with the smaller, less organised, forces of Pakistan, who were without the commitment to an unpractical objective. As the line became stabilised the advantage to Pakistan increased. Pakistan could choose her point of attack from any one of several centres, and not have far to move her troops in doing so. In contrast, in order to avoid setting foot on Pakistan soil, India could only confine her movements to the long line up from Amritsar to Poonch. For Pakistan it was an advantage not unlike that enjoyed by the North Koreans in their knowledge of the immunity of Manchurian soil across the Yalu River; and it was a very real advantage.

The initial airborne operation to defend Srinagar had all the elements of an exciting adventure. But the Indian troops had little heart for this further stupidity. They were slow over the massive hills as compared with their lighter opponents, while many of them could happily not forget that until recent times they had all been part of the same Army. Indeed, on one occasion two companies of the Guides Infantry found themselves in opposition and came to a friendly arrangement about jamming each other's wireless messages! Their lack of mobility could in some measure be compensated by the use of their air arm, a use which inevitably resulted in the bombing of some inoffensive targets, including the well-known summer leave station, Murree, with consequent Pakistan protests. General Bucher deplored the use of the air arm, and Nehru was in general agreement with him. But there appears to have been no tight control exercised over the Indian Air Force, and local demands for air support were easily put through. At one stage in the summer of 1948, on General Gracey's signal that he could arrange with the Azad forces for the safe evacuation of the Indian garrisons in Poonch, General Bucher approached Nehru, who gave his consent to a " cease-fire "; but the Azad irregulars were enjoying themselves too much, and it was effective for only a few days.

I would not wish this comment in any way to be interpreted as a reflection on the fighting qualities of India's Army as compared with the forces of Pakistan, for we know well enough the qualities which made distinctions invidious in the days when in peace or war they were one brotherhood. But I do assert that the motive to fight in the case of Pakistan was more vital than that in the case of India, with obvious repercussions in the two armies which any soldier will appreciate.

The initial instruction to Pak Army [1] by their Government was " to prevent India obtaining a decision by force of arms ". Having in view the wider implication of avoiding as far as possible direct conflict between the two armies, this instruction imposed a basically defensive role on Pak Army. It was therefore decided that the best method was to force India to disperse her troops and reserves on non-vital objectives, and beleaguered Poonch provided the perfect answer.

If Poonch was captured the political repercussions in India would be considerable. India was therefore bound to use up a good deal of strength in at least maintaining the garrison, and if possible effecting its relief. So long as she had this burden on her hands it was unlikely that, with her limited resources, she would be able to sustain a strong offensive in other more vital directions, such as the Jhelum River at Muzzaffarabad or the canal headworks at Mangla. [2] In general terms this " running-sore " strategy worked, and the diversion of India's effort on Poonch was certainly enough to detract considerably from her intentions elsewhere.

In the north on 19th May the Indians struck against Uri simultaneously with an outflanking move directed on Tithwal. The Uri thrust was held after some determined and confused fighting. But the outflanking move met with practically nothing except tribal opposition, and Tithwal was reached without difficulty. Pakistan's situation was now grim, and had India only used air supply more aggressively to maintain the impetus of this outflanking success they would so severely have threatened Muzzaffarabad as to force a Pakistan withdrawal from the whole northern sector. Luckily for Pakistan they paused, and 10th (P) Brigade, relieved from elsewhere and already tired, under Brigadier Haji Iftikar Ahmed, was rushed up the track from Muzzaffarabad towards Tithwal, and not only held the Indian advance but counter-attacked and recaptured some vital ground. Pakistan's rescue of her situation was the turning-point in a very unfortunate campaign.

The advance of 10th (P) Brigade beyond Muzzaffarabad was carried out in the face of great difficulties, not only administrative but also of terrain, and Pakistan certainly owes a debt of gratitude to this fine formation and the cool determined leadership of its commander. Brigadier Haji, to give him his familiar name, was a cavalry soldier with little or no infantry experience. He here found himself confronted with an infantry

[1] The military abbreviation in common use.
[2] The Mangla headworks control the Upper Jhelum Canal, which irrigates a great area in the north of West Pakistan.

situation in mountainous country. That he solved it correctly is an illustration of a simple principle of application outside its purely military context, that character and judgment are the masters of textbook knowledge.

When the threat to Tithwal was at its height, Pakistan was confronted by two alternative plans. The first was to withdraw the Uri front on to Muzzaffarabad, and then fight it out in a full pitched battle. The second was to abandon Muzzaffarabad and hold a token area of Kashmir within the area Kohala–Bagh–Palandi–Bhimbar. From this confined area guerilla operations could then be used to effect.

The implications of adopting one plan or the other were so great that the decision was felt to be a political one, and was accordingly referred to the Cabinet. Fortunately for Pakistan they chose the first plan, with the result described, by which 10th (P) Brigade retrieved a desperate situation.

By June it had become obvious that one Division could not continue to hold the Pakistan extended front, and so with effect from 20th June the 9th (Frontier) Division moved to Abbottabad and took over the line from Bagh up to Tithwal. Thereafter two Divisions were the basis of the Pakistan defence.

As 1948 wore on the general course of operations in the south-west of the State hardened to a stalemate. The tribesmen's psychology was hardly suited to a standstill war. The chance of snatching a quick victory had gone, and the tribes had no wish to be tied down to a desultory campaign in the south of the State. A diversion was therefore sought, and with the melting snows they carried out a rapid move round the north of the Kashmir Valley and appeared in strength at the south exit from the Zojila Pass north of Srinagar. The Indians were quick to meet the new threat. A squadron of light tanks were accordingly rushed to the Zojila. It was General Bucher's suggestion that in order to lighten the weight sufficiently to enable the bridges to be crossed the turrets should be removed. The tanks were therefore dismantled, and reached their mountain battle-ground in time to be reassembled on the Pass. Armour has certainly never operated before or since at an altitude of over 10,000 feet, and the Indian Army rightly takes pride in the achievement. The threat evaporated, but not until a great tract of country in the north of the State, including the Gilgit Agency and the tributary States of Hunza and Nagar, had thrown in their lot with Pakistan.

By the end of August the Pakistan Sappers had driven a road through Palandi towards Poonch. It was a rough-and-ready job of work, but it did enable them to run a 25-pounder gun to within range of the Poonch airfield. With the road open once again in October, the Pakistan Command contemplated an attack on Poonch, which throughout the year had served as a magnet for both sides. India, however, had pushed a relief force vigorously forward from Rajauri who were able to effect the relief of the garrison before the Pakistan attack could be mounted. With Poonch relieved, Pakistan could no longer rely on her "running-sore" strategy, and it was accordingly decided to act more aggressively and create a threat against some vital point of the Indian communications. By November the Pakistanis felt they could afford to take the risk—and it was considerable—of withdrawing forces from their Lahore front where Indian forces faced them, and concentrating in the area of Jhelum and Gujerat.[1]

The obvious area to harass the Indian lines of communication was somewhere between Pathankot and Jammu, in the neighbourhood of Akhnur, where the new road was carrying the full maintenance of a Corps of two Divisions. It was, however, realised that an Indian counter-attack, if successful, would have carried the war on to Pakistan soil, with all the fatal consequences of a full-scale inter-Dominion war. A point was therefore chosen between Jammu and Poonch, where the vital bridge at Beri Pattan provided a target which could be attacked from bases in Pakistan territory. The attack was originally planned for 8th December, but was delayed on account of political negotiations. On 13th December the Royal Indian Air Force successfully bombed the Pakistan dump at Palak on the Kotli line of communication, thereby providing Pakistan with an excuse for retaliatory action. It is significant of the usual conditions that at least excuses were still regarded as useful sanctions to begin a battle! By now the Indian Intelligence had a shrewd idea of the Pakistan intention. Their pilots were busy, and the Pakistan gunners were being shelled; and so on 14th December 1948 Pakistan staged their final threat. In a thirty-six hour bombardment the Pakistanis not only shattered ammunition dumps and communications, but successfully searched out the Indian Divisional Headquarters at Naoshera. A point on which General McCay is most emphatic is that neither this engagement nor any other exchange of fire initiated from Pakistan soil. The dispositions behind the front line obviously involved movement within Pakistan. But no gun was fired or attack launched from inside Pakistan territory, and the control of actual operations was also conducted from within Kashmir.

After the battle General Bucher's first inclination was to call upon armoured units from India and push them south from the road into Pakistan. But his armour was widely scattered and the chances for a quick decision for either side had passed. Bucher doubtless realised also that as Commander-in-Chief of the Indian forces he was no longer merely concerned with the eviction of wild tribesmen from a State which he regarded as a legal unit of India; he had now to prevent a war between two Dominions. In these circumstances he approached Nehru with the suggestion that he should signal Gracey and that they should in mutual co-operation effect a cease-fire.

---

[1] The Pakistan concentration consisted of 10th Brigade (made available from 9th Division), a parachute brigade, two field regiments R.A. and a medium battery R.A.

The credit for the cease-fire has been given to the United Nations Commission, and it is not generally known that in fact it was British initiative which should receive the honours. Bucher realised that Gracey would almost certainly support the proposal. He knew, too, that the United Nations Commission were about to make their own proposal, and that it was in the mutual interests of both India and Pakistan that the initiative should come from one of the contestants. He must also have known that if this war were to continue, India's honour would almost certainly now require to be satisfied. That satisfaction could only involve carrying the war on to Pakistan soil, a commitment which India was neither politically nor physically prepared to sustain. Having therefore obtained Pandit Nehru's approval, on the afternoon of 30th December Bucher sent Gracey the telegram which is reproduced as an Appendix. This suggested that if Gracey was prepared to reciprocate, Bucher would immediately order his troops to remain on their present positions and cease fire. Gracey agreed, and thus the craziest of wars was brought to a halt. The cease-fire was not difficult to implement. As has been pointed out, the opposing forces had but recently been one army. Many of the commanding officers had been colleagues together at Sandhurst or the Royal Military Academy at Dehra Dun. Sometimes they discovered that they were brother officers of the same unit. In such circumstances it certainly seemed folly to fight. The significance of the situation was just that the worthy envoys from Lake Success were comparatively inactive passengers so far as any influence on events in Kashmir was concerned.

There is one aspect of the military situation over which Pakistanis brood with bitterness. It concerns the award of the Gurdaspur District under the Radcliffe Award. It will be recalled that the statement of the British Government known as the " 3rd June Plan " announced arrangements by which the members of the Punjab and Bengal Legislative Assemblies should each meet in two separate portions to decide their fate on partition. The portions comprised members respectively from Districts holding Moslem and non-Moslem majorities. If either portion then voted for the division of their Province, the Province would be divided. This, in fact, happened; and so the Punjab—that magnificent administrative creation of British enterprise—was torn in two. The point is that the basis of the decision to divide was the District, and in an appendix to the plan the Districts with Moslem majorities according to the 1941 Census were enumerated. In the Lahore Division the Gurdaspur District carried a Moslem majority. A glance at the map will show that had this District as a whole been awarded to Pakistan, the position of troops landed by air in Kashmir from India would have been quite untenable.

The Gurdaspur District consists of four *tehsils*; Batala, Shakargarh, Gurdaspur itself and Pathankot. Of these, the first three had Moslem majorities, and only the Pathankot *tehsil* had a Hindu majority. Had

therefore the three Moslem *tehsils* gone to Pakistan, the maintenance of
Indian forces within Kashmir would still have presented a grave problem
for the Indian Commanders, for their railhead at Pathankot is fed through
the middle of the Gurdaspur *tehsil*.   It was Radcliffe's award to India of
the Gurdaspur and Batala *tehsils*, with Moslem majorities, which rendered
possible the maintenance of an Indian force at Jammu based on Pathankot
as railhead, and which enabled India to consolidate her defences south-
wards all the way from Uri to the Pakistan border.[1]

The cease-fire came into effect on 1st January 1949.   On the Pakistan
side there were then certain tribesmen and Pakistan Nationals inside the
State, together with the troops of Pakistan's Army and the Azad Kashmir
forces.   On the Indian side were the troops of the Indian Army, troops
of the State Army, and of the newly raised State Militia.

With the new year of 1949 the military aspect of the Kashmir problem
faded into the background, leaving the arena clear for the political attack
and counter-attack.   It had been the most absurd of wars.   There can
be no precedent in history for a situation in which armies commanded
by two senior British officers in telephonic communication were res-
trained with difficulty from closing with each other.   The reactions of
the commanders themselves were by no means simple.   General Gracey
was most certainly able to identify himself completely with the Pakistan
case.   A few minutes' conversation with him was sufficient to convince
me that here was a man who would be ready to risk his reputation for a
cause in which he sensed an injustice to the side which fate had chosen for
his championship.   His situation differed in several respects from that of
General Bucher.   By geographical circumstances he was in close
proximity not only to the troops he commanded, but also to the general
pulse of local sentiment.   At Rawalpindi he lived and worked on top
of the situation, in contrast to General Bucher, whose direction was
necessarily distant and who had to interpret events after rather than before
they had been subjected to political scrutiny in Delhi.   Bucher could
communicate with Gracey with complete freedom.   At the Pakistan
end the wires were safe and "top secret" messages were respected.   The
reverse process was by no means so certain.   But above all, Gracey was
struggling to establish an army which had to start from nothing, whereas
Bucher's forces merely evolved from a process of mathematical subtraction.   In the circumstances it was hardly just to blame Gracey for a
failure to control wild hordes of frontier tribesmen.

There remain to be recorded some aspects of the Kashmir War which
might be considered as of particular interest for soldiers.   Pakistan
suffered severely from the improvised nature of her war-machine in
contrast to a functioning concern. Until 1st November 1948 both the
Pakistan Divisional Commanders were commanding administrative

---

[1] The award of the greater portion of the Gurdaspur District to India is discussed
in detail in Chapter I.   Only the Shakargarh *tehsil* west of the River Ravi was left
with Pakistan.

Districts in Pakistan, with responsibility for their lines of communication, in addition to conducting operations in Kashmir.   The complete Indian monopoly of the air imposed movement by night on Pakistan, and their commanders have testified to the great strain to which troops were constantly subjected.   But perhaps the greatest disappointment for Pakistan, was the comparative insignificance, from a purely military point of view, of both Azad forces and tribesmen.   The former were brave enough in defence of their native soil, but they lost value in inverse proportion to the distance they were called on to fight from their villages.   The latter, by their indiscriminate slaughter of both Moslems and Hindus, had by December 1947 successfully antagonised the entire Kashmir Valley, without any appreciable military contribution for the assistance of the gathering Azad forces.   At the same time Pakistan was unable to spare aders which she could have hoped for to organise and lead either n or Azad Kashmiris.   It had been thought that the mere of the Pakistan Regular Army would galvanise the Azadis n into action.   Instead the contact operated merely to affect ps adversely.   Pakistan Commanders found the passive war forced on them by political considerations extremely plain to their own troops, let alone to the irregulars.   In ces it is remarkable that Pakistan officers could continue to confidence of their men in the manner they did.   To sum an Regular Army had fought a war with one ally of ue, and one as a definite liability.

ease-fire came, Pakistan senior commanders were confident ould have achieved the rapid collapse of the whole of Kashmir lia could have obtained important results in Pakistan itself. ll be thousands of Englishmen who are thankful that their was not to be tested.   Pakistan had laid open her Lahore front, dia still had two armoured Brigades on the Pakistan frontier. r-Dominion war, then as now, would have put the clock back, sastrous results for millions.   Perhaps the happiest aspect of an y year was the fact that the commanders on both sides were always ious of their grave responsibilities and the need to limit operations. Until November 1948 to seek a show-down with India was for Pakistan not only bad politics, but also bad strategy.   For India, too, operations in Kashmir were an unwelcome background to a situation in Hyderabad and on the economic front at home.

In this account of the most curious of wars I would emphasise that I have not told the story as a detective searching for clues in a crime.   But I do believe that by exposing the outline of truth the foundations for any future settlement must be made more secure than by allowing suspicions to linger on.   There we may leave the military situation, and pass on to note the confused tactics of the political entanglement.   In the shooting which never really merited the term of " war ", and which was officially never declared as such, we were aware that so long as British senior officers commanded the opposing forces, sooner or later the brake to a show-down could always be applied. But in the political arena it is difficult to see any finality, and we tire of the wearisome arguments. Yet we cannot avoid them; for more is at stake than just peace for the long-suffering Kashmiris.

CHAPTER SEVENTEEN

UNITED NATIONS INTERVENTION

THE story of international negotiation starts early in 1948. We have seen that December 1947 was not a good month for India's Army in Kashmir. They managed to relieve Kotli, which had been hard pressed by raiders for thirty-one days; but apart from the initial advance from Srinagar described in the previous chapter, the Azad Kashmir troops were hitting back at many points along India's tenuous lines of communication. There was therefore relief in Delhi when the Indian Government decided on 1st January 1948 to take the issue to the Security Council under Article 35 of the Charter of the United Nations.[1]

This decision is often spoken of as deriving from Indian initiative. In fact, it appears to have been one of mutual agreement.[2] Early in December Mountbatten prevailed on the two Prime Ministers to meet for the first time since the Kashmir accession. With the help of Lord Ismay, a formula was produced by which the United Nations Organisation would be asked to send a Commission to conduct a plebiscite in Kashmir and to make recommendations covering its fair and free execution. A few days later agreement was nearly shattered when Patel and Baldev Singh, the Sikh Defence Minister, appeared before the Defence Committee and gave lurid accounts of atrocities of which they had had direct evidence after their recent visit to the front. So often in the dreary record of dissension the two chief actors in the drama have been ready to agree, only to be forced to continue the struggle by the weight of either Cabinet or public opinion.

On 15th January 1948 the Council heard Sir Gopalaswami Ayyangar present the Indian case, and on the following day they listened to Sir Zafrullah Khan's reply for Pakistan. The one bright feature among a crop of fresh accusations was the fact that both delegates seemed glad enough to unburden their woes to the Security Council. Ayyangar

[1] The reporting of situations likely to endanger the maintenance of international peace and security.

[2] Some doubt has surrounded the question as to who took the initiative in an appeal to the United Nations. On inquiry it appeared that Pakistan made the first move. At a Press Conference on 16th November 1947 the Pakistan Prime Minister suggested a reference to the United Nations. The proposal was formally made to the Prime Minister of India in a telegram dated 19th November, in which Liaquat Ali Khan said, " In view of the stand you have taken I see no other way to a peaceful settlement except a reference of the whole question to UNO." This was rejected by the Indian Prime Minister in his telegram dated 25th November. It would therefore appear that the subsequent Indian appeal was in some measure borrowed from Pakistan initiative.

confined his argument to the presentation of a picture of the people of Kashmir rescued from the depredations of a desperate invader by the Indian Army. The first and last task of the Security Council was there-fore to effect their withdrawal. Sir Zafrullah Khan, in contrast, sought to cover the whole field of Pakistan's grievances, including India's failure to implement her financial obligations. He asked that the Security Council should extend its inquiry to cover all these matters. The sum of his argument concerning Kashmir was that the accession, together with the massacre of Moslems in East Punjab and the neighbouring Sikh and Hindu States, were factors in one vast plot. He concluded with a suggestion that India's appeal to the Security Council was due to the failure of her Army to enforce a decision. In this there was certainly an element of truth.

Though the two advocates had spoken with little evidence of tolera-tion, there was hope in that they both welcomed the prospect of United Nations intervention. On 20th January the President therefore an-nounced that India and Pakistan had agreed to the appointment of a Commission to mediate between them. Both countries would choose one member, and the countries chosen would then select a third—a method which was later discarded in favour of the appointment of a large Commission.

In the meanwhile the Council made efforts to effect a direct agreement between the representatives of the two countries. Abdullah himself was now available to present the Kashmir case. But it was not a very con-ciliatory argument. He had not a magic lamp, he said, with which to discover what Pakistan had done and was doing in Kashmir, but he could assure the Council that "the souls of Hitler and Goebbels have trans-migrated to Pakistan"! He said that when the Kashmiris had gained their freedom it would be for them to vote on the question either of accession or independence. The reference to independence as coming from Abdullah seems at that early stage to have attracted surprisingly little attention. Others have turned it over in their minds, but almost certainly with different interpretations of its meaning.

On 6th February 1948 the Council, still hoping for a direct agreement, invited the assistance of the President, General McNaughton of Canada and Mr. Van Langenhove of Belgium. But the deadlock was complete. Sir Gopalaswami Ayyangar, on behalf of India, refused to abdicate responsibility for the maintenance of law and order by withdrawing Indian troops when the fighting ceased. They would remain in Kashmir until the plebiscite had been held. He then asked for an adjournment in order to return to India to consult with his Government. Although the initial submission by India had been favourably received, a second impression of this first skirmish seemed in favour of Pakistan. The Council was not disposed to take action against Pakistan and effect the withdrawal of her forces without reference to the conditions of an eventual plebiscite.

The United Nations Commission [1] disembarked on the Indian sub-Continent in August 1948. They were a mixed bag, and it certainly went against the grain to watch the representatives from Latin America seeking to get on level terms with a problem which so many Englishmen might have regarded as their preserve. The pattern of military operations produced only one fresh element of embarrassment since the Commission's appointment. This was the fact that in May 1948, for the first time in fear of a threat from India's Regular Army, Pakistan had moved units of her Army into Kashmir.

A feature of the Kashmir situation is that the student can put it aside for months at a time and return to find exactly the same arguments and accusations being tossed backwards and forwards from one side to the other or thrown into the arena of the United Nations. The leading articles in *The Times*, which may be depended upon to produce a fresh aspect when justified by events have for many months found nothing new to add to the general monotonous picture of stalemate. There is therefore little profit in following the detailed course of the Commission's inquiries in the first months of their survey. The conditions were to some of them strange and quite outside their previous experience. Few of them could have had any knowledge of the historical background to the elementary problem of Moslems and Hindus on the Indian sub-Continent. Their survey of the situation eventually resulted in the formulation of two resolutions which ever since have been the basis of discussion. These are the resolutions of 13th August 1948 and 5th January 1949. Together they provided for the demilitarisation of Kashmir, pending a plebiscite, in two stages. The presence of Pakistan Regular troops on Kashmir soil was tactfully recognised as a "change" in the situation since the initial presentation of the Pakistan case. The first stage should therefore be the withdrawal of the Pakistan troops, the Pakistan Government using its influence to effect a similar withdrawal of the tribesmen or anyone else who had entered the State for fighting. The Commission would then report the completion of this process to India, who would proceed to withdraw the bulk of her own forces. Certain regular forces, however, were to be left behind by India to assist local authorities in the maintenance of law and order. On the Pakistan side the territory evacuated was to be administered by the local authorities under the supervision of the Commission. The accession of Kashmir to one State or the other would subsequently be settled "through the democratic method of a free and impartial plebiscite". The pattern of this plan has remained unchallenged in the subsequent years. A "truce" period has been recognised as covering the withdrawal of troops, whether effected in one or two stages, to be followed by the "plebiscite" period. During the latter period the plebiscite administrator is empowered to direct the final disposal of all forces remaining in the State for the

[1] UNCIP (United Nations Commission for India and Pakistan). See Kashmir, Appendix.

Q

plebiscite, an arrangement which, as will be seen, was open to different interpretations.

India and Pakistan accepted these resolutions in substance. But it is one thing to accept the principle, and quite another matter to agree on the detailed method of carrying it out. India, for instance, wished to leave behind troops to control the northern passes into Baltistan and Astor, and demanded the disbandment of the Azad forces rather than their withdrawal. Nor did a joint letter from Mr. Truman and Mr. Attlee to Pandit Nehru in any way soften the Indian approach. Nehru's difficulties must be appreciated. He was under heavy fire from the Hindu Mahasabha, who had attacked his Government for their handling of the campaign. In their view the fighting should never have been carried into the snow-clad hills. For them the home of the enemy in the plains was the correct objective. Kashmir was part of "Bharat Mata". Under pressure of such irresponsible raging, Nehru himself was rash enough at Allahabad in September to claim Kashmir as "part of India". Why, then, had he accepted the United Nations Commission's two resolutions of August 1948 and January 1949? Was it wise to admit four Kashmiri representatives to the Indian Constituent Assembly after the principle of a Kashmir plebiscite had been accepted?[1]

On 10th September 1949 UNCIP proposed the American, Admiral Chester Nimitz, as an arbitrator, adding that his decision would have to be accepted as binding. India immediately objected, saying that this would tend to reopen questions which had already been settled, such as the disbanding of the Azad forces. The truth was that the Commission had worked itself into an ambiguous confusion over this particular question, India believing that the Commission had agreed to the disbandment of the Azad forces and the handing over of their territory to Abdullah as the appropriate "local authority" for administration. Pakistan, in contrast, placed a quite different interpretation on the intention, believing that the Azad forces could remain on the ground to hand over to the Azad Government before withdrawal. In admission of failure and frustration, the Commission in their third interim report in December asked the Security Council's Canadian President, General McNaughton, to take up private discussions with the contestants. Sheikh Abdullah and Sardar Ibrahim accordingly both travelled to Lake Success.

[1] In taking note of this, UNCIP reported that India's action was undesirable, but difficult to oppose on legal grounds. The Belgian representative submitted a minority opinion, adding that if this led to elections in Kashmir in the parts under Indian control there would be grave consequences. Eventually the Kashmir Constituent Assembly on 25th March 1951 elected ten persons to represent the State in the Indian Parliament : four for the Council of States and six for the House of the People. These included three nominations of individuals normally living in the Pakistan-held areas and four who were not members of the National Conference Party. For the Council of States, two members are Moslems, the other two being Hindu or Sikh. For the House of the People there are four Moslems and two Hindus. All the Kashmir representatives are technically nominees of the President of the Indian Union on the recommendation of the Kashmir Government.

General A. G. L. McNaughton, whose term of the presidency expired at the end of the year, was prevailed on by the Council to continue his efforts to arbitrate into 1950. McNaughton's suggestions were for a progressive withdrawal of the regular armies and the disarming and disbandment of the Azad forces. Admiral Nimitz would then work with the Azad Government on one side of the dividing line and with Abdullah's Government on the other. India objected that this would condone the original Pakistan aggression, would limit Abdullah's authority, and ignored India's claim to the northern passes. Pakistan accepted the proposals, holding herself responsible for the disarming of the Azad forces.

On 6th February 1950 Nehru in Delhi permitted himself a comment, ominous and familiar in another context. "My patience is getting exhausted," he said. McNaughton's patience apparently was exhausted, for the following day he reported his own failure. The most formidable of India's objections had been her refusal to recognise any administration in the northern areas except that of Abdullah as the lawful authority for carrying on the administration. The "defence" of the area—a loose term open to several interpretations—should be vested in the Government of India.

Early in February 1950 Sir Benegal Rao took charge of the Indian case at Lake Success. A greater sense of urgency possessed the Council, but by now the feeling was abroad that the obstacles to progress which India was increasingly discovering derived from motives which were obscure, and therefore not above suspicion.

The next attempt at settlement arose from a resolution at Lake Success sponsored by the curiously mixed family of the United States, Britain, Cuba and Norway. Their proposals were based on General McNaughton's negotiations, to which they appeared to adhere closely. The progressive withdrawal was to be effected over a period of five months, and Sir Owen Dixon, a Judge of the Australian High Court, was charged with the task of demilitarisation. Both India and Pakistan accepted the resolution on 14th March, so that demilitarisation was due to be achieved by 14th August. Sir Owen's appointment was announced on 12th April, and a rare optimism for a time was injected into the discussions. *The Times*, reflecting the new sense of hope, wrote, "The way should now be prepared for Admiral Chester Nimitz to take up his functions as plebiscite administrator. British efforts behind the scenes have contributed to the happy outcome."

The terms of Sir Owen Dixon's appointment set the plebiscite as the main objective. But, in the nature of an afterthought, he was empowered to "make suggestions at variance with that objective" if he felt the plebiscite to be impracticable. In other words, the possibility of some form of partition as a last solution was not excluded, an aspect which was resented by Pakistan, who held to the mutual acceptance of the plebiscite as the one common denominator over many months of disagreement. Solution by partition was, however, not seriously advanced at this stage, and it remains to be seen if, with the prospect of eternal frustration and the consolidation of the areas already held by the two contestants, this logical form of settlement may come forward again for serious discussion. I shall return to the issue before closing the story.

By the end of July Sir Owen Dixon had exhausted his inquiries. He had travelled by car and jeep over much of the country and flown over the northern areas. His final conference with Liaquat Ali Khan and Nehru had failed. On 22nd August he issued his gloomy statement: "I have come to the conclusion that there is no immediate prospect of India and Pakistan composing any of their differences over Kashmir. No purpose can be served by my remaining longer in the sub-Continent." He had in fact examined the possibility of partition. He had thought that if each side could agree to absorb those areas where the wishes of the inhabitants were known, the way might then be left for a plebiscite in the residual territory. But since the nucleus in dispute proved to be the Vale of Kashmir itself, negotiation failed, because both sides regarded this central heart, with its 1,800,000 inhabitants, as a prize equal in value to the whole of the rest of the State. After thanking both Governments for their kindness and courtesy, Sir Owen regretted that the one element which had been missing in his mission had been any positive proposal from the Governments themselves. He then recommended them to return to the barren consolation of their own ways and means. He had made a gallant and determined effort, but the conclusion undoubtedly appeared in the nature of an anticlimax. This first statement, written before the detailed report, held one useful feature, in that it gave the Security Council fresh food for thought. Was some form of partition, after all, so improbable? It had one great merit. It would obviate those mass movements of refugees which any total award resulting from an overall plebiscite would be bound to engender.

On the sub-Continent Sir Owen Dixon's failure was at first more deeply resented in Pakistan than in India. This was natural. Throughout the hazards of negotiation, the spokesmen of Pakistan have repeatedly accepted international or Commonwealth proposals, while India has refused them. It is the exhaustion of Pakistan's patience which frankly would seem to carry the greater sanction. The fact that India held so much of the territory in dispute only added to Pakistan's frustration. Sir Owen Dixon, it was said in Karachi, had convicted India but punished Pakistan. In the circumstances the bazaar rumours of a fresh *jehad* were regrettable, but hardly unexpected. More formidable was a certain amount of wild talk of the need to seek fresh alliances and to consider the abandonment of the United Nations.

The publication of the detailed Report added fuel to the fire. It appeared to recommend the acceptance of the existing cease-fire line as the starting point for partitioning the State. For the Pakistan Press it displayed also an unwelcome readiness to describe the tribal invasions of

1947 and the subsequent use of Pakistani troops in 1948 as contraventions of international law. In fact, Sir Owen Dixon had never offered unqualified condemnation of Pakistan as an aggressor, and Sir Zafrullah Khan was himself later able to shed light on Dixon's attitude. Sir Owen he pointed out, had, as a matter of practical convenience and in order to make any progress in negotiation possible, been prepared to assume a *de facto* act of aggression.[1] This was a very different matter from a verdict pronounced after judicial investigation, which was no part of his commission. Nevertheless, the less responsible elements of the Pakistan Press readily fanned the flames. It was therefore with relief that an anxious public within Britain and the Commonwealth read of Liaquat Ali Khan's sound and steadying survey in the Pakistan Assembly on 5th October. He pointed out that it was unfair to judge the Security Council before it had acted. The Council could not and would not divest itself of its responsibilities : but if it was again to refer the matter to arbitration, then the decisions of the arbitrator must be enforced. The machinery of enforcement is, as we know to our cost, a very nebulous factor in international negotiation. There would seem little prospect for an arbitrator's solution which, however just, is so fraught with practical difficulty in its implementation.

The venom was reserved for the Prime Minister of India. " The world now knows what value to attach to his oft-repeated advocacy of self-determination for the peoples of Asia." Here was bitterness likely to attract attention in a wider circle of international debate.

There followed a long delay of two and a half months before the Security Council again displayed interest in the Kashmir question, a delay which only served to emphasise the failure of the Council at the other end of the world to appreciate the international significance of events in this most beautiful of Asia's isolated potential Utopias. Mr. Mohammed Ali, Secretary-General of the Pakistani Government, returning from Lake Success to Karachi, told of a new plan round the corner, but its discussion was to be postponed pending the meeting of the Commonwealth Prime Ministers in January 1951 in London; and in the meanwhile it was known that Liaquat Ali Khan intended to raise the question at that meeting.

The effect of wearisome delay was beginning to be felt in the arena of international power-politics. At a time when a united voice on the great sub-Continent could have played its part in Asian affairs, and more particularly in the political background to the Korean war, the two countries were, through mutual dissension, losing prestige and authority. It was at this stage in the last days of December that the British Government seemingly quibbled over the propriety of the Commonwealth Prime Ministers taking up a matter of domestic disagreement. It just was not done, was the attitude : and very naturally Pakistan's Prime Minister stated that the Conference therefore held no interest for him.

[1] Sir Zafrullah Khan, Security Council, 6th March 1951.

Scruples were finally overcome by arranging for Kashmir to be covered in informal discussions, avoiding the inclusion of so delicate a subject on the formal agenda.   Accordingly, at the last moment Liaquat Ali Khan on 6th January 1951 flew to London.   A sad reflection on the deterioration in Commonwealth relations crept into *The Times*.   Speaking of the reactions of responsible Pakistanis to Liaquat's attitude, their Karachi correspondent on 7th January wrote:

> " A complete boycott of the Commonwealth Conference would, they feel, have lost him sympathy abroad and possibly have brought him to the point of no return in Pakistani relations with the Commonwealth—a connection whose benefits many of the more soberminded Pakistanis still recognize!"

The Prime Ministers met, they discussed and they dispersed; and Kashmir remained unsolved.   But at least men who should long ago have been in intimate deliberation had learnt something of each other's manners and methods.   The right note had been set by Mr. Menzies, who, on his way to London from Australia, took the trouble to make the journey to Delhi and Karachi and acquaint himself with his two new colleagues; and so Liaquat Ali Khan was able to leave at least with a full appreciation of the sincerity of the Commonwealth leaders.   Before he left London he revealed something of the nature of the Kashmir discussions in a Press Conference on 18th January.   Starting from the point of India's contention that her troops could not be withdrawn from Kashmir for a plebiscite, since India was responsible for the State's security, three alternative proposals had been mooted.   These were: (*a*) The maintenance of forces in Kashmir by Commonwealth countries before and during the plebiscite, at their own expense.   (*b*) A joint force of Indian and Pakistani troops under a common command in occupation during the plebiscite.   (*c*) A local Kashmiri force raised by the plebiscite administrator for security, enabling all other forces, regular or irregular, to be withdrawn.   Liaquat claimed that he had in turn accepted all these solutions and that, with familiar consistency, Nehru had refused them.   Earlier the same day Pandit Nehru had given nothing away at a Press Conference, and it was clear he regarded Liaquat's statement as a breach of confidence.   In the meanwhile in Bombay Sheikh Abdullah on 8th January in a statement to the Press set out four conditions for a settlement which bore little relation to the substance of the London discussions.   The withdrawal of all Pakistan forces, the entire State of Kashmir to come under the control of its legally constituted Government, the liquidation of the Azad Government and his own administration then to be given time to establish its authority and to rehabilitate the people: these were his conditions for a plebiscite. India's sincerity could well have been demonstrated by a mild repudiation of terms so far removed from the situation as understood at the United Nations.

And so the endless quest returned again to Lake Success. This time it was Britain, supported by the United States, which tabled the resolution. They had had a long trail of experience on which to draw. They threw in the suggestion of a United Nations force to hold the ring. They left partition aside as a solution and clung to the common commitment to the overall plebiscite. Finally they proposed to elect yet another arbitrator, Dr. Graham, to arrange demilitarisation and prepare a detailed plan for a plebiscite. After three months it would be his duty to report to the Council on outstanding points of disagreement. These would be settled by arbitration on reference to a panel appointed by the International Court of Justice. In short, they added a few ingredients to a meal which was already cooked, for time had shown that it was out of the question to prepare a fresh meal. Their resolution was adopted on 30th March.

Once again Sheikh Abdullah appeared to pursue the course of his own choice. It was now his announced intention to stage elections to a Kashmir Constituent Assembly within the areas which he controlled. It is a sad reflection on the ineptitude of our international machinery that, in spite of the repeated protests of the Security Council as voiced by the British representative and supported by the most powerful nation in the world, Abdullah was able to see the election of his doubtful Assembly through to its conclusion.

The immediate reactions in Delhi and Karachi to the new proposals were exactly as foreseen. To India they were " wholly unacceptable ". In particular they refused the principle of arbitration on points of disagreement. To Pakistan they were insufficient. The Indian case as presented by Sir Benegal Rao was, in effect, a plea to return to the direct negotiations advocated by Sir Owen Dixon. The entry of foreign troops could not be accepted, nor could the lawful Government of Kashmir be superseded. There was, in fact, nothing new. Sir Zafrullah Khan, in contrast, would have armed the United Nations arbitrator with dictatorial powers. The good name of the Security Council was at stake. Only by asserting its authority could the Council discharge its duty. India and Pakistan should be called on to withdraw their forces and offer their full co-operation to the mediator. At one point Sir Zafrullah's forensic logic forsook him. It was when he looked back to the original Indian occupation and sought to prove a conspiracy between the Maharaja and the Indian Congress leaders. This hardly strengthened his case, for it furnished Nehru with effective material to refute so slender a charge with justifiable indignation.[1] His lengthy statement, which was

[1] Speaking in the Constituent Assembly, Nehru said Sir Zafrullah Khan's insinuation was nothing but a figment of his fertile imagination.
" No member of the Indian Cabinet or our General Staff had even thought of this as a remotest possibility till after the invasion of Kashmir by Pakistan—that is during the last week in October 1947. There was a British Commander-in-Chief then, and a British Chief of the General Staff. It is easy to find out what the facts were and how this question first arose before us after the invasion started."

concluded on 2nd April, fully accepted the new proposals. On the same day from Srinagar came the report that Nehru had addressed a closed meeting of the Kashmir National Conference and told them that the Security Council resolution could not affect the holding of elections in Kashmir.

In Delhi the Security Council was denounced as a partisan body, and the Soviet abstention from voting was warmly praised.[1] It was not surprising that so much of the goodwill which India had reaped through her brilliant advocacy of the Chinese case at Lake Success in the autumn of 1950 was now dissipated in a suspicion that in the isolated issue of Kashmir she was displaying that imperialistic intolerance which she had so frequently criticised in others. More in sorrow than in anger we watched the process, for India's contribution to international harmony has been broad and constructive, and can be so again.

[1] The *National Herald* wrote: " To the Soviet's credit it may be said that it has so far taken little interest in the strategic or political possibilities of Kashmir, further that it is undue Anglo-American interest which provokes Soviet intervention anywhere." Quoted by *The Times* Delhi Correspondent, 1st April 1951.

CHAPTER EIGHTEEN

DR. GRAHAM'S ARBITRATION

O N 30th April we learnt that, in accordance with the Council's resolution of 30th March, Dr. Frank D. Graham of the United States Defence Manpower Administration had been appointed as arbitrator, but it was not until 30th June that he arrived at Karachi, and not until 2nd July that, in the absence of Pandit Nehru on holiday in Kashmir, he met President Rajendra Prasad in Delhi. In accordance with the modern tendency, the appointment of one individual did in fact involve the employment of twelve secretaries, political and military advisers and administrative assistants. It was an invidious task that Dr. Graham faced. After a long period of quiescence in Kashmir, there had been a sudden spate of raids across the cease-fire line, and Major-General Nimmo, the United Nations' Chief Military Observer, was kept busy with visits to the two armies. If Dr. Graham was merely to ascertain the points of disagreement and refer them after three months to the United Nations for arbitration, he would be leaving matters in a worse state than when he arrived. He could expect little co-operation from India, who, though giving him a polite welcome, never officially recognised his appointment. In Kashmir, in defiance of the Security Council, the Constituent Assembly had been convened.[1] He entered into his deliberations in an atmosphere charged with fresh Pakistani accusations of Indian Army concentrations along the Punjab frontier. At the same time Nehru was retaliating with stories of unnecessary assistance afforded by British officers to Pakistan. Khan Abdul Qayyum Khan, the zealous Chief Minister of the Frontier Province, hit out at India and Britain with equal ferocity, and Nehru returned to the attack with a story of a Pakistan brigade moved from Peshawar to Rawalkot, within 15 miles of Poonch. Seldom could the conditions for moderation and tolerant discussion have been less auspicious.

Early in September Sheikh Abdullah staged his elections. In an Assembly of seventy-five, forty-five seats were reserved for Ladakh and the Kashmir Valley, and, of these, forty-three returned Abdullah's candidates unopposed. The elections would have been more convincing if the Opposition could have claimed at least to have been allowed to exist, and it was difficult not to recall the familiar methods of other ideologies. This one measure perhaps stirred the Security Council to censure more

---

[1] Convened by the Yuvraj Karan Singh, son of Maharaja Hari Singh. The former has acted as Regent and Head of the State ever since his father finally left Jammu for Bombay on 20th June 1948.

than any other recent action of the contestants. On 30th March 1951, before the convening of the Kashmir Assembly, the Council had passed a resolution to the effect that they would not regard action taken by a Constituent Assembly as in any way determining the future disposition of the State. Later in November, when Dr. Graham's interim report was being considered, Sir Gladwyn Jebb found consolation in a statement by Nehru. " We have made it perfectly clear in our statement in the Security Council that the Kashmir Constituent Assembly, so far as we are concerned, does not come in the way of a decision by the Security Council; that stands completely." Thus spoke India's Prime Minister, and we would like to believe in the sincerity of this unambiguous declaration. Yet we are left bewildered. For if it means what it says, we are to assume that Mr. Nehru must wish to avoid a clash as between a Security Council decision and the will of the Kashmir Assembly, in which case he surely could have obviated such a possibility by opposing the Assembly's establishment with the weight of his authority and advice.

Dr. Graham set about his task in the only way possible, which was to hold separate informal discussions with each Government. On 7th September he was able to write to them from New Delhi, setting out his conclusions.

After careful thought he said that there was reason to believe that a compromise could be reached by which both Governments could implement their respective commitments under the UNCIP resolutions of August 1948 and January 1949. He then requested them to consider certain proposals. First, they should reaffirm their determination not to resort to force, coupled with an undertaking to restrain within their frontiers the Press, the radio and all organisations and responsible leaders from incitement to force. Secondly, they should reaffirm their will to make the cease-fire effective from 1st January 1949. Thirdly, they should reaffirm their faith in a free plebiscite, under the auspices of the United Nations, to decide the fate of the country. Dr. Graham then proceeded to outline his proposals for the demilitarisation of the State, to be achieved within three months. This was to be effected as a single continuous process. On the Pakistan side all Pakistan regular troops and all tribesmen were to withdraw out of the State, and the disbandment and disarmament of the Azad Kashmir forces were to be well in hand. On the Indian side the " bulk " of the regular forces was to withdraw. There would then be left a specified number of regular and State forces on the Indian side and a civil armed force on the Pakistan side of the cease-fire line.

The reaffirmations required were readily forthcoming. But the old objections and suspicions were immediately in evidence when it came to comments on demilitarisation. Pandit Nehru was not satisfied with the proposed commitment to state the number of Indian troops remaining after the " bulk of regular forces " had withdrawn. He indicated that he wished to retain a Division of sixteen battalions without commitment as to its withdrawal, a force which he claimed would be inadequate for security if Pakistan failed in her part of the bargain.

The two previous UNCIP resolutions had contemplated demilitarisation in two stages. First the Pakistan troops and tribesmen were to withdraw, since their presence had been India's declared reason before the Security Council for the presence of her own troops. Secondly, on completion of Pakistan's withdrawal, the Commission was to report to the Indian Government, who would then initiate their own withdrawal by stages. In contemplating one single operation Dr. Graham's proposals therefore represented a considerable modification of India's previous demands. India had at last accepted a simultaneous withdrawal. But this surrender was to some degree negatived by the demand, already noted, to leave behind a considerable number of troops.

Yet another matter of contention was the meaning of the term " disposal " in relation to the power of the Plebiscite Administrator over the forces remaining in the State during the plebiscite stage.[1] Pakistan assumed this to mean their disbandment. India, on the other hand, was prepared to recognise the term as covering disbandment when applying to the Azad forces, but held that the meaning and intention in application to her own forces only concerned the placing of troops into barracks and camps. Location rather than disposal was their interpretation.

Pakistan's general views, submitted simultaneously and without knowledge of the contents of the Indian reply, were that approximately equal forces of four battalions of Azad Kashmir troops and Indian regulars should remain on either side of the cease-fire line after the demilitarisation period of ninety days. Nevertheless, in general terms Liaquat Ali Khan's reply constituted a full acceptance of Dr. Graham's proposals. He particularly emphasised the need for the Plebiscite Administrator to assume his office as soon as possible after the initiation of demilitarisation. With this partial acceptance by India and comparatively full acceptance by Pakistan, Dr. Graham sailed for Geneva on 12th September to complete his report. On 15th October a first instalment of this was made available. It told us nothing new, and requested the Security Council for an extension of six weeks in which to be allowed to make renewed efforts for a detailed agreement on the process of demilitarisation.

On 17th January 1952 [2] Dr. Graham presented his second report to the Security Council, and at the same time admitted his failure to achieve agreement on certain fundamental principles. So far as the scope of demilitarisation was concerned, two points defied solution. First was

[1] UNCIP Resolution of 5th January 1949 stated that the Commission and the Administrator, in consultation with the Government of India, would determine the final disposal of forces, " With due regard to the security of the State and the freedom of the plebiscite ".
[2] The written report had previously been released on 21st December 1951.

the problem of disarming and disbanding the Azad Kashmir forces. Since to the Pakistanis these were the manifestation of the faith and resistance of a Kashmir in bondage, the difficulty in obtaining their agreement on this point can be appreciated.   Secondly, it seemed impossible to decide the moment within the period of demilitarisation when the plebiscite Administrator would take up his appointment.   Dr. Graham's own view was that he should start work at the end of the demilitarisation period, which was assumed to be not later than July 1952. In regard to the more vital question of the numbers of regular troops to be left behind, India sought expert advice.   Accordingly, General Jacob Devers, the military adviser to Dr. Graham, held separate talks with the representative of the two countries, as a result of which he was successful in inducing India to agree to withdraw an additional 7,000 troops.   This reduced the Indian and State forces to a Division of 21,000 troops exclusive of the State militia of 6,000 which Abdullah's Government had raised in the early days of the campaign.   To balance these on the Pakistan side were to be left three regular battalions, four battalions of Azad forces and a civilian Police force of 4,000, which in turn was to be subdivided into no less than four categories.   The Devers plan was communicated to both Governments on 29th November 1951, and in substance appears to have been accepted by India.   When therefore on 21st January 1952 a different form of the plan was published purporting to be the original agreed upon, India emphatically denied all knowledge of it.   The new plan reduced the disparity of forces on either side to about 4,000.[1]   This would have satisfied Dr. Graham's view that the ratio of troops remaining on either side of the cease-fire line should be the same after withdrawal as it was on 1st January 1949.   Exactly how the misunderstanding arose is one of those matters of academic consequence which will remain buried in the files, for the doubts round the Devers plan are now regarded as a storm in a tea-cup.

Since, in spite of all Dr. Graham's tact and patience, he had made little headway on fundamental principles, the subsequent explosive contribution from Mr. Jacob Malik on behalf of the Soviet did less damage than might have been expected.   Breaking the Soviet silence of four years, Mr. Malik did full justice to his country's fertile imagination in the discovery of Anglo-American motives.   Apparently Kashmir was really intended as a " trust territory " under Anglo-American control.   Its ultimate fate was probably to form an armed base for Anglo-American troops with air-bases from which the capitalists could strike at China. The proof of it all was the British and American objection to the convening of a Kashmir Constituent Assembly.   Unfortunately, the outburst produced the impression that Britain and America had decided to put Kashmir into cold storage.   The Pakistan Press were accordingly completely bewildered.   On the one hand there were bitter words for the two great Powers who repeatedly shelved their responsibility.   On the

[1] India, 13,800; Pakistan, 10,200.

other hand there was equally severe censure of Mr. Malik for not having taken the trouble to discover Pakistan's real attitude to Abdullah's spurious Assembly. The Soviet intervention remains another of those inexplicable intrusions designed apparently to complicate international situations. A fair guess would be that the intention was to influence voters in the Indian elections in favour of the Communists. Certainly the Indian National Congress could hardly have regarded it as a move to their advantage. In justice to Mr. Malik, it must be said that he had received some provocation from Abdullah himself. In the latter's opening address to his Constituent Assembly in the previous November the offer of Commonwealth forces for the plebiscite was referred to as "imperial control by the back door". Their presence would have created suspicion among Kashmir's neighbours that Kashmir was allowing itself to be used as a base for possible future aggression against them. This would easily have turned Kashmir into a second Korea. What more suggestive language could have been chosen for Mr. Malik's purposes!

Mr. Malik's wild talk was accompanied by accusations of a personal nature directed at Dr. Graham. This, however, did not prevent the Security Council from extending his term of office for another two months from 31st January 1952 and requesting him to make a final attempt to effect agreement. Accordingly, Dr. Graham returned to the sub-Continent for a short period from the 29th February to the 27th March. He then went to Geneva to complete his third and last report. This was published on 22nd April. Previously he told the Press that he had noticed a general lessening of tension between the two nations. He was confident that one day a settlement would be reached. We are grateful for such imperturbable optimists, even though they fail to produce signatures on an agreement. Nevertheless, it was difficult to resist the reflection that Dr. Graham was clinging to a situation in which he was reluctant to admit his own failure. The publication of his final report revealed that of the original twelve points of disagreement, only four now remained unsettled; and of these only two really mattered. But if Dr. Graham had been prepared to face the position with unspectacular honesty he would have had to admit that one of those two points—the numbers of troops to remain at the end of the truce stage— was as important as the sum total of the remaining eleven judged together. Instead he preferred to draw attention to the fact that India had decided to withdraw forces from the Pakistan border in the neighbourhood of Amritsar to distances varying from 70 to 450 miles. The Pakistan view that Graham was using the Indian withdrawal as a cover for his failure to achieve agreement on the one vital issue received little publicity. Moreover, the Pakistan contention was that Indian troops in Kashmir had not been withdrawn, but merely relieved, leaving the total forces in Kashmir unchanged. This would presumably be the kind of matter to which the Observer Corps would know the answer, and one presumes that Graham would have verified his data in consultation with

General Nimmo. The optimism of Dr. Graham was faithfully reflected in the comments of the British Press, *The Times* correspondent in Karachi alone voicing the bitter disappointment in Pakistan.

The second point on which Dr. Graham failed to gain Indian assent was the timing of the arrival of the Plebiscite Administrator. He reported that the situation was now at the stage when he could call on Admiral Chester Nimitz to join in the discussion. It would seem a matter of common sense that if Nimitz was to be in a position effectively to control a plebiscite from an agreed date, that control should be based on his own ideas of its previous development. He would need, in common parlance, to be "in the picture". The Indian objection seemed barely intelligent. In London, *India News* on 3rd May 1952 commented :—

> "It is India's view that the time for appointment of the Administrator is after the demilitarisation scheme has been agreed to and they feel that if Admiral Nimitz should get involved in any prior controversies, which are bound to arise in the course of the negotiation for demilitarisation, it would prejudice his position as Administrator. Any man taking an active part in the parleys will be forced to take sides at some stage and that will at once disqualify him from his exalted office as Administrator, because he would have lost his impartiality. . . ."

If a senior United Nations official is not to be trusted to maintain impartiality previous to the commencement of his task, one wonders how it is logical to suppose that he will remain impartial while actually shouldering responsibility for a subsequent plebiscite!

The report closed with a recommendation that he, Dr. Graham, should be allowed to continue to negotiate with a view to achieving agreement on the outstanding points. It is not difficult to imagine the alacrity with which the Security Council seized on this amiable suggestion. Echoing the negotiator's optimism, *The Times* in a leader of 1st May commented, "The one thing which the Security Council must avoid is another full-dress debate now on Kashmir." It was certainly the one thing which they wished to avoid!

The Pakistan Government were very reluctant to discuss the matter further. They felt it was purposeless to meet again until India agreed to Graham's proposals. But diplomatic pressure was brought to bear on the Pakistanis, and Mohammed Ayub, the Joint Secretary in the Ministry of Kashmir Affairs, left in the third week of May for New York, where he was joined by Mr. A. S. Bokhari, the Permanent Pakistani United Nations Delegate. In reluctantly accepting a decision representing procedure which was never foreshadowed in the original intention, Pakistan would have had in mind the fact that after the Indian elections a happier atmosphere for negotiation might develop. Graham might even be in a position to stage a meeting of the two Prime Ministers—an accomplishment which was known to be constantly in his mind. But if and when the defeat is final, the Pakistan demand for an unequivocal statement from the Security Council to cover the future will have to be faced in wider interests than those of mere equity in the present case. The alternative is for the Council to lose what little respect it still commands in the Moslem world eastwards from Tunisia. How long the Pakistan Government are prepared to wait remains to be seen.[1] Meanwhile Dr. Graham was again able to entice deputations from the two countries to Geneva, where it was hoped that the happier atmosphere of Swiss neutrality and pleasant scenery might help his perseverance.[2] The British Press were optimistic. But they failed to take note of the Pakistan Prime Minister's reference to Kashmir in his public address on Independence Day (14th August 1952). "We have not accepted the accession of Kashmir to India and notwithstanding anything that Mr. Nehru may say, we will never accept it." If Khwaja Nazimuddin meant what he said, there is little prospect of a settlement. For it is impossible to foresee the circumstances in which either Pandit Nehru or Sheikh Abdullah would risk a verdict adverse to their interests.[3]

I had closed this chapter when yet another attempt by Dr. Graham suddenly demanded a record. We are reminded of the opera star who cannot resist the temptation to repeat the farewell performance! On this occasion he returned as a result of an Anglo-American resolution before the Security Council in December 1952. The resolution called on the two countries to enter into immediate negotiations in New York to decide that elusive twelfth point—the strength and character of the forces to be retained after the main forces had withdrawn. It was difficult to read any imaginative thinking into this restatement of proposals, which appeared to be of a similar nature to the previous conclusion of Sir Owen Dixon. Nevertheless, early in February 1953 Dr. Graham met Sir Zafrullah Khan and Sir Girja Shankar Bajpai, not in New York, but in Geneva. They then duly recorded the usual monotonous failure. One slight variation in the pattern of argument governed this final effort. Based on the data of Dr. Graham's last report, the Anglo-American resolution suggested compromise figures for the respective forces; and at one time it appeared that India had only to accept a figure of 18,000, as

[1] A period of one month was mentioned by Sir Zafrullah Khan, which has long since been exceeded.

[2] Talks started on 26th August 1952. For India Sir Gopalaswami Ayyangar (Minister of Defence) was assisted by Mr. D. P. Dhar, Deputy Home Minister, Kashmir Government. Sir Zafrullah Khan led the Pakistan delegation.

[3] Subsequently certain further developments added or subtracted little. On 6th November 1952 Sir Gladwyn Jebb put forward an Anglo-U.S. proposal before the Security Council that both countries should reopen direct negotiations at United Nations Headquarters, confining themselves to the one point of the size of the forces to be left behind during the plebiscite. They were to report back within thirty days. On behalf of the British Government Sir Gladwyn indicated that any plan outside the scope of the familiar pattern of negotiation would be welcome, if it provided the possibility of acceptance.

against her previous minimum of 21,000, for the two sides to reach agreement. But a more interesting development was a sudden offer of Sir Zafrullah Khan to accept 28,000 Indian troops and a withdrawal of all Pakistan Regular troops, if India would agree to leave the Azad forces intact. The nature of this suggestion was hardly apparent to a neutral observer. Pandit Nehru saw in it a device to leave Pakistan regular troops behind disguised as irregulars; and he spoke of a consequent threat of 20,000 to 30,000 armed Azad men who would face India's forces. There was no indication on what evidence he based his figures. And so another round in the contest ended in the same monotonous inconclusion.

One new feature of the final report escaped attention. Dr. Graham wrote that it was his firm conviction that there were other factors " which have a bearing on demilitarisation which need to be taken into consideration. The United Nations representative is not at the present time in a position to give a considered statement on all these factors."

My information is that whereas Dr. Graham has on occasions met Sheikh Abdullah, official discussions with him, indeed the whole issue of a contribution to the fate of Kashmir from either Abdullah or the Azad Government, have hitherto lain outside the scope of his brief. It is to those " other factors " that I now turn. The recitation of the story of political negotiation has proved a thankless task, approached in a sense of duty rather than pleasure. Too often it seemed to be a cycle of India's objection, followed by a proposal, followed by an objection to the proposal on the ground that issues already agreed upon were being reopened. We now leave the dismal train of bargain and negotiation for matters of theory, speculation and personalities.

CHAPTER NINETEEN

PERSONALITIES AND PLANS

Apersonality who has not yet figured overmuch in the Kashmir dispute is the young Yuvraj Karan Singh, only son of Maharaja Hari Singh, and now accepted as the Constitutional Head of the State. I had the pleasure of meeting him on 6th January 1952 at his house in Jammu. It is possible that he may be destined to play his part, for he has charm and ability with little of the traditional background of hostility to social change which prohibited his father from accommodation with Sheikh Abdullah. He has suffered cruelly from ill health and accident, and he was hurried out of Srinagar in an army lorry on 26th October 1947 and dumped down in Jammu bound up in plaster-of-Paris. Subsequently he went to America for treatment and study, and he took his degree in political economy in Srinagar having worked under private tuition.

I was curious to discover his exact relationship with his Prime Minister. Since 20th June 1949 he has acted as Regent, for it was finally on that date that it became obvious that his father could no longer remain in the State. He described relations as "excellent". He was prepared to remain a Constitutional Ruler. He received an adequate privy purse and he looked forward to assisting the democratic progress of his people. He seemed to be a young man who in normal times would have been the focus of the affection of his subjects, capable of leading Kashmir forward to a happier destiny of freedom. It was therefore disappointing to find later in the day, in talking to Sheikh Abdullah, that the Sheikh did not appear to reciprocate this friendly approach. He recognised monarchy as a necessary evil appendage of Government at that stage, but I fancy he would be quick to abolish it on provocation if the fate of a united Kashmir could first be settled to his satisfaction.

Abdullah did in fact openly express his views when addressing his Constituent Assembly in Srinagar on 5th November 1951.

"So far as my Party is concerned, we are convinced that the institution of monarchy is incompatible with the spirit and need of modern times which demand an egalitarian relationship between one citizen and another. The supreme test of a democracy is the measure of equality of opportunity that it affords to its citizens to rise to the highest point of authority and position. In consequence, monarchies are fast disappearing from the world picture, as something in the nature of feudal anachronisms."

Abdullah continued with a picture of the circumstances which had finally rendered Maharaja Hari Singh's position untenable. Having well prepared the ground for an extension of his attack to fit the existing conditions, he rather surprisingly paid a warm tribute to the Yuvraj.

"Our judgment should not be warped by ill-will or personal rancour. During our association with Yuvraj Karan Singh these last few years, I and my colleagues in the Government have been impressed by his intelligence, his broad outlook and his keen desire to serve the country. These qualities of the Yuvraj single him out as a fit choice for the honour of being chosen the first Head of the State."

In conclusion Sheikh Abdullah was willing to recognise the Yuvraj as a "fitting symbol". It was as a "symbol" that India was prepared to recognise the Crown in her relationship with the British Commonwealth, and the conception may have proved infectious. Whatever may be Abdullah's personal appreciation of Yuvraj Karan Singh, his official attitude seems charged with that ambiguity which surrounds all his future intentions.

That was my assessment of the Yuvraj's situation in March 1952, and as the months went by the tendency to which I have drawn attention seemed to be developing into a crisis. It did not take quite the form which might be expected, for there was little public evidence of any ill feeling between the Yuvraj and Abdullah. Instead it accentuated the doubtful relations with India. Early in June, as Chairman of the Basic Members Committee of the State Constituent Assembly, Abdullah was able to announce that his Committee recommended the abolition of hereditary rulership and the future appointment of the Head of the State to be elective. In India many felt that these developments represented a situation far beyond the nature of the accession in 1947. A Kashmir deputation was accordingly summoned to Delhi and Abdullah and his party answered the call with definite reluctance. It was the most obvious open clash of mutual interests hitherto recorded. The Kashmir Assembly in the meantime confirmed the decision, which ran contrary to the provisions of the Indian Constitution. Simultaneously and without outside consultation they adopted their own flag,[1] a gesture which was criticised in Delhi as contrary to the Constitution and an ominous pointer to future dangerous intentions.

In so far as the two Governments are concerned these matters were finalised in an eight-point agreement which Pandit Nehru announced in the House of the People on 24th July.[2] In spite of the Prime Minister's

[1] A white plough on a red background. Three equidistant white vertical stripes run parallel to the staff. Sheikh Abdullah's explanation is that the plough represents the peasants who form the backbone of the country, the stripes symbolise the geographical regions—Jammu, Kashmir, and the Frontiers—and the red background stands for labour.
[2] The agreement covered the following points:

ability to silence criticism, we cannot feel that the foundations for agreement are secure. Vigorous opposition came from Dr. S. P. Mukerjee, President of the Bharatiya Jan Sangh, who naturally resists any tendency to deprive India of opportunities for expansion. But it is the uncertainty of Abdullah's intentions which must lend definite commitments the nature of doubt. Nevertheless Abdullah and his deputies left Delhi in an atmosphere of mutual congratulation, and for a time there will be a truce to controversy.

The immediate status of the Yuvraj is not affected by the change, for he has been elected Head of the State. But on his death all association of Kashmir with the Dogra House of Gulab Singh will cease. The final resolution providing for an elected Head of the State to be known as " Sardar-i-Riyasat " was adopted by the Kashmir Constituent Assembly on 21st August 1952. It provided for a five-year appointment. Previous to accepting the appointment the Yuvraj had obviously been in some doubt as to his position. If he could perform no useful purpose he was not prepared to play the role of a complete puppet. He appears to have received reassurances from Delhi, but it remains to be seen if he will be allowed to maintain a position of any dignity or influence.[1] Should the

---

1. Citizenship. A common citizenship was recognised, with special privileges for State subjects.

2. The Head of the State to be recognised by the Indian President on the recommendation of the State Legislature. The State to decide the process of election of the Head of the State. Appointment to be for five years.

3. For " historical and sentimental reasons " a State flag to be recognised, but the Indian national flag to continue to have the same status as elsewhere in India.

4. The President of India to retain powers to reprieve and commute death sentences.

5. The President of India to exercise his emergency powers under Article 352 of the Indian Constitution in such matters as invasion and external or internal disturbances, in Kashmir. But in the case of internal disturbance, action to be taken only with the concurrence of the State.

6. The application of principles of Fundamental Rights, as defined in the Indian Constitution, to apply in Kashmir subject to certain modifications. For example, the Kashmir decision not to award compensation to dispossessed landlords is contrary to the Indian guarantee.

7. The Supreme Court of India to retain original jurisdiction in respect of disputes mentioned in Article 131. Such disputes are those between States or between a State and the Government of India. The State Advisory Tribunal to be abolished and its functions are to pass to the Supreme Court of India. This in effect makes the Supreme Court the final Court of Appeal in all civil and criminal matters.

(The Kashmir Government seemed uncertain over their final consent in this matter, and in his statement Pandit Nehru inferred generally that the agreement covered principles but not details.)

8. Financial arrangements between India and Kashmir have still to be worked out.

[1] Karan Singh was formally sworn in as " Sardar-i-Riyasat " on 17th November 1952. On that occasion he spoke of the Kashmir dispute in terms which allow for no optimism : " The unfortunate tendency to equate the aggressor and aggressor's

circumstances ever arise, the Yuvraj, if he chose, could command a considerable following among his Dogra subjects, and, for that reason I could not entirely agree with *The Times* correspondent in Delhi that the move would enhance Abdullah's popularity. A more probable development would seem that it might further widen the gap between Srinagar and Jammu.

In my meeting with Sheikh Abdullah I had been prepared for a more aggressive personality, and the Sheikh's approach, which, though stubborn, was quiet, took me somewhat by surprise. He repeated the well-known argument. A plebiscite could be held only when a reunited Kashmir came under the administration of his legal Government. He stressed that even Pakistan had not recognised the Azad Government. He must be given the chance to re-establish his administration over the whole. He would agree to allow " local authorities" to function in Azad Kashmir who would be responsible to the United Nations; but they must be nominated by his Government. After a conversation of over an hour I found myself wondering what would be the nature of his relations with the Government of India if ever the circumstances permit him freedom of choice in action. In discussing the choice before his country his final words to me were, " My mind is open ". Whether he meant it, I know not. In Pakistan I found opinion divided about Abdullah. There were those who regarded him as a tool of India, and a traitor to Islam. There were others who admitted that his influence was something more than that of a political mountebank. Not a few seemed to harbour some secret appreciation of the man. Others would have me believe that the real power lay with his Deputy, Bakshi Ghulam Mohammed, and that Abdullah was to Bakshi as Hindenburg to Ludendorff.

Abdullah is in fact something of an enigma. Born in 1905 in a village on the outskirts of Srinagar, his father, a shawl weaver, had died before his birth. After graduating at Aligarh University he became a school teacher, and rapidly developed an intelligent interest in practical Socialism. Indeed, the squalor of Srinagar was just the environment for the exercise of his urge to reform, and while others merely talked of Dogra oppression, the secular welfare state became his dream. Whether his political courage deserves the title " Sher-i-Kashmir " which his more adulatory followers have bestowed upon him is open to doubt. The lion in him certainly has much subtlety in his make-up. He conveys an impression of some conceit and opportunism. He has an acute sense of the technique and value of propaganda, and lustily but shrewdly blows his own trumpet. Through the screen of his exaggerated oratory there is yet perceptible the spark of an ideal. The preamble to his resolution before the Kashmir National Conference in 1944 speaks of a " determination to make this our country a dazzling gem on the snowy bosom of Asia ", which

victim has led to a deadlock and it is hoped that this attitude will once and for all be laid aside. Any attempt to impose an arbitrary solution seeking to circumvent this fundamental aspect cannot be acceptable to us."

adequately enough conveys the synthesis of idealism, showmanship and
material ambition which governs the lives of greater men than Abdullah.
His declared devotion to everything secular, and his abhorrence of everything communal should command the respect of all those who in the
West have tasted the barren futility of physical or mental communal
strife.

Whatever may be the truth concerning this rather baffling individual,
he is a Kashmiri; and as a Kashmiri we need to think of him in relation
to the problem of his country. For years his life was one of tough
and unrelenting struggle against the Government of Maharaja Sir Hari
Singh. Once this background of conflict is understood we can appreciate
how the Indian National Congress rather than the Moslem League always
attracted his loyalty. We should be prepared to accept his genuine
concern for Kashmiris as such, without communal bias. His whole
outlook is one of advanced Socialism, impatient at the limitations of the
communal mentality. Nevertheless he is a Moslem who commands the
loyalty of numbers of Moslems, for his present Government includes at
least a dozen Moslem colleagues.[1] It was this evidence of genuine
secularism in a Government containing many Moslems which leads us
to doubt the infallibility of the Moslem League claim to forecast accurately
the sentiment of the Kashmiri Moslems of the Valley. It was the fact of
Moslems in Government which also led me to suggest that perhaps the
solution lay in bringing the leaders of Azad Kashmir and members of
Abdullah's Government together in conference. In January 1952, when
Mohammed Ibrahim and Chaudhri Ghulam Abbas were in disagreement, the Azad Government was led by Mir Waiz Mohammed Yusuf,
a Kashmiri of Srinagar.[2] Here, it seemed, was the chance for two
Kashmiris, both Moslems from the same city, to meet and negotiate,
not as rival envoys of Pakistan and India but as Kashmiris seeking to
reunite their divided country. Such an approach would in effect be but
an effort to bring together the Moslem and National Conferences which
had gone their separate ways in 1938. Cordial messages of an unofficial
nature have been exchanged between Abdullah and Abbas; and it appears
that at one time or another Pakistan and India would have welcomed such
a meeting. But apparently they never both felt the same way on the
matter at the same time!

The difficulties are obvious, and we are in deep waters directly we
consider the form which such a settlement could take. Furthermore,
there is the certainty that while the Kashmiri leaders talked, the two great

[1] Sheikh Abdullah is married to a former Christian, a grand-daughter of the well-
known Swiss proprietor, Mr. Nedou, of Nedou's Hotel, Srinagar. His children
attend the C.M.S. school in Srinagar.
[2] I have found it more convenient to separate the involved affairs of the Azad
Kashmir Government from the main narrative. The disagreement between
Ibrahim and Ghulam Abbas is obscure. But it appeared that the latter received
some support from certain Pakistani Ministers at the expense of the former at a time
when the late Liaquat Ali Khan was in America. The story is told in Appendix VII.

neighbours would never be content to lay hands off the country, and Kashmir would internally be rent in two by political factions seeking to undermine unity in their own interests. The conception of a settlement of, for, and by Kashmiris then becomes a mental exercise rather than a practical contribution. It raises more problems than it solves: and yet this matter has lingered on now for years, so that it would seem right to explore any untested approach. Certainly in February 1952 no official steps had been taken to encourage an all-Kashmiri settlement.

As I went from the Government officials on one side to those of the other, yet another proposition seemed not to have received full consideration. India's claim to maintain a large force in her portion of Kashmir, after the withdrawal of the greater portion of her forces, is based on a fear that once again aggressive action by the other side might result in a sudden descent on Kashmir which would wrest the country by force. This is a polite way of defining her fear of a double-cross. It surely disregards the fact that Pakistan could never afford to defy the force of world opinion, which through the United Nations would then be directed against her. Nor can one believe that Pakistan would ever wish to do so. Nevertheless, the Indian objection remains. Furthermore, India regards foreign troops, whether of the United Nations or of the Commonwealth, on the territory she holds, as an infringement of her sovereignty. Pakistan, in contrast, has accepted every proposal that the United Nations have submitted. The immediate object is to achieve a plebiscite. Would the Pakistanis be prepared to go to the length of accepting the presence of foreign troops on their soil—and on their soil only—if India would then agree to withdraw all her troops under international observation, leaving behind only a token force such as Pakistan has already recognised as reasonable?

Such an approach might well be regarded by Pakistan as an insult. Is not the acceptance of an alleged insult worth the indignity, if, after these years of frustration, it leads to the attainment of the object? I put this question to leaders on both sides, and their reactions were sufficiently non-committal to make me believe that here was a diversion which might with diplomacy be developed to practical purpose. I was told that in the early negotiations of UNCIP, Sir Zafrullah Khan had accepted some such proposal. The Pakistan Prime Minister's reaction to the suggestion was cautious. Pakistan could not again accept terms which would subsequently be refused by India. This process would only lead to his country eventually becoming the butt of international ridicule. I replied that naturally the success of the plan would be conditional on India's simultaneous acceptance, and that neutral observers would be on the spot, as already agreed, to report the progress of demilitarisation and watch the intentions of both sides. Khwaja Nazimuddin's last word was that if such a proposal came in the form of an offer from India it would have to receive consideration. I discussed the plan with other senior Pakistani officials, who certainly gave it no refusal, while one immediately gave it his personal consent. "Speaking for myself . . ." were the words he used, and in the public interest it must be left at that.

In India I confronted both Sir Girja Shankar Bajpai and Sheikh Abdullah with the proposition. The latter was obviously taken by surprise. It is, after all, extremely difficult to find an objection from the Indian point of view. Abdullah gave me the impression that he was searching for the catch. After some minutes of evasion he eventually submitted, without conviction, the argument that since he had never recognised Azad Kashmir as other than territory which by right should be under his administration, the presence of foreign troops on Azad soil would constitute an unlawful occupation. This had been his attitude in all public utterances for some time past. Bajpai was in some doubt, and I felt that while he could in no way commit himself to an opinion, as an official spokesman of great authority he certainly gave the proposal no direct condemnation. He repeated that the United Nations could not impose a settlement on one side or the other and that direct negotiation was a more hopeful method for success. On return to England it was disappointing to discover that a suggestion which had seemed new to many of those closely concerned on the spot, had apparently been discussed and abandoned after the Commonwealth Conference of Prime Ministers in 1951.

No one can appreciate better the lost unity of the Kashmiris than the few officers of the United Nations Observer Corps whose task it is to see that the terms of the cease-fire agreement are adhered to. The cease-fire demarcation was, after all, a red line drawn on the map without relation to any political or administrative cohesion whatsoever. It represented a military situation, and a military situation only. Moreover, a cow or a goat is not over-concerned with a boundary drawn on the map, whether it be political or military. Consequently the owners living on or near the line might be forgiven if they, too, sometimes forget the political restrictions created for them and in innocence find themselves more concerned with their ownership than with the polemics of Kashmir. When the cease-fire line was first established no one in the area for a moment thought that it would still be separating Kashmiris from each other after four long years and more; and so innumerable petty local situations involving grazing rights, the irrigation of fields or—in one case—the possession of an island in the middle of the Jhelum, were at first ignored, only to accumulate as time passed, for the general irritation of the people and the United Nations observers.

My first encounter with the observers of the United Nations was on a Sunday morning in Jammu, where I woke up a sleepy American officer to try to find out something of his work and the manner in which he set about it. I had no luck. He and his Belgian colleague had had strict orders to give nothing away to inquisitive tourists or journalists, and I was wasting my time. A few days later, however, in Rawalpindi I found General Nimmo,[1] the Chief Observer, most informative and helpful.

The Observer Corps started in a small way under UNCIP in 1948. In January 1949 General Delvoie, a Belgian, took over control, and by July the Corps had accumulated thirty-two observers from the United States, Canada, Belgium, Mexico and Norway. Delvoie handed over to Brigadier Henry Angle from Canada in January 1950; but the latter was tragically killed in an air crash in July, when General Nimmo took charge.

Nimmo and his officers have hardly an enviable duty to perform, for both sides regard them as a nuisance. Yet they have received the fullest co-operation from the local commanders. One Pakistani Brigadier in fact let it be known that he would remove any officer who infringed the rules. On either side of a central line for a distance of 500 yards is a neutral no-man's land. Here and there, however, certain obvious positions within the neutral zone fall to one side or the other. No new defences may be dug and no increase of troops within Kashmir is allowed. It is in supervising this work and in smoothing out unofficially innumerable local situations of friction that Nimmo's team of observers discharge their very important responsibility. Behind the front line the Corps is organised in teams at centres of communication, where they live and mess with the troops. Teams are in wireless communication with each other, so that when trouble arises they can quickly meet and settle a dispute by mutual discussion. In order to obviate the possibility of succumbing to the temptations of partiality, observers are moved from one side to the other every three months; while General Nimmo himself spends the winter in Rawalpindi with Pakistan and the summer in Srinagar with India.

General Nimmo performs no political function. His men are there to observe, and if the two armies were ever ordered to engage each other in battle his work would cease. He maintains a group at Azad Kashmir headquarters in Muzzaffarabad, and, with his own international operators on their wireless sets working in code, he can effectively keep in touch with the scene as a whole so long as it remains static. From his headquarters he is in contact with the Indian and Pakistani Chiefs of the General Staff, while his link with the outside world is direct with the Secretary-General of the United Nations, to whom he renders a fortnightly report. His group, which in 1951 numbered thirty-five officers, was at his request to be increased to sixty-five in 1952. It can hardly be a life of comfort or exhilaration for those on the spot: and yet for a young officer out for a new experience the year's duty with the Observer Group is not wasted. Some of them in their eagerness chafe at inactivity, and one or two no sooner report back from a distant corner of Baltistan than they demand to be ordered on to a new beat on the line. Nimmo himself has stories of curious and unexpected personal attentions of kindness and charity for

[1] Major-General R. H. Nimmo, C.B.E., of the Australian Military Forces. Commander of the Northern Command, Australia, until 1950.

him and his men from the troops on both sides. It is in such ways that we are prevented from despair in our distant hope that one day there will be no problem.

While I have emphasised that in no way is the Observer Group entangled with the political settlement, it would hardly be illogical to assume that Dr. Graham or General Devers had never sought out the opinion and advice of those who have been so intimately concerned with the Kashmir dispute on the spot. General Nimmo's official role remains that of observing and reporting. But we would like to think that one day his very valuable estimate of the whole problem could be placed at the disposal of the authorities at the United Nations. For certainly there could be no more balanced or sympathetic counsellor than this very kindly and conscientious international observer.

CHAPTER TWENTY

THE FRONTIER AREAS AND LADAKH

GLANCE at the map of Kashmir indicates that great tracts of country in the east and north of the State have received comparatively little publicity. Controversy has tended to centre round the perpendicular arm of the cease-fire line. It is to these distant territories that this chapter is confined.

By no stretch of the imagination could the Gilgit Agency, including the feudal States of Hunza and Nagar, be considered as owing loyalty to a Government in Srinagar. In 1842 Raja Gulab Singh overran this rugged country with the customary success associated with his dynamic ambition, and Lord Hardinge confirmed the territory to him in 1846. Six years later the Dogra garrison was wiped out by a local leader, Gaur Rahman, the ruthless chief of Yasin. After Gaur Rahman's death Maharaja Ranbir Singh regained a loose control. But it was left to the British to consolidate the vague understanding with the Dogra regime in Kashmir. In 1889, in face of the increasing threats of Russian expansion, the British occupied Chitral and at the same time established the Gilgit Agency. Two years later an expedition to Hunza and Nagar brought these small States under Gilgit, and thereafter they paid an annual tribute to Kashmir State. A British Political Agent at Gilgit was responsible to the British Resident in Srinagar, and represented the loose titular allegiance of the Gilgit Agency to the Maharaja.

In August 1947 the end of British supervision in Gilgit was the obvious opportunity for a very individual Shiah Moslem community to break away. A few days before partition Gilgit was handed back to the Maharaja, whereupon the Gilgitis quietly staged their own peaceful revolt without assistance from Pakistan and set up a Republic. Pandit Nehru protested. The Agency, he maintained, should have remained with the British to be disposed of between Pakistan and India. Previously the Maharaja had optimistically appointed his own Sikh Governor. But it was too late. The Sikh Governor arrived and was held hostage, imprisonment probably saving his life. The Gilgit Republic, under their leader, Shah Rais Khan, then invited the intervention of Pakistan. Pakistan complied, and a single officer, Sardar Mohan Aman, was flown in from Peshawar to take control. It was typical of the sense and honesty of the people that he was able to take over the Gilgit Treasury untouched since the first days of the revolt. Weeks later the Gilgitis undertook the occupation of Baltistan. Thus it was that Pakistan acquired the great mountain wastes of northern Kashmir, with all the semblance of perpetuity.

It should be understood that the Gilgit Agency is in no way associated with the Azad Administration at Muzzaffarabad, although in Pakistan as late as March 1952 followers of the Azad Kashmir leader, Ghulam Abbas, were agitating at Jhelum for Gilgit to come under their control. The former functions of the British Resident of Kashmir are now exercised by a permanent Secretary who works in the Pakistan Ministry for Kashmir Affairs with its Headquarters at Rawalpindi.[1] But with the old route in from Srinagar denied to Pakistan communication is a problem. Twice a week planes of the Pakistan Airways fly in and out on one of the most hazardous air routes in the world. A road capable of taking light motor traffic was hurriedly being constructed over the Balusar Pass in the spring of 1952. Perhaps the building of roads remains the one progressive and practical legacy of so much human folly. This brief account should be sufficient to indicate that the men of the Gilgit Agency are never going to allow themselves to be subject to control from either Srinagar or Delhi.

There is no more rigid ethnographical division in the country than that which separates north and south Ladakh. In the north the Skardu *tehsil*, with its population of 106,000 Moslems, is controlled by Pakistan.[2] In the south the two *tehsils* of Kargil and Leh are under Abdullah. The Kargil *tehsil* is mainly Moslem while the Leh *tehsil* of eastern Ladakh has a population of 40,000 Buddhists.

The Buddhists of Ladakh are racially and culturally closer to Tibet than Srinagar. Indeed, until Raja Gulab Singh conquered and annexed Ladakh for the Sikhs over a century ago, they were politically integrated with their Tibetan neighbours. Buddhism has flourished in Ladakh since A.D. 400, and for centuries Leh has been ecclesiastically subject to Lhasa. Early in the seventeenth century a Mohammedan invasion of Ladakh by Baltistan, when Leh's temples were plundered and destroyed, successfully confirmed the complete division, ethnographical and geographical, between the Balts and the Buddhists. The legacy of those events is that today Ladakh has made it clear that if there is any question of conditions demanding the area to be handed to Pakistan, the people would abandon both Pakistan and India and return to the ancient association with Tibet. This is the declared intention as defined by their chief spokesman, the Lama Bakula of the Spitok monastery. Whether or not the choice in that form would ever present itself, the links with Tibet present sinister political problems. The hand of Communist China now stretches over the roof of the world to the Indian frontiers. To discover a welcome in Ladakh would be but a logical extension of Chinese hopes.

---

[1] In February 1952 the Secretary for Kashmir and the northern districts was Mr. Mueenuddin, to whom I am indebted for his clear exposition of the situation. The Minister for Kashmir Affairs was Dr. Mahmud Hussein, whose secretary, Mr. Mohammed Ayub, acts as liaison officer with the Pakistan staff at the United Nations.

[2] Skardu is sometimes referred to as the capital of Baltistan. Baltistan, however, is an area rather than an administrative unit and its boundaries are vague.

The position of the Buddhist hierarchy of Ladakh is not enviable. In the face of Abdullah's agrarian reforms, the monasteries retain their lands precariously. The Shushok Lama Bakula,[1] who attends the Kashmir Assembly on behalf of his people, carefully watches their rights. He has successfully recruited Ladakhis for the State Militia and in return the State representative at Leh sees to it that Ladakh receives a generous share of cloth, sugar and kerosine oil. But theocratic societies are hardly compatible with the new winds that blow from Srinagar. Yet if the Tibetan loyalties were revived it would in time prove but a case of exchanging the frying-pan of Abdullah for the fire of Peking.

In June 1952 Abdullah spoke out in the State Assembly in spirited defence of his policy in Ladakh. A factor in the poverty of the people, he said, was the practice by which the managements of the *Gumpas*[2] received grain from their tenant-cultivators and then loaned it back to them at exorbitant rates. The Government would hold the law of transfer of land to the tribes in abeyance in view of the peculiar conditions.[3] The "pernicious" practice of requiring a definite quota of transport ponies and porters at different stages on the Srinagar–Ladakh route for tourists, officials and traders would cease. He then listed a number of advances which his Government could record in their administration. It appeared that previous to 1948 no forest operations of any kind had existed in the district. Veterinary services were to be improved and agricultural research undertaken. The area was rich in mineral resources which would be exploited. Already a start had been made on sulphur and borax mines. Samples of salt from the lakes had been sent to Delhi for analysis. Two new high schools had opened up in Leh and Kargil, and a teachers' training-class was to follow. It all looks as though the primitive slumbering content of the Ladakhis is to receive a jolt; and a feature of the new initiation paradoxically is that the Kashmir war proved an incentive. Recruitment in the local Militia brought regular wages to the landless labourer. The army brought with it its own communications, the telegraph, the telephone and, more important, a few roads.[4] Early in 1948 a handful of Indian troops pushed over the Rohtang Pass from the Kulu Valley up to Leh and saved it from falling into Pakistani hands. The construction of a rough road followed. The journey from Srinagar to Leh through Dras and over the Zoji La, which formerly took over two weeks,[5] thanks to the Indian Army can

---

[1] "Shushok" or "Skushok" means "living Buddha".

[2] The Ladakh term for "monastery" is "*Gumpa*".

[3] This apparently referred only to land held by the *Gumpas*. In July 1951 *The Times* special correspondent in Leh reported that under a National Conference official, Khwaja Sahib Ghulam Qadir, the abolition of landlordism had proceeded apace, 25,000 out of 30,000 acres having passed to peasant proprietors.

[4] Telegraph offices which had been destroyed by enemy action were restarted at Leh, Khalsi, Kargil, Dras and Machol.

Emergency telephones were installed in sixteen stations.

[5] Dras and the Zoji La were both recaptured from Pakistani irregulars in November 1948.

now be covered in seven days. The Indian Air Force Transport Command operates an airlift between Leh, Kargil and Srinagar, comparable to that of the Pakistanis' into Gilgit. But more interesting than the technical benefit derived through an army of occupation is the psychological effect of new contacts. Forget the limitations of communalism and there is no better ambassador of India than the Sikh or Dogra or Mahratta sepoy. Contact with the Army may well have contributed to the tendency for Ladakh to seek a direct approach with Delhi, a tendency which receives encouragement from the increasingly ambiguous nature of Abdullah's own contacts with the Indian Government. Yet if Abdullah is to keep Ladakh within his fold he can hardly afford ambiguity with either India or Ladakh. The undefined frontier between southern Ladakh and Tibet is of vital importance to the Indian defensive system, and it is not difficult to visualise the circumstances in which India might insist on its adequate protection being under direct control from Delhi. It would seem that this wild, unknown country, in spite of its mediaeval theocracy, is itself in a key position; and it is something of a paradox that, more than in any other portion of the State, the conception of a plebiscite in its scattered, snow-bound hamlets appeals to our sense of the ridiculous.

It may be that in discussing the intentions of either Ladakh or Kashmir or India we are a long way from reality, for sometimes it seems that the shape of things to come may, alas, be moulded at Chinese dictation in Lhasa. The immediate result for Ladakh has been to kill her former trade with Yarkand, and the only travellers through from Sinkiang have been 175 Kazakh refugees, who after months of persecution and endurance trickled into Ladakh in October 1951 from western Tibet.

The Iron Curtain has descended; and yet the very isolation of the country offers limitless opportunity for infiltration to those who seek to work within the gullible Indian framework. Maybe that the first taste of Communist technique within the Assembly in Delhi will act as a timely warning. Certainly the refugees who filtered through from Sinkiang brought with them their quota of poison; and so we note another corner of the earth's surface ripe for the familiar contamination.

CHAPTER TWENTY-ONE

THEORIES AND SOLUTIONS

MANY Englishmen are coming to believe that the days when our intervention in this dispute could be effective are gone. Only the two nations themselves can now solve their own problem. If this is true, what should be the attitude of Britain? It can be argued that to remain outside the discussion without any expression of sentiment or opinion is the only course. Let us not give one side or the other the excuse to accuse us of partisanship. It would certainly save a lot of trouble. And yet I can see little merit in isolation. Apart from a suggestion of laziness and fear of responsibility, we should undoubtedly receive blame from both sides. Bolder, yet more honest, would be to throw the weight of our opinion—and I emphasise of our opinion only—on to the side which we consider carries the greater authority to be closely associated with Kashmir. In this we should be guided by the desires of the Kashmiris; and our dilemma is that we cannot know those desires until a free plebiscite is held.

Hitherto we have mainly considered a solution in terms of the accepted pattern of a withdrawal of troops and an overall plebiscite. Let us then turn away from the orthodox plan to other possibilities. We have noted that when Sir Owen Dixon was briefed for his task he was empowered to make suggestions " at variance with the object ", which was then still regarded as a decision of the people as a whole. In these months of 1953 we know well enough those areas in Kashmir where the results of a plebiscite are a foregone conclusion. The 40,000 Buddhists of East Ladakh, who occupy nearly one-quarter of the State, have declared their intention to throw in their fortunes with India. The Moslems of Gilgit, Hunza and Baltistan, now on the Pakistan side of the cease-fire line, have found the fulfilment of their desires. In the south we know the wishes of the men of Poonch, while the Jammu province is evenly divided between a Moslem majority in the west and a Hindu majority in the east. These are the known factors, nor is either India or Pakistan really going to challenge the claims of the other in the confirmation of desires already known. It was this element of certainty which Sir Owen Dixon had hoped to exploit. What, then, are we or Pakistan or India arguing about? Only the residue, the Vale of Kashmir with its 1,800,000 inhabitants. Well might it be called " Valley of Indecision ". Unfortunately, the one issue on which there is complete agreement between the two contestants is their unqualified refusal of any form of partition; and it is the barren folly of the legal approach on both sides, divorced from reality, and the insistence on treating a geographical expression, Kashmir, as one political unity, which remains our constant despair and exasperation.

What of this valley? Can we today know what exactly its people desire? The Pakistanis well recognise and fear those circumstances to which I have referred. They know that time is on the side of Abdullah and the consolidation of his administration.[1] You cannot introduce sweeping land reforms without winning popularity.[2] Nor if you operate a very comprehensive State broadcasting system to effect, as Sheikh Abdullah with his high sense of the modern power of propaganda and publicity has done, can you fail to dominate the malleable mind of the Kashmir peasant.[3] Finally, the real mind of the Kashmiri will not be known while troops of either India or Pakistan or the State Militia are on his doorstep. Writing as an international observer Sir Owen Dixon made that quite clear in the following terms :—

> " I had formed the opinion that it was not easy to exclude the danger that the inhabitants of the valley of Kashmir would vote under fear or apprehension of consequences and other improper influences. They are not high-spirited people of an independent or resolute temper. For the most part they are illiterate. There were large numbers of regular soldiers of the Indian Army as well as of the State Militia and Police and more often than not they were under arms. The State Government was exercising wide powers of arbitrary arrest. These are not matters that the Kashmiris inhabiting the valley could be expected to disregard in choosing between voting as the Government of Kashmir asked them and voting for accession to Pakistan."

Thus wrote Sir Owen Dixon in his report, and anyone with acquaintance of the country will endorse his opinion. In doing so, we need cast no reflection on Indian troops themselves, so long as they remain under their present leadership. Hitherto it has been their presence, and not

---

[1] There is evidence that Ibrahim, the Azad leader, himself fears this situation.
[2] The " Big Landed Estates Abolition Act, 1950," expropriated all land exceeding $22\frac{1}{2}$ acres. One acre can be retained for residential use. The Government stated that they would pay compensation on a sliding scale, payment being made for three years, and being reduced to half the former revenue in the third year. In no case could compensation exceed Rs. 3000 p.a. All declarations were subject to confirmation by a Committee of the Kashmir Constituent Assembly. The Committee subsequently recommended that no compensation should be paid, and this was confirmed by the Assembly. The principles of a further measure, the Tenants' Rights Bill, were announced by Sheikh Abdullah in Delhi in July 1951.
[3] Radio Kashmir controls some 500 community receivers in the villages, and the service is constantly expanding. It is owned and serviced by the State. The programme, " Awami Raj Zindabad " (The People's Programme), must in time come to be accepted as a voice beyond reproach by a large ignorant and innocent peasant audience.

their behaviour, which has operated for the intimidation of the timid Kashmiri.

The sentiments of Moslems within the valley are therefore an uncertain factor. In and around Srinagar, Abdullah's following is probably secure without yet assuming the aspect of permanency. The tribal invasion, with its indiscriminate slaughter of Moslem and Hindu, undoubtedly prejudiced the cause of Pakistan for months to come. Nevertheless, the appeal of the secular State will still be meaningless to many thousands. For Pakistan an undoubted element of fear is a modification in the ratio of Moslems to non-Moslems in Abdullah's areas since 1947. While in no way admitting the Pakistan charge that a policy still exists to alter the population so as to increase the non-Moslem proportion, it is obvious that many Hindus availed themselves of new opportunities of immigration into the Kashmir Valley; and this will continue until the distant day of control by a plebiscite administrator.

But we have still to view the question of the attitude of a British Government to this greatest of Commonwealth crises in the face of so much confliction and argument. Assuming that the Security Council can offer little more than a solemn but ineffective pronouncement of blame for the past and remedy for the future, a British Government could continue to work to the goal of the limited plebiscite on the basis of partition. I have said enough to indicate that as time passes, and Abdullah's hold is consolidated, the results of a vote in the valley must become more obscure, in so far as Englishmen are able to judge. If so, it seems logical that the process of lending the weight of our opinion to influence the situation can continue only for a few more years. In the unknown future we face a new set of imposed circumstances. All the more urgent is then the case for a plebiscite within months, in the interests of justice and equity: and if the normal conditions for a free expression of the people's will are then refused, there is no possible remedy short of force which a British Government can offer. The days of force in such situations are gone for ever: and so, if world opinion in general and Commonwealth opinion in particular are disregarded, India and Pakistan can only be left to work out their own salvation in their own frustrated way. Such a diagnosis lends weight to the view that neither side wants a settlement—a proposition which we will examine before the story is ended.

We have noted that the ties of race, religion and economy at present indicate an accession to Pakistan as logical, and we must therefore assume that if and when all efforts for mutual agreement fail, the weight of our opinion and authority must in the last resort support the Pakistan case. But a world of argument still separates us from that final position, for whether or not we have lost faith in Abdullah's intention ever to allow the plebiscite, the fact remains that the prospects of a plebiscite are still the basis of such vague agreement as exists.

Those Englishmen who in no small measure share a sense of frustration with Indians and Pakistanis are naturally thinking in terms of the effect of so much dissension within the family of the Commonwealth. The problem for us is political. In contrast, for the other two partners the more sinister effect is to keep alive communal passions which otherwise might have faded away. So often on the sub-Continent I heard the view that once Kashmir was in the background there would be a new era of understanding between Hindu and Moslem.

Sheikh Abdullah's own views on the communal aspect have been skilfully presented to indicate the wisdom of an open mind. In an interview with the British Press in Delhi on 1st December 1947 he said:

> "The Kashmir episode may well have paved the way for communal peace in India. The accession of Kashmir, which has an 80 per cent Moslem majority, to the Indian Union will depend upon the goodwill shown to Moslems by the Hindu majority in India. Our present accession to India is only tentative and is subject to confirmation by referendum. If India wants the people of Kashmir to elect for accession to India, there must be communal peace in India." [1]

It was easy enough in the capital of Delhi, when in constant contact with his colleagues in the Congress, for Abdullah to throw out a plausible smoke-screen. But his more accurate reactions were revealed when he was asked the direct question as to whether the overwhelming Moslem majority would not prefer association with Pakistan.

> "Our economic interests lie with India. Our trade connections are here and we have here extensive markets for our goods. But all that will be of no avail if we cannot come to India and live here in peace. . . ."

Kashmir's main economic interests do not lie with India. Her trade connections are with Pakistan, as are her extensive markets for her goods. Karachi is her natural port. Her fruit is sold in Rawalpindi. The logs from her rich timber forests float down to depots at Jhelum and Wazirabad. Just as Kashmir looks to Pakistan, so does Pakistan in no small measure look to the waters of two great rivers, the Jhelum and the Chenab, to satisfy the thirsty soil of the Punjab. The headworks of the Upper Jhelum Canal at Mangla are actually on Kashmir soil.[2] Such a suave contradiction of fact could only betoken a frame of mind which can never be prepared to sanction the free plebiscite to which lip service is paid.

I discounted British active intervention as neither effective nor practical. But to withhold the power of our sincere opinion, sheltering in the fear

---

[1] In justice to Sheikh Abdullah we should note that in April 1952 he was still adopting this approach (see Footnote 2, p. 278).

[2] The published figures for the Kashmir budget of 1953–54 reveal a deficit involving a subsidy from India of £1,530,000. This hardly indicates conditions of the natural flow of trade between the two countries.

of an accusation of partiality, is to watch the fortunes of our Commonwealth drift until the day when we might discover there was no Commonwealth to argue about. Great issues are certainly at stake, for we might endanger the continued membership of one or other of the two Dominions. I have sought to deal with that dilemma elsewhere. Here, I would only claim that if we believe on the balance that Kashmir's adherence to Pakistan is the more rational settlement, we should state that belief. First reactions may often be unpleasant. But honesty usually pays a final dividend.

As a Commonwealth we cannot afford to neglect the strategic dangers of this running sore. The possession of Kashmir by either Dominion gives it a back-door entry to the other Dominion. The rival claims therefore cancel each other out, and the remaining factor is only the comparative difficulty of India's strategy in placing an Indian Kashmir in defence as compared with the task of defending it from Pakistan. That is the problem, by no means hypothetical, mutual to India and Pakistan. But when we turn to consider the defence of the sub-Continent as a whole from external aggression, it is clear that a system which places responsibility with India for guarding the northern Kashmir passes, while the old Khyber and Quetta areas remain a Pakistan liability, is surely fraught with difficulties. Apart from technical difficulties, the integration of the northern territories by India for purposes of defence is, as we have noted in the preceding chapter, quite unpractical for more forceful reasons of race, religion and a complete lack of identity of interests. What more simple and sound premise could there be than the blue-print of a plan by which the Army of Pakistan assumes the familiar role of covering troops, the forces of India comprising the Field Army? It then becomes a matter merely of Pakistan extending the frontier network to cover Gilgit, Hunza and the distant inaccessible passes of the Karakoram Range. Already through Chitral she has access to that unknown piece of country which, like a curved finger, barely separates the Gilgit Agency from the U.S.S.R.

When the Commonwealth Prime Ministers met in London in January 1951, after much hesitation they considered Kashmir. Liaquat Ali Khan had previously signified his intention of staying away unless he could have the matter on the agenda. The Prime Ministers met. They covered the problem from every angle and they dispersed with no solution. Yet nothing but good came from that meeting, for Liaquat was able to leave the conference table convinced at least of the good faith and integrity of his colleagues. It is this understanding between men who speak the same language which we should continue to hope may prove the means by which a plebiscite may yet be staged. Certain it is that the chances of agreement are more auspicious in the intimate atmosphere of Commonwealth discussion than in the glare and publicity of the United Nations, with its quite impersonal approach. When the three alternative methods of staging the plebiscite were mooted, Mr. Menzies went so far as to advocate the use of any international force in the world which might prove acceptable to India. Let Dutch or Belgian troops hold the ring if there were objections to others. But it is the method which contemplated Commonwealth troops in use which appealed to all those who felt that this matter should have been essentially one of a family putting its own house in order. Certainly I believe it is the method which would have been most acceptable to the villagers of the Kashmir Valley.

It has been noted that on one occasion Sheikh Abdullah spoke of an independent Kashmir. He obviously had in mind an independence of his own particular administration. But there is another form of independence, and the difficulty is to find men with the courage and ability to support it. I have in mind an independence under Commonwealth or British trusteeship, which would not only operate for the contentment and advancement of the Kashmiri, but could also act as a bastion of strategic and political stability in the general entanglement of Pakistani-Indian relations. In such a solution there would be a place for Indian or Pakistani ability. Indeed, the status of independence could be the means by which an administration might be based on a unique relationship of equality between Indians, Pakistanis and Englishmen in the government of Kashmir: a condominium, but of three partners sharing responsibility. The goal would then be to lead Kashmir forward in the fullness of time to its own choice, and the analogy of the Sudan naturally comes to mind. The one situation which such an arrangement could not sanction in the true interests of the Kashmiri would be that he should be thrown on his own resources and left to work out his own immediate independence. The great merit of a triangular administration would be that for some years the Kashmiri could have the opportunity of watching Moslems, Indians and Englishmen working in harmony for his benefit, and there might thus be time for him to forget much of that communal background which has hitherto dominated every aspect of his life.

Alas, the prospects for such a sane solution are slender in view of the practical difficulties. For example, can it be offered to the Kashmiri as an alternative choice in a plebiscite? Who is in a position to present such logic to the people? For its acceptance by their free vote would certainly be the happiest way for its introduction. Equally certain it is that Abdullah's Government would never allow its presentation. My own belief is that there are many Indians and Pakistanis who would be prepared to join Englishmen in so great a project if leadership could be afforded the initial opportunity.

My condominium may be a castle in the air; yet it is right that it should be remembered. History repeats itself mainly because men do not study it. History is in fact the history of men learning only through their own experience, which is another way of saying, by their own folly. Somewhere and at some time in the distant future of other days there may be another Kashmir, another Britain and another divided sub-Continent.

For the benefit of that situation I ask indulgence for the sanest, yet most improbable of solutions for Kashmir.

In the meanwhile, in so far as the day-to-day unchanging stagnation is concerned, I would offer this comment. If Pakistan is right she has nothing whatsoever to lose from a frank and graceful admission of the degree of help which she afforded to the frontier tribesmen in those early days; and in so far as in law aggression was committed, let her acknowledge it. It will in no way jeopardise the result of a free plebiscite or affect world opinion. It might soften Indian leadership to a more compromising approach. To admit a mistake is sometimes the highest achievement of statesmanship, rare enough in any stratum of national or international polemics. For India I would reserve this reflection : that if alternatively she is right then she, too, has nothing to fear from a plebiscite held under any conditions which an outside authority may care to dictate. Pandit Nehru has consistently refused proposals, on the grounds that the legal sovereignty of the present State Government must be preserved. The Government is there, and its replacement in this or that area for the purposes of a partial plebiscite or its preparation is an unconstitutional act of impropriety. Well it may be, but the fact remains that a plebiscite is the test of a people's will, and whatever the conditions of its conduct, Sheikh Abdullah will be back again in office for as long as he cares to stay if, as he claims, his Government is really based on popular support.

The argument has been advanced that if religion is to be the basis of nationality—and Kashmir is the test case—then some 40 million Moslems in India and 14 million Hindus in east Pakistan immediately become semi-aliens. The honest endeavour of Indian leaders under Nehru to establish the truly secular State certainly betokens wisdom and statesmanship. Unfortunately in so far as Kashmir is concerned, its Hindu rulers were ignorant of the meaning of secularism, and the result is that for the Kashmiri Moslem today the secular State still remains something of a myth.

There is, however, one aspect of secularism to which the case of Kashmir draws our attention, and I am referring to the activities of a certain Pandit Prem Nath Bazaz, a Kashmiri Hindu, who from Delhi quite fearlessly advocates his country's accession to Pakistan. Prem Nath Bazaz, who has been freely quoted by Sir Zafrullah Khan at the Security Council, leads an organisation, the Kashmir Democratic Union. In May 1946 he attended the plenary session of the Kashmir Kisan Mazdoor Conference at a village in the Anant Nag district of Kashmir Province. This meeting, he claims, gave birth to the Azad movement. Prem Nath Bazaz was charged with the preparation of a manifesto explaining the constitution of a free Kashmir which his party proposed to adopt. Before he could start work, India was partitioned, and Bazaz and his colleagues were thrown into prison, where they spent the next three years. He is now not allowed to enter Kashmir, and he devotes his time propagating the cause of the Azad Government and attacking Sheikh

Abdullah.   The gist of his highly scientific argument is on the following lines.   India's claims to champion true secularism in Kashmir are hollow. Why?   Because if, as India asserts, it is wrong for Kashmir to accede to Pakistan, then in the truly secular and democratic State an honest democrat is just as much entitled to make his wrong choice as he is to make a right one!

Yet of Abdullah's own sincerity of belief in the secular State there is no doubt.   Indeed, if by chance a really free vote was to endorse his leadership, something more than the purely political matter of Kashmir's choice would be at stake.   The creation of Pakistan was the result of a recognition of the claim that Moslems should receive their separate political identity as a religious community.   A verdict in favour of Abdullah could call into question the validity of the whole case of Pakistan's existence; for here would be the first serious negation of the religious State.   Moslems frequently invoke the Prophet himself in support of a contention that the Islamic State is also the true interpretation of democracy.   It is an inspiring theory, but in practice it hardly seems to work that way, any more than did the old Indian Congress claim to impartiality impress us in the 1930s.   In the case of Kashmir the fact that the terrors of communalism might one day be replaced by an even more oppressive political tyranny count for nothing.   Only the immediate triumph of Abdullah's secular State, constituting the basis for a wider challenge, matters.

Whether or not such vague fears have sheltered in recesses of the Pakistan national mind, their case is patently more desperate than that of India.   If there was one clear impression which I carried away out of so much mental confusion, it was the different approach of the two countries.   In despair the Pakistanis would repeat that war was the regrettable but inevitable solution.   In optimism the Indians would argue that it was impossible.   "It must happen" and "It can't happen" might well represent the contrast in the two approaches.

The many talks I had with Indians and Pakistanis confirm the view generally held that when this one issue is settled, all other pieces in the puzzle will find their allotted place.   The vital eagerness of the two countries to press on with all those dreams and schemes of progress which they so rightly cherish is a very effective deterrent to war.   Yet while 60 per cent of India's central budget and 70 per cent of that of Pakistan support armies on the alert for a war in Kashmir, much of that progress and urgent reconstruction remains in abeyance.

Liaquat has passed on, and Nazimuddin has taken his place.   Perhaps the most practical contribution which Englishmen close to the scene can make is to lend their energy and diplomacy to assisting constant and free discussion between the two leaders.   This is what Mahatma Gandhi might have expected of them and us; for when wise men see enough of each other, mutual wisdom slowly but surely defeats those emotions which are stimulated and which flourish by the outside world's endeavours.

I wonder if either of the countries has paused to consider the British action if, in defiance of either Commonwealth or international endeavours, they were to be plunged into a Kashmir war. One immediate decision would certainly be the withdrawal of all British officers from both sides. Another would be the refusal of all arms and military supplies. If the mild expenditure of some ammunition and the loss of a few good lives satisfied national pride, it is hardly cynicism to believe that this might prove a solution. Saving face is, alas, a recognised technique in international relations; and if the opening moves of a war proved the only means by which leadership can discover a way out of its dilemma, then the cheapest and quickest results might obtain from the most illogical of solutions. There are still too many bonds of family and sentiment across the Indian–Pakistani frontier to allow a sub-Continental war to drag on in futile mutual destruction. This is not a happy conclusion, yet India and Pakistan are no better nor worse than a number of other countries who fail to settle their differences: nor can a Security Council which is unable physically to implement its decisions blame member nations if they take the law into their own hands. Experience is sometimes a bitter but effective medium of instruction.

And if, in contradiction to this unhappy solution, both countries should, in the wisdom of fear, just rest content to remain through the years on a cease-fire line, we would have to admit that there was some logic in the view that neither side really now wants a settlement.[1] Time becomes the great healer, and gradually the *status quo* comes to be accepted. Passions are not exorcised, but driven inwards to infect the national thought and development in a process which substitutes mental damage for its physical counterpart. We could accept this solution for Abdullah. Time, as we have seen, is on his side. We could believe it of India, and indeed sometimes we are led to believe that this is their goal. But can we believe this of Pakistan? I think not; and while one will not accept time as the healer, the other cannot do so.

Looking back through these pages, the general effect is of a vast uncertainty; and as the months pass the obscurity increases. Abdullah's own ambitions seem sometimes to lead him further from the Indian Government into isolation. At other times, when it suits him, he is ready enough to use the Indian association.[2] Perhaps the most em-

[1] This argument was developed by the Editor of the *New Statesman and Nation* in the issue of 16th February 1952.

[2] On 11th April 1952 Sheikh Abdullah made a speech at Ranbirsinghapura, a village on the Kashmir–Pakistan border, which the Pakistan Press were quick to seize on as an indication of dissension between Abdullah and India. "Kashmir's accession to India will have to be of a restricted nature so long as communalism has a footing on the soil of India." Abdullah continued to describe the full application of the Indian Constitution to Kashmir as "unrealistic, childish and savouring of lunacy". He then returned to the theme of doubt as to whether communalism had finally been exorcised in India. He again reminded his audience that Kashmir had acceded in respect of three subjects only. It was a speech calculated to create a sensation without any commitment as to future intention. On 11th June 1952 the

barrassed of negotiators in these developments is the Indian Prime Minister. On 26th June 1952 Hindu nationalists demonstrated their disapproval of a Kashmir flag and the abolition of hereditary rule in no uncertain manner outside the Parliament building in Delhi. Inside, Mr. N. C. Chatterjee argued that a republic within a republic hardly made sense, and Dr. S. P. Mukerjee alleged discrimination by Sheikh Abdullah against Hindus. In defence Nehru found scapegoats in the Maharaja and the United Nations.[1] He confirmed that in the particular case of Kashmir, accession related to the three fundamental subjects which " could be interpreted to mean a little more or a little less ". But the accession was complete. He went on to praise the Kashmir land reforms. He thus effectively pacified his listeners, yet left them guessing. At least there is one certainty. While agreeing for obvious reasons to accede in defence, foreign affairs and communications, Abdullah wishes to leave all further relations on as tenuous a basis as possible. Particularly he seeks to avoid entanglement in such matters as the Indian fiscal and judicial systems. In view of his surrender of external affairs, he could not, if he is to be consistent, defy a solution for his country after its acceptance by India. Nor, conversely, can India claim immunity from responsibility on the grounds that a decision is unacceptable to Abdullah. Control of external affairs is constitutionally India's affair, though there is un-doubtedly room for much political exploitation and elasticity within the constitutional arrangement.

The interest for us is in the point raised by Mr. Chatterjee. An Indian Republic was accepted as compatible with the loose demands of the Statute of Westminster. Would not India extend the same indulgence to Kashmir? A Kashmir in treaty relationship with India would then enjoy that happy status of " independence plus ". A republic within a republic is not so fantastic a conception as Mr. Chatterjee believed.

There is yet another uncertainty which concerns Kashmir itself. The story began with a Raja of Jammu who found himself in possession of a kingdom, Kashmir. Would not the Dogras of Jammu wish to see it end that way? There is much evidence to the effect that just because the present conditions reverse those loyalties, the Dogras are not going to rest content to watch a National Conference Party dictate its will from Kashmir. Srinagar should once again be ruled from Jammu, and not Jammu from Srinagar; and since on such an issue neither side would be prepared to give ground, the logic of the situation can only indicate that both would go their separate ways. It is this kind of thought which

---

Kashmir Constituent Assembly, without reference to India, abolished the hereditary rule of the Dogra dynasty.

[1] The Prime Minister's own approach was on this occasion sometimes inconsistent. " The Kashmir Constituent Assembly has every right to frame its own Constitution, but so far as we are concerned, we would not be bound by their decision, because the question is before the Security Council. . . ." (*India News*, of 28th June 1952, did not give the particular occasion or date.) Such an approach seems an attempt, in words, to reconcile the irreconcilable.

comes to mind as we read of the activities of the "Praja Parishad" movement in Jammu and the ruthless steps taken for its suppression.[1]

There we will leave the Kashmir issue in the doubt which governs speculation until the end. When, in the past, nations have resorted to war in dispute of territory, the land in dispute has seldom been articulate in the heat of controversy. So it would seem with Kashmir. At least two political parties within the State, two neighbouring members of the Commonwealth, the whole of the Islamic world, and the machinery of the United Nations are concerned with the future. Yet the boatmen on the river and the craftsmen in the bazaar might, if they could voice their desires, sometimes evince a craving for the freedom of a land of no politics or national aspiration. Such is the folly which men perpetrate in the name of political consciousness and conscience, with their futile emotions and selfish ambition. If the Kashmir episode can in any way contribute to the education of a world whose poverty of political morality must amaze the hosts of heaven, then perhaps somewhere there is compensation for so sad a story.

[1] On 1st December 1952, on the occasion of the arrival of Karan Singh, in his new capacity as " Sardar-i-Riyasat " in Jammu the Praja Parishad staged a demonstration at which many arrests were made. Defying a Government order, they held a meeting at which Abdullah's regime was roundly abused. There followed incidents such as the replacement of the State flag by the Indian national flag, the emphasis being always on the complete " Indianisation " of Kashmir.

In February and March 1953 there were grave disturbances in Jammu, Ministers of Sheikh Abdullah's Government being attacked by members of the local Praja Parishad. This movement regards Abdullah's administration as a Moslem tyranny dominating the Hindu Dogra community of Jammu. In Delhi the Right-wing Hindu orthodox parties rose in sympathy with their Jammu compatriots. The result was the arrest of Dr. S. P. Mukerjee (Jan Sangh), Mr. N. C. Chatterjee (Hindu Mahasabha) and Nand Lal Sharma (Ram Rajya Parishad), after extensive rioting. They were subsequently released on 12th March on a technical point. But the latest information was that Dr. Mukerjee was again courting arrest, presumably in the determination to act the role of a martyr.

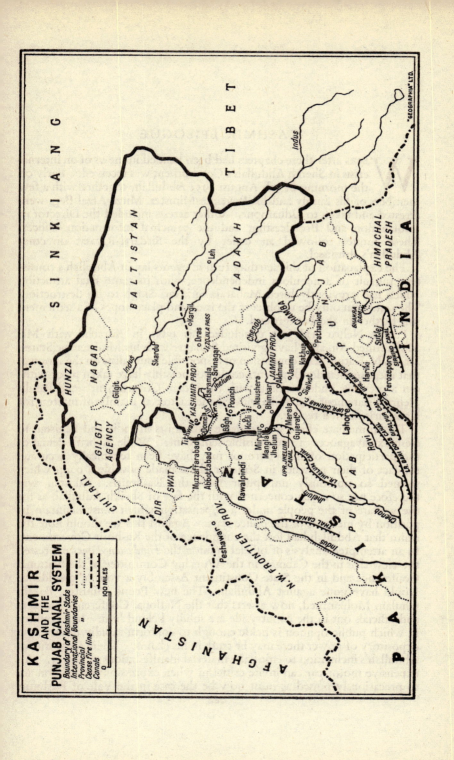

KASHMIR
AND THE
PUNJAB CANAL SYSTEM

Boundary of Kashmir State ———
International Boundaries —·—·—
Provincial   "   —··—··—
Cease Fire line ·············
Canals ————

0   100 MILES

"GEOGRAPHIA" LTD.

T I B E T

S I N K I A N G

NAGAR

HUNZA

BALTISTAN

LADAKH

CHITRAL

GILGIT
AGENCY

SWAT

DIR

N.W. FRONTIER PROV.

AFGHANISTAN

P A K I S T A N

KASHMIR PROV.

JAMMU PROV.

CHAMBA

HIMACHAL
PRADESH

P U N J A B

I N D I A

°Leh

°Kargil
ZOJI-LA PASS
°Dras
Skardu°
°Gilgit
Titwal°
Muzaffarabad°
Domel°
Baramula°
Srinagar°
°Poonch
Abbottabad°
Bagh°
Kotli °
°Naushera
Bhimbar°
Rawalpindi°
Mirpur°
Mangla°
Jhelum°
Gujerat°
Merala°
Akhnur°
Jammu°
Sialkot°
Kathua°
Pathiankot°
Peshawar°
Lahore°
Ferozepore
Harika
Indus
Indus
Indus
Chenab
Chenab
Jhelum
Jhelum
Ravi
Sutlej
BHAKRA
DAM

UPR. BARI DOAB CAN.
LR. BARI DOAB CAN.
UPR. CHENAB C.
LR. CHENAB CAN.
UPR. JHELUM CANAL
LR. JHELUM CANAL
THAL CANAL
BIST DOAB DIALPUR CANAL
SIRHIND CANAL

KASHMIR EPILOGUE

WEEKS after these chapters had been handed in, news of an internal crisis in Sheikh Abdullah's Government was received. Early on the morning of 9th August 1953 Abdullah, together with a few members of his family and his Revenue Minister, Mirza Afzal Beg, were arrested and taken to Udhampur. Other arrests included the Director of Information and Broadcasting and the principal Information Officer. These moves followed an order by the Sirdar-i-Riyasat directing Abdullah's dismissal.

The explanation of this startling turn in events lay in Abdullah's consistent pursuit of a nebulous independence, with its same fatal attraction which had previously lured Maharaja Sir Hari Singh to his destruction. The result can only be to obscure the issue and place hopes of a settlement still further in the background.

Pandit Nehru had just concluded his talks in Karachi with Mr. Mohammed Ali, after having visited Srinagar with his Minister for States, Dr. K. N. Katju. The conclusion of responsible journalists on the spot was that these sudden developments could not possibly have taken place without a previous understanding with the Indian Government: and Pandit Nehru's statement that India viewed the matter as mainly of interest for Kashmiris, lacked reality.

The immediate effect was to drive extremists in India and Pakistan to fresh extravagances of irresponsible sentiment. While Nehru's denial of the participation of Indian troops may have been technically accurate, the fact of their presence in Srinagar alone made possible a coup which seemed so obviously unpopular with the Kashmiris. Pakistan was therefore not so much concerned with the fate of Sheikh Adbullah as for the welfare of the people under a dispensation which must maintain its position by methods of the police state. Against this we should note the claim that Abdullah had lost the confidence of the Kashmir Government. In an attempted analysis of official opinion the *Hindustan Times* expressed the view that in the Cabinet, in the Working Committee of the National Conference and in the State Constituent Assembly a vote of confidence would have gone against Abdullah. The new Prime Minister, Bakshi Ghulam Mohammed, now asserts that the National Conference workers and officials out in the countryside are solidly behind him. In a country in which public opinion is fickle enough to conform rapidly to any new depository of power there may be truth in his claims. There are stories of Abdullah's inclination to enjoy the material manifestations of power. An expensive motor-car can invite criticism when expressions of opinion are so precariously poised as must now be the case in the Vale of Kashmir.

Bakshi Ghulam Mohammed was an unknown quantity until 1947, when Abdullah himself set him on the path to power. In contrast, Abdullah had at least pursued a consistent fight for the welfare of Kashmiris ever since the 1930s, and the necessity for the police to open fire in the spasmodic rioting which followed his arrest was the measure of the acceptance he had won in the bazaars and out in the fields of the valley.

Quite suddenly in August, Abdullah threw ambiguity aside and in a speech just before his arrest he spoke openly of repudiating the accession. He was also bold enough to refer for the first time to discrimination against Moslems in the state administration. In all probability his accusations were near the truth, for the death of Dr. Mukerjee only a few weeks previously had driven the Jammu Hindus into paroxysms of communal excitement.

The Pakistan Press told of Moslems being " mown down " by Indian troops. The Indian Press retaliated with fantastic stories of an international plot. When I first heard of the rumours that Abdullah had been in league with a foreign imperialist Power, my reaction was that he had been caught out in negotiation with the Soviet. I rubbed my eyes when I read that the villain was Mr. Adlai Stevenson alleged to be plotting on behalf of the United States of America!

These fabrications could only have worried and embarrassed Mr. Nehru; and it is to the great credit of both Prime Ministers that they refused to tread the path down which popular sentiment would have led them. *Dawn* indeed advocated the abandonment of negotiation; and Mr. Mohammed Ali's courage in moderation could well merit the label of true statesmanship. Mr. Nehru has years of established prestige and public recognition behind him. In contrast, Mohammed Ali is an unknown quantity not even claiming the background of a popular election. With him, to pursue the wisdom of compromise through negotiation is to accept a certain risk. In doing so the good wishes of a wide circle of observers far from Delhi or Karachi will be with him.

A future more uncertain than ever invites speculation. Bakshi Ghulam Mohammed's position may be compared with that of Colonel Nasir in Egypt. They both hold the power, but not the popularity. Nasir will continue so long as Neguib is there to invite the applause. In Kashmir the focus of applause has been removed. If it be true that the President of the Kashmir Assembly, Ghulam Mohammed Sadiq, is to step into the post of Deputy Prime Minister, it would seem clear that the new Government will assert its authority with resort, if necessary, to the extreme measures of Communist technique. For Sadiq is reported to be an unashamed Communist. Our immediate hope must be that India will not permit the new Prime Minister to indulge in excesses for the enforcement of his will.

Of the more distant negotiations, in my view a fair comment came from Mr. Suhrawardy, President of the Jinnah Awami League, in which capacity he was not necessarily supporting the views of his Government.

He pointed out that India's acknowledgment of a plebiscite assumed a recognition of the right of the people to choose. All shades of opinion should therefore be allowed their freedom of expression, and steps to educate the electorate in the nature of their choice would not only be justified, but should logically be a *sine qua non* of the present situation. Yet Abdullah, whom India had previously supported as representing the will of the people, had been removed immediately that will seemed out of step with India's desires. To suppress slogans in favour of Pakistan in the streets was to deny the plebiscite itself.

According to Mr. Rawle Knox of the *Observer*, the Bakshi Sahib announced, on the assumption of power, that the Kashmir Constituent Assembly as " elected representatives of the people " would ratify the accession to India in October. What, then, is left for Mr. Nehru to discuss ? Will he in turn have the courage to risk unpopularity ? Such are the tests of greatness, and in the case of Mr. Nehru I hazard that he is sufficiently entrenched in the affections of his people to withstand the noise from his more communal nationalists, and take the risk.

Perhaps the saddest reflection in these new developments derives from a warning by Bakshi Ghulam Mohammed that United Nations Observers must " keep away from disturbed areas ". For in this threat to the perfectly legitimate functioning of the Security Council through its local representatives is summed up the impotence of international arbitration when co-operation is not in the interests of one of the parties to a dispute.

APPENDICES

THE INDIAN CONSTITUTION

The Union Government

1. *Upper House. Council of States.*

Part A States	145
„ B „	49
„ C „	10
	204

2. *Lower House. House of the People*

Part A States	374
„ B „	90
„ C „	25
Nominated for Andamans and Kashmir	7
	496 [1]

3. *The State Legislatures*

Part A

	Legislative Assembly [2]	*Legislative Council*
Assam	108	—
Bihar	330	72
Bombay	315	72
Madhya Pradesh . .	232	—
Madras	375	72
Orissa	140	—
Punjab	126	40
Uttar Pradesh . . .	430	72
West Bengal . . .	238	51

[1] These figures include seventy-two seats reserved for scheduled caste representation and twenty-six reserved for scheduled tribes. The final results of the 1952 elections in the House of the People were

Congress . .	362	Communists and Allies .		27
Socialist . . .	12	Scheduled Caste Federation .		2
K.M.P. . . .	10	Krishak Lok Party .	.	1
Jan Sangh . .	3	Akali Sikhs . .	.	4
Independents . .	36	Miscellaneous . .	.	32

[2] These figures include a total of 477 seats in the Assemblies reserved for scheduled castes and 170 seats for scheduled tribes.

Part B.

	Legislative Assembly	Legislative Council
Hyderabad . . .	175	—
Madhya Bharat . .	99	—
Mysore . . .	99	40
Pepsu	60	—
Rajasthan . . .	160	—
Saurashtra . . .	60	—
Travancore-Cochin .	100	—

Part C.

Ajmer	30	—
Bhopal . . .	30	—
Coorg	24	—
Delhi	48	—
Himachal Pradesh . .	36	—
Vindhya Pradesh . .	60	—

Electoral Colleges (thirty each) for Kutch, Manipur and Tripura are formed for the election of the six members from these three States who sit in the House of the People.

Summary of the Constitution

Preamble.

Part I.	The Union and its Territory.
Part II.	Citizenship.
Part III.	Fundamental Rights.
Part IV.	Directive Principles of State Policy.
Part V.	Chapter I. The Executive.
	Chapter II. Parliament.
	Chapter III. Legislative Powers of the President.
	Chapter IV. The Union Judiciary.
	Chapter V. Comptroller and Auditor-General of India.
Part VI.	The States in Part A of the First Schedule.
	Chapter I. General.
	Chapter II. The Executive.
	Chapter III. The State Legislature.
	Chapter IV. Legislative Power of the Governor.
	Chapter V. The High Courts in the States.
	Chapter VI. Subordinate Courts.
Part VII.	The States in Part B of the First Schedule.
Part VIII.	The States in Part C of the First Schedule.
Part IX.	The territories in Part D of the First Schedule and other territories not specified in that Schedule.
Part X.	The Scheduled and Tribal areas.
Part XI.	Relations between the Union and the States.
Part XII.	Finance, Property, Contracts, Suits.
Part XIII.	Trade, Commerce and intercourse within the territory of India.
Part XIV.	Services.
Part XV.	Elections.
Part XVI.	Special Provisions relating to certain classes.

T

PREAMBLE TO THE CONSTITUTION OF PAKISTAN

In the name of Allah, the Beneficent, the Merciful;

WHEREAS sovereignty over the entire universe belongs to God Almighty alone and the authority which He has delegated to the State of Pakistan through its people for being exercised within the limits prescribed by Him is a sacred trust;

This Constituent Assembly representing the people of Pakistan resolves to frame a constitution for the sovereign independent State of Pakistan;

WHEREIN the State shall exercise its powers and authority through the chosen representatives of the people;

WHEREIN the principles of democracy, freedom, equality, tolerance and social justice as enunciated by Islam shall be fully observed;

WHEREIN the Muslims shall be enabled to order their lives in the individual and collective spheres in accord with the teachings and requirements of Islam as set out in the Holy Quran and the Sunna;

WHEREIN adequate provision shall be made for the minorities freely to profess and practise their religions and develop their cultures;

WHEREBY the territories now included in or in accession with Pakistan and such other territories as may hereafter be included in or accede to Pakistan shall form a Federation wherein the units will be autonomous with such boundaries and limitations on their powers and authority as may be prescribed;

WHEREIN shall be guaranteed fundamental rights including equality of status, of opportunity and before law, social, economic and political justice, and freedom of thought, expression, belief, faith, worship and association, subject to law and public morality;

WHEREIN adequate provision shall be made to safeguard the legitimate interests of minorities and backward and depressed classes;

WHEREIN the independence of the judiciary shall be fully secured;

WHEREIN the integrity of the territories of the Federation, its independence and all its rights including its sovereign rights on land, sea and air shall be safeguarded;

So that the people of Pakistan may prosper and attain their rightful and honoured place amongst the nations of the World and make their full contribution towards international peace and progress and happiness of humanity.

THE ARMIES OF INDIA AND PAKISTAN

INDIA

Armoured Corps [1,2]

President's Bodyguard	(P.B.G.)	The Deccan Horse	(9 HORSE)
Skinner's Horse	(1 HORSE)	The Scinde Horse	(14 HORSE)
2nd Lancers	(2 L.)	16th Light Cavalry	(16 CAV.)
3rd Cavalry	(3 CAV.)	The Poona Horse	(17 HORSE)
Hodson's Horse	(4 HORSE)	18th Cavalry	(18 CAV.)
7th Light Cavalry	(7 CAV.)	The Central India Horse	(C.I.H.)
8th Light Cavalry	(8 CAV.)		

Engineers [3]

MADRAS Engineer Group

BENGAL Engineer Group

BOMBAY Engineer Group

The greater portion of the Bengal Sappers went to Pakistan, a new group being raised at Roorkee in India. The other two groups remained with India, although the Bombay Group previously enlisted Punjabi Moslems. The Madras Group were and still are largely composed of Madrasi Moslems.

Foot Guards

1st Battalion The Guards (PUNJAB)
2nd Battalion The Guards (GRENADIERS) [4]
3rd Battalion The Guards (RAJPUTANA RIFLES)
4th Battalion The Guards (RAJPUT)

Infantry

The Punjab Regiment	The Assam Regiment [7]
The Madras Regiment	The Bihar Regiment
The Grenadiers	The Mahar Regiment
The Mahratta Light Infantry	The Sikh Light Infantry [8]
The Rajputana Rifles [5]	The 1st Gurkha Rifles
The Rajput Regiment [5]	The 3rd Gurkha Rifles
The Jat Regiment	The 4th Gurkha Rifles [9]
The Sikh Regiment	The 5th Gurkha Rifles
The Dogra Regiment	The 8th Gurkha Rifles
The Garhwal Rifles	The 9th Gurkha Rifles
The Kumaon Regiment [6]	The 11th Gurkha Rifles

PAKISTAN

Armoured Corps

5th K.E.O. Probyn's Horse	12th Sam Browne's Cavalry
6th D.C.O. Lancers	(Training Centre)
10th Q.V.O. Guides Cavalry	13th D.C.O. Lancers
11th P.A.V.O. Cavalry	19th K.G.O. Lancers

Infantry

1st Punjab Regiment [10]	16th Punjab Regiment [10]
8th Punjab Regiment	Pathan Regiment [12]
10th Baluch Regiment [11]	East Bengal Regiment [13]
14th Punjab Regiment	12th F.F. Regiment [10]
15th Punjab Regiment	13th F.F. Rifles
(Machine Guns)	1st, 2nd, 3rd Bahawalpur Infantry [14]

The Frontier Corps

Northern Scouts	South Waziristan Scouts
Gilgit Scouts	Zhob Militia
Chitral Scouts	Pishin Scouts
Khyber Rifles	Makran Levies
Kurram Militia	Chaghai Levies
Tochi Scouts	Kelat State Forces

[1] In addition to the cavalry regiments, a few horsed cavalry units—e.g. Mysore, Patiala and Gwalior Lancers—have been absorbed into the Regular Army.

[2] The Armoured Corps publish an excellent quarterly journal from their centre in Ahmednagar.

[3] The Indian Army has its complete ancillary services—Artillery, Signals, A.S.C., A.M.C., A.O.C., E.M.E., Pioneers, Postal and Provost Units.

[4] The four battalions of Guards are all class units based respectively for training and development on the Punjab Regiment, the Grenadiers, the Rajputana Rifles and the Rajput Regiment. Height limits are laid down for each battalion, the 1st Battalion being 6 feet and over, the others being scaled down to a minimum of 5 feet 6 inches.

[5] The Rajputana Rifles include men from Rajputana. The Rajput Regiment includes Gujars, Rajputs, Jats and Bengalees.

[6] The 1st Battalion is the "Kumaon Rifles".

[7] Raised in the war from the hill tribes of Assam (Nagas, Chins, etc.).

[8] Re-raised at the beginning of World War II from the Mazbhi and Ramdasia Sikhs (Sikh Pioneers).

[9] 2nd, 6th, 7th and 10th Gurkha Rifles transferred to the British Army. Each Regiment has two battalions.
(I have used the familiar spelling, although in November 1948 the Indian Army officially reverted to a previous spelling "Gorkha").

[10] 1/12 F.F. Regt., 3/1 Punjab Regt. and 3/16 Punjab Regt. were formerly parachute units.

[11] Pathans formerly in 10th Baluch Regiment were transferred to Frontier Force units, their place being taken by Brahis from Baluchistan, Hazaras and Sindis. In 1948 and 1949 unsuccessful efforts were made to recruit Sindis. But in the case of Sind new settlers from the Punjab are now coming forward for enlistment.

[12] Consists at present of one battalion. Has two companies Punjab Moslems and two companies Pathans in which Mahsuds are predominant. Took in N.C.O.s from the Frontier Force.

[13] Two battalions raised after partition.

[14] State troops, but trained and administered by the Pakistan Army.

Commanders-in-Chief, since 15th August 1947

INDIA

Field–Marshal Sir CLAUDE AUCHINLECK, G.C.B., G.C.I.E., C.S.I., D.S.O., O.B.E.

General Sir ROB LOCKHART, K.C.B., C.I.E., M.C.: 15th Aug. to 31st Dec. 1947.

General Sir F. R. R. BUCHER, K.B.E., C.B., M.C.: 1st Jan. 1948 to 15th Jan. 1949.

General K. M. CARIAPPA: 16th Jan. 1949 to 15th Jan. 1953.

General MAHARAJ SHRI RAJENDRASINJHI, D.S.O.: 16th Jan. 1953 to

PAKISTAN

General Sir FRANK MESSERVY, K.C.S.I., K.B.E., C.B., D.S.O.: 15th Aug. 1947 to 15th Feb. 1948.

General Sir DOUGLAS GRACEY, K.C.B., K.C.I.E., C.B.E., M.C.: 16th Feb. 1948 to 17th Jan. 1951.

General MOHAMMED AYUB KHAN: 17th Jan. 1951 to

INDIAN AND PAKISTANI POLITICAL PARTIES

INDIA

(a) *Indian National Congress*. Founded 1885. Assumed the leadership of Indian political thought and activity working for independence. Was returned in overwhelming strength in the non-Moslem Constituencies at the elections in 1946 for a Constituent Assembly. Confirmed in power in the 1952 elections with 362 out of 496 seats in the House of the People.

Strongest in Uttar Pradesh, Madhya Pradesh and Punjab. Comparatively weak in Orissa, Hyderabad, Pepsu and Rajasthan.

Policy:—Progressive socialism. Nationalisation of heavy industries concurrent with scope for private enterprise. Stands for the secular State.

President: Pandit Jawaharlal Nehru.
Secretaries-General: Messrs. Balwantrai Mehta and S. N. Agarwal.
Working Committee of twenty-one members.

(b) *Socialists*. Left the Congress in 1948. At the 1952 elections stood for the abolishment of *zemindari* without compensation, the nationalisation of foreign capital and the creation of a third Asian bloc in international affairs. Its programme was Utopian and academic. Though polling the largest number of votes after the Congress, they obtained only twelve seats in the House of the People. (The socialist poll of nearly 10,000,000 was almost double the poll of the Communists who secured twenty-seven seats.)

Leader: Mr. Jaya Prakash Narayan.

(c) *Kisan Mazdur Praja Party* (Peasants', Workers' and Peoples'). Broke away from the Congress in the summer of 1951. Claimed a greater devotion to the principles of Gandhi. Obtained ten seats in the House of the People.

Leader: Mr. Acharya Kripalani, formerly of the Congress Working Committee.

(d) *The Praja-Socialist Party*. Both (b) and (c) above have now combined to form this new Party which, with twenty-two members in the House of the People, is the third largest organised Party. Early in 1953, on Mr. Nehru's initiative, the Congress Working Committee took up the question of a possible merging of the Praja-Socialists with the Congress.

Leaders: Messrs. J. P. Narayan and A. Kripalani share the leadership.

(e) *The Jan Sangh* (National Peoples' Association). The former Hindu Mahasabha under a new name. Stands for the Hindu theocratic State, though it does not necessarily support orthodoxy. Is violently anti-Pakistan. Obtained only three seats in the House of the People.

Leader: Dr. Syama Prasad Mukerjee. Was arrested in March 1953 in connection with disturbances organised in Jammu, but subsequently released.

(f) *Ram Rajya Parishad.* Orthodox Hindu. Opposes cow-slaughter, divorce and inheritance by daughters. Was recently successful only in Rajasthan, where *jagirdars* of influence stood on R.R.P. tickets.

Secretary: Mr. Nand Lal Sharma.

(g) *Hindu Mahasabha.* The former stronghold of a Hindu renaissance. Dr. S. P. Mukerjee was a former President. Was recently successful only in the Gwalior area of Madhya Bharat. Opposes the Hindu Code Bill.

President: Mr. N. C. Chatterjee.

(e), (f) and (g) constitute the three Hindu communal parties.

(h) *Communists.* By concentration secured twenty-seven seats in the House of the People in the recent elections. Yet in numbers this represents only 5 per cent of the total vote. In certain areas their position is strong, and in Madras and Travancore-Cochin they could conceivably win sufficient power to take control. In the south Communist-inspired groups such as the " United Front of Leftists " and the " People's Democratic Front " constitute an effective bloc of fellow-travellers.

Leader: Mr. A. K. Gopalan (in the House of the People).

(i) *Scheduled Castes Federation.* Represents, under its respected leader, the isolation and separate representation of the Scheduled Castes (Untouchables). Yet it recently secured only two of the seventy-two seats reserved for its community in the House of the People, seventy seats being captured by nominees of the Congress Party.

Leader: Dr. Ambedkar, who was himself defeated.

(j) *Akali Sikhs.* Since the 1920s this party has stood for Sikh nationalism, while during the last ten years it has at intervals claimed a separate Sikh State. In the Punjab Assembly at the recent elections it won thirteen seats out of fifty-eight contested. It is confined to the Punjab and Pepsu. (See Glossary.)

Leader: Master Tara Singh.

PAKISTAN

(a) *Moslem League.* Founded 1906. Gradually assumed the role of the protection of Moslem interests throughout British India. In 1926 the late Mr. Mohammed Ali Jinnah was elected President, and he continued to lead it until his death. Stands for the establishment of Islamic principles of democracy and social justice. Continues to enjoy popular support in Pakistan and constitutes the Central and all Provincial Ministries. (A small section of the League captured five seats in the recent Indian elections in Madras.)

(b) *Jinnah–Awami League.* A splinter Party from the Moslem League sponsored by Mr. H. S. Suhrawardy in 1951. Claims to interpret the principles laid down by the late Mr. M. A. Jinnah more faithfully than rival Moslem Parties.

Advocates Pakistan leaving the Commonwealth and following an international policy of neutrality. Aims at more effective agrarian reform. Little influence in rural areas and of significance only in the Lahore urban constituencies.

Leaders: Mr. H. S. Suhrawardy and Khan Iftikhar Hussein Khan of Mamdot.

(c) *Anjuman-i-Shabal-Muslimeen* (Moslem People's Organisation). Aims at the establishment of a Moslem bloc in world affairs by non-violent means.

Leader: Chaudhri Khaliquzzaman, a former President of the Moslem League. Appointed Governor of East Pakistan in succession to Malik Firoz Khan Noon in March 1953.

(d) *Azad Pakistan*. Claims that it represents the interests of the masses in contrast to the Moslem League, which is only concerned with classes of privilege. Aims at the elimination of all foreign influence. Asserts that British political and economic control over Pakistan continues under the Moslem League Government in the same way in which it was exercised before partition. Claimed that the provincial elections in the N.W.F.P. in 1951 had been rigged, and demanded that the Province be placed under Section 92A administration. May be regarded as fellow travellers with the Communists.

Leader: Mian Iftikaruddin, formerly President of the Congress Party in undivided Punjab, owner of a controlling share of the *Pakistan Times*.

(e) *The Communist Party*. In the Punjab the Party is confined to a group of intellectuals in Lahore.

It is active in East Pakistan, where the proximity of Burma and West Bengal offers opportunities for local encouragement. Separatist tendencies in East Pakistan also provide a convenient background.

The Communists appeal to Moslem opportunists who normally would have little interest in Communism and who seldom have any knowledge of Marxist theory. The Rawalpindi conspiracy case provides examples.

Sujjad Zaheer, a scholar of Oxford and son of a former Chief Justice of the Oudh Chief Court, is the Secretary. He previously edited *Naya Zamana*, a Communist weekly, in Bombay. He came to Pakistan in 1949 and was arrested in April 1951.

(f) *Ahmadiyyah*. This is not a political Party. But since the Ahmadiyya movement early in 1953 was the cause of dissension and rioting, a brief note on its meaning is necessary. The Ahmadiyyahs are centred on Qadian, 70 miles east of Lahore, where the family of the present head of the Community (Bashir-ud-Din Mahmud Ahmad) have been settled for four centuries.

The late Hazrat Mirza Ghulam Ahmad, born in 1835, was a profound student of the Holy Quran, who undertook to reawaken interest in and vindicate Islamic doctrine in a massive publication of four volumes. The Mirza Sahib founded the community in 1889, and at the same time claimed, through divine revelation, to be the promised Messiah and successor to the Prophet himself. The Mirza Sahib's claims brought a storm of protest and opposition; and the subsequent expansion of the movement both within and outside Pakistan has only served to increase suspicions that a separate and parallel religion is being established. The present head of the Community is Hazrat Mirza Bashir-ud-Din Mahmud Ahmad, who continues to claim that the movement is one of unswerving loyalty to Islamic principles.

(g) *Ahrar Movement*. Founded in the Punjab in 1934. A Moslem group formerly in sympathy with the Indian Congress. The latter used it as a handle to counter the claims of monopoly of the Moslem League. Opposed the establishment of Pakistan. For a time went " underground ", but within the last year has actively interfered in politics, particularly in violent opposition to the Ahmadiyyah movement. Is strictly orthodox and opposes all progressive reform which could possibly be interpreted as in conflict with religious instruction. Invited vehement attacks in Lahore in March 1953, which resulted in much hooliganism and bloodshed.

Leader: Attamullah Shah Bokhari (at the present moment in gaol).

(h) *The Congress Party*. A " hang-over " from partition. Represents minority interests in the Central Assembly. In effect this is a group of about ten Hindus from East Bengal. Has no political programme and opposes Government legislation as a matter of routine.

Leader: Mr. Chattopadhya (Bengal).

LEADING ARTICLE, THE *PAKISTAN TIMES*, 17 JANUARY 1952

THE MAGHREB AND THE MIDDLE EAST

The Churchill–Truman declaration on the Middle East, which rules out the possibility of the U.S. remaining neutral in the Anglo–Egyptian conflict and which reaffirms the West's desire to *impose the Middle East Command on the States of that* region, has evoked *strong protests from the Egyptian opinion* and the Press. A wave of disillusionment in regard to the sincerity of American democratic professions has swept the Arab world and even those elements who used to favour a pro-American orientation of Middle East politics have been constrained to express their disappointment. The struggle between imperialism and newly awakened nationalism is the sharpest in Egypt and it is in that country that the Anglo–American declaration of " *a complete identity of aims* " in the *Middle East has been regarded as necessitating a reconsideration of basic* policies. The popular reaction in other Arab States and in those lands which are directly under the imperialist sway cannot naturally be far different from that reported from Egypt. Muslim countries from Morocco in the West to Iran in the East are today engaged in a straight fight with Western imperialism over the question of national rights and complete independence. *The effect of the Churchill–Truman declaration has been to warn them that they must cherish no illusions about the U.S.A.* coming to their aid or becoming an ally in their bid to attain independence. The great upsurge of patriotic and nationalist sentiment in countries of Arab North Africa and the Middle East, which began in the post-war period, has now reached a stage which is of decisive importance for the realisation of national aspirations. Egypt and Iran, which are in the forefront of the fight to banish colonialism, are making enormous sacrifices to achieve the laudable aims they have set themselves. *With every fresh aggressive deed perpetrated by the British occupation forces* in Egypt, *the people renew their vows that they will rid their* country of the unwanted presence of *foreign troops.* The past few months have witnessed an unprecedented awakening among the Sudanese people, who are determined to seek their national salvation, notwithstanding hypocritical expressions of British *solicitude* for *Sudanese self-determination.* Only the other day all Sudanese political parties agreed to set aside their differences to raise the demand unitedly that the Sudanese will about their future destiny, be ascertained by the holding of a free and unfettered plebiscite. It is not surprising that Britain, which has always exploited differences among the Sudanese, has not cared to take cognizance of this consensus of opinion. With the Iranian rejection of the scheme submitted by the *American-controlled International Bank for Reconstruction,* the Anglo–Iranian dispute has remained where it was. *British intrigues and manoeuvres in Iran are, however, responsible for a fresh crisis leading to the Iranian demand for the closing down of all British Consulates in the country by January* 21. An important new development is the suspension of U.S. military

" aid " to Iran following the Iranian Government's refusal to accept the *humiliating conditions that go with the so-called Mutual Security Pact*. These conditions in effect require a prospective beneficiary to *toe* the American line in foreign policy, fulfil military obligations and use American " aid " in the manner indicated by American advisers and agencies. While Britain is making frantic efforts to retain its stranglehold over Middle East States where it has got economic, political and strategic stakes, France is no less eager to prevent its large North African Empire from falling to pieces. A reign of repression and terror has accordingly been established in Morocco, Algeria and Tunisia to suppress the freedom movement and to make it impossible for patriots to carry on the freedom struggle in a lawful manner. The antagonism between imperialism and the people's urge for freedom is the sharpest in Algeria where France has been tenaciously pursuing its policy of cultural assimilation. The so-called constitutional reforms introduced by the metropolitan Power in these three countries have totally failed in their purpose of blunting the edge of the anti-imperialist movement. The latest reports indicate that a fresh crisis is brewing in Tunisia and two Tunisian Ministers have asked the U.N. Security Council to consider Tunisia's appeal for independence following breakdown of negotiations with France.

The freedom struggle of the peoples of North Africa and the Middle East has not failed to impress the world's freedom-loving peoples. Now that this struggle has entered a critical phase it is but natural that the imperialist offensive should be intensified. A situation has now arisen when to counter and defeat the plans of the forces of colonial slavery all Governments and peoples pledged to uphold the cause of national liberation should extend full support to the hard-pressed peoples of these colonial and semi-colonial countries. This view is very widely shared in this country and there is a growing realisation of Pakistan's moral and political responsibility effectively to help the fighting peoples of the Middle East and the Maghreb. *One wonders if the Pakistan Government are fully alive to the need of expressing their loyalties in this conflict in a more pronounced manner.*

PORTUGUESE AND FRENCH TERRITORIES ON INDIAN SOIL

The Portuguese territories in India are three.   They are

Goa	. . . .	541,000
Daman	. . . .	60,000
Diu	. . . .	19,000

The settlement of Goa was established by Alfonso d'Albuquerque who at the head of 20 ships and 1200 men carried the small town by force in 1510, and founded a Christian city which by the middle of the 16th century had risen to become one of the most prosperous cities in all India.

In March 1951, the Portuguese Government passed an amendment to their Colonial Act by which Colonies were to be renamed " Overseas Provinces ". The Portuguese method has always tended towards an exaggeration of the French system by which the life and fortunes of the colonial population become merged in that of the metropolitan power.   A visit to Goa is today in many respects identical to a visit to Portugal, and racially the Portuguese and Goans have become very intermixed.   In May 1952 the Portuguese Minister for Overseas Territories, Sarmento Rodrigues, visited Goa and spoke publicly of the traditional friendship between Portugal and India and his country's desire to continue the policy of a good neighbour.   His reiteration of the " one nation " theory in his country's colonial policy failed to satisfy the Indian Press, and in particular angered *The Hindu.*

The passage in the amendment to the Portuguese Act which called for Nehru's caustic comment was one which spoke of Portugal's historical mission of " propagating the benefits of civilisation " and the " Exercise of moral influence deriving from Portuguese patronage ".   Perhaps, he suggested, the people of Goa were now ready to forgo this beneficence?

The small territory of Chandernagore near Calcutta which was formerly French held a referendum in June 1949, as a result of which under a Treaty signed in Paris in February 1951 it passed to India, most of the French Community then seeking their fortunes in Calcutta.   Today only such evidence as the words " Patisserie " and " Café " on the shop fronts remains to remind the visitor of former days.

The French territories remaining on Indian soil are

Pondicherry	. . .	220,000
Karikal	. . .	70,000
Mahé	. . .	18,000
Yanam	. . .	5,800

Letters were exchanged between France and India concerning their future in June 1948.   In March and April 1952 a delegation of neutral observers appointed by the International Court of the Hague visited the territories. In their short stay the delegation came to the conclusion that so intense was the atmosphere in which polemics concerning the future of these territories were conducted, that at present it was quite impossible to hold a fair referendum. On the one hand there was French official pressure. On the other hand there was aggressive Indian infiltration. This resulted in so-called political parties which could command gangs of terrorists for purposes of intimidation. Such teams of *goondas* frequently changed masters and were used to attack political adversaries at election time, selling their votes and services to the highest bidder. In addition Indian customs restrictions had resulted in much smuggling between Pondicherry and India, particularly in wine, with incidents on the mutual frontiers of a serious character. Until normal economic relations between India and the French enclaves were restored and until steps had been taken to ensure the exercise of the vote without intimidation, a referendum to decide the choice as between a future within India or continuation with France would be useless.

The attitudes of Portugal and France differ in that whereas the former refuses to recognise a modification of the status of her territories, the latter recognises India's claims. Mr. Nehru has made it clear that while India will not resort to force, the claims will never be renounced.

APPENDIX SEVEN

KASHMIR

Rulers of Kashmir

1587. The Moghul Emperor Akbar. The State continued under Moghul control until 1752.
1752. Durani conquest. (Rule from Kabul.)
1819. Maharaja Ranjit Singh. (Sikh Rule.)
1846. Maharaja Gulab Singh ⎫
1857. Maharaja Ranbir Singh ⎬ (Dogra Rule.)
1885. Maharaja Pertap Singh ⎪
1925. Maharaja Hari Singh ⎭

Note.—Maharaja Hari Singh is the son of Raja Amar Singh, a brother of Maharaja Pertap Singh.

2. *Population*

	Mohammedans	Non-Mohammedans [3]	Total
Jammu Province [1]	1,215,676	765,757	1,981,433
Kashmir Province	1,615,478	113,227	1,728,705
Frontier District [2]	270,093	41,385	311,478

3. *Telegram sent from India to Pakistan which Effected the "Cease-fire" on 1st January 1949*

From Ind Army	Date	Time
To Pak Army	30	1710

Top Secret 220835/MO3

Bucher to Gracey. In view of political developments my Government thinks continuation of moves and countermoves too often due to misunderstanding accompanied by fire support. Seems senseless and wasteful in human life besides only tending to embitter feelings. My Government authorises me to state I will have their full support if I order Indian troops to remain in present positions and to cease fire. Naturally I cannot issue any such order until I have assurance from you that you are in a position to take immediate

[1] Includes the Jagir of Poonch, administered by the Raja of Poonch as Jagirdar subject to the sovereignty of the Maharaja of Kashmir.
[2] Consisted of Ladakh, Baltistan and the Gilgit Agency. Previous to August 1947 the latter owed a limited loyalty to the Maharaja of Kashmir but was administered by a Political Agent of the Government of India. The population is predominantly Shiah Moslem, but Eastern Ladakh includes some 40,000 Buddhists, who have declared their attachment to India.
[3] Includes approximately 807,000 Hindus and 66,000 Sikhs. Hindus are concentrated in and around Jammu.

reciprocal and effective action. Please reply most immediate. If you agree I
shall send you by signal verbatim copies of any orders issued by me and will
expect you to do the same.

(*Sgd.*) Shej Manekshaw
Brig.
Acting C.G.S.   30th December 1948.

4. *Composition of Gurdaspur District.*   (1941 *census*)

Tehsil			Hindus	Sikhs	Christians	Moham-medans	Moslem percentage of tehsil
Gurdaspur	.	.	56,979	76,695	23,323	171,498	52·1
Batala	.	.	33,430	116,413	20,753	209,277	55·96
Shakargarh	.	.	116,533	20,573	4,779	149,600	57·3
Pathankot	.	.	76,227	7,580	2,673	59,548	38·3

5. *Original Composition of the U.N.C.I.P.*

Argentina { Minister Ricardo J. Siri.
Minister Carlos A. Laguizaman.

Belgium { Ambassador Va de Kerchove.
Minister Egbert Graeffe.
Mr. Harry Graeffe.

Czechoslovakia { Ambassador Joseph Korbel.
Ambassador Oldrich Chyle.

Colombia { Minister Alferedo Lozano.
Mr. Hernando Samper.

United States { Ambassador J. Klahr Huddle.
Mr. C. H. Oakes.
Minister Robert Macater.

All the chief Representatives with the exception of the Argentina representative
were replaced during 1948 and 1949.

6. *The Azad Kashmir Government.*

The affairs of the Azad Kashmir Government are most involved. To understand the story we need to go back to 1938. Previous to that year Chaudhri
Ghulam Abbas and Sheikh Abdullah had both been prominent in the leadership
of the Moslem Conference. Outside influences had, however, been at work
capturing their loyalties. Ghulam Abbas gradually turned to Mr. Jinnah and the
Moslem League, Abdullah to Jawaharlal Nehru and the Indian Congress. Nor
was Abdullah averse to an understanding in 1938 with Sir Gopalaswami Ayyangar,
Prime Minister of the State. Years later Ayyangar was appointed head of the
State Ministry in Delhi, when naturally his previous acquaintance with Abdullah
would have stood him in good stead.

In 1946 the leaders of both the two Kashmir political organisations were in
gaol, their common opposition to the Maharaja's Government providing the
only element of agreement between them. It was during this time that Mohammed

Ibrahim, an unknown assistant District Advocate in the Maharaja's Government, was given his opportunity of stepping into the vacuum and accepting the leadership of the Moslem Conference. It will be recalled that Abdullah was released in September 1947. Ghulam Abbas, however, was not to have his freedom until March 1948, by which time Ibrahim had come to be accepted by a large section of the Moslem Conference. Sheikh Abdullah appears to have made approaches to Ghulam Abbas after his release, but without success. Abbas found his way over to the Pakistan side, and there followed some polite negotiation between him and the new Moslem Conference leader. With a gesture of magnanimity, Ibrahim surrendered the leadership to the former leader, Abbas accepting it with a similar gesture of appropriate reluctance. The exchange was not a success, and an arrangement was worked out by which throughout 1948 Abbas reassumed the titular head of the Moslem Conference, Ibrahim remaining the administrative head of the Government of Azad Kashmir.

Throughout 1949 Abbas and Ibrahim continued to drift apart, largely through the enthusiasm of Abbas's followers. The late Liaquat Ali Khan found a formula by which both leaders could call themselves Presidents, the Azad Government, however, being responsible to the Moslem Conference. It was as if a Cabinet was not responsible to Parliament as a whole, but to the particular Party in office. For a time this arrangement provided the answer. But in 1950 Abbas started to meddle in the administration, and the Pakistan Government found itself in the embarrassing position of a choice for its support between the rival leaders. Ibrahim resigned, and a new Government was formed. Ghulam Abbas took the title of Supreme Head of the Azad Government, Colonel Ali Ahmed Shah of Mirpur assuming the role of President. This understanding was operative until December 1951. In the meanwhile Ibrahim's supporters in Poonch had been making trouble. The Pakistan Government were again about to intervene and Liaquat Ali Khan was on the point of negotiation when he was assassinated. In December Abbas, discontented with the frustrations of political jealousy, resigned and announced his intention of withdrawing from politics. Previously he had nominated Mir Waiz Mohammed Yusuf Shah as President of the Moslem Conference for the year. Yusuf had hitherto been more interested in religious speculation than politics. The Pakistan Government accordingly took advantage of the situation to ask Yusuf to form a Government, a task which he undertook in some sense of duty. At the present time he appears successfully to steer a caretaker Government at Muzzaffarabad, and he has the support of refugees from Indian-held Kashmir.

Whether or not Ghulam Abbas intends to re-enter the political contest remains to be seen. But his followers hardly seem inclined to allow his cause to lapse by default. From Lahore one of his lieutenants, Chaudhri Hamidullah, at the head of the Moslem Conference Plebiscite Board (M.C.P.B.), carries on a campaign of more zeal than discretion.[1] The Indian Press have naturally been quick to draw

[1] The Pakistan Government set up an official Plebiscite Board to undertake research for future purposes. The original intention was that the M.C.P.B. was to work in liaison with the official organisation. Apart from the M.C.P.B. the Kashmir Moslem Conference has its representation in Pakistan. Its agents tend to drift away from their official function and join forces with those organisations which draw confidence from pictures of imaginative Islamic blocs of powerful dimensions (e.g. Lahore 23rd Jan. 1952. Sardar Mohd. Alam Khan. Resident, Lahore Circle, All-Jammu and Kashmir Moslem Conference. " The only course before us and

attention to this trail of intrigue. Pakistan officials themselves sadly admit that the cause of Azad Kashmir has suffered through the narrow ambitions of poor leaders. For myself, I could yet wish that some external influence could be exercised to bring Sheikh Abdullah to talk either with his former colleague Ghulam Abbas or the now approachable Mir Waiz Mohammed Yusuf Shah.

the Moslems of Iran, Egypt, Morocco and Tunisia is to forge a united front against the Western imperialists who have always been using the Moslem countries for their imperialistic intrigues ").

GLOSSARY

OF INDIAN WORDS AND ABBREVIATIONS

Achkan: long coat, closed at the collar. Usually black. Worn in the evening.
Akali: lit. " Eternal One ". Originally a Sikh devotee of Guru Govind Singh.
Now the adopted title of Sikh nationalists.
Akhand: unified, united.
Auqaf: plural of *Waqf,* meaning " religious endowment ".
Azad: free.
Azam: great.

Bagh: garden.
Baniya: a Hindu merchant.
Bara Khana: lit. " big dinner ". Hence, a feast.
Batai: the old agricultural system of the East, by which the products of the land
are divided equally between landlord and tenant.
Batti: a lamp.
Bharat: the old Sanskrit word for the sub-Continent. Now adopted by India.
Bharatiya Jan Sangh: lit. " National People's Party ".

Chappattee: a thin form of pancake which is the basis of a meal all over the sub-
Continent.
Chaprassi: an office messenger.

Dal: party (Punjab).
Dewan: Chief Minister.
Dogra: a Hindu Rajput hill clan sprinkled along the Punjab–Kashmir border.
Durbar: any public occasion on which authority meets the community it governs.
Usually of a ceremonial nature.

I.N.A.: Indian National Army. Raised from Indian prisoners of war under
Japanese patronage for operations against our armed forces in Burma.

Jagir: a gift of land.
Jagirdar: holder of a gift of land.
Jana: people (Jan Sangh, People's Society).
Jehad: a war undertaken as a religious obligation. A holy war.
Jirgah: a meeting of tribesmen on the North West Frontier.

Khassadar: a Frontier tribesman paid by Government for local " protection "
services.
Khidmatgar: a table servant (*khidmat:* service).
Khud-kasht: land cultivated by the owner (*khud:* self. *kasht:* cultivation).
Kisan: peasant.

Lashkar: armed band.

Madhya: central. "Madhya Pradesh" was constituted a State out of twenty-two former Princely States of Central India, June 1948.

Mahabharata: the great Hindu epic relating the struggle for power between the Panchalas and Pandavas, two peoples in the area around Delhi. Period about 1000 B.C.

Mahratta: martial Hindu clan of the Western Ghats, who under their great leader Siva-ji broke the power of the Moghuls in Southern India.

Mahsud: tribal clan of West Waziristan.

Malik: owner.

Mullah: Moslem religious leader.

N.D.A.: National Defence Academy (India).

Panchayat: the ancient village Council of five. Now being revived and expanded to meet modern needs.

Panth: The Sikh tradition and religion.

Parishad: Assembly.

Patel: the term for "village headman", in Gujerat. Adopted often as a surname.

Patwari: village official concerned with land administration.

Pepsu: Patiala and East Punjab States Union.

Pradesh: Province or State.

Praja: subjects of a State or Ruler. (*Praja Parishad:* Assembly of subjects.)

Purdah: curtain.

Quaid: leader. (*Quaid-i-Azam:* Great Leader.)

Rajpramukh: Governor.

Ramayana: the second of the great Hindu epics, concerned with the story of Rama and Sita.

Ramzan: the Mohammedan month of fasting. Known also as the *Roza* Known as *Ramadhan* in the Middle East.

Rashtrapatti: President.

Rashtriya: National.

R.S.S.S.: Rashtriya Sewam Sevak Sangh (National Self Service Society). Formerly a militant Hindu organisation. Now claims a background of social activity.

Sahib: Sir.

Sangh: Society or Association.

Sari: dress of Indian women which falls gracefully down from the head, covers the body and is tucked in at the waist.

Satyagraha: non-co-operation.

Saurashtra: formerly the name of the Kathiawar peninsula. The term was in use before A.D. 740. Megasthenes refers to the "Orostrae" who have been identified as the "Saurashtras", a tribe inhabiting part of the Kathiawar area.

Sepoy: soldier.

Sewam Sevak: self service.

Shariat: Moslem Law.
Sher: lion. (*Sher-i-Kashmir:* Lion of Kashmir.)
Shri, Sri: Hindu term of respect. Sir, Mr.
Sikh: martial community which broke away from Hindu orthodoxy under their
 founder, Guru Nanak, in the fifteenth century.
Sunna: traditions of the Holy Prophet, Mohammed.
Suttee: the former practice of Hindu widows throwing themselves on the burning
 funeral pyres of their husbands.
Swami: Master.

Tamasha: display, public entertainment, festive occasion.
Tehsil: sub-division of a District.
Tehsildar: official in charge of a tehsil.
Thana: Police station.
Tonga: small two-wheeled conveyance pulled by a pony.
Topee: European hat designed for sun-protection. Now falling into disuse.

Uttar: North.
U.P.: Uttar Pradesh: Northern Provinces (formerly United Provinces).

Vindhya: the ancient name of the small mountainous system of central India
 from which the State, Vindhya Pradesh, takes its name.
V.C.O.: formerly Viceroy's Commissioned Officer, now termed Junior
 Commissioned Officer (J.C.O.).

Zemindar: agricultural land owner.
Zenana: the portion of a house reserved for women.

INDEX

309